FILMMAKERS SERIES
edited by
ANTHONY SLIDE

Directing

Learn from the Masters

Tay Garnett

Edited by Anthony Slide
Foreword by François Truffaut

Filmmakers, No. 48

The Scarecrow Press, Inc.
Lanham, Md., and London
1996

SCARECROW PRESS, INC.

Published in the United States of America
by Scarecrow Press, Inc.
4720 Boston Way
Lanham, Maryland 20706

4 Pleydell Gardens, Folkestone
Kent CT20 2DN, England

Copyright © 1996 by Tiela Garnett Fazio

British Cataloguing-in-Publication Information Available

Library of Congress Cataloging-in-Publication Data

Siècle de cinéma. English
Directing: learn from the masters/[edited by] Tay Garnett
p. cm.—(Filmmakers: no. 48)
1. Motion picture producers and directors—Interviews. 2. Motion pictures—Production and
direction. I. Title. II. Series: Filmmakers series : no. 48.
PN1998.2.S52313   1995   791.43'0233—dc20   95-42831   CIP

ISBN 0-8108-3046-9 (cloth: alk paper)

⊖™ The paper used in this publication meets the minimum requirements of
American National Standard for Information Sciences—Permanence of
Paper for Printed Library Materials, ANSI Z39.48–1984.
Manufactured in the United States of America.

This book is reverently dedicated to

C. B. DeMille   1881–1959
Victor Fleming   1883–1949
James Cruze   1884–1942
D. W. Griffith   1885–1948
Ernst Lubitsch   1892–1947
Frank Borzage   1893–1962
John Ford   1895–1973
Sergei Eisenstein   1898–1948
George Stevens   1904–1975

Contents

Foreword—"The Old, Laughing Mariner"

In Fellini's film *8 1/2,* the director, Guido, asks an old crew member, an ancient mariner, to do a few tap-steps for him. More than Guido himself, this graceful sailor represents Tay Garnett. He was thin, laughing, rugged-featured. Like Hitchcock, his film career began in title-writing for silent films. As nearly all his colleagues of the Silents, he was athletic, a flyer, an adventurer; like them, he was an intellectual without wanting to be.

His modesty forced him to use the term "Masters" in regard to the directors interviewed here and yet, if such a number of filmmakers the world over answered him without haggling, it was because they were moved and proud to see their existence was known to the man who had created *Her Man, One Way Passage, Seven Sinners, The Postman Always Rings Twice, Fireball,* etc.

In Hollywood, where everyone is rich, Tay Garnett was the only filmmaker who was poor—he spent his money on friends and women. When Henri Langlois, in 1977, had a plane ticket sent to him to be on the jury at the Festival of Tours, Tay Garnett accepted without suspecting that he would learn of the death of Henri Langlois upon landing at Roissy.

He saw also, in his stay in France, an opportunity to enrich this book on which he never stopped working, as if he couldn't resolve to part from it. This book, which you now hold in your hands, has become a posthumous work through the normal course of events. The conception coming to him the day of John Ford's death, this devoted work could not reach its logical end without the death of its creator, Tay Garnett, one of our masters.

—François Truffaut

Introduction

Tay Garnett (Los Angeles, June 13, 1894—Sawtelle, California, October 3, 1977) was one of that special bred of Hollywood directors who could turn his hand to any type of film project with enthusiasm and with honorable results. "The most important attribute for a motion picture or television director is the ability to shift your mental gears," he commented in 1969, "For you never know what the bosses will throw you next." His studio bosses through the years threw him film scripts in any variety of genres. In all, he directed 43 feature films, including *China Seas* [1935] with Jean Harlow and Clark Gable, *Seven Sinners* [1940] with Marlene Dietrich and John Wayne, *Bataan* [1943] with Robert Taylor and Lloyd Nolan, *Mrs. Parkington* [1944] with Greer Garson and Walter Pidgeon, *A Connecticut Yankee in King Arthur's Court* [1949] with Bing Crosby and Rhonda Fleming, and *One Minute to Zero* [1952] with Robert Mitchum and Ann Blyth.

Unlike most of his contemporaries, Tay Garnett grew up in Los Angeles, and he entered the film industry as a title writer and gagman for Mack Sennett and Hal Roach. He became a writer-director in 1928 with *Celebrity*, and directed his first sound films *The Spieler* and *Her Man* in 1929 and 1930 respectively. If there is any ongoing link in his films it is a strong melodramatic streak, found as early as *Her Man* in 1930, and continuing through Garnett's classic *film noir The Postman Always Rings Twice* in 1946.

Tay Garnett made an easy transition to directing for television, and his name appears on many episodes of *Bonanza, Gunsmoke, The Untouchables, Wagon Train, The Loretta Young Show, Death Valley Days*, and other classic series.

There are obvious comparisons to be made between Tay Garnett and his friend John Ford both in terms of length of career and prolificity of films. Both men were adventurers, and at one time Garnett was known as the Richard Halliburton of Hollywood, a reference to the virtually forgotten handsome, daredevil explorer of the early years of the 20th Century. Like Ford, Garnett had his own boat, in which he sailed around the world in 1935 and 1936, gathering film footage for his 1939 feature film *Trade Winds*, starring Fredric March and Joan Bennett. Whereas Ford was often gruff and uncommunicative, Garnett was happy to share his reminiscences and thoughts on the film industry which so obviously he loved. It is ironic that John Ford, a man who dismissed all attempts to study film as an art form or an academic exercise, should have been the catalyst (in death) for Garnett's conceiving of book such as *Directing: Learn from the Masters*.

At the time of his death, show business biographer Charles Higham, who was a close friend to the director, commented, "Tay's comedy-melodramas represent him, I believe, at his most characteristic. He was a happy man. He was surrounded day and night by loving friends. He was happy and beloved because he was devoid of a sense of self-importance, because, like so many rollicking Irishmen of his generation, he didn't take himself too seriously. Unlike most famous and gifted men, he was more interested in others than in himself. It was typical of him that his last, unfinished task was completing a book in which great living directors of many countries would reply to questionnaires he had prepared."

And so we come to *Directing: Learn from the Masters*, a textbook that could not have been compiled had not Tay Garnett been considered on a par with many of those who responded to his questionnaire. As a working film director, he had the foresight to ask the right questions, questions which help the reader understand the concept of filmmaking, and were not foolish or academic as are so many questions asked by interviewers outside the industry.

One might have wished that John Ford was alive to answer Garnett's question-naire. Perhaps he would have refused. Or that Orson Welles did not somehow slip through the cracks. Nevertheless, there are responses here from awe-inspiring names such as Clarence Brown, René Clair, George Cukor, Federico Fellini, Lewis Milestone, Satyajit Ray, François Truffaut, Raoul Walsh, and Fred Zinnemann. Jean Renoir's responses are curt and very much to the point, while others, such as Claude Lelouch ramble on. For reasons unclear, the William Wyler reply is in the form of an essay by Tay Garnett, and Samuel Fuller also refused to respond to the questionnaire, instead submitting an essay in which the director appears obsessed with a comparison between the print and film media. How fascinating to read Steven Spielberg's comments so early in his career, or Raoul Walsh's concerns over nudity on screen which make him sound prudish and old-fashioned.

Represented here are the genuine masters of the cinema, such as Howard Hawks and Jean Renoir, and also the journeymen film directors without whom there would have been no American film heritage: Allan Dwan, Henry King, etc.

As an author, Tay Garnett had credentials, although perhaps not as meritorious as his credits as a filmmaker. As early as 1935, he published a novel titled *Man Laughs Back,* and three years earlier, he had produced *Tall Tales from Hollywood,* a parody on the history of the film community. In 1973, he had commenced work on a novel *Death Plays a Dual Role,* based on the William Desmond Taylor murder mystery. His autobiography *Light Your Torches and Pull Up Your Tights,* co-authored with Fredda Dudley Balling and published by Arlington House in 1973, is a fascinating collection of anecdotes. It takes its title from the order by an assistant director on the 1925 Lon Chaney vehicle *The Hunchback of Notre Dame.* And, of course, Garnett's first wife was the leading lady in that film, Patsy Ruth Miller.

Like so many American directors of his generation, Tay Garnett was revered more in Europe than in his own country. There was a major retrospective of his work at the Cinémathèque Française in Paris just months before his death. It should not be surprising, therefore, that this book was first published in French translation, thanks to the efforts of Garnett's daughter Tiela, and a French editor Thierry de Navacelle. At the time of his death, Tay Garnett was in the final stages of preparation of the book, which it was thought would be published by Prentice-Hall. One suspects that he was having too much fun in compiling the material and constantly held off delivering a manuscript in the hope that there might be one more director, one more completed questionnaire.

Directing: Learn from the Masters is now published for the first time in English, the language in which it was compiled, and in much the manner that Tay Garnett hoped it might appear. The intervening years since its compilation by Tay Garnett have not diminished the book's value. It remains a primary sourcebook for film historians and scholars, and a working textbook for students of film and film production at any level.

Anthony Slide

Genesis of a Textbook

It was due to the death of John Ford, that this encyclopedia of the modes and philosophies of some of the world's greatest motion picture directors was conceived.

John and I first met at Universal Studio in 1915, where his brother, Francis Ford was directing a serial. I believe it was called, *The Broken Coin*, and it co-starred Francis Ford and Grace Cunard. John Ford was the Assistant Director. I was a writer/cartoonist on a magazine called *Photoplayers' Weekly*, and had been assigned to interview John and do a sketch on him. I was completely charmed by his intellectual scope and his grand sense of humor. A warm and abiding friendship was inevitable from the instant we met.

Over half a century later, I found myself faced with the necessity to adjust to the shattering realization that this cherished friend was gone. My grief was amplified by the nagging regret that I had never taken time out to sit with Jack, and dig into that brilliantly creative mind, to uncover his innermost thoughts—the philosophies which guided his approach to his craft—to try to identify the skills and devices with which he contrived to make his films so outstandingly individualized.

Out of this torment a resolve emerged: there would be no more of the truly great Directors now living, in any land in the world, who would pass on without my having made every effort to record, for history, their thinking on filmmaking.

Obviously, for me to reach the greats of many countries for personal interviews, was impractical. Then came the thought—something I knew personally from my many years of filmmaking—that there are certain definitive questions which every Director must answer for himself, before, during and after the filming of a picture. A questionnaire based on these fundamental questions should engender information of inestimable value to historians and film students.

In the interest of brevity and the forestalling of possible student hernias, it was decided to limit our questions to 23 in all. The first two should be designed to give us an insight to the personal background of each Director—to acquaint ourselves with those elements in his life which may have had much to do with bringing his latent genius into lush fruition.

This accomplished, we are ready to get on with our 21 *cardinal* questions. The following (numbered) questions are phrased exactly as they were when presented to our master directors.

The Questionnaire

Please answer all questions by their numbers, as fully and in as much detail as your time and inclination will permit. Rest assured, your views will be quoted verbatim unless you wish it otherwise.

1. What was your personal background (your vocation) before entering this field of endeavor?

2. What was your first position in the movie business? Were you an assistant director, a cameraman, an actor, a writer, a film editor, an agent, or other? Please indicate the steps that led to your directing.

3. What is your philosophy regarding your film: your aim or purpose in making it? Is there an underlying objective beyond providing entertainment?

4. In seeking a story on which to base a film, in what particular genre do you hope to find it?

5. Have you a preference as to the source of your story material: story or script written directly for the screen, a play designed for theatrical use, or a story (fact or fiction) intended for book or magazine publication? Please explain reasons for your choice.

6. In any of the above cases, do you prefer using another screen dramatist to prepare the actual shooting script, or do you choose to do that work yourself?

7. If you do use another scriptwriter, do you like to work closely with him (or her) as a co-writer, or do you elect to allow the writer to express his views fully, then ultimately do the final script polish yourself?

8. Does it please you to have all the action (business) worked out fully on paper before you start shooting, or do you prefer to improvise?

9. Is there one specific component involved in the creation of a film, which you regard as transcendent in importance: story, script, (or scriptwriter), star or stars, cast (as a whole), film editor, art director, or cameraman?

10. Do you work with a producer? If "Yes": what functions do you expect from him? If "No": would you care to explain?

11. Do you use a dialogue director, if only to save time by making sure that all the actors know their lines? Or, if you use one, is it because you feel that he brings other values to your operation? Kindly elucidate.

12. Do you like to have your writer or producer on your set while you are rehearsing or shooting?

13. Do you work closely with your cameraman prior to shooting: planning effective dramatic and mood lighting, predetermining every camera set-up for effectiveness dramaturgically as well as composition-wise, and in blocking out all camera movements in minute detail? Or, do you again prefer to extemporize?

14. How closely do you supervise the casting of your films? Do you pay particular attention to the proper casting of the more important roles, then allow

your casting director to set the other parts, or do you maintain rigid control of setting the entire cast, down to the one-line bit parts?

15. In considering actors, do you prefer working with the seasoned "technician," or with the more "instinctive" type? Would you care to express your views toward the "method actor"?

16. Is it your practice, before rehearsals—even before the actor has had a chance to form his own image of the character or to absorb his lines—to discuss with him, in depth, your concept of the character or the relationship of that part to the play-structure as a whole? Or is it your position that, having chosen the actor, you would be better advised to let him exercise, uninhibited, those qualities for which you selected him, thus allowing for the possibility of his bringing to the characterization, a plus which is entirely his own?

17. Some very fine directors believe in long rehearsals, covering the entire script with the complete cast, as one would in a theatrical production. Others, perhaps equally talented, shun this method on the theory that "Too much rehearsal flattens out spontaneity." Many hold their rehearsals to a minimum, on the theory that by "shooting rehearsals" they avoid the possibility of leaving the player's best performance on the rehearsal hall floor. What is your view on this subject?

18. Do you insist that an actor adhere meticulously to the script—lines and business—or do you accept the position of some very able actors, that a slight change here or there, can damage nothing, but will enable them to bring more realism, color or effectiveness to the character being portrayed?

19. To what extent do you supervise the editing of your film? *Note*: I recall one director—one of the all-time great American Directors—who loathed viewing his own rushes. He preferred to allow his editor to make his own first rough cut. Then the director would move in and live with the film until a final editing was achieved that presented the picture to a viewer precisely as he had intended as he shot it.

Will you kindly express your views as to the importance of this phase of picture-making, and your individual approach to it?

20. How vital do you believe the musical score to be, as an adjunct in emphasizing the emotional, dramatic or comedic values of a picture?

21. Are you deeply involved in the preparation and recording of the musical score for your films? *Note*: Obviously we are not dealing with filmed opera or musical comedy at this point.

22. Do you exercise final control as to which scenes are to be scored, and which are to be played *a capella*?

Do you have a fixed rule by which you determine this for yourself? If so, would you care to elaborate?

23. We who have directed silent pictures are inclined, perhaps, to overestimate the importance of sound effects, particularly in action sequences. What is your viewpoint on this? To what extent do you participate in the recording and dubbing of the sound effects in your films?

Note to Director-Contributors

After you have completed the questionnaire, if you feel that you have left unsaid, anything that you believe could be vital to the growth and development of the Student Director, please write whatever you have in mind, as fully as you can spare time to do it.

It is quite possible that such thoughts from a man of your standing might well exercise tremendous influence on the lives and careers of a number of future filmmakers.

Hal Ashby

1. BACKGROUND?

I've had very many jobs. I traveled around just trying to find what I wanted to do. This is prior to getting into the motion picture field, and becoming a director. I finally got into film editing. I was a film editor for about ten years and found it to be an excellent background.

2. FIRST FILM JOB?

My first position was running a copy machine making copies of scripts at Universal. I got that job from the State Employment Office in Van Nuys. I went there because it was a free employment agency. I remember sitting there, waiting for about an hour. I told the lady who interviewed me that I wanted to get into the film industry. She looked at me like I was crazy.

From there, I wanted to become a director. I thought, at that time, the quickest way to directing was to become an assistant director, but everyone I spoke to said, "Get into editing. With editing, everything is up there on film for you to see over and over again. You can study it and ask why you like it, and why you don't."

All this took a long time. The biggest break came for me when, after two years, I worked with William Wyler on *The Big Country* [1958]. I was, like, the fifth assistant on it. Those people opened all the doors for me. They really encouraged everyone to get their ideas out. What a blessing it was; the experience changed my life.

3. YOUR GOAL IN FILMMAKING?

My philosophy is what I like to call preoccupation with the "human condition," which can, of course, mean a lot of things. It's basically the relationship between people. I like to do that with entertainment. I just can't get into the idea of pure entertainment. If something is really good, even if someone approaches it with pure entertainment in mind, I think it will have an underlying theme. If I'm dealing with characters that I don't particularly like, I try to be kind with them. If I like the characters, I'm very hard on them.

4. IN WHAT GENRE DO YOU SEEK A STORY?

I look everywhere for my source material. It doesn't matter what genre it might be. Whatever comes along that interests me, I'll do.

5. STORY SOURCE?

I believe an original story would be my preference, because it starts right out with the idea of film in mind. I find that I have to read a script two or three times to fully understand it and bring it to life.

Other things happen with novels; I find I get too emotionally involved in reading a novel. Transposing that to a screenplay is difficult.

A short story might be interesting, and that's one thing I haven't done.

I think there's very little relationship between the stage play and film. I think the best thing you can hope for out of a stage play is to get some very highly emotional things like the delivery of dialogue.

6. USE A SCRIPTWRITER OR DO IT YOURSELF?

I prefer to use another screenplay writer. I like that input, and objective viewpoint.

7. CLOSE COLLABORATION WITH THE SCREENWRITER?

I let them have as much freedom to create as they need, and I will sit with them at the end, and use what I want. I've found with film that the more creativity you can get out of other people, the better chance you have of making a good film.

8. PREPLAN OR IMPROVISE?

The structure of the script is very important to me, so I don't start messing around with that while I'm shooting. If a scene isn't working, I might get into improvisation as long as I know what the obligation of the scene is. I like the spontaneity of films, so I don't like to get it down exactly as the script reads.

9. MOST IMPORTANT COMPONENT OF YOUR FILM?

All of them. The guard is just as important as the quarterback. It's a communal operation to make a film.

10. WORK WITH A PRODUCER?

The function I expect from the producer is to try to get me what I need, and to take a lot of pressure off me. On a more important level, I want that producer's creative input, because he usually feels as close to that story or film as I do, and should have a lot of things to say about it. I look for those things to be said. I expect to have him take care of all the business end of things. Also, I try very hard to work with my producers.

If I were a producer and director on my own films, I would get a sensational production manager and let him become, in effect, an associate producer, and let him produce the film himself.

11. USE A DIALOGUE DIRECTOR?

I haven't used a dialogue director yet.

12. WRITER OR PRODUCER ON THE SET?

That's entirely up to them. If the writer or producer would like to be on the set, they're more than welcome. Certainly with _Shampoo_ [1975], Robert Towne was on the set most of the time, along with Warren Beatty.

13. WORK CLOSELY WITH THE CAMERAMAN?

I don't block out my camera movements in advance. I work very closely with the cameraman before shooting and we talk concept of the overall look of the film; at that time we sometimes make a test to have something concrete to look at. Sometimes he'll make the set-up to see if I like it, and if it feels comfortable.

When we start shooting I'm probably closer to my cameraman than anyone else in the crew. I always make sure I ride to work with him, or come home with him, so we can talk. I've found that the more freedom a cameraman has, the better he works.

14. SUPERVISION OF CASTING?

I maintain a tremendous control on casting. I work very closely with my casting director. Casting is one of the toughest things in the film for me. Casting the major roles can become really frustrating, because it's the first major decision. You have human beings out there waiting to get work.

On _Bound For Glory_ [1976], I used my advent television screen and my video recorder! I had my casting director, Lynn Stalmaster, tape interviews with all the one-liners and one-day players. I was shooting in Stockton and Bakersfield, so he would send the tapes up to me at night. I could play them, run them back and forth until I got a good look. It was a good technique, because those being tested were far more comfortable with the casting director than they would have been with me.

15. PREFERENCE OF ACTING STYLE?

I have no preference. When an actor is good all I know is that I get excited. Whatever it takes for the actor to get where he or she wants to go, it doesn't matter to me how it's done, as long as it works. But he has to have some of the instinct. I do, too. One can have all the "method" there is, but if the instinct isn't there, it's nothing.

16. PRECAMERA WORK WITH ACTOR?

I believe that actors are intelligent people and are capable of giving a character more study, more thought, and more levels than I ever could. If they're good actors, they'll explore many different ways. Take Jack Nicholson in *The Last Detail* [1973]; before shooting, we talked about five or ten different approaches to his character. We talked concept. I never want that exploration to stop. I always encourage my actors to look at the dailies.

Again, with Jack, if he noticed some little mannerism he did, and it worked, he would continue to do it. It was much easier with Jack sitting there with me than if I approached him the next day and said, "You know that little thing you did yesterday..."

17. IMPORTANCE OF REHEARSALS?

I'm more for spontaneity. I think rehearsals are good if you have something complicated that needs to be worked out. It's best to work things out on a Sunday, before you start shooting on Monday morning. That's better than, say, working out something eight weeks in advance, then—ready to shoot—you're standing on the set saying, "Gee—what was it we did eight weeks ago?"

18. ADHERENCE TO SCRIPT?

What ever more color and realism an actor can bring to a script with slight alterations, I'm for. Considering the number of people involved in making a film, it doesn't make much sense to insist that every word must be spoken exactly as it was written.

19. EDITING SUPERVISION?

I do like to look at my dailies. I let the editor have free reign to put the stuff together in a way about which he feels strongly. I did that myself as an editor. It all has to do with getting maximum creativity out of all the elements involved in making a film.

Nowadays, an innovation helps: we have those tabletop editors that are just fantastic. I was raised on the old moviola. I started to use the tabletop on *Harold and Maude* [1971].

20. ROLE OF MUSICAL SCORE

The musical score is vital, I think. You just have to be careful not to overdo it.

21. INVOLVEMENT IN PREPARATION OF MUSICAL SCORE?

I'm very much involved, at least in discussion of what I feel the music should be. I usually find records, and track a portion, a melody or a theme—not to guide or hamper the composer's freedom—but to give him an inkling of what I'm trying for. Over a period of time, I've had the opportunity to experiment with a number of different musical approaches.

22. WHAT SCENES SHOULD HAVE MUSIC?

I have no fixed rule. I usually sit with the composer and pick the areas where I think we should have music. Most composers won't get too alarmed if you should drop something (that they've done) when you get to the mix.

23. SOUND EFFECTS?

Because I've come out of the editing field, I've been very fortunate in knowing some very good sound effect editors, and I've been lucky enough to get them on my films. I know I'm going to have an excess of what I need, but the fact stands that sound effects are very important to the film.

COMMENT

I'd like to impress the importance of a certain openmindedness to be maintained by a newcomer toward the thoughts and ideas of others. Don't ever limit yourself to saying, "This is exactly what I want. You move here, you move there, and speak these words." The result tends to be "locked in" and rigid. On *Harold and Maude* Colin Higgins, the author, was supposed to direct the film.

I went to Robert Evans and said, "Let Colin direct."

Evans said, "No."

I left it up to Colin, who was sitting beside me, as to whether he wanted me to direct the film.

He said I was to do it; Colin was made co-producer; in that capacity, he was able to remain on the set and watch the film being made.

There were times when it was really hard for him to stand by and watch the necessary changes being made. I would say to him, "Try to keep an open mind about these things." He tried, but it wasn't easy.

Then, by the time we got into the editing, he began to understand why certain things were done and why certain other things were not done. I think he was pleased with the result.

So, in making films, it's very important to keep an open mind.

Alessandro Blasetti

1. BACKGROUND?

I was brought up in a middle class family: parochial school, military academy, Army Reserve officer, college. Vocation: show business, since I was five years old.

2. FIRST FILM JOB?

In 1919, just after I was discharged from the army, I worked for a few months as an extra and a bit player, then as critic for a daily newspaper.

After that, I was the founder and editor of two magazines, *The Screen*, and *Cinematography*, which formed the first group of cinema intelligentsia (Libero Solaroli, Mario Serandrei, Francesco Pasinetti, Umberto Barbaro, Aldo Vergano, headed by Massimo Bontempelli: 1926-1930).

In the height of the crisis of the Italian film industry, the work in these magazines triggered the proposal, and then the foundation, of a corporation through which I went directly to directing the motion picture *Sun* [*Sole,* 1929-1930].

3. YOUR GOAL IN FILMMAKING?

I think that making a film by just worrying about the audience's reaction is like getting a gun without the bullets. By the same token, to worry about only the subject of the story—whatever it may be—is like getting the bullets without a gun.

4. IN WHAT GENRE DO YOU SEEK A STORY?

I seek a story having to do with the truth of life, whatever kind (even fable or fantasy), whatever the setting, whatever the time. A fundamental theme: antiviolence in any form and expression.

5. STORY SOURCE?

I have no preference whatsoever with regard to the source of the material on which to base my stories.

6. USE A SCRIPTWRITER OR DO IT YOURSELF?

As far as the screenplay is concerned, I always need some collaboration. This goes for any other director, even for those who turn the function of the collaborator into the so-called "wall," which represents the refraction of what the director says, the reaction to what he proposes.

Chaplin himself—according to what he told me—shared with other people the ideas that came to his mind, the themes he selected, the details he wished to carry out. Those who listened and gave him their comments were just "walls," from which Chaplin got a "bounce back," a reference—a form of collaboration.

I had the honor of spending a few hours with Mr. Chaplin, the greatest artist in the entire history of motion pictures, during his visit to the Experimental Center of Filmmaking (Centro Sperimentale di Cinematografia) here in Rome.

I asked him how important he thought the stories of his films were in relation to the direction. He answered, verbatim: "It takes me two years to prepare a film and two months to make it."

7. CLOSE COLLABORATION WITH THE SCREENWRITER?

There are periods of close collaboration with the screenwriter, which lead to another stage of work, when the screenwriter works by himself, developing the story line as previously agreed upon with the director. Afterwards, writer and director together rearrange and give the final touches to the screenplay.

8. PREPLAN OR IMPROVISE?

With the exception of stories of great inquiries and great explorations, in most cases the fundamental scenic effects in connection with the story and the relative dialogue must be established in the screenplay with the utmost precision.

This does not exclude that, when actually making the picture, the director may give his personal, original touch to the tempo and the tone of an actor's performances and may change some action or business involved in the scene. In the course of amending and developing the story, the director may also make all adaptations to action and dialogue as suggested by unforeseen reality or fantasy. However, this does not mean that I indulge in improvisation, which is certainly *not* my choice.

9. MOST IMPORTANT COMPONENT OF YOUR FILM?

In this century of collectivism and technicalism, I think that cinema was born to express these concepts with the language of art, so that they don't wither the harmony and despoil the free trip of the human being through life.

This is why I think that the aesthetic rules which control other forms of art don't apply to cinema. The concept of collaboration with others does not go with painting, sculpture, poetry, writing and music, while it is congenial and inevitable in the cinema, even at the highest level, that of Charlot (Chaplin).

The director is the sole author of a movie *only* when this is a flop, because the errors of the collaborators fall on the person responsible for hiring and guiding them. However, when a movie is successful, the director will have to acknowledge the work performed by the screenwriter, the actors, the creators of the sets, and of the general atmosphere—namely the set designer, costume designer and cinematographer. Each personal contribution forms an essential and inseparable part of the entire work, even if such contributions are secondary (although not in all cases) to the work of the director.

The weight of such contributions will undoubtedly vary according to each different case. However, the director, under whose name the work is know, should recognize each of them and have the wisdom to praise all of them.

10. WORK WITH A PRODUCER?

This collaboration is based on professional intuition or on the intellectual level of the person in question. When such collaboration is possible—though not easy to find—it gives very good results. Why? Because it involves an understanding which starts with the preparation of the picture, when the actors are cast and the crew selected, thus avoiding the inconvenience of difference, conflicts and polemics. When the atmosphere on the set is serene, free from stifling contentions, in most cases the work proceeds quicker and secures more and convincing results.

11. USE A DIALOGUE DIRECTOR?

I use a dialogue director only in order that the actors learn and say their lines according to the timing and in the way I previously decided, and that was agreed upon with them.

12. WRITER OR PRODUCER ON THE SET?

It varies according to the individuals, namely according to their disposition, and the kind of friendship that binds me to them.

13. WORK CLOSELY WITH THE CAMERAMAN?

It goes without saying. Collaboration with the cinematographer is fundamental, as collaboration with the screenwriter, with the set designer, and with the cast.

Of course, the director and the cinematographer decide together not only the tone and the character of the lighting, but also all the different sizes of shots and camera movements in detail. Collaboration in the making of a film is inevitable. By the same token, the collaborator must not be left to work alone, because not even a shadow of unity of style and content must be lost.

14. SUPERVISION OF CASTING?

I always get the assistance of a casting director. However, I personally select all the cast, down to the last extra—let alone the leads!

15. PREFERENCE OF ACTING STYLE?

I don't follow any particular rule. At times, the solution is in the full maturity of the actor, let's say of a well-trained professional with intelligent and proficient acting experience. In other cases, absolute freshness of spontaneity is indispensable.

The method I used when I was appointed to create the First Italian School of Filmmaking at the St. Cecily Academy of Rome—which later became the Experimental Center of today—was to take all students (directors, actors, men and women) to jails, to hospitals, to mental institutions, to the morgue, so that they could meet face to face with criminals, dying people, prostitutes and madmen. The effect was prodigious.

I never used any French, Russian or American methods; not because I didn't approve of them, but because I was not quite familiar with them.

16. PRECAMERA WORK WITH ACTOR?

I tell the actor immediately how I want his character to be portrayed, and why he was picked for the role. Nearly always the choice is motivated by the personality, the qualities and even the shortcomings of the actor as a person. This is the only way I ask an actor to give me something that's "entirely his own," thus letting him free to give me just what I always wanted.

17. IMPORTANCE OF REHEARSALS?

Naturally only with regard to scenes with difficult dialogue, I tend to have as many rehearsals as needed to achieve tones and rhythm of acting which can express the characters and that particular moment in their lives, just as it was written in the screen play. Only after he masters the mechanics of the dialogue, can an actor capture the meaning of his lines and give them the right feeling.

However, when the actor reaches such a stage of perfection, he also has a tendency to become mechanical. In such cases, I wrap up the day's work without shooting that particular scene.

Next morning, the actor—rested and with the dialogue still vivid in his mind—will deliver his lines with the feeling and the freshness I always wanted.

18. ADHERENCE TO SCRIPT?

When I care a great deal about a picture, or about a particular segment of a picture, I don't like any actor (as great as he may be) to give me a different version from the one that I studied and decided—together with the screenwriter—unless the change improves what was previously established.

19. EDITING SUPERVISION?

I think that the director is often the main author of his films, yet *never the only one*. However, I am also convinced that, from beginning to end, from the very first idea that motivates the motion picture to its final editing, *the work of the director is the determinant in all phases of the making of a film*.

Should it be possible to grade the importance of these phases, *editing* would come first. Editing is where everything can come into right perspective (and can be corrected), where everything can be ruined or saved.

Frankly, I must say that I don't understand that great director, who—without looking at the dailies (and ignoring whether or not they were true to his intentions)—leaves the editing completely to a person who knows these intentions only indirectly, and therefore approximately. I don't mean to say that I don't understand the principal of this method chosen by a man of talent who intends to achieve the interesting result of reading his ideas in the mirror of another person's mind. However, this other person may discard some material that the director might have chosen, or may give the film a rhythm that could be opposite of what the director himself had in mind.

What I really don't understand is how, even after some personal retouching by the director, the film comes out "exactly as he had it in mind while he was shooting it."

My system is very different. I select the dailies, in fact I start cutting scenes while I shoot, in very close collaboration with the editor, whose work is previously agreed upon on the set when I decide on different angles.

20. ROLE OF MUSICAL SCORE

This is undoubtedly the field that less frequently requires the creative work of the director. Therefore, here he may be less determinant than in the fields of screenplay, selection and direction of the actors, set designers, costumes, photography and editing.

The director can only, and should, avoid permitting the musical score to overcome or distort the real meaning of the story. This is why many great directors have resorted to classical music, which offers great selection and no surprises.

However, I must say that often there are cases of lucky encounters between director and composer. The result may then be very effective, because the musical contribution becomes more harmonious, more appropriate, and plays an important part in the film. I had this experience with Maestro Alessandro Cicognini [*Quattro Passi fra le Nuvole/Four Stages in the Cloud*, 1942; *Ettore Fieramosca*, 1939; *Prima Communivre/Father's Dilemma*, 1950].

21. INVOLVEMENT IN PREPARATION OF MUSICAL SCORE?

I do become involved, and as thoroughly as I possibly can.

22. WHAT SCENES SHOULD HAVE MUSIC?

I control the score together with the composer. Everybody has his own rules in order to decide when a musical score is helpful, or when it is superfluous or harmful. Only one rule applies to all: moderation in emotivity and volume. The best music is often the silence in the variety of the different atmospheres.

23. SOUND EFFECTS?

In my opinion, the director must not delegate any of his work to others. Not even when it is a matter of footsteps, the galloping of a horse, the opening and closing of a door or a drawer, the scratching of a pen on paper.

Anything can be annoying–namely, incorrect, excessive or insufficient, i.e. anything not in gear with the atmosphere we intend to create.

COMMENT ON A QUESTION WHICH WAS NOT ASKED

Q. Which is the most essential thing required to become a film director; which is the right way to follow?

A: The essential thing is to know that, if one wants to go on climbing, the road must be long and tough. When the shining talent of a young man makes the road quick and easy, quick and easy will also be the downfall. This philosophy is proved by countless examples.

Clarence Brown

1. BACKGROUND?

By 1910, having graduated from the University of Tennessee, I became an automobile mechanic. Within a few years, I owned my own automobile agency in Birmingham, Alabama. My business was doing well, but I was restless. I spent my lunch hour each day, watching movies. In those days, movies were shown in empty stores with the windows blacked out; a few rows of chairs were lined up for the audience; a sheet of white cloth served as a screen; a makeshift projection booth housed the projector, and sound was provided by a lone piano player.

I really got hooked on movie business. The work of the directors particularly fascinated me. I took to studying their work avidly. Finally it dawned on me that I, too, could learn to direct. At that point I was no longer a fan; I was a student-observer, analyzing, trying to see how dramatic effects were achieved. One name began to loom large in my mind: Maurice Tourneur, a Frenchman whose work, in my opinion, was vastly superior to any other of the directors whose work I had studied.

Finally, determined that moviemaking was the business for me, I dropped everything and hightailed it for Fort Lee, New Jersey, and the great Tourneur. I laid everything out for him, right on the line. At first he seemed disappointed in my total lack of experience in the motion picture business, but before the interview was over he had hired me! At the staggering sum of twenty dollars per week! Which brings me right up to answer Question Number Two.

2. FIRST FILM JOB?

My first job in the picture business was as assistant director to that wonderful pioneer filmmaker, Maurice Tourneur. That job, in those days, was not very closely related to the position as we know it today. In addition to the duties which we now regard as the normal functions of the assistant director, I was expected to take a hand in everything that needed doing.

Then, when the picture was finished shooting, I would work in the cutting room with Mr. Tourneur, helping him edit.

It was not too long before I was doing all the editing myself. Shortly after that, when we were viewing the previous day's work, if the boss saw a scene that displeased him, he'd turn to me with, "What did you think of that?"

Usually, I'd say, "Looks okay to me."

He'd answer, "It's bad. Tomorrow *you* shoot it over."

So, the next day, scared half to death, I'd go out and reshoot the scene. Strangely enough, he usually liked what I shot. Soon after that, he inaugurated a new system: sending me out to shoot all the location stuff. He always said that it was because he loathed shooting anywhere but in the studio. I often wondered how true that was, because he was a kind and generous man.

World War I came along and I went to work as a flight instructor. When the war ended, I returned to Fort Lee to discover that my friend and benefactor had joined the great trek to Hollywood. I followed.

In Hollywood, Tourneur helped me in my search for the story for my first movie—as a director. We found an idea in a news story about a cowboy-artist who, having been jailed for some minor offense, brightened his cell walls with drawings.

In 1920, this idea hit the screen as a prison-melodrama entitled *The Great Redeemer*. It was a commercial success. However, The *New York Times* commented patronizingly, "It might have been a great deal better, but also it might have been much worse." Not an auspicious beginning, but at least a start.

3. YOUR GOAL IN FILMMAKING?

My primary objective in making a film was always to provide entertainment. In my opinion, the only accurate barometer we had for judging the entertainment value of a picture was *audience reaction*. There seems to be a tendency today, among producers, to forego the obvious advantages of the preview, preferring to trust their own judgment implicitly. I am convinced that this is a serious mistake. It is *audience reaction* which ultimately translates into box-office dollars, in direct ratio to the degree of theatregoers' acceptance.

At no time had I any interest in making a film for the purpose of imposing my views, political or social, on an audience that had *paid* to be entertained. However, were I to have found a fine story in which an integral part of the yarn expressed my views on a controversial subject, I would not have hesitated to film it. My only example (one of the last pictures I made) was *Intruder In the Dust* [1949]. It won a "Picture Of The Year" award from the British Academy [of Film and Television Arts].

If ever I had made a film for purposes of propagandizing my views, I would have announced it as an educational or a documentary.

Regarding what constitutes entertainment in movies, I would say, "The story with which the people in the audience can *identify*." The little shop girl thrills to a picture in which a poor girl like herself, through courageous effort, becomes the wife of the governor. Pollyanna, of course, but the basic principle touches the innermost hopes of a large percentage of an audience. Most of us, young or old, have our "Impossible Dreams"; the optimistic type of story gives us reason to hope. Our super-sophisticates are very outspoken in their scorn for "escapist" thinking, but Mr. Average American knows that, every four years, in this country, someone is elected president. Mr. Average American knows, also, that a very small percentage of the men so elected, have come from rich or powerful families.

Obviously, I can't buy the theory that, to represent life, a story must be one of futility, or that it must be loaded with obscenity or violence, and generously spiced with intimate sex exposure. Our daily bathroom duties are certainly a vital part of life, but I can visualize no way in which they can be photographed so as to qualify them as *objects d'art.*

4. IN WHAT GENRE DO YOU SEEK A STORY?

It has been said that much of my best work has been in the field of Americana. If that is true, it was not due to a conscious effort on my part. It is a fact, however, that I thrilled to stories involving American people, American spirit, and the great American dream. It is quite possible that my vulnerability to situations involving these elements influenced my choice of picture story material.

5. STORY SOURCE?

I've had no preference as to the source of story material. Any place I found an idea from which I believed a good picture could be developed, I've latched onto it, be it a flop play, a new novel, a passage in a history book, or an obituary column.

I've made many films from "originals" over the years. From Broadway plays, I've had such great properties as *Ah Wilderness* [1935] and *Anna Christie* [1930]—both by Eugene O'Neill—and *Idiot's Delight* [1939] by Robert Sherwood. From novels came such films as *Anna Karenina* [1935] by Count Leo Tolstoy, *National Velvet* [1945] by Enid Bagnold, and *Intruder In The Dust*, by William Faulkner.

Actually, I find it impossible for me to express a preference. Tomorrow, even though I have long been retired, I might become quite excited over an idea gleaned from an article in a medical journal, or a bit of California real estate development literature. If I did happen across such an idea, I'd undoubtedly give it to one of my younger friends.

However, it's an even money bet that the one to whom I gave it, would never see in it the things that had excited me. Picturemaking is a highly individualized operation, and for every idea there are as many concepts as there are directors to whom the idea is presented.

6. USE A SCRIPTWRITER OR DO IT YOURSELF?

I am not a writer. I can imagine no circumstance under which I would undertake to write a script for myself, or for anyone else.

7. CLOSE COLLABORATION WITH THE SCREENWRITER?

I can only repeat that I was, in no sense, a writer, although I prided myself on knowing good writing when I saw it. Consequently, I did work very closely with my writer. My reason for desiring this close collaboration was an obvious one: from the outset I always had a clearly visualized plan for the unfolding of the story.

When, under such joint endeavor, a script was completed and shooting started, there were often instances when scenes did not play as I had believed they would. If the changes involved only *business*, I handled the adjustments myself. If the indicated alterations were concerned with dialogue, I sent for the writer.

8. PREPLAN OR IMPROVISE?

It verges on the impossible for any picturemaker to block out detailed physical action in advance, with any degree of accuracy. Experience has taught us that, until we have rehearsed a scene with the first string players, on the set or on location, any preconceived bits of action or business are quite likely to prove unworkable, or at least far from the effective bits we can come up with. Many times the actors themselves will *feel* something that prompts a suggestion. In many cases, a rehearsal of a scene exactly as written will make a clearly defined demand for whatever is lacking. I have always felt that this sort of improvisation was a matter of necessity—not of choice.

9. MOST IMPORTANT COMPONENT OF YOUR FILM?

There has been no doubt in my mind that story and the scriptwriter are the all-essential starting points. If you're wrong in those areas, no matter what you do in an effort to overcome your mistake, you'll never come up with a really good film.

However, prior to shooting, the selection of stars and cast, the choice of cameraman, art director, recorder, editor—each in turn assumes the position of prime importance. It is true that a fine actor or actress can, in some instances, lift an uninspired scene to great heights momentarily, but to escalate a weak story into a good picture is an impossibility.

We hear of an actress who can read aloud from a telephone directory, and move her listeners to tears. Such a reading is comparable to playing one scene, one minute or so, not to building a dramatic structure which will hold an audience for an hour-and-one-half, or two hours....

Now let's stroll briefly down the other side of the street. A weak or incompetent star or cast can emasculate a fine director's work, using the best script ever written.

When shooting is concluded, the film editor takes the stage. There's no doubt that a sensitive and intuitive editor can work wonders with a film. However, there's an old saying in the business: "If it ain't on the film, you can't put it there."

To summarize: it is my opinion that, from the director's viewpoint, although all the crafts involved are vital in determining the quality of the finished picture, the story and script are transcendent in importance.

10. WORK WITH A PRODUCER?

Over the years, I have worked with many of the great producers, and a lot of others who were something less than great.

As to what functions I expected from a producer: I expected him to assist me in any way he could in the preparation of the script. It was the generally accepted practice for a producer to deal with the multitude of problems, large and small, which seem—inevitably—to plague the preparation of a picture.

When shooting started, I expected the producer to continue to run interference for me.

11. USE A DIALOGUE DIRECTOR?

I can't recall ever having used a dialogue director. I know that many of the old-time directors, from silent picture days, were disturbed by the switch to dialogue. Some of them used dialogue directors—men with theatrical experience—at first as a safety precaution. Most of them discontinued the practice as soon as they had adjusted to the added dimension of sound.

As for bringing "other values" to my operation: I have never felt that this was necessary. I expected each film I made to be an accurate and undistorted reflection of that particular story exactly as I had visualized it.

Regarding the idea that a dialogue director could save time by making certain that all the actors knew their lines: my casts, including the stars, were—with a few exceptions—selected from the ranks of highly trained professionals. Among other assets, one is entitled to expect from a professional actor a thorough self-discipline. Such discipline should render it most unlikely that an actor report for work without being properly prepared.

12. WRITER OR PRODUCER ON THE SET?

The writer was always free to come and go on my sets. During the shooting of most pictures there seems, inevitably, to come that moment when something doesn't play as we had anticipated. At such a time, a writer is doubly welcome.

As for producers? The wise and knowledgeable producer knows that he is not needed on the set, and he usually has plenty of things on his mind, so that he doesn't need to go about looking for trouble.

13. WORK CLOSELY WITH THE CAMERAMAN?

I always enjoyed a close relationship with my cameraman. Together, we planned dramatic and mood lighting. However, I did not attempt to predetermine every camera set-up and movement prior to shooting. Long experience had taught me that such a procedure is not very practical.

In the matter of photographic composition, my cameraman and I collaborated very closely. I wouldn't have a cameraman who didn't have an eye for composition.

Also, I consider myself fairly able in this area, having absorbed a lot of it from that great artist, Maurice Tourneur. An example: when working out a set-up for a full or medium shot, I'd often use a masking piece in close foreground, in half-tone, to lend depth to the set. It was one of the first things Tourneur taught me about composition.

It had been my good fortune to have worked with some of the all-time greatest cameramen. I have learned much about composition from them, and—I like to think—they have profited by the association as well.

14. SUPERVISION OF CASTING?

There are no "unimportant parts," even including the one-line bits. I always exercised the utmost care in the selection of every member of the cast. There were no exceptions. The student would do well to remember that one line, improperly read, can hurt a scene badly.

15. PREFERENCE OF ACTING STYLE?

Naturally, it was to my advantage to use experienced actors whenever suitable types were available.

The seasoned actors, even those of the more "instinctive" type acquired, through experience, a solid *technical foundation*. The actor who works completely within the framework of a technique, will give you the identical performance of any given scene again and again, once he is set in it solidly. This has obvious advantages. The director, as well as the other actors in the scene, will know exactly what to expect from the technician.

Conversely, the "instinctive type" actor is unlikely to play the same scene in exactly the same way on any two occasions. He plays it as he "feels" it. As a scene builds through rehearsal, he changes with the mounting emotion of the scene. As a result, the other participants in the scene—including the director—never know exactly what the instinctive performer will do. Yet, whatever he does, it will register with inspired integrity.

Viewed from every angle, I much prefer the seasoned instinctive type. The man I regard as by far the most consummate actor with whom I have worked, was utterly unpredictable. He'd be on the phone on the sound stage, placing a bet with his bookie. The assistant director would call him for a shot; he'd hang up, step into the set and into his character as you and I might slip into a coat someone was holding for us. His dialogue would be letter perfect, and his performance brilliant. Of course, there was technique involved, but no amount of technique could ever have delivered the impact he brought to the scene.

I am not an advocate of the "method" school of acting. In watching these actors perform, I sensed a certain sameness about their performances. Most of them seem to have a high disregard for diction. Actually, in many cases, the "Method" seems to stand out much more clearly than does the characterization.

16. PRECAMERA WORK WITH ACTOR?

I didn't do too much with the actor until rehearsals started. I wanted to get all each performer had, so—on my first rehearsal—I turned the actor loose.

In that way, I found out very quickly what he was bringing to the character: richness, color or an added dimension. It often proved, in some way, better than the concept I'd had in mind. At such times, I'd take the good things he did, and blend them with my own thinking. The results were usually very satisfying.

17. IMPORTANCE OF REHEARSALS?

Certainly I have always believed in rehearsing each sequence fully, until I was thoroughly satisfied. This doesn't mean that I concurred with the practice of rehearsing the entire screenplay as one would a play for "live" theatre. I found, over the years, that I achieved my best results through rehearsing each scene fully, just prior to shooting it.

As to the question of over-rehearsing and the danger of leaving the actor's best performance on the rehearsal-hall floor, one often hears a knowledgeable director say, "We'll shoot a rehearsal."

In most cases, when a director says that, it is because he feels the scene is ready to be shot, but suspects that an announcement of the fact might have the effect of tightening up the performers. Personally, I've never called for a "take" until I believed the actors were at their best for the scene.

18. ADHERENCE TO SCRIPT?

I've never had an irrevocable rule about an actor adhering meticulously to the script. There are so many variables involved that it would have been most difficult to do so. So much depended on the individual actor who was suggesting the deviation. There are many actors—particularly those of super-star status—who, through training or instinct, never suggest even the simplest dialogue or business change that can, in any way, injure the intent of the scene or the storyline.

Unfortunately, however, there have always been some actors who appear to have very little interest in the story as a whole. Their concern would seem to be involved only with the character they were doing. Such people would try to slip in a line or a bit of business that they believed would fatten their part, regardless of the impact on the story.

I have even known actors who seldom read an entire script that they were doing, starting with the first line and absorbing the story to final fade-out. Those people are dangerous. The knowledge that people of that sort are to be found at every level of the acting craft keeps the director constantly alert.

To return, momentarily, to the *real professionals*—who far outnumber the "Bad Guys"—one would do well to give close attention to anything the real professionals suggest. They are *thinking actors*—people who study each character they play, and the kinship of that character to the story. These "Good Guys" often come up with suggestions which prove to be valid and of great worth to the picture.

19. EDITING SUPERVISION?

From the moment I first ran my rushes, I began explaining to the cutter precisely how I intended that the film be assembled. Together, the editor and I would run each sequence as soon as it was put together. After the running, we would discuss means of tightening the scene, where close-ups were needed, or whether I felt they should be eliminated. By this method, I was usually able to view the whole picture, in rough cut, soon after the conclusion of shooting.

Then, the real editorial work began. If I was pleased with the first cut, it became a matter of tightening up the whole show so that it flowed smoothly, and the dramatic elements drew together inevitably, closer and closer. This process continued until the film finally crystalized into the picture I had originally visualized.

I am convinced that there is no function more vital for the director than the editing of his film. I have seen pictures with excellent potential rendered dull and totally lacking in vitality by insensitive or unimaginative cutting.

On the other side of the ledger, I have seen pictures previewed before they were properly edited. They were dismal flops. I have seen films, after they'd been sweated down, previewed again as fine, entertaining movies.

By the term "sweated down," I mean run again and again _ad infinitum._ Usually, when you rerun a film often enough—even one you have considered polished—you will find a cut here or there that smooths the flow and snaps up the pace materially.

I am convinced that, no matter how well a story is directed, it still requires the concentrated attention of the director during the editing to bring a film to its full potential.

20. ROLE OF MUSICAL SCORE

Used judiciously, music is one of our most potent of dramatic tools. In "action" scenes, a well-done score can add immeasurably to the excitement. A haunting love theme, properly reprised, can bring added tenderness to a romance. However, many pictures have been injured by too much scoring.

I have always worked very closely with my composer and scorer, both in advance of shooting and right on through the actual recording and dubbing sessions.

21. INVOLVEMENT IN PREPARATION OF MUSICAL SCORE?

I repeat: there is no operation involved in picture-making to which I do not give my total attention. Obviously, scoring falls into this category. Fortunately, I have worked with some of the greatest motion picture composers in the world. It was my practice, always, to sit with my composer after he had familiarized himself with the script. Together, we would discuss the picture. By the time these sessions were concluded, he knew exactly where, and to what purpose, I had visualized scoring. He'd have made his recommendations, and we'd have reached a mutual agreement.

The usual practice was to overscore, on the theory that if you didn't like it, you could cut it out. After a preview, it was not at all unusual for a composer to say, "We've got to lose that musical bit. The scene will play much better without it."

I don't believe I ever disagreed with a composer on that point.

22. WHAT SCENES SHOULD HAVE MUSIC?

As regards my exercising final control as to which scenes are to be scored and which are to be played *a cappella*, I must state unequivocally that Mr. Composer and Mr. Preview are both my ardent advocates in my exercise of this final control.

23. SOUND EFFECTS?

I do not subscribe to the theory that having directed many "silents," inclines me to overestimate the importance of sound effects. If anyone doubts the value of sound in "action" sequences, I suggest that he view a gun battle, an automobile chase, or even a rough-and-tumble fist fight, silent; then run it with proper sound effects. The question will be eradicated from his mind, permanently

As regards my involvement in the recording and dubbing of the sound effects: it was exactly parallel to my involvement in every other phase of my approach to filmmaking: I stayed on top of it until I was completely satisfied with it.

René Clair

1. BACKGROUND?

I was a journalist and writer, before entering the cinema world. In fact, during the first two years of my association with the film business—acting and composing screenplays—I also worked as a writer of the film section of the magazine, *Théâtre et Comedia Illustrés*, even though I was constantly growing more intrigued with the screen art.

2. FIRST FILM JOB?

My first contact with the cinema was as an actor—a juvenile lead with directors [Yakov] Protazanov and Louis Feuillade in serials. The following year, becoming more than ever fascinated by cinema, I worked with director Jacques de Baroncelli, composing screenplays. In 1923, I directed my first film: *Paris Qui Dort* [*The Crazy Ray*].

3. YOUR GOAL IN FILMMAKING?

As with the novel, the play, the poem, or the musical composition, the prime purpose of the cinema is to entertain. In some of my films, there is an underlying objective, but—for God's sake—no message. Many films give the illusion of importance because their makers include a glimpse of a message. However, the illusion of importance does not necessarily imply entertainment.

Over the years, in my films, I have tried with constant determination to keep the cinema as an art, free from contamination from foreign elements of any nature. I have made some films in my career for the wrong reasons—films that didn't spring from my heart—that I now completely disown.

Thus, I would advise students of filmmaking: whatever you do, know it, love it, and be faithful to it.

4. IN WHAT GENRE DO YOU SEEK A STORY?

In fifty years of filmmaking, I have experimented with many types of material and background. With experience, it soon became evident to me that, of all the dramatic fields, comedy was the one toward which I was drawn. To my delight, I had discovered that I was able to find humor in almost any subject with which I was dealing, no matter how somber that subject appeared. Comedy, and the rhythm of comedy, were my genre, right or wrong.

5. STORY SOURCE?

I much prefer a story and script written directly for the screen for obvious reasons: I am convinced that theatrical plays have been a hindrance rather than an aid to the growth and development of the cinema.

In the theatre, because of the distance separating the players from the audience, the facial expressions of the actors are, at best, dimmed or minimized from the viewer's standpoint. Consequently, the theatrical tale must be unfolded and dramatized, largely through the use of dialogue and exaggerated gestures.

Film, even though it may talk, remains a medium of expression that affects the eye more strongly than the ear—*sight* as opposed to *sound*! The playwright is constricted to dramatizing his story within the narrow bounds of his set (or sets), and with minimal physical action; whereas, for the screenplaywright, visual action is his vividly articulate means of communication with his audience. For sets: he has the world—without limit!

6. USE A SCRIPTWRITER OR DO IT YOURSELF?

In the making of a film, I have found that I can approach the actual shooting with more ease and confidence if I have prepared the final shooting script myself, with or without a collaborator.

No other person can possibly have any cognizance of a director's previsualization of the finished film—*and that completed film is solely the director's responsibility!*

However, once I have had a good talk with a prospective collaborator, revealing to him my complete plan for the story development, the characters, and the subtler nuances which give color and life to both, then if he (the writer) understands and concurs, I know we are on the right track.

Of course, if he does not agree with my approach, then I would be better advised to do that work myself. Under the stress of final script preparation, I don't need a devil's advocate, thank you!

7. CLOSE COLLABORATION WITH THE SCREENWRITER?

As indicated in the foregoing, I like to work very closely with a co-screenwriter. After I have briefed him thoroughly on my thinking, and made quite sure that he agrees as to how the script should go—then, and *only* then—do I know that we are ready to start...together.

All of this does not mean that I do not listen and weigh whatever suggestions the writer has to offer. So long as the suggestions do not violate the boundaries, structural and characterwise, on which we have agreed, I am most grateful for any suggestions that will enhance the artistic, dramatic or entertainment values of the film.

Lest this sound too arbitrary, let me explain. Fortunately, or unfortunately, this seems to be the only way in which I can function at my best. My film must be an expression of the *best* of what I think and feel...and perhaps dream. Then, good or bad, it is mine!

8. PREPLAN OR IMPROVISE?

In the beginning, probably due to uncertainties arising from inexperience, I liked to have everything worked out on paper. Later, I improvised more. By that time, experience had taught me that it is impossible for one to sit in an office and anticipate the exact conditions or limitations a set or a location can impose on one, or the situations which can arise from the actors themselves—a scene which read so well, but just doesn't play, or in which seasoned actors feel awkward and ill-at-ease. At such times, the director is out there on his own, and extemporization is his only solution.

However, in extemporizing, there is one particular pitfall against which one must be constantly on guard: no improvised alterations of action or dialogue must ever be undertaken until the filmmaker has fully assured himself that the proposed change can in no way disturb the carefully designed dramatic structure of the screenplay.

This is by no means an imputation of extemporization. Actually, some of our most effective ideas come to us inspirationally, under the stress of actual shooting. We must woo the muse constantly and ardently. But, again, a word of warning: we should never allow the exultant thrill of inspired improvisation to lead us astray. It is imperative that we proceed with great caution. *One does not improvise dramaturgy!*

9. MOST IMPORTANT COMPONENT OF YOUR FILM?

All the listed elements are essential to film realization. However, a picture may be magnificently acted, superbly directed, recorded and photographed, but if the story and script are not worthy, the picture is doomed. Of what good is a building—even though it is superbly constructed, of the finest materials, by master-craftsmen—if it is erected on a flimsy foundation? I have never heard it said of a picture that it was well-written, but badly directed!

10. WORK WITH A PRODUCER?

Most of the opinions expressed herein are based on retrospective evaluation of many years of experience as a writer-director, and often as co-producer in France.

Of course, my position was not the same in Hollywood, where the directors, working for the great companies, have less independence and liberty. Naturally, given the choice, I prefer to function as director and producer.

It does not require more than one skilled musician to compose a superb sonata, nor does it require more than one able writer to produce a fine French novel; nor have I heard that the *Mona Lisa* was created by a committee. As in these art forms, it is my opinion that the making of a picture is singularly a one-man responsibility. The cameraman, the electricians, and the director's assistant, are all vitally important, but they do not make the film. They, with the cast, constitute the tools and raw materials with which the director works to achieve the ultimate manifestation of his dreams.

From my personal viewpoint, the producer is in no way as vital to the quality of the film as any of those mentioned above. If I do have a producer, I ask of him, *only* that I be left alone. Then, be the final result success or failure, the responsibility is mine.

As far as I have been able to learn, there is no fail-proof formula for making a success. I guess we have all tasted the acrid futility of a flop.

11. USE A DIALOGUE DIRECTOR?

I did use a dialogue director occasionally when I was making pictures in English, because of my lack of familiarity with the language. However, in French—NEVER! I can imagine no way in which another director could be of any possible benefit to me or to the film.

12. WRITER OR PRODUCER ON THE SET?

There's no possible reason why I should object to having the producer or writer on my set, so long as he (or they) do not impair or in any way interfere with what I am trying to do. However, regardless of visitors, *that set is the director's domain*—a fact that must be respected at all times!

13. WORK CLOSELY WITH THE CAMERAMAN?

As stated earlier, there are times when, despite the most careful advance planning, improvisation becomes imperative. Particularly is this true in the areas of camera movement and visual composition. Frequently we find that our thoughtfully planned camera action just doesn't work. Ergo: we must extemporize.

However, in my experience, this lacks much of being the "kiss of death." There's something—possibly it's the thrill of seeing one's dreams actually pulsing into life, in the background one had visualized—that gives a powerful spur to the imagination in those emergencies. Not infrequently, the inspirational thing that one does at these moments emerges bright and gleaming with qualities one had scarcely dared hope for. I must confess in this area I prefer to extemporize.

14. SUPERVISION OF CASTING?

Close supervision of the casting—big parts, small parts, one-line bits, no-line bits, even atmosphere, when particular types are required—seems to me to rank high among the director's duties. In this way he manages to avoid most of the unpleasant surprises that one must surely encounter if he were to leave any part of the casting to another person. Even the most insignificant bit must have its one unique form in order to fit in and complete the jig-saw puzzle; which is the completed picture. If a bit is less essential than that it should not be in the script.

15. PREFERENCE OF ACTING STYLE?

Great actors are instinctive as well as being thorough technicians. Most of the truly fine performers are born with an instinct for knowing how the other fellow reacts to any given set of circumstances—how he thinks and feels. This is the quality, incidentally, which enables him to slip into a character—"feeling it" every step of the way, and which—in the theatre—enables him to give an identical performance every night.

One of the greatest difficulties a director faces, even with good actors, is to find the way between what he visualizes within himself, about the part, and what he feels the actor can *do*.

There is still another type actor who warrants mention because, unfortunately, he seems to be with us in rather large numbers—not, however, in important roles, thank god! This is the person who, as far as anyone can determine, is without natural gifts, but is heavily endowed (or cursed) with an overpowering exhibitionism and its accompanying self-assurance. Beware of these people. They are dangerous. They are likely to have mastered a technical smoothness which is quite effective in the smaller parts in which they are not required to do anything involving too much honest emotion. Don't be fooled by their smoothness and apparently effortless charm.

I honestly don't know what is meant by "method actor."

16. PRECAMERA WORK WITH ACTOR?

I never discuss characterization in depth with an actor, or the relationship of his part to the whole. If he is really a good, professional performer, he will know these things very definitely as soon as he has had an opportunity to study his script.

Of course, there are those actors who, after the first quick reading—interested only in *their* parts—never again glance at anything in the script but their own lines or cues. These people should be avoided whenever these facts are known about them. There is seldom room for a soloist in a dramatic motion picture. Obviously, I do not refer to musicals—only to straight dramatic or comedic cinema.

17. IMPORTANCE OF REHEARSALS?

I don't believe in rehearsals without a camera. By that, I mean that I prefer to rehearse only when I am on the set or location in which the scenes are to be shot, with the actors and the entire crew.

Between the brain that conceives it, and the screen that finally reflects it, there is a plethora of problems, any one of which may upset the most skillfully devised program of operation.

The ablest, most resourceful and experience of filmmaker can't possible anticipate every obstacle which can arise to harass him; camera movements and lighting effects that just won't work, readings and business for the actors—perfect on paper and in rehearsal, refuse stubbornly to adapt themselves to their new surroundings; at least a hundred other equally frustrating impediments can intercede. In such cases, the time devoted to prior rehearsals is not only wasted, but additional quantities of that precious commodity are consumed by actors and technicians unlearning much of the useless procedure acquired in premature rehearsals.

18. ADHERENCE TO SCRIPT?

Among the many duties of the cinema director, there is none more vital to the ultimate quality of the film than that which demands that he bring out the best performances of which his actors are capable.

Furthermore, the cinema actor seldom has an opportunity to build and play out an entire scene. He can express only fractions of the emotions, which, when properly connected to one another later on, will form a succession, the quality of which cannot be completely or accurately evaluated before this assemblage is accomplished.

The cinema actor's job is a complex one. Consequently, I agree to any slight change here or there—anything that will enable the actor to feel at ease in his part—as long as the change does not damage anything. As to the likelihood of such damage, I, as the director, must retain the right to be the final judge.

19. EDITING SUPERVISION?

Film editing has been defined as: "The essence of the cinematic art." It is, in fact, a procedure peculiar to the cinema, which has no equivalent in any other art form. Certainly there is no phase of filmmaking more essential in determining the flow, the vitality and dramatic impact of the completed picture.

All the time our eyes are open to the light, they never record anything but an uninterrupted succession of images. Now, editing permits the eye of the camera to effectuate arbitrary cuts—compressions in time and place, in a fraction of a second. Thanks to the first craftsmen who juxtaposed and intercut various scenes, or shots, taken at different distances at different times, editing manufactured the language of the cinema. Until then, film had been only photography in motion.

The infinite advantages this procedure offers can become disadvantages if the process is used unthinkingly or immoderately. Disorderly editing can give rise to confusion that makes the viewer wonder: "Where are we? What is taking place?"

I am aware that a certain amount of confusion is not always sneered at in our day, but this fashion will pass, as does everything that is based on artifice.

It is in the nature of every beginner to be tempted (as I was), by some of the startling effects of editing. That is a facile procedure of which you can soon tire. When you have thought about it for awhile, your greatest hope is that every filmed sequence, no matter how intercut it is with different shots, will look as if it had been cast in a single piece. The best editing job is the one that is so right, you do not notice it.

I supervise the editing of my films very closely, of course.

20. ROLE OF MUSICAL SCORE?

There is no doubt that music can be a decided adjunct when used with discretion and taste. However, it is my considered opinion that music has injured, seriously, more scenes than it has benefited.

Naturally, there are exceptions—pictures in which the director had definitely anticipated help from the composer in emphasizing certain dramatic moments. But these things are designed; they are not accidents.

The greatest injuries brought about by unwise or overzealous composers is most frequently seen in sentimental moments or bright comedy dialogue scenes.

21. INVOLVEMENT IN PREPARATION OF MUSICAL SCORE?

As indicated previously, I am always vitally concerned with every aspect of my pictures. Naturally, I am quite deeply involved in the preparation and recording of the score for each of my films.

At the advent of sound, it was fervently hoped that sound-cinema would give rise to an entirely new type of music, conceived for the microphone and the loudspeaker, and so intimately tied in with the film that it would be almost impossible to separate them.

Now, it has to be admitted, that outside of a few exceptional cases, nothing like that has happened, and that the music for films is not outstanding for its originality. The score that Erik Satie wrote for my *Entr'acte* in 1924, to accompany a silent film, is more "cinematic" than many of the scores written today for sound-films. Ah well, we can always hope.

22. WHAT SCENES SHOULD HAVE MUSIC?

Yes, I do exercise control as to which scenes are to be scored, and which are to be played *a cappella* in my films. In order for me to even approximate the film as I have visualized it, it is essential that I control every phase of the picture's realization, from its earliest concept to the completed cinema.

It seems to me that there can be only one author fixed rule by which one can determine this for himself: one must weigh each scene and sequence, to decide whether music will enhance the dramatic or comedic values or each, or whether it will, instead, actually deplete the basic values in them. Often, this decision becomes a matter of pure instinct on the filmmaker's part.

23. SOUND EFFECTS?

Organized sound (music or the human voice) lends itself to an infinite number of combinations, whereas the number of *natural sounds* that can be used for dramatic ends is exceedingly small. It is because of the poverty of the catalogue of noises, that music is used so frequently, and—in my opinion—so arbitrarily in most films.

In the early days of sound, the *Tower of Babel* seemed to be the symbol of the "talkies." Added to this "babel," every opportunity to use sound—at its most ferocious level—would add to the din. The effect on the viewer was most abrasive.

It was not until 1929 that a significant breakthrough occurred in the use of sound. In *The Broadway Melody*, director Harry Beaumont found its form for the first time, neither cinema nor theatre, but a new genre.

The immobility of the shots—the flaw that had marred talking pictures—had disappeared. The camera was mobile, the shots as fluid and varied as in good silent films. The sound effects were used with restraint and intelligence. If some of them seemed superfluous, others would be held up as models. For example: the sound of a car door being shut, and the car pulling away (all off-screen), are heard under a close shot of Bessie Love, in anguish, as she watches the unseen departure from a window.

In another scene, Bessie Love is in bed, sad and pensive. The viewer felt that she was about to cry, but—as she puckered up her face—the image disappeared into the shadow of a fade-out, and from the screen, which had turned black, issued the sound of a single sob.

Both of the above scenes carried tremendous emotional and dramatic impact. Since that time there have been remarkable refinements in the sound system; such as *sound perspective* and the added fidelity of sound on magnetic tape.

However, I feel that there is still much to be accomplished by the unrestricted use of the imagination that these facilities afford us.

Jack Clayton

1. BACKGROUND?

I didn't have a vocation. At the age of fifteen, I ran away from school. In fact, I ran away three times, and because I had such a wonderful mother, she said if I found myself a job, I needn't go back to school. I got a job as someone who made the tea for Alexander Korda, head of Korda Films. I was fifteen at the time. Alexander Korda was a wonderful man and it so happened that he loved children—and that's the only reason I got the job from him.

2. FIRST FILM JOB?

I started as a gofor. Then I became a second assistant director. Then I went into cutting—then camera work. A little incident at this time took five-and-one-half years of my life. It was the Second World War. I was in the Air Force and managed to get into the film unit where I photographed bombing raids.

When I eventually started to direct films, I'd been through virtually every department of films, and strangely enough, got sidetracked most beautifully into being a producer before I was a director. I was also, at one time, a production manager and an associate producer. I have never done anything in the film industry that I couldn't personally enjoy. When I became a producer, I would always be tearing my fingernails off, because I knew that I always wanted to be a director. I took a very long way around to becoming a director.

3. YOUR GOAL IN FILMMAKING?

As you know, I've not done a lot of films. I have five-and-one-quarter to my credit. Basically, I've only made a film on the average of one every three years, and sometimes even longer.

The philosophy is possibly in the choice. I have to choose something a) different from the previous film I did, and b) subject matter with which I associate emotionally, or for which I have some great personal feeling. I definitely do have other objectives than providing entertainment, but—more than anything—I would love the idea that any one of them is entertaining.

4. IN WHAT GENRE DO YOU SEEK A STORY?

Absolutely any source is acceptable. I wish I were like so many wonderful directors who can turn almost any idea into a film. I think that's the finest way of doing it. I'll do anything, but I like the original script written directly for the screen.

5. STORY SOURCE?

I seriously consider almost anything, including a one line statement, if it has one really substantial idea in it. I prefer novels to plays, but I don't think one can be over specific about it.

6. USE A SCRIPTWRITER OR DO IT YOURSELF?

I've worked on every screenplay that I ever made, but I always work with another writer, although I don't consider myself a writer. I do consider myself, as I think every director does, a substantial contributor to the ultimate script.

I did a script once with Harold Pinter called *The Pumpkin Eater* [1964]. He very kindly offered me a co-screenplay credit when we were finished with the picture. I worked very hard on that script, but I didn't accept the credit. I consider the work on the script as important to the director as the shooting is. I consider it as part of my directing job, and I don't want another screen title.

7. CLOSE COLLABORATION WITH THE SCREENWRITER?

I don't, personally, like the idea of a screenwriter left totally alone to produce something without a lot of guidance. The way that guidance is given depends on the way the writer likes to work. I will always adapt to the way in which the writer feels more comfortable and likes to work. I'm in close contact with the writer the whole while, so by the time the first draft emerges, it will emerge as the basic principal of what I think it should be, having been written by him. After that, any polishing job we'll do together.

8. PREPLAN OR IMPROVISE?

Fifty-fifty is the answer. When you, as a director, work on a script so closely that you know it as well as the writer, you devise many of the scenes yourself. You say, let's change this scene or this scene. When you do something like that, the idea for the scene is already in your mind as a director. It has to be. It's a visual thing, and you have to, basically, know what to do. I know exactly how I will shoot many scenes before going on the floor.

However, for the other fifty percent, I like to have freedom, so that my artists (when I'm working on a script, I don't know who they'll be) can, by the chemistry of their personalities, give me a cocktail of some magic. The moment I start to rehearse a certain type of scene in which acting personalities can take over, in some way, I can totally change my mind on how I'm going to do it, and absolutely improvise it on the spot. Suddenly, they've given me new ideas.

With *The Pumpkin Eater*, I had two marvelous actors: Anne Bancroft and Peter Finch. Their reaction to each other, as actors, was absolutely wonderful. I wrote the screenplay with Harold Pinter long before I knew I was going to have Anne or Peter Finch. In certain scenes they actually created a magic which I had never envisioned before. They provided a different dimension. I'd rehearse a scene and probably have most of it planned in my mind. Yet, when I started to see the possibilities of certain little subtleties I could introduce, I'd change the whole concept of the shot to suit them. What they were giving me was more important than what I had originally thought or planned.

9. MOST IMPORTANT COMPONENT OF YOUR FILM?

I think the first ingredient, obviously, must be your basic story. After that, I would say that everything has an equal importance. That's the great thing about filmmaking: it's a combination of so many different components, which—fortunately—are under the control of the director.

I wouldn't single out any specific component, other than that the story is transcendent.

10. WORK WITH A PRODUCER?

I mentioned earlier that I used to be a producer. I have produced, as well as directed, all of my films. That's only because I was a producer first, and not because I like doing it. I would prefer not to produce the film, because it's basically too much hard work. A good producer should be right in there, doing that hard work.

When I was doing both jobs, the time I would have liked to have been in the cutting room, I had to spend working out exactly where we were on the budget, working out schedules, etc. I can still do all that, but I prefer not doing it now. I like directing, and prefer doing just that.

11. USE A DIALOGUE DIRECTOR?

I've never used a dialogue director, nor would I. If I felt that a dialogue director could bring values to me, I would feel that I was no longer qualified to be a director. I have my own mental vision of what I want the actors to do. I don't want, or need, anyone else interfering with that vision.

12. WRITER OR PRODUCER ON THE SET?

I don't mind having the writer or producer on the set, if they like to be there. I certainly don't require their presence, but I have absolutely no objection if they want to have a bit of fun.

13. WORK CLOSELY WITH THE CAMERAMAN?

I work extremely close with the cameraman because, again, I was in that department and loved it. I'm quite a good technician. In the beginning—before the film starts—I talk to the cameraman or write him a rather long essay on it. I cover the feel of the atmosphere to be created.

Basically, I do all the set-ups myself, the moment I get on the set. I think composition is as important as the acting.

14. SUPERVISION OF CASTING?

I have total control of all casting. To me, a one-line part—while he is on camera—is as important as the star. I will go around, personally, and choose all the extras.

15. PREFERENCE OF ACTING STYLE?

I have absolutely no preference regarding "technicians" or "instinctive actors." I want a beautiful actor who is totally right for the part, and for my conception of that part. The style of acting doesn't interest me at all. I have every reason to believe that I will be able to get the best out of each actor I choose, regardless of acting style or methods.

I'm not sure what a "method actor" is. I've worked with some marvelous actors who will improvise all the time. It doesn't worry me at all, because when it's good, I allow it. When it disturbs either the scene or the other actors, I'll cut it out.

16. PRECAMERA WORK WITH ACTOR?

Absolutely both. I always discuss in advance all the principals involved in playing the part. At any moment that an actor can introduce something that is better than I thought of, I love it. I've made two films with children. One was with children who had never acted before. You must really get their confidence. It's fascinating, because there are moments in which you'll get magic.

17. IMPORTANCE OF REHEARSALS?

The only chance I've had to rehearse beforehand was on *The Great Gatsby* [1974].

I personally like rehearsal. I always say, "Now, don't stop for anything; let's just make it through. Then, if I feel we can improve it, I would love to do it again."

I have no rules about rehearsing. I'll rehearse as much as I feel is necessary.

18. ADHERENCE TO SCRIPT?

Unless the line or lines are changed so that they don't fit the character or scene, I will always let the actors make changes with which they're comfortable.

19. EDITING SUPERVISION?

I'm heavily involved with the editing. If I don't see my rushes, and there's been a mistake made, how am I going to reshoot it?

I always see my rushes as well as supervising the entire editing process.

20. ROLE OF MUSICAL SCORE?

The score is, without a doubt, very important. Music can help your mood, obviously, and provide certain dramatic effects. I would personally—if asked for guidance as to how music should be used in a film—say automatically "use as little as possible."

21. INVOLVEMENT IN PREPARATION OF MUSICAL SCORE?/22. WHAT SCENES SHOULD HAVE MUSIC?

Yes, I am deeply involved in the preparation and recording of the score for my films. I love this side of it. I choose the places where the music should go. I have my own system of communicating what I want to the composer. I love music, but I'm not musical.

I'll lay a track on the film of all types of "canned" music, which I feel conveys emotionally what I want the scene to be. It could be some great jazz, or a classical theme. The concept is that it will give the composer a feeling of what kind of mood I want. I've done it on all my films and it always seems to work.

23. SOUND EFFECTS?

Unless you're doing *Earthquake* [1974], where, obviously, the enormous volume of noise is having an effect on the audience, I think sound effects should be used in a most limited way to get the greater effect. I'm not actually present when the effects are recorded, but I've already run the film endlessly with the dubbing editor, and gone over exactly what effects I want, and at what point they should be used.

COMMENT

I've had the great good fortune to start very early in the industry, and to be able to work in very many areas of filmmaking. Perhaps some people don't require that knowledge. I know directors who have never been in the camera department, or the editing department, and seem to do very well.

However, if one has a love and understanding of all these areas, one will always do well at them. I know there is a feeling that "something new" is made by breaking rules. Yet I believe that, before one intends to break the rules of cinema, one should know those rules very well.

Luigi Comencini

1. BACKGROUND?

My activity as a film director is the fruit of a youthful infatuation. I saw filming as a liberating, marvellous, and fascinating activity. Until I was able to direct films, I had been a movie fan; I devoted myself to movie history. I founded a film library, I lived among old films; I wrote (and talked a lot) about films.

2. FIRST FILM JOB?

I arrived quite rapidly to film directing. Occasionally, I realized (in Milan) a short documentary on children in cities destroyed by bombing. It obtained a lot of success, and—immediately—a producer asked me to make a full-length film (about children, naturally). Before that I had been once an assistant director, and I had collaborated on two scripts.

3. YOUR GOAL IN FILMMAKING?

I think that the unconscious (or conscious) aim for anyone who makes a film, is to communicate with an audience which is thought, by the author, to be *very* large. The fact that the audience has to be *entertained* is a reality which conditions me, of which I feel concerned, but it is never the immediate reason which urges me to plan one film more than another. Therefore, I will answer the question, overturning it. I do not have a secondary aim besides the primary one which is to entertain; but the necessity to entertain conditions my primary aim which is to communicate something: the knowledge I have of reality.

4. IN WHAT GENRE DO YOU SEEK A STORY?

It is very hard for me to imagine situations and stories which do not have a humorous or an ironic side. Besides this, I do not believe in a rigid division of "genres," and I can imagine all kinds of stories, tragical, comical, sad or funny.

5. STORY SOURCE?

I have even used, for some of my films, very famous novels (*Pinocchio*), but generally I have based myself on subjects written for the screen by me or by others.

It has not been a choice, but a consequence: I have not found in Italian literature many books suitable for transposition onto the screen (suitable *or* available.)

I think that to have a novel as source of inspiration facilitates my work a lot; but a film is valid if the film director (or the author of the film) can propose a *personal* vision and not a faithful one, which might result in a flat transposition of the book.

6. USE A SCRIPTWRITER OR DO IT YOURSELF?/7. CLOSE COLLABORATION WITH THE SCREENWRITER?

I have always written the scripts of my films, whether they were drawn from original subjects or from novels, with the collaboration of other scriptwriters. Even when I have committed the drafting of my scripts to a scriptwriter, without collaboration, afterwards I have always revised and changed it before or during the shooting. But I usually prefer to collaborate with the scriptwriter since the beginning.

8. PREPLAN OR IMPROVISE?

The script has to be a story of the film, the dialogue being possibly definitive, and the action described clearly. All the technical indications are superfluous, and would have to be precisely indicated after the scene had been built or chosen, and after it has been rehearsed with the actors; in other words, the technical indications should be put after the film has been shot!

What, in your question, is called "improvisation" is for me the film director's real creative moment. The purpose is to tell with images what was before described with words, to commit to actors, to their gestures and to their words what has been committed before the reader's fantasy. The same for the scenes, the landscapes, the movements, which the film represents definitively (therefore leaving little space to the spectator's fantasies).

Then, the object is to give back space to their mutilated fantasies, by creating, with images, another mystery, another ambiguity, which can stimulate the spectator so as to live the film not only with his eyes, but also with his mind.

9. MOST IMPORTANT COMPONENT OF YOUR FILM?

All the persons mentioned are important. It is difficult to establish a classification. The collaborators with whom I have a closer relationship are, first of all, the scriptwriter, and then the cameraman.

10. WORK WITH A PRODUCER?

I have always worked with a producer and I think that his function is to worry about the film making good receipts. In this role he is very useful. If I see him interested in artistic questions, I get alarmed and become suspicious.

11. USE A DIALOGUE DIRECTOR?

I think that one of the most interesting functions for a film director is to *direct* the actors, which means I will never be able to use a dialogue director. To be sure, if the actors do know their lines by heart, the script girl is sufficient.

12. WRITER OR PRODUCER ON THE SET?

I prefer not to have spectators on the set while I work. While organizing and shooting, prompting the actors, the film director ends up clowning; I prefer not to have observers, especially if they are concerned with the film. I also think that the film director is the only one who can "see" in his mind how the film will be when achieved. The producer is interested in commercial results, and the scriptwriter, who is jealous of what he has written, can draw—observing the film director's work on the set—wrong impressions, which can lead to useless and annoying discussions.

13. WORK CLOSELY WITH THE CAMERAMAN?

As I have already said, the cameraman is, for me, one of the most important collaborators. With him, I decide the camera movements and set-ups even in detail. The fact that I, personally, observe the rehearsals through the viewfinder depends on the level of harmony I have with the cameraman. When it is a collaborator with whom I have already done films, we understand each other right away, and all the work turns out to be easier and faster.

14. SUPERVISION OF CASTING?

I usually do not use a casting director. The main cast is fixed with the producer. The minor roles are chosen by me, with the collaboration of my assistant—we make proposals.

In any case, I believe that the cast is an element on which the film director has to keep a strict control, because the choice of the cast is the first act which determines the style of a film.

15. PREFERENCE OF ACTING STYLE?

I do not really know, because I do not believe in such a clear division; anyhow, both types can be interesting.

I would rather say that there are actors with whom it is possible to build a character with their conscious collaboration, and actors with particular characteristics which you have to use without their knowledge, to secure a result of which they are not totally conscious.

16. PRECAMERA WORK WITH ACTOR?

I have partly answered in the preceding statement. The preliminary discussion about the character—with the actor—seems to me to be an abstract exercise, mainly because I think that the script, if well done, should really give, in an exhaustive way, not only the physical side, but also the nature of the character.

When both the actor and the film director find in the script this description, the best thing is to start to rehearse the scene. The way of acting, of behaving with things and with people surrounding the actor, will come by itself if the actors and the film director will start with the idea that from the voice to the body movement, everything has to be suggested by the character described in the script.

Naturally, there are several ways of describing the aspect of a character, from the most obvious to the most subtle. In the choice of the way employed to say the same things, the quality of the film can already show up.

17. IMPORTANCE OF REHEARSALS?

I am not used to rehearsing the entire script as in theatre. But I also do not think that the fact of not rehearsing and shooting unprepared, gives an impression of greater spontaneity.

This rule might be valid with children (with whom I have, considering the films I have made, a vast experience). I have always started with the assumption that children must never "act," that is, to pretend attitudes or reactions that are not proper to them. With children, the decisive step is the choice of the actor. The child has to behave in life as the character in the film, so that he can live this character, and not pretend to perform it.

Therefore, the film director's task is to introduce the child in the film as a game, trying to shoot practically with no rehearsals, so as to record his spontaneous reactions.

18. ADHERENCE TO SCRIPT?

The script is not the Bible, and the changes which can improve it are welcome— *even* if suggested by actors! The danger is when the actor suggests changes which can be useful to *his* role in that particular scene, but not to the film as a whole. Therefore, I would say: change the script while shooting, *only* with caution.

19. EDITING SUPERVISION?

I prefer to let my reliable film editor, with whom I have worked for many years, make the first rough cut. After that, my presence next to the film editor is continuous until the final editing.

20. ROLE OF MUSICAL SCORE?

There are no rules in use of the musical score. There are beautiful films with no musical score; others need music. The important thing is for the music to be a structural component of the scenes, and not to be added only to *underline* effects which already exist independently from the music.

21. INVOLVEMENT IN PREPARATION OF MUSICAL SCORE?/22. WHAT SCENES SHOULD HAVE MUSIC?

Even the musician is a collaborator with whom it is important to establish a continuous relationship. Nobody can carry on an autonomous work in a film.

It is important to settle with the musician the function of the musical score; the idea that the music represents, how the presence of the music can be effective (themes, instrumentation, etc.). I'll never stop repeating that every contribution to a film must have a creative value, and that the opposite of *"creative"* i s "obvious."

A gentle music which scores a gentle scene is an obvious, stupid, noncreative choice.

23. SOUND EFFECTS?

The sound effects are always important; in some films, they are practically essential. If I have efficient collaborators with whom I have already worked, I can also rely on them to do the recording. In any case, I control them before the mixing.

George Cukor

1. BACKGROUND?

I was born in New York City, and I was always mad about the theatre. Pictures were around, of course, but that really didn't interest me. Yes, I would think I was rather highbrow, and I wanted to be in the theatre.

I was, for several years. First, I was a stage manager on Broadway. Then I became a director, under the very distinguished auspices of Gilbert Miller. I directed Ethel Barrymore, Laurette Taylor, and other people. In the summer I ran a stock company in Rochester—a most valuable experience. Then came the "talkies," and Hollywood yelled for all of us who knew dialogue, so I came west in 1929. A lot of theatre people, after reaching the West Coast, fled or died. Maybe I'm thick-skinned, but I remained here, and I'm fascinated by pictures. Isn't it a glorious thing when you can work, and it's exciting, and you keep that freshness and enthusiasm through the years!

You have referred to me as a fine director of women. I'm very pleased about that. In the days of the great movie queens, that was very good indeed. I've worked with all the super-star ladies. I've worked with the gentlemen, too, because where there was a lady, there was a gentleman. I've worked with—this sounds awfully stuffy, like the composer who says, "And then I wrote...." but I have directed Spencer Tracy, John Barrymore, Ronald Colman, Jimmy Stewart and Jack Lemmon—all of them, I guess.

I don't think there's really a hell of a lot of difference in working with men or women. The big difference is that they used to write parts for women. Now they don't.

2. FIRST FILM JOB?

When I was a young director on the stage, I thought I was awfully smart. Then I came to Hollywood, and I had to learn everything again. I was in a completely alien field.

Fortunately, "talkies" had just come in, and everybody was *thrown*. We all had to make a fresh start.

You remember, Tay, I believe you and Frank Capra both came out of Mack Sennett's around that time. Mack Sennett's! *There* was a school for moviemaking. You learned it the hard way, and you learned to get on with it and get it done.

As for the steps leading to my directing pictures, I started as a dialogue director at Paramount. I worked on a picture with Buddy Rogers. Then, through David Selznick, I met Lewis Milestone. David said, "Milly, why don't you use George as a dialogue director?" So I had the wonderful experience of working with Milestone, who was *truly* a *master*. I learned an awful lot from that very talented man, a man of enormous skill and vigor. It was wonderful! He gave me full opportunity to make tests of people, and also to work closely on the intimate scenes. It was very good training.

You know, when I see *All Quiet on the Western Front* [1930]—for its time it was so innovative, so extraordinary, had such vigor—I like to think I helped. But the vigor, the truth and integrity, the size of it all—that was Milly.

Then, just ahead of *All Quiet, Two Arabian Knights* [1927]. It had a kind of rough-and-tumble thing going, but also there was a lot of humor, and always a sense of good taste. Milly was a sensitive man—a man of great dignity. Strangely enough, he was a very funny man, too. He could do comedy beautifully.

3. YOUR GOAL IN FILMMAKING?

I don't want to sound pompous, but you've got to satisfy yourself or you can't do any really good work. The first thing you do—you have to be true to yourself. Then, of course, you hope the public will like the film, too.

I don't believe anyone knows for certain what's going to be a success. There is now abroad, somehow, this great thing that if a picture is a commercial success, it's ignoble or wrong, and I think that's a very stupid, impractical thing.

As for the second part of the question: I have no purpose beyond entertainment. I am an apolitical creature. I am very interested in politics, but generic man and the human heart, plus man's struggles which are common to everybody, interest me far more. If, incidentally, it happens that you make certain points with political implications, you must make them very lightly and tactfully. I don't think that people go to the films to be instructed or preached at.

4. IN WHAT GENRE DO YOU SEEK A STORY?

As I said before, for me to choose a story from which to make a film, I have to find something which attracts me, something about which, in my secret heart of hearts I think, "I can do this better than anybody." (That's a delusion of mine.) But you must really be honest with yourself, and you must say, "I *think* I could do this. I have an aptitude for it, and a real interest in it."

Now there are often things, highly varied, that I've read which interested me. I've said to the people who wanted my reaction, "Listen: I like this, but you can get a much better guy to do it, better than I in this instance. I'm not suited for it. I could do a competent, workmanlike job, but that's what you'd wind up with: a 'competent' job, but certainly not a brilliant one."

As a director, a man should always select something for which he feels a real compatibility. Also he should avoid falling into odd traps. When I came out here from Broadway, I was inclined to be funny—at least I *tried* to be funny. I still think laughter is the common denominator, the bridge to getting to know people.

When I was new in town, people were solemn about certain things, so I would make wisecracks to ease the tension. I hoped to be witty. The result? Important people would say, "Well, you've got to give him only sophisticated things to direct."

In those days "sophisticated" meant "it has no heart." So I was boxed in flippant things.

Then, by some fluke, I did a couple of sob things. You know: *David Copperfield* [1935] and *Little Women* [1933], then I was put in the sob box.

For some reason, people try to put limits on you. We all have our limitations, but no one can outline them for us. Also, our limitations change. Sometimes I think, "This picture no longer interests me."

Another consideration is that a great many subjects really don't interest me. I'm bored to death with crooked policemen and violence. You know, Spencer Tracy and Jimmy Stewart appeared in a picture in which they were gangsters. Spencer Tracy had a talent for being terrifying. Very few people have that ability, but he made it look genuine. When he saw the rushes, he said, "Good Lord! I look like someone's old grandfather with a backache."

The thing that I cannot emphasize too strongly is that, in seeking a story, a director must be sure to choose one which he can truly make his own, emotionally and intellectually.

Do the thing you know about! I saw a young man do a film, and it was very interesting. It concerned his experience in going to see his grandmother in a rest home. It was very moving, because he knew what he was talking about.

However, there's one thing we must be careful to avoid: falling into clichés or going into things that are fashionable at the moment. One must be careful to ask oneself, "Do I really *know* about this?"

5. STORY SOURCE?

I think every possible source should be explored. First, let me talk about plays. It happens that I've put a great many plays on the screen. That was tricky, because plays don't have the visual thing—the action or movement—so a great deal of creative work must be done in that area. Let's take *Born Yesterday* [1950]. It was a one-set play, hence static. You can't keep a film interesting in one set.

Garson Kanin, the author, came to New York and we worked things out together. We went out of the set for locations whenever it was the harmonious and valid thing to do.

A well-written scene is a great help to a director, but one must watch that a film does not become too verbal. Obviously, you use less talk than one would in the theatre. Also, the talk must be good talk—lively and interesting— and the people who speak the lines must be good.

I recently made my first television picture—for ABC-TV [_Love Among the Ruins,_ 1975]. I had two young beginners: Katharine Hepburn and Laurence Olivier. Naturally, I had to coach them, but I believe that both have a future. Seriously, they knew how to make dialogue fascinating, effective and funny. It was a very exciting experience for me.

To sum it up: everything should be grist for the director's mill. I've done them all: plays, novels and original screenplays. One should not neglect any of the potential sources; it is a constant search, because you never know when or where you'll find the perfect vehicle.

6. USE A SCRIPTWRITER OR DO IT YOURSELF?

I suppose I am the only living director who is not an _auteur_. I seem to hear nowadays of directors who not only direct brilliantly, but who can write anything.

Alas, I cannot. I wish I could. I have a great respect for the writer, and I do know that I am not one. I work with the writer, but I am not so equipped as to do the job alone. As a matter of fact, I work so closely with the writer as to be a nuisance to him, in all probability.

I know that there are times, when I am shooting, that people breathe down my neck, and I wish they'd leave me alone. An author's concentration should be respected, too. Actually, I feel that there must be a close collaboration between director and writer, as well as mutual respect.

7. CLOSE COLLABORATION WITH THE SCREENWRITER?

I don't really polish a script, but the writer and I discuss it ultimately. I give him all my thoughts on the story; he goes away and write it.

When it's all together and done, I let him do the editing, but I'm present. I don't like to mess with a man's work. I let him do it. That's what I expect him to do with me. I certainly don't want it taken out of my hands.

All this is assuming he is a good, _competent_ writer. If he's incompetent, a director simply should not work with him.

8. PREPLAN OR IMPROVISE?

You should have an idea in your head—a sort of optimal thing, a target to shoot at, but I do not have every move worked out. Some production designers will draw up a shooting plan most meticulously. Such things can be very good guidelines, but you must never allow yourself to be restricted by them. My practice is to work along guidelines as far as it serves my ultimate purpose, but one must always allow for improvisation, the actual creative thing that happens on the set with an actor or a director.

Naturally, you give the better actors leeway, but remember, that, too, is a dangerous thing. You must have enough authority not to let the thing get out of hand. It's up to the director to set the tone of the whole thing, and if any actor behaves like a fool, then you've got to pull him in. I've found that the better the actor, the more open he is to suggestion.

If the director is smart, he will know when to shut up—when the scene's as good as it's going to be. Also, one works differently with different actors. When you work with experienced actors, you realize it, and adhere to an established pattern to save time.

9. MOST IMPORTANT COMPONENT OF YOUR FILM?

Every facet of picturemaking is vitally important—it's a collaboration. First you've got to select the right subject—one that you know something about—then you work from that.

Let's not kid ourselves; we've got to have all the assistance we can get. I always try to have the best script, the best star, the best cast, the best film editor and cameramen in the world. Then, of course, I'm a goddamned good director!

I've worked harder—and failed—on stories that didn't hold water. I've made many such mistakes, so I suppose it boils down to one thing: story. Without a damned good one, you're sunk, regardless of the other elements. That takes a long time to realize. Sometimes there's something about he story that attracts you, and you kid yourself by saying, "Hell, I'll do it. It has something."

Then comes the cold light of dawn, and you're on the set, the people are on their feet, and suddenly you say to yourself, "This is a phoney-baloney! It hasn't a chance."

You do all sorts of tricks to keep the ball in the air, but if the story isn't on the level, you're a dead duck.

As a director, you must regard yourself with great importance, but you must also realize that your work can only be done well with a LOT OF HELP. These alleged geniuses who can write everything and do everything, including directing usually they fall flat on their asses.

In brief, the prime essential in turning out a fine picture is collaboration. Filmmaking is a team sport.

10. WORK WITH A PRODUCER?

I like to work with a producer who's intelligent, who's a help. Now, there's a tendency to put down the producer, by people who've never worked with a *good* producer. Capable producers really helped pave the streets of Hollywood. A lot of them are fine showmen, and the intelligent ones are very, very intelligent.

However, there are still a lot of stupid jerks putting down producers. When people say to me, "Oh, I just loved that picture!" I answer, "You do know, of course, that the film was made under that terrible system you talk about, in which we were all in slavery."

That's a kind of myth that's grown up, and I think it should be destroyed. It infuriates me when people make wisecracks about [Jack] Warner and Harry Cohn. It's stupid, because the gossips don't know what the hell they're talking about.

Those people—the producers—brought order to the picture business, and helped make great careers for a lot of people. I've never found producers to be restrictive. I've had rows with them, but I've had rows with everybody. I'll wind it up by saying that I've found producers to be of enormous help, *if they were intelligent.*

11. USE A DIALOGUE DIRECTOR?

I came from the theatre, so I'm supposed to know something about dialogue. First of all, I want people to be prepared when they come on the set. I get terribly exasperated if they come unprepared; it's highly unprofessional and second rate. I expect actors to study and work, and know exactly what they are going to say when they report for shooting.

As a director, I don't want people to give the actors their readings. Nor do I want anyone to give me their hot ideas while I'm doing a scene. I don't really need that.

I've done a hell of a lot of plays, which means an awful lot of dialogue. Also, I don't see how anyone can separate dialogue from action. I think it's all one thing. Of course, they must be blended together, and tempo is awfully important. I always say, "Pick it up quickly. Get on with it." I'm terribly impatient with the pomposity and slowness of some players. A drama has got to move, and it should be perfectly integrated, just like a human face and body.

Only the director can control that, and he must not be seduced, fall in love with one portion of the play and be swept into it. He must rigidly avoid such self-indulgence. It's a real booby-trap—we love this scene or that concept—we must all goose ourselves now and then to avoid detours, and to keep the thing rolling.

12. WRITER OR PRODUCER ON THE SET?

No, no, no! A good producer doesn't come on the set.

In every instance, while a film is being shot, you are required to use your judgment, saying, "That's played too slowly," or "That was done too fast." You can't have someone second-guessing you.

Authority is essential. Anything that compromises it threatens the development and the validity of what you are trying to do. None of the really able producers want to be on the set any more than you want them to be.

As for a writer since I can't write clever stuff, I like to have a writer on hand, but I don't want him defending his stuff while I'm shooting. What we must have is mutual deference: I think he's a good writer or I wouldn't be working with him, but I don't like having him on the set; rather, I'd say, on standby.

13. WORK CLOSELY WITH THE CAMERAMAN?

To come on the set without knowing what you're going to do, or what the cameraman is going to do, is the kiss of death.

What I really prefer to do is to rehearse the mechanics thoroughly in advance. However, you can't really do that until you're actually in the set, ready to shoot. Rehearsal, therefore, is a great luxury; failing that, you should know in general what you're going to tell the cameraman that you feel might interest him. If he's an intelligent man, he'll be very helpful. Our relationship is, ideally, one of mutual trust, mutual respect.

I begin by telling a cameraman what I hope to get; he must know what a scene is all about—its place in the story and the desired impact. I don't want something beautifully photographed that has nothing to do with the script. When a cameraman slips in one of those atmospheric specials, he's merely being self-indulgent.

I think one must make suggestions as to movements, but most good cameramen are *awfully* smart: often I am quite pleased, because I get a better result than I had hoped for.

Everybody on the set must serve the picture, and be on the level. No one should do tricks or didos to star themselves—neither the actors, the director, nor anyone else. The film should be all of a piece.

Integrity does photograph, as does common sense.

14. SUPERVISION OF CASTING?

I guess I'm rather a problem to a casting department, because I really stick my nose into that phase of picturemaking. I always have definite qualities I'm looking for in a player, and no one else can see exactly what those qualities are.

I do exercise full control, but it's a flexible control, particularly if I'm working with a good casting department that knows something about what, in general, I require.

I love to have new actors around; I get a big kick out of working with young, untried people. It so happens that I've done the "first" directing with so many of them that I've lost count.

Naturally, I also enjoy working with experienced people, because you never know when you may uncover a new facet of their talent.

15. PREFERENCE OF ACTING STYLE?

I think that if you are aware of an actor's technique, it's not very good. Acting should include freshness, realism and truth. A mechanical actor I don't like.

On the other hand I certainly don't like people who have no discipline, and spill all over the place with self-indulgence.

Now, the "Method" actor. There are an awful lot of young people who indulge in a great deal of scratching and egotistic behavior, yet have no sense of pace. This happens to be the fashion now.

I simply do not stand for people who attitudinize and are difficult. I think a director must establish quickly that he is not going to have any nonsense with actors giving him stupid arguments. In such a case, I just say, "Why don't you shut up? We'll do the scene, and I'll watch you. I'm very sharp, and I'll understand what you're trying to accomplish. I think talking about it will let the magic out of it."

I find it fascinating to have people talking *about* their art, but not about a scene we're about to shoot.

I recall a talk I had with Ronald Colman. I often told Ronnie, "You're a master at acting FOR the camera. You never act to the camera. It would be instructive for you to tell young actors what you've learned about your craft."

As far as I know, Ronnie never got around to it. A pity.

16. PRECAMERA WORK WITH ACTOR?

It's a combination of both, and depends on the actor. I don't think you should talk an actor to death. I'm inclined to be rather a definite person, but I curb myself, because I want to see what the hell the actor is bringing to the part.

Some actors are creative; I sometimes have a little chat in hope of stimulating the actor, firing his imagination; in return, the actor often stimulates the director. If the actor responds, I most certainly let him exercise his qualities uninhibited.

One should be aware—as far as possible—of the range and scope of each actor the director is working with; that being the case, the director can multiply and magnify those qualities he wants in a characterization.

A director has to know when to talk, and when the scene is as good as it's going to be. That's all a question of the director's experience and discretion, and the individuality of the actor. The creative actor must be given a climate in which to function comfortably.

In the case of some actors, you can give them all kinds of instruction and nothing happens. There's a great cliché to the effect that "You can't give an actor a reading of the lines." Every once in awhile, some actor will throw that at you. I consider it the old "horse to water" problem. I answer, "Why can't I? You misread the line, and you'd better read it this way."

In the final analysis, it boils down to necessity for rapport between director and actor. There must be no pomposity on either side, no rigidity of behavior—you play it by ear.

17. IMPORTANCE OF REHEARSALS?

I believe that rehearsals are good for the mechanics of a script. A scene only springs to life when the cameras are going, so you rehearse the scene, smooth out the mechanics, let the actors get the feel of the thing, but you do not rehearse it to death. It is not like a play. I like to rehearse up to a certain point, then I stop, and let it happen, because all of us in pictures realize that we rise to the challenge of the moment. If you rehearse the hell out of a scene, it simply doesn't come off.

On the other hand, I had an alternate experience with *My Fair Lady* [1964]. Rex Harrison had not before played in a film based on something he had done previously in the theatre. He was terribly concerned that it *must* appear to be spontaneous. The solution of that mental hangup was reached when I suggested that he *imagine* the whole thing as being fresh, as if playing it for the first time, although—in the back of his mind—he knew the values of every scene.

Rehearsals also depend on what kind of subject you're doing. If it's a thing with a lot of verbiage, extensive rehearsals are a help. Yet the chips are down only when the action gets to the camera. Until then it never comes fully to life.

18. ADHERENCE TO SCRIPT?

Let's talk about lines. You usually do a script that you respect; it has been very carefully prepared by talented people. Consequently I *do* insist that the actor respect the words. Otherwise the work becomes sloppy and tempo is lost. If I'm doing a script that I respect, I expect the actor to respect it, too: I think it's impertinent to change a well-written script.

As to the "business"—if one can do business that illustrates the thing, I'm all for it, but I do not encourage an actor to make up business as we go along.

However, there are exceptions in all cases. Often, during the shooting of a scene, I've seen things happen by accident that made the scene come alive. I've always said, "Keep it in!" I'm not stupid, not rigid.

There was a scene in *The Actress* [1953] with Jean Simmons and Spencer Tracy that illustrates what I mean. In the story, Jean was a young girl who had just spent fifty cents on a magazine, when money was scarce. Now, Tracy was formidable, you know—bad-tempered. When we rehearsed it, he became really violent in this scene—verbally, of course. Jean huddled on the bed and giggled.

Spencer looked at me and said, "Look I may not be good, but she doesn't have to laugh at me."

I said, "Jean, keep it in the scene." My reasoning was that a young girl, absolutely petrified of the guy, would be too frightened to cry, so—out of nervous tension—she would giggle. It played effectively.

Then there was a scene with Judy Holliday and Jack Lemmon in a play in which they had a big row, according to the script. We rehearsed it several times, then I said, "I'm sorry, but I just can't believe you. It isn't effective." I turned to Lemmon and asked, "What do *you* do when you get furious?"

"I get sick at my stomach," he admitted.

I said, "Do it."

So we did the scene that way. They started a frightful row, then Jack pressed his stomach and sat down, continuing to yell his opinions while he was doubling over with terrible cramps. It was damned funny.

19. EDITING SUPERVISION?

In regard to editing, you're referring to John Ford, of course. He was truly a master.

As to how I do it: I see the rushes, and I talk to the cutter after the running. I let him make a first assembly. Then, with trepidation, I go see it, and put in my two cents' worth here and there.

Next, I get down to the meticulous things, with particular emphasis on a choice of angles. Many directors have started as cutters, so they cut the film as they shoot it. Milestone is the perfect example.

I am not of that school. I shoot the picture as I hope it's going to be, and then allow the cutter a certain latitude. However, I always "advise" him. I try to shoot master scenes, always, so I tell the cutter, "Look at the master scene. That is the way the scene should play. And, for God's sake, don't lose tempo. Also, don't put a different emphasis on the scene than that intended."

There's a scene in *My Fair Lady* in which Harrison has been working with the little Cockney for hours, but she can't get the phrase right. Harrison delivers an inspiring speech about the beauty and nobility of the English language. It's three o'clock in the morning, everyone is dog tired, yet he says, "All right, go ahead!"

After all the times she's tried to say "The rain in Spain," etc, and failed miserably, she says it correctly.

In the first assembly, they cut to a close-up of her saying it correctly. I said, "No, no." You must not indicate to the audience that she's going to say it right. If you cut to her, they'll know something is going to happen. So...in the long shot, she says it correctly. The first one to react is Rex Harrison, who's been struggling so hard with her diction. Rex, incredulous, says "Again!" So she says it again correctly. *Then* the camera closes in. This is an example of the use of close-ups for dramatic emphasis. Had we cut to her in the first place, as she said it right, the entire climax would have been dedramatized.

In cutting, you sometimes get some very pleasant surprises. Occasionally, when I'm cutting and it's not going too well, I ask the cutter to run the take outs to remind myself what I was trying to accomplish. In that way I pull myself back into the feeling of what I was after when I was shooting it.

You see: nothing is sloughed off. In editing, the final decision is up to the director. He's not always right, but he must have the final say-so.

20. ROLE OF MUSICAL SCORE?

Fashions in musical scores have changed. Pictures used to be drowned in all kind of lush melodies. When you did a scene with a horse, they wrote horse music; when you did a scene about a dog, they wrote dog music. In fact, you were going everything twice: you were seeing it, and you were hearing it.

Audiences today are more sophisticated. However, I do think music is of vital importance to a film, emotionally and comedically—as necessary. In the latter area, one must be careful not to allow the music to "Mickey Mouse"— it.

Of course, if you do a thing with much dialogue, the music needs to be used unobtrusively. For a visual thing, you will probably use a hell of a lot of contributory sound.

21. INVOLVEMENT IN PREPARATION OF MUSICAL SCORE?

I respect composers. Naturally, I try to get the best available composer to do the scoring; I tell him of my hopes, and what I want him to accomplish; then I step back and cross my fingers.

I think it would be an impertinence of me, being a non-musical person to give him a lot of hot tips. I *do* give him a notion of the picture as I intend it, and let him embellish it. That's my involvement—as far as I go.

22. WHAT SCENES SHOULD HAVE MUSIC?

I don't want any scenes to be deluged in music, and I pray the composer will have the discretion to abide by my attitude in that area. I'm glad to say that they no longer use those great, lush orchestras, because the audience think that's absurd, and so do I. That was a hang-over from silent pictures; everything had to be done musically in those days; when talk came in, they kept on with the lush music until there was both industry and audience rebellion.

23. SOUND EFFECTS?

I was not in Hollywood during the silent picture era. However, I think that—as in everything else—the use of sound effects should be discreet.

For example, exterior scenes are likely to have those damned cricket and other familiar cornball sounds. We must be realistic about what is heard in the background.

In response to the second part of the question as to what extent I participate in the recording and dubbing—I am very careful about that. I sit in the recording room, sometimes week after week, remembering what I did, and guarding it jealously.

Only the director himself, can tell whether the thing comes off correctly. He's heard it when it was shot; he's heard it in the rushes; he's heard it in the first rough cut, and it's through his ears, only, that the fidelity of the work can be judged.

Sometimes it's a nuisance, but it's the final obligation, and I don't think that, after all the throes of production, that ultimate detail should be neglected.

Allan Dwan

1. BACKGROUND?

I was educated at Notre Dame University in Indiana where I divided my time between football and engineering. I graduated in 1907, with a baccalaureate degree in mechanical engineering. During my junior and senior years, I worked with Steinmetz, the celebrated scientist who was head of the electrical department of Westinghouse. Because I wanted to specialize in illuminating engineering, he introduced me to the head of Cooper-Hewitt Company.

After my graduation, I was employed by Cooper-Hewitt and helped develop the mercury-vapor (fluorescent) tube. A man who saw these tubes asked if they would be good for use in photography and asked me to develop a bank of them to be used in his studio on Ivar Street in North Chicago. So I designed, had the factory build some of these banks, and delivered them.

While I was supervising the installation of these lights, I saw this group of people making silly pictures and asked, "But where do you get the stories you're shooting?" I was told they bought them from any source whatsoever, paying as much as twenty-five dollars for each.

Well, I had written some short stories for *Scholastic* magazine at Notre Dame, so I brought in thirteen of my honest efforts, and sold them at the going price. Whereupon, the management asked, "How'd you like to be our scenario editor?" I had no idea what that was, but I was attracted and the salary was substantial. Compared with what I was making at Cooper-Hewitt, the prospects were appealing, so I accepted.

2. FIRST FILM JOB?

As I've indicated, my first position in the picture business was as scenario editor. When a group of the executives at Essanay left to form the American Film Company, they offered me twice the salary Essanay was paying to join them as scenario editor, which I did.

I was sent to California, because American had a company there which was supposed to be making films, but the films were not forthcoming. I searched all over Los Angeles (there was no Hollywood then)—no studios. After extensive questioning and exploration, I finally found my company in San Juan Capistrano.

They were holed up in a little hotel, waiting for their director to dry out, and return, sober they hoped, from Los Angeles.

I wired headquarters in Chicago, suggesting that they disband this unit, because of the total absence of a director. Back came their answer, "You direct."

That was a shock, but I called the actors together (J. Warren Kerrigan was our leading man) and said, "I'm your director or you're out of work."

They said in chorus, "You're the best damned director we ever saw."

Then I asked, "What do I do?"

They said, "Come with us." They assigned me a chair and a megaphone, and said, "Now, pay attention. You've gotta learn three words: you gotta be able to say, 'Camera,' and 'Action.' After you've got your action, you've gotta say 'Cut'!"

So I practiced, and finally I was able to say those three words with authority. I was a director!

3. YOUR GOAL IN FILMMAKING?

In answer to that rather profound question, I would say—to be frank—that my reason for making motion pictures in the silent era, and later, was to make money for myself, and to entertain the public.

I should like to point out that the difference between my early methods and today's practice is that I had absolutely no autonomy over my pictures. I did not select the stories or the casts; I did not determine the budget; I simply made what was given me to make by the people employing me, which I enjoyed because it made my life comfortable.

In talking to students of motion picturemaking, I'd say that what you should have in mind in preparing to make a film is *decency*. I base my judgment of decency on a fundamental group of laws known as The Ten Commandments. By no means violate them on the screen, unless it is done to point a great moral.

4. IN WHAT GENRE DO YOU SEEK A STORY?

In selecting a story, it's important to consider two things: (1) are you selecting a story for the story's sake, one that *you* can put into script form, or that your choice of writer would select, or (2) are you trying to find a story that will fit a certain star that you're stuck with, or—on the other hand—a star that you're fortunate enough to be associated with.

Let's say you're going to pick a story for the story's sake—possibly the story of Queen Esther. Naturally, you think of the story first, and you think of the characters in the story: Malachai and Esther, and the others. You consider what actor you could get to play Malachai, and what woman would be appropriate to play Esther. You begin to build these personalities into your idea of how the story of Esther should be told.

On the other hand, let's say you have Gloria Swanson as your star, which I did frequently; you look around for something that will fit her. You don't force her into a story; you find a story to build around her. I picked stories like *Zaza* [1923] and *Manhandled* [1924] and others that were good for her, and she did well by them.

However, I would much prefer to select a good story for the story's sake, then find actors to play the parts. That would be the ideal way to do it—story first, because "The play's the thing."

5. STORY SOURCE?

Well, a story is a tale told, and the manner in which it's told is extremely important; first, the style of the writer is important, the plot is very important, but, above all, the outstanding factor in any story is the *central character*. If we find a central character—an interesting person with an interesting life, one who does interesting things, possibly historical things—then we have an interesting story to tell, an interesting picture to make.

Unless there is such a character, augmented by lesser characters of challenge, I would say we have nothing. The average story of a girl and a boy can be very dull if it's just the usual girl-boy experience. If the girl is unusual, unique in some way, then the story can be outstanding. The same thing goes for the other characters.

Today, as I watch television, I see a police story; if I turn the dial, I'm likely to see the same story, the same policeman, and often the same actor playing the lead in each. It's hackneyed to me; it's dull, because they're not outstanding characters.

In considering a story for production, I prefer, if possible, to see it in print, to read it, to be able to discuss its effect on other readers. A play is a good thing, because I can hear it and see it, and watch the characters develop; also, a play is finished and solid. Just the suggestion of a story isn't of interest to me.

Occasionally someone will come up to me and say, "I've got a fine idea for a picture!" He will rattle off a few sentences, and ask, "Isn't that good?" It's interesting, but it isn't good until it's complete.

In summary, I prefer a well-written book or short story, or a well-written and well-played play.

6. USE A SCRIPTWRITER OR DO IT YOURSELF?

I much prefer to use a dramatist. If he's a good one, he'll come up with great ideas to enhance the story. That is, if he's in sympathy with the story. Of course, he can be as miscast as the wrong actor in the wrong part.

A good writer who likes the story—that's my preference; I don't want to write anything myself.

7. CLOSE COLLABORATION WITH THE SCREENWRITER?

If a writer is available, and he's going smoothly along, I like to have him finish the script in exactly his way; if he's stumbling or has met a blockage, I prefer to have him confer with me as to which way he should go. Then I like to read the finished script, and discuss it with him, suggesting any changes that I might desire, or at least argue about them, or fix them. I'd say, yes: I like to have a finished script, then put in my own little touches here and there, if I feel they're needed.

8. PREPLAN OR IMPROVISE?

I much prefer to improvise for various reasons. In the first place: it's impossible to dope out all your action before you start actual shooting, especially if you're on location. Conditions you meet will often dictate what the action must be.

I really prefer not to have the action described in detail in the script, because I may be intending to do something else. If the action is written out, the actors and everyone else may have a firm idea that we are going to do exactly what is written, which is usually not the case.

9. MOST IMPORTANT COMPONENT OF YOUR FILM?

In my opinion, any motion picture that's any good is a result of team work. There are a good many people involved, and they're all important, extremely important, to the final success of the picture.

But, taking the other elements in their proper order, I would say again, "The play's the thing." If it isn't a good story, it won't be a good picture. When I say "a good story," that means a good script, which means a good scriptwriter. A good script needs a good storyteller.

Photography is important. The movement that is given the actors by the director is extremely important. Acting, in all of the roles, is very important. But the most important factor in the art of making a picture is the *star*, and public acceptance of that *star*. When you go to spend your money at the box-office, you go because a well-known story is being shown, or a well-known star is appearing.

That is the order then: story, number one, and star, number two. The combination is perfect.

10. WORK WITH A PRODUCER?

A producer's first responsibility is getting the money with which we can make a picture. The second factor is: has he enough influence to get a good release (or other efficient method of distribution) for the picture. The third is: has he enough wisdom to respect your ability to make the picture for him? If he hasn't, then he becomes the director, and you become the office boy.

My experience has been that producers are good business men. I've worked with both artistic producers, and with commercial producers. I prefer the commercial; I'll be the artist.

11. USE A DIALOGUE DIRECTOR?

This question has two heads. In the first place, I don't want a dialogue director to do more than assure me that when an actor comes on the set, he'll know his lines.

I don't want him to tell the actor how to read them, or interpret them. I insist that inflection, interpretation be worked out between the actor and me.

On the other side of the coin, an actor will often come up with some valid ideas that will lend color or conviction to the character he is playing—ideas that will coincide perfectly with my thinking.

I'll give an example of what I'm talking about: when I started to cast *Sands Of Iwo Jima* [1949] and decided to use John Wayne, he came to us fresh from another picture. He read our script. It was excellent—beautifully dialogued—but for some reason the words didn't fit Wayne's face. We allowed him to bring his own pet writer, James [Edward] Grant, with him. Grant knew Wayne so well that he could and did, quite easily, change our dialogue to suit Duke's style of speech. It was a great help to all concerned. He hadn't changed the meaning of any part of the dialogue, but he had enabled Duke to get an Academy nomination for the part.

12. WRITER OR PRODUCER ON THE SET?

I think that, whenever possible, everybody connected with the picture—the cameraman, the gaffer, the electricians—should be present from the beginning to see what our problems are, and to work with us to correct them. So, yes; I would like to have the writer there. I'd like to have the producer present to understand what our problems are (if I'm not the producer.) Once again—it's a "Yes" and "No" question. Yes, if you can afford it; no, if you can't.

13. WORK CLOSELY WITH THE CAMERAMAN?

If a cameraman is assigned to my picture in time, and I have a chance to catch him before we go to work, which isn't very often, I like to sit down with him and work out movements. Especially is this important because it influences what we will need in the way of booms or dollies, etc. I like the cameraman to understand in advance, whenever possible, what I plan for camera movements. I also like to get his ideas of lighting—mood-lighting in particular.

Cameramen are so different, one from the other, that you have to be cautious about that. For instance, I was using Jimmy Howe [James Wong Howe], who, in my estimation, was one of the greatest cameramen we've ever had. I once walked onto my set and asked him why he hadn't lighted the set for the master scene.

He replied that it was already lit. You see, he used so little light, compared to the other cameramen, that even I was baffled. One of his tricks, as he explained it to me, was this: that when you use back-light, you have to enhance it with front-light; the stronger the back-light, the stronger the frontlight must be. There-fore, he used very little back-light, and practically nothing from the top of the set. As a result, his front-light was soft and beautiful, so that his photography was out of this world.

Now another man might have an entirely different idea; he might use a strong front-light, so much so that it would hurt my eyes to look at the set, but still, his photography would also be excellent. In brief, you must talk over every phase of your problem with your cameraman—really get acquainted with him. It will simplify your shooting immensely, once you know that he is fully aware of exactly what you want from him.

14. SUPERVISION OF CASTING?

Personally, I believe that more attention should be paid to the one-line bit parts than should be paid to the stars. The stars have usually been chosen in advance when the package was put together, and you have little to say about them. In addition to that, they have their own way of performing, and their individual personalities to project.

However, those little fellows—the people who come in and say, "Madam, the carriage awaits without," and she says, "Without what?" and they answer, "Without horses," or something of the sort, are important. If they gum up one little scene, they can ruin the entire structure. Consequently, I feel it important to pay great attention to the bit parts, and trust my luck with the stars.

15. PREFERENCE OF ACTING STYLE?

Beginning at the end of your question: I honestly don't know what a "Method Actor" is. I've been told that certain actors are "Method Actors" and that they're really a pain in the differential. I wouldn't care for them.

Instinctive actors, I think, are fine. Why not? What else is there, if he's good. I would say that, taking it all in all, I like the instinctive actor, and I'm sure that they become fine technicians, given enough professional experience.

16. PRECAMERA WORK WITH ACTOR?

That's really an academic question. I suppose it could be answered easily in about four volumes.

When I talk to an actor about the script, I try to explain how I see the character, and how I believe the writer sees him—which usually parallels my own view.

In an effort to determine whether or not the actor sees it as I do, we discuss it—not rehearse it—just discuss it. Then, if possible, and we all get together—especially if it's on a set and we're about to do a scene (which is generally the time I really get a chance to know the actors)—we run through it. I explain to each actor what his character is, and what portion of the picture we're about to make. The toughest part of making a motion picture is that you do not shoot in continuity.

You're highly likely to find your characters well-developed in the first scene you shoot, on about Page 31 in the script. Next, you shoot Page 172. (You have to assume that your actor has read the script up to that point.) You've got to know where your actor is in character development, and try to explain it to him—make it easy for him— and at the same time make very certain that he knows precisely what he is doing. You have to fill him in on all the stuff he hasn't done yet, but will do, perhaps weeks later.

It's extremely rough on the actor not to know where he is with his character development—if he's just starting to build to a climax, if he's really reached a climax, or if he's falling apart. If he's a sick man, how sick was he on Page 35? How sick was he on Page 10? Page 10 may be shot five weeks after Page 35 was finished.

Those are your problems, and you've got to have your head about you; you've got to know pretty well, how far along you want to actor to be with his development at any given moment.

As I indicated at the outset, it isn't easy.

17. IMPORTANCE OF REHEARSALS?

I must say that I've never enjoyed the luxury of having full rehearsals before shooting—all I have are those brief moments on each set-up prior to calling "Camera!"

As far as rehearsing a picture all the way through is concerned—ironing out all the kinks as it's done in the theatre—I'd like to call attention to the fact that the motion picture is not made inside a proscenium arch, nor is your background a fixed set. You can't possibly know what problems you're going to run into, in the way of movement and business, until you are on the set where your scene is to be played.

When I say "set," I mean scenic background—wherever you're going to work, whether it's on the seashore, in a beautiful garden, in the desert or the mountains. You're affected too by the movement the scene may call for: whether you're on horseback or in a car, and at what speed. These things influence your action.

A love scene can be played by two people sitting on a couch, or it can be played along a beautiful lane shaded by gorgeous trees, passing lovely wild flowers on a dolly as they walk and talk. He picks a wild flower and puts it in her hair, for example.

These are the times when you invent business that you've never thought about before—things that come to you out of the blue, perhaps on a run-through just for camera movement. These things are inspired by the set itself, and could not possibly have been rehearsed in advance.

If you had rehearsed the scene fully in advance, until the actors were "set" in it, then you went to location and started putting in business, you'd only manage to confuse the actors, possibly even to the point of destroying the spontaneity of the scene.

Obviously, your bits of business must come easily—seem spontaneous—as everything in your picture should seem spontaneous.

18. ADHERENCE TO SCRIPT?

I certainly believe the actor should have some leeway in his lines, and his opinions should be respected if he's a good actor, an experienced actor, and his concept valid.

That's his art—his profession—he's perfected it. He knows more about acting than you'll ever know. Your responsibility is to be a good listener and be able to say to him, "I like it. It pleases me. How do you like it?"

If he likes it, let it go. Let the actor express himself, if he's a good one.

19. EDITING SUPERVISION?

I am of the opinion that, of all the director's many duties, there is—perhaps—no one single function that is more vital to the ultimate quality of the film than the editing.

I have always believed that the director should have the final say regarding the cutting, in order to bring the film to its full potential.

There's no doubt that a good editor can enhance a director's work immeasurably. Nevertheless, I always stayed as close as possible to my film throughout the entire editing process. Because of my long and intimate knowledge of every facet of the story, I knew the values to be derived from the many little touches I had added during the shooting, and I knew how to jockey them around to take maximum advantage of them—perhaps to eliminate a dull spot, or to pick up the pace.

In my opinion, to be a good director, one must have a pair of scissors in his brain at all times while shooting. He must know exactly why he makes every camera set-up.

I think editing is a terrifically important part of picturemaking, but, no matter how talented an editor is, the quality of the finished film is the director's responsibility and, it's his picture!

20. ROLE OF MUSICAL SCORE?

I think the musical score is extremely important, and if it's good, it's a great asset to any kind of picture. I'm all for it.

21. INVOLVEMENT IN PREPARATION OF MUSICAL SCORE?

When you ask if I'm deeply involved, I'm not involved at all until the picture is finished and the editing has begun, unless there is a musical moment in the picture that's important to it, for instance a song like "Love Is A Many-Splendored Thing." That was a theme, and it was important in building the scene's sentimental values. Long scenes could be played silently because of that gorgeous theme under them.

However, if you were just dreaming that you'd have music under silent scenes, the scene wouldn't be played properly. You've got to know that audience emotions are being stirred by the music.

I'll say this: if a scene is to be played silently, with a musical background, it would be fine to have the actual music pre-recorded, even if it was a temporary recording of the proper length, and done well so that even the actors themselves could hear it while they were doing the scene. It would be as inspiring to them as it would be to the eventual audience.

22. WHAT SCENES SHOULD HAVE MUSIC?

In scoring a picture, I usually rely on the musical director, and if he's a man with whose work I'm familiar, if I like him and know I can trust him, I let him alone; afterward I attend, or try to attend the scoring sessions.

There, I quietly make suggestions to him; often he'll try it another way. For instance: three or four times I'd hear too much brass, and I'd say, "Can you give me more strings in there and less brass?" He would, and the result would fit what I thought the mood should be.

Other than that, I didn't influence the scoring. If I had a favorite air that I would like to hear, I'd ask him if it was free—if we could us it. If it was free, I'd prefer to use it.

Yes, I attended those sessions, and enjoyed them, occasionally making a contribution.

23. SOUND EFFECTS?

Sound effects are extremely important, because anything that touches our senses contributes to enjoyment when we're viewing a picture.

However, any disturbance is bad. The person sitting next to you can destroy a mood by rustling a paper.

I have one reservation about the present inclination to use sound to a point where it is harmful. If it's too loud or raucous it can be annoying, in which case you've lost your audience.

Some of our people seem to think that the louder, the more exciting it is—like a chase, or a railroad train roaring toward some grim disaster. It merely annoys me, because it hurts my sense of feeling. Maybe my ears are too sensitive, but I think sound effects, as well as all other elements, should be used within conservative limits.

COMMENT

My only suggestions for directors of today and tomorrow are two.

First: be involved in every step of your production, the cast, the story, the script, the sets and locations, the photography, the sound effects, the music, editing, advertising, credits, selling—everything.

Second: As the director, you are only one of the many specialists essential to the making of a picture. Some of the others are also referred to as directors, i.e. art director, director of photography, costume director, director of this, and director of that.

However, always remember that you are the captain of the ship, and don't you ever forget it!

Blake Edwards

1. BACKGROUND?

I had no vocation before entering this field. As the only son of a third generation film family, I can't recall wanting to do anything other than working in films, aside from wanting to be a fireman at age five, or a John Dillinger at age six.

I never thought specifically about what job I would do. I didn't realize that I would begin as a writer! Shortly after leaving the Coast Guard, I went to work in the script department at 20th Century-Fox. I delivered scripts to various people and departments on the Fox lot. I didn't enjoy that very much.

When Henry Hathaway started production on a film titled *Ten Gentlemen from West Point* [1942], my father, Jack McEdwards, who was then an assistant director, suggested that I try to get a job as an actor on that film. Years before, when I was quite young, I had done some extra work at the same studio.

2. FIRST FILM JOB?

I can elaborate a bit more on the steps that led to my directing. I continued being an actor (not a very good one) for sometime. I played a minor lead in a "B" film called *Strangler of the Swamp* [1945]." I did a second lead in *Leather Gloves* [1948], which was Richard Quine's first directing chore.

At that time, I decided I could be a writer, so my good friend, John Champion, and I sat down and wrote a screenplay which we called *Panhandle* [1948]. Eventually, it was produced by Allied Artists. I know that's a small statement for a very big step.

After that, because the film was successful, Allied Artists let us do another which we called *Stampede* [1949]. That film was moderately successful. Because John and I were now established young Hollywood producers, we thought, we decided that we would do better to go our own ways. We broke up the act, and I went into the terrible Hollywood jungle. Predictably, Hollywood was not interested in an out-of-work young producer who had produced a couple of Allied Artist Westerns. So, after a considerable time of scrounging around, trying to make ends meet, I fell back on writing.

I was encouraged to do so by a young lady I was keeping company with. I criticized a radio show in which she was involved; she told me I had no right to speak my mind, because I lacked proper professional credits. She added that if I thought I could do better, I should sit down and write a show of my own.

I did, and as it turned out, my show was better. She showed it to the producer of the radio show, Nat Wolff. He signed me and a few weeks later brought me to meet Don Sharp, who was then a producer for the Dick Powell radio program. Nat Wolff asked if I had written anything that might resemble a show which Powell did, called *Rogue's Gallery*. I said, of course, I did, and I'd get it to him tomorrow morning. We made an appointment for ten o'clock.

I went home, sat down at a typewriter and wrote the show that I had said was lying on my desk all the time. It turned out to be *Richard Diamond, Private Detective.*

From there I became a rather prominent radio writer and wrote a show for CBS, while continuing to write *Richard Diamond.* There was one month when I was writing three half-hour radio shows a week. I gave that up one morning at three when I fainted. I was advised to cut down my work load, even if I had to support a rather large apartment, several ladies, and a convertible Cadillac. I was really living high on the hog back then, but my energy was low, and there was no choice but to cut down.

Now, about this time Richard Quine came along. He was just getting his chance to direct his first film at Columbia. Quine graduated to a better company, so I was the logical person to fall heir to those few remaining "B" film commitments.

So I became a director. I had already decided that I wanted to get into directing. I didn't like sitting alone in an office at a typewriter. I envied the directors on the stage, and their power. I wanted that power, and that kind of creative arena to express myself.

I directed a few low budget features for Columbia. At the same time, film television was really coming in; Dick Powell and David Niven formed a company called "Four Star Playhouse" for which I wrote and subsequently directed. I was getting all the action necessary to push myself along toward being a writer and/or director.

3. YOUR GOAL IN FILMMAKING?

I'm not at all sure there is an underlying objective beyond entertainment. I don't approach a film or any project, thinking first: this is going to be entertainment. I *hope* it entertains the public, thereby becoming a commercial success. That's implicit, to be sure.

I think the first consideration for me is whether or not I'm turned on to a particular project. There have been times when I wasn't at all turned on with a project, but I took it with the hope that, through it, I would get to a project that I really wanted to do. I guess that most of us have made that sort of compromise.

There was a period in my career when I wasn't so lucky as to be able to pick and choose what I wanted to do, so I had to do things in which I had little interest. If I could pick and choose, I would start out, as I think most directors do, deciding whether I was turned onto the project or not. If it really turned me on, I would investigate it further and eventually make the film. In my case, most of my projects have been a total package: writing, producing and directing. Eventually, the writing and producing parts are over, and I must walk on the stage and direct. At that point, I think it's not so much a professional indulgence with me, as it is a kind of intellectual challenge. I come equipped, knowing the script intimately, because chances are that I've either written it myself or co-authored it.

It's interesting to me that I can always cancel the memory of those words. I know generally what the scene is about. The actors perform my words, but it almost seems they are coming to me for the first time. It is very beneficial, because I don't judge them by preconception; I really judge their value on the set.

I think the underlying objective is to do something that I want to do desperately. I hope the public is in agreement with me, and that the film is moderately successful. Then I can go on and do another one. I'm quite sure that's my entire motive because I've ventured into so many fields. Comedy seems to be the most natural for me, but I've done heavy drama with *Days of Wine and Roses* [1963], and suspense with *Experiment in Terror* [1962]. I've done all those things, because I want to try my hand at everything. I don't think that I will ever be content to be totally a director of comedy or suspense. I hope I will always be able to experiment.

4. IN WHAT GENRE DO YOU SEEK A STORY?

I suppose if there was emphasis on any particular genre, for me it would be the novel, although so many films have been original screen plays from either my head, or from the head of another writer who has been encouraged by me. I suppose every genre has contributed to my films. I read a lot of novels and galleys that are sent to me. That seems to be the most convenient way of finding a story.

5. STORY SOURCE?

I really don't have any choice. If I had to make a choice, I would say a story written directly for the screen. However, some of the best material I've had has come from other media.

6. USE A SCRIPTWRITER OR DO IT YOURSELF?

I prefer to work with someone else. Working by oneself is a very lonely occupation. Working with a good writer provides me with companionship and an arena in which I can air my views and battle for my opinions. A great number of my films have been written in collaboration.

7. CLOSE COLLABORATION WITH THE SCREENWRITER?

I like to work very closely with a collaborator.

8. PREPLAN OR IMPROVISE?

A little of both really, particularly in the case of comedy. I don't like to bring too much business to the set. If you do bring too much business, you might detour an actor from giving you his best performance. Good actors bring an awful lot to a scene, and I prefer to go on the set, knowing that my actors have learned their words and know what the words are all about. Put them in an environment which is familiar to them only in that they have read the words of that script, and see what problems that environment poses. Really, in effect, turn them loose and say, "Okay, show me your stuff. What can you bring to this moment?"

Then I become almost an editor. I sit back in judgment and listen and watch, and hopefully take what they bring and mold it into the final result. Quite often, they will come up with something startling that I never even conceived of when I wrote the scene. That's terrific.

The only problem occurs if you've got someone who is not capable of bringing that much to a scene. I always try to get the very best actors I can, knowing that if I'm on my toes, they'll make me a hero.

In the "Panther" films, there is an enormous amount of improvisation. The scripts only indicate the physical comedy. [Peter] Sellers and I enjoyed improvising so much that we did a film called, *The Party* [1970], which was almost entirely improvisation. The screenplay was only seventy pages, and we actually made up the rest.

9. MOST IMPORTANT COMPONENT OF YOUR FILM?

I suppose if there was one component, transcendent in importance, I would say it was the script. You can have a great script, but not the best director, only an average cameraman and average actors, yet you still may be able to get away with something that people might find interesting.

However, nothing will save a bad script. Film is a director's medium, to be sure. He runs the show, and makes a script live. He makes the performances work, yet he can only go so far if he hasn't got the material, and that's not far at all.

All the ingredients that go into filmmaking are very important, but if I had to choose the one vital element, it would be the script.

10. WORK WITH A PRODUCER?

I really don't work with producers anymore. I have very capable production people who physically produce my films for me. There are only a few talented creative producers around, and they haven't sought me out!

11. USE A DIALOGUE DIRECTOR?

I used to use one. He was very good, and was also a very good actor. When he wasn't acting, he would often work as a dialogue director on my films. He was valuable, because the actors respected him. He has since passed away, and I haven't used anyone since. A really good dialogue director can help a lot.

12. WRITER OR PRODUCER ON THE SET?

I don't mind having my writer on the set. I've worked with very few, and they've been close friends so they know how I work. I'm not bothered by anyone on the set as long as they don't interfere. There have been times when a producer has been a disturbing experience. Those times I eliminated the interference by talking it over with them, or suggesting that they remove themselves from the set.

13. WORK CLOSELY WITH THE CAMERAMAN?

I work very closely with my cameraman. As I mentioned before, I don't have many preconceptions beyond what is indicated in the script. I prefer to go on the set—turn the actors loose—rehearse, and see what happens. I'll get everything together with my cameraman watching, and then I'll pick my set-ups. We, obviously, have general conversations prior to the production—particularly if I'm doing something that might call for an unique overall pictorial concept. Mainly, as I do with my actors, I'll get the best available people.

When you have really good people around you, there doesn't have to be too much conversation. I've been lucky and worked with some great camerapeople. When you work with an expert you don't have to spend that much time verbalizing about set-ups and lighting. I'll pick a set-up, and know that it may well be modified, if the cameraman comes up with a better idea. I don't really get into specifics about lighting, but will speak generally about what I want. I do not block until the actors and I have rehearsed a scene, getting the words and the moves down—then I pick the set-ups.

14. SUPERVISION OF CASTING?

I maintain rigid control of the casting. I'm totally involved in casting all of the parts. Only a few times have I had to rely on a casting director to cast a few bit parts.

15. PREFERENCE OF ACTING STYLE?

I find it hard to differentiate between the two. All good actors, whether they be seasoned or not, are instinctive.

As far as "method" goes: I know that years ago some actors coming out of the [Lee] Strasberg school were labeled "method" actors, but it becomes such a complex subject that I can talk only about what I personally consider to be a good actor, versus the not-so-good actor.

Those good actors can be coming out of the "method" school, or they can be the Spencer Tracys who have been around the block enough times to know their craft so thoroughly that we might say that they're "seasoned technicians."

I think that when I look back on working with someone like Jack Lemmon, who is a fine seasoned actor, I would also have to say that his instincts are supreme, and he's had very little to do with "method."

On the other hand, if you could label Marlon Brando, it would be "method." I would like nothing better than to work with Brando. I could say a lot about other actors who are not in the same category.

In my book, it boils down to if he's a good actor—I can't care less how he got to be that way.

16. PRECAMERA WORK WITH ACTOR?

I really prefer to let an actor bring to me that which he has extracted from the script. I certainly don't hesitate to give him the benefit of my understanding of the character—if he wants it. But, in the beginning, I want to see what he or she brings to the character. Then we can go on from there.

17. IMPORTANCE OF REHEARSALS?

I don't believe in "long rehearsals" or in "short rehearsals" *per se*. It all depends on what I'm trying to achieve in a particular scene. Quite often there will be, maybe, a five-page sequence that becomes very involved movewise, and that demands, obviously, a longer rehearsal, because it's more involved. It's very necessary to get my moves down so my cameraman can get his set-ups.

Generally speaking, if I had to choose between short and long rehearsals, I would pick the short rehearsal if I had my moves down and rehearsed on film. Quite often something magical will happen and it should be on film. I try not to let my actors get totally into it. We will work until the scene takes shape, but like an athlete who can continue to train, but not give his fullest until the gun goes off—I try to get my actors to cool it until everything is ready.

18. ADHERENCE TO SCRIPT?

I don't insist that an actor adhere meticulously to the script. Hopefully, the script is a good one, and that's why the actors really want to do it in the first place. Therefore, it follows that most of the lines and action will be acceptable to the actors.

It's always a revelation to walk on the set for the first time, and face the environmental requirements, and speak the character's words. It doesn't always work. It may need modification.

I make it very plain that my actors have the latitude they'll need. We try what is there first, and if it doesn't work—we seek the best way of making it work...and change it.

19. EDITING SUPERVISION?

I'm very much like that American director. I don't mind looking at my rushes. I do mind being the one to say how they go together. I much prefer letting my editor make the first cut, and then get involved, really heavily involved, from there on. If I'm lucky, I can get the best editors. These people will know their jobs. I may not agree with something that they do, but I can guarantee what they do is going to be damn good going in. All I have to do is give them the benefit of my reaction to what they have done, and we start working from there. Quite often, a first cut is so good because I have given my editors that latitude.

20. ROLE OF MUSICAL SCORE?

It's extremely vital. There have been times when I've felt that the musical score has contributed as much as 50 percent of the end product. I have been closely associated with Henry Mancini for many years, and his contributions to my films have been enormous. I can't speak too highly of him. I've seen examples where his music has saved a sequence for me.

21. INVOLVEMENT IN PREPARATION OF MUSICAL SCORE?

I'm not at all deeply involved with the recording. I'm not a musician. I have a great respect for the musicians, and love to go to the scoring sessions as much as I enjoy anything else connected with making a film.

22. WHAT SCENES SHOULD HAVE MUSIC?

I've only worked with a few, and they are musical authorities—much better suited for deciding what should be scored and how it should be scored. I can only suggest certain changes, but mine will be decisions of little consequence.

23. SOUND EFFECTS?

I do best when I let other people show me their wares. That also goes for dubbing engineers. I sit through a sound-running of the film and discuss what effects I envision, but in the final analysis, I leave all that up to them to show me. They'll set up a reel according to how they feel it should be dubbed. Then I view it and start to make suggestions.

Because we are not making silent films—we are dealing with sight and sound—the sound is an integral part of the end product. A really good dubbing engineer is worth his weight in gold.

COMMENT

I have always been one to speak up, and *have* spoken up in defense of the creative individual's right not to be interfered with by management, by people who control the purse strings and therefore think they have a better right to judge the creative end result than the man who created it.

Luckily, I feel that more and more of that power is being transferred from the unqualified managerial forces into the hands of the creative artist. I think we are seeing better quality product because of it.

There are still those in power who control the purse strings, yet who are unqualified to direct or write a film, or cut a film—people who have less credentials than a first year cinema student. They continue to impose their judgment on the creative product.

They claim it is their right, and they do it in the name of good business. That's the ultimate madness. Every day, some executive tells some director that he, the director, is too close to his product. That he can't make an objective judgment, and now the great men in power will judge what the final product will be.

Just once, I would like to see a qualified filmmaker in a position of authority in a major studio. I would stop complaining, or at least I wouldn't complain so much....That will be the day...!

Federico Fellini

1. BACKGROUND? / 2. FIRST FILM JOB?

I reached cinema through screenplays, and these through my collaboration in humorous publications (*Marc' Aurelio* in particular) for which I wrote stories, columns and drew cartoons. If, one day, [Roberto] Rossellini hadn't invited me to collaborate on the screenplay of *Roma, Città Aperta* [*Rome, Open City,* 1945], I would have never even considered cinema. Rossellini helped me go from a foggy, apathetic period to a stage of cinema. It was an important encounter, but more in the sense of my future destiny than in that of an influence. As far as I'm concerned, I recognize his is an Adam-like paternity; he's sort of a forefather from which many of my generation descend. Let's say I was open to that endeavor, and he appeared at the right time.

But I wasn't thinking of becoming a director then. I felt I lacked the director's taste for being tyrannically overpowering, the coherence and fussiness, the ability to work hard, and—most of all—the authority; all endowments missing from my temperament. The conviction I could direct a film came later, when I was involved and could no longer pull out.

After having written many screenplays for Rossellini, [Pietro] Germi, [Alberto] Latuada, I wrote a story called *Luci del Varietà* [*Variety Lights,* 1951]. It contained my recollections of when I toured Italy with a variety troupe. Some of those memories were true, others invented. Two of us directed the film: Lattuada and I. He said "Camera," "action," "stop," "everyone out," "silence," etc. I stood by his side in a rather comfortable and irresponsible position.

That same year I wrote a story called *Lo Sceicco Bianco* [*The White Sheik,* 1952] together with [Tullio] Pinelli. [Michelangelo] Antonioni was supposed to direct the film, but Antonioni didn't like the screenplay, so [Luigi] Rovere—the producer— told me to film it. I can therefore state I never decided to be a director. Luigi Rovere's rather reckless faith induced me into it.

The vocation was altogether rather mysterious. As I said, my temperament led me elsewhere. Even today, when a film is finished, I find myself wondering how the devil I could have been so active, gotten so many people into motion, made a thousand decisions a day, said this yes, that no, and not have fallen madly in love with all those beautiful women that actresses are.

3. YOUR GOAL IN FILMMAKING?

I don't know how, exactly, to answer this question. I make films because it seemed to me that everything naturally led in that direction. I said before that I would have never expected to become a director, but then—from the first day, from the first time I said "Lights, action, camera..." it felt as if I'd always been doing it, and that I would never have been able to do anything else. That was me. That was my life.

Therefore, when I make films, I propose nothing more than to follow this natural inclination. In other words: telling stories with cinema...stories I feel are congenial, that I enjoy telling with an inextricable mixture of sincerity, invention, desire to astound, to shamelessly confess and absolve myself, to be liked, to interest, to moralize, to be prophet, witness, clown...to make people laugh and to move them. Are any other motives necessary?

4. IN WHAT GENRE DO YOU SEEK A STORY?

From one time to the next, one year after the other, I do the story that seems inevitable to me. I believe it's a reciprocal thing: it's not only the author who chooses his story, but also the story and characters who choose their author. At least, that's how it seems to me.

In any case, the decisive element to oblige me to define a story, is the advance on the contract!

5. STORY SOURCE?

My preferences generally go to original subjects written for the screen. I don't think cinema needs literature. It only needs cinema authors. In other words, people expressing themselves with rhythms and cadences special to cinema. Cinema is an autonomous art that doesn't need to be transposed into an illustration. In the best cases, it will always, and only, be illustrative.

Each work of live art lives in the dimension it was conceived in, and in which it expresses itself. What can be taken from a book? Some situations. But situations in themselves have no meaning. It's the feeling with which they're expressed—the fantasy, the atmosphere, the light—that count. In the end, the interpretation of these facts. Now, the literal interpretation of these facts has nothing to do with the cinematographic interpretation of these same facts. They're two completely different means of expression.

6. USE A SCRIPTWRITER OR DO IT YOURSELF? / 7. CLOSE COLLABORATION WITH THE SCREENWRITER? / 8. PREPLAN OR IMPROVISE?

I don't know what you Americans mean by "screen dramatist."

As collaborators, I call one or two screenwriters I esteem, and who are good friends. When I have an idea for what might be a new film, I talk to them about it as if I were telling them about something I partially caught a glimpse of, partly dreamed, and partly really happened to someone I know, who could also be me.

From that moment on, we try to organize our encounters. In other words, we try to see each other as little as possible and when we do see each other, we try not to create a real work atmosphere. We talk about everything but the film. Or, at the most, we hint at the thing, but as if to exorcise it, to keep it in line so it won't make us suffer too much. A bit like homework.

The realization of a film has different and—in a certain sense—successive phases. To remain too long in one of these various phases out of doubt, lethargy, or exterior impediments, always involves a compromise of the successive phases. The operation takes shape and grows if the passage from one phase to another is tempestive—in other words, determined by spontaneity, by naturalness. In this sense, an inalterable priority, a rigid chronology of the various phases doesn't even exist. What I mean is that the importance lies not in the consequentiality of the phases, but in the changes, in the constant movement of the film toward its own concretization. Certainly, if we remain immobile for too long, inert in one of these stages (the set and figurative design for *Casanova* [1976] was meticulous beyond all limits) then there's a risk of getting bogged down, or rotting. In this case, the only precaution to be taken is to no longer think of the film.

That's what I did for *Casanova*. I decided not to think about it any more. It may be that, from the pits of this kind of inertia, getting bogged down generated new forces, elaborates new contents, but Heaven forbid letting myself go to the consolation of such a forecast. It, too, can become a trap…a snare that keeps one from moving on.

There's only one thing I have to worry about: to *make* the film, because an image, a phantasy, a sentiment (even a feverish disease) born and conserved in your imagination becomes vital for others and healthy for you *only* in the moments you make it a reality.

I don't think it's a good idea to appear in front of your actors, in order to give the story shape, and to be intransigent, with steely limits, saying, "This is what we've accomplished on the work table, and *this* is what has to be done." No. I believe we must be humble enough to leave a door open to all the possibilities of the imagination at the moment of realization. The film cannot but be helped by it.

Sorcery is necessary in cinema; the real effort does not consist in wanting to be first, or later precise, about the choice of a type or what the type must say. The decision will come, and it will be right, *only* if you have known how to create a vital atmosphere in which something can grow.

Everything can be brought into play to create this atmosphere that first surrounds you individually, and then the set where you work. When I say "everything," I also intend some negative things: misunderstandings, difficulties, slow downs. There comes a moment, each time, where I feel the insufficiency of the screenplay, the uselessness of continuing further on a literary level.

It's then I open the office, start to call people, have hundreds of faces file past me. It's a kind of propitiatory rite to create an atmosphere. I see hundreds to put two into a film; I assimilate clothes, dialects, moustaches, nervous tics, attitudes. At a certain point I've had enough of the office and the people filing past, so I start tests. It's the definitive phase of the ritual. At this point I know I have to start the film before long. When we start, if the atmosphere is just right, there are no problems.

The real efforts all come first, in the alternation and intertwining of the preparatory phases. If everything has gone as it should, even with accidents and contradictions, if the oxygen starts to circulate, then nothing more is needed: the actors, the places, the lines...everything can be changed. Everything is born, in fact, by NOT respecting what you've prepared. At this point it's useless to remain faithful to the steps you've taken, to choices made the day before yesterday, to a script written five months earlier.

For a week or two I must wait to see if the film has been born, and where it's going. It's the film directing me, not I the film. The filming process is a trip, and one doesn't travel in the abstract, but keeps track of the needs it determines from hour to hour—of one's mood, of unexpected things. You just have to be very open to it, let yourself be carried away. Or, more exactly, put yourself at the service of what is about to be born.

9. MOST IMPORTANT COMPONENT OF YOUR FILM?

No. In the different moments of the making of a film, all these "specific components" are important.

10. WORK WITH A PRODUCER?

I expect the producer to finance the film and show up on the set as little as possible. The relationship between director and producer is almost always dramatic. In any case, it can't be formulated in terms of collaboration—even the most tenuous and moderate possible. This relationship is always one of slyness, of high and low blows, of pathetic persuasions or showy threats.

The director-producer relationship is among the most comic, deep-rooted ones of our time. It's spoiled at the roots by an incongruous defect. On the one hand we have the man with his ideas and his stories (sometimes he's an artist); on the other there's the producer who believes he's the mediator between the director and the public. He believes it with the kind of inspired fury of certain Greek temple high priests who would not allow any control over their relentless dialogue with the Gods.

Producers are these mad poets of public intuition; the beauty is that their idea of the public, their dialogue and their intuitions are almost always inexact and unfortunate. They harbor within themselves a concept of what's "commercial," of what's "publicable" that's a real maniacal excogitation—an abstract scheme, spoilt by a kind of plebeian intellectualism and categoric mysticism stemming from a nonexistent, counterfeit reality they invented themselves. They almost always end up making not very commercial or intelligent films. The cinema producer is one of the most typical figures of modern capitalism.

There are no bad films that weren't made through fault of the producers, because of intellectual lasciviousness. Or, if the films are good, they were made *notwithstanding* the producers. We must also consider the fact that lit screen is by now a rite to which huge masses meekly submit; so he who makes consumistic cinema determines the direction taken by mentality and costume, the psychic atmosphere, I'd say, of entire populations that weekly visit images displayed on screens.

In other words, I'd say that on commercial scales—and only on those—cinema is an unjustly authorized, justly bogged-down cocaine vending place, considering its profits. Cinema poisons the blood like work in a mine, and it corrodes the fibers. It's a collective art in the sense that it's born at the center of a "knot of relationships," mutual exchanges and infinite ties. But it can soon become a "game of relationships." It can announce new times when it breaks free of this "yoke" (see neorealism, all of it). The new and real directors are the authors of artistic revolutions; producers are often the authors of unartistic reactions.

Having said all this, I'm obliged to add that I, personally, really need a producer. Not only because of the advance (very important!), but to be stimulated to defend my creature; to protect the film I want to make from all the attacks, the tricks, the distortions, the dangers masked as affection, the betrayals and the impositions threatening it from the very moment the producer on the one hand and I, on the other, have decided to give birth to it.

This struggle with the producer to defend the film is an advantage for the film, because to fight means to charge oneself with aggressive energies, and energies are good, honest, vital things for creativity. Viva the producer!

11. USE A DIALOGUE DIRECTOR?

I don't use the collaboration of a "dialogue director." It would feel like having a friendship through someone else or to make love by correspondence. This last situation may sometimes be handy, but the post offices in Italy don't work very well.

12. WRITER OR PRODUCER ON THE SET?

I like to have people around me when I work...lots of people obeying the sign that is shown from time to time on which the word "APPLAUD" is written!

13. WORK CLOSELY WITH THE CAMERAMAN?

This seems like an almost offensive question to me. Cinema is images. And an image is made of light. Therefore, light is everything in cinema: ideology, feeling, tone, color, depth, atmosphere, style.

Light can do miracles: add, cancel, reduce, enrich, shade, underline, allude, make the fantastic and dreamed become credible and acceptable. On the contrary, it can give oneiric magic transparencies to the dailiest realities. With a reflector and a couple of flags, the most opaque, inexpressive face can become intelligent, mysterious, fascinating.

The most elementary or roughly made set can, with the help of light, reveal unexpected perspectives and lend a suspended, disquieting atmosphere to your tale. Or, by moving a five thousand watt a little bit, and turning another on in backlight, suddenly all sense of anguish disappears and everything has become serene, friendly, comforting. A film is written with light. An author's style is expressed with light.

The film's cameraman—he who must set the lights up—must, therefore, try in every way to understand what the author wants to express and try to realize it at all costs, even though it might go against his knowledge or technical experience. Those things count, but only up to a certain point. Also, those things can be limitative, and testify to a pale terror of taking risks.

Also, with regard to setting up the shots and the camera movement, it seems incredible to me that one can think that someone who is not the film's author can prepare or suggest them.

14. SUPERVISION OF CASTING?

I, myself, choose even the face of the least important extra, even the faces of those extras in the middle of a crowd that won't be visible in projection. But how else could it be? Forgive me, but would you ask a painter if someone else chooses the colors for one of his paintings? Would you ask a writer who chose the adjectives and the adverbs in his latest story?

I would like to add one more thing: the protagonist is sometimes found while choosing extras' faces for a scene's human tapestry. But then, I've said it—I don't know how many times—choosing the faces for the characters of a new film is the most important and delicate operation of all to me.

It's the real beginning of the trip. It's beginning to catch a glimpse of the film's appearance—the film as it will be, not as you imagined it up to that moment while cradling it tenderly in the cotton folds of your complacent imagination! Do those hopeful or threatening faces staring at me from beyond my small office table belong to me or to my film? Are those gazes, those smiles, those silences, those hoarse or trilly voices, those ostentatiously nonchalant puffs of smoke, are they signs of shyness of anxiety? Do they have anything in common with the characters I'm looking for? I alone can tell. How could someone else do it?

15. PREFERENCE OF ACTING STYLE? / 16. PRECAMERA WORK WITH ACTOR? / 17. IMPORTANCE OF REHEARSALS? / 18. ADHERENCE TO SCRIPT?

There are no fixed rules. Having said that, I have a certain preference for "instinctive" actors. The moment of choosing the actors is the most dramatic for me; the only moment of discomfort I feel during the preparation and realization of a film. For instance, suppose you have written that a particular character is a tall, pale, distinguished-looking type. Then, when you start looking for an actor for that role (I have actors and extras, who have read a newspaper ad and come to seek work, filing past my work table) I let myself be influenced by the living reality of those authentic characters—by the breath of humanity their presence communicates to me.

Therefore, if I find myself in front of a small, rubicund, perhaps gross type who fascinates me, I instinctively think: Perhaps he's just the right type for that part.

In other words, the type I had in mind is a phantom, but the one filing past the table is a real, authentic creature with hairy hands, and a dialectical inflection to his voice that moves me and makes me laugh...a live, concrete human presence seems to fit better than a character living only in my head. I never commit the mistake (and perhaps this is the only system to be discovered in my method of work) of adapting the actor to the character. I do the opposite: I make an effort to adapt the character to the actor.

I never decided to choose an actor because I was attracted by his talent or his professional capacity; on the other hand, I've never hesitated to take a nonactor because of his inexperience. For my films I go looking for expressive, characterful faces that say everything about themselves the first time they appear on the screen. I tend to underline with make-up and costume, everything that can show up the type's psychology.

As for making the choice, I have no system. The choice depends on the face of a person, usually unknown to me that I'm seeing for the first time, and how much I can guess there is *behind* that face. If I make an initial error, if I attribute a significance to a face it does not really have, I usually realize it at the first "ciak," then I change the character. I don't force the person interpreting the part to enter in ill-fitting clothes. I prefer to have him express what he can. Most of the time I don't say anything, so as to avoid reticence, modesty, resentments. But then I could always tell the actors in my film "Be yourselves and don't worry about it." The result is always positive. Each one has the face he's supposed to have; he can't have another. And all the faces are always right. Nature never makes a mistake.

I don't feel much trust for actors who think about their character for a long time, who soak it up and then come on the set the next day with their ideas, the script memorized and perhaps corrected, rewritten by them.

I always try to explain they're wasting time, because I often change the lines, enrich them or cut them. My work with actors never derives from reasoning, from discussions. It's articulated, rather, in a series of banal suggestions deriving from an observation of common life.

A resource for me in this field is observing the actor while he's not working; at the dinner table, when the personal confidences begin or the political discussions, when he's talking with the crew. That's when I see how I want him. I often find myself saying—it's a recurring sentence: "Do like you did that time when..."

That time might be, for example, when he argued with a waiter in a restaurant. To the actor who has to tell his lover or his son, "Another night like this is atrocious!" I suggest, "Do like the time you told the waiter, 'The rice you brought was overcooked.'"

As a matter of fact, I even get to the point of having an actor say, "You brought me overcooked rice!" instead of saying, "Another night like this is atrocious!" Dubbing will put everything back in order and the atrocious night will take the place of overcooked rice.

19. EDITING SUPERVISION?

From their vaguely inquisitory tone, these questions surprise me a bit, and make me feel a little awkward and ridiculous with my answers, because I suddenly feel *observed*—like a fanatic and presumptuous man trying to pass himself off as someone who does everything himself when it's a well-known fact that's not true. So an attempt is made—with a trap of well thought up questions—to get him to contradict himself, and finally admit that he does almost nothing in the film...it's the others who do everything!

But I'm sticking to my guns; I'm not going to give in and tell you that I do the editing *too*, deciding on frame after frame, meter after meter, naturally with a faithful, intelligent editor next to me. In my case, it's Ruggero Mastroianni, Marcello's brother. I also have a couple of expert, precise, affectionate, maternal women assistants with me. If they've a pretty ass, so much better....

I want to add one more thing, which is certainly obvious, but I feel it's the case to say it anyway: editing is one by the film's author when he's shooting, on the set, or even before as he's imagining his film. Later, at the moviola, he's only sticking the various shots together, and ...here and there correcting his creature's breathing.

I don't believe at all in those films that are born at the moviola. That's not cinema. It's eye-tickling at the best for (and not even that anymore) television publicity.

20. ROLE OF MUSICAL SCORE?

Many music themes of my films are composed (I intend by "composed"—created, written, and recorded) before I start filming because I feel the necessity of shooting certain scenes with the help of rhythm and musical suggestion. I must say this way of filming always gives very positive results. The action, camera and actor movements, the entire expressive atmosphere of the scenes are enriched; as if fixed in more precise rhythms and cadences, inevitable, I would say.

Therefore, I'm led to conclude that the sequences that will be, in mixage, underlined by music, are usually known to me in the screenplay. On the other hand, I don't at all consider the music a more or less ruffian effect to be added, post-editing, to underline a sequence in a sentimental, comic, or emphatic way after it has turned out to be a bit weak or disappointing in projection.

Music is an integral part, a vital expression in my films; as much a part of the tale as light, set perspectives, costumes, dialogue, and actors' faces.

21. INVOLVEMENT IN PREPARATION OF MUSICAL SCORE?/22. WHAT SCENES SHOULD HAVE MUSIC?

Yes, I'm deeply involved in the preparation and recording of the musical score for the films. There's complete understanding between my habitual musician—Nino Rota—and me. He's very close to my world, to my stories. We work together very well. Nino lives inside his music; Nino is *made* of music; Nino *is* music; therefore I feel very, very fortunate to have met him. Obviously, I don't suggest music themes to him. I'm not a musician.

But, since I usually have very clear ideas on what the film I made is all about, I work with Rota just as I would with the screenwriters on the screenplay. I sit next to the piano he's working at, and try to express the film's necessities and what music can do, must do. Obviously, I don't dictate themes, but I guide him, telling him what I want. Nino's music is extremely suggestive and functional, even if he hasn't seen the film, and sometimes he doesn't even really know what it's all about. But it doesn't matter. Nino knows me, and I know him.

As an element of my work—if I have to take care of it for a film—then I let myself be totally absorbed by music. I abandon myself to it without reservations, without effort; with Nino, I can spend entire days listening to him at the piano in the attempt to get a precise motif, to clear up a musical phrase so it will coincide as exactly as possible with the sentiment, the emotion I want to express in the film. The recording process is always a very exciting, liberating moment. In this case it's as if my participation was protected, absolved, by objective necessity which re-routes the direct, and always overwhelming, impact of the music onto the film.

But, outside my work, I prefer not to listen to music. It dismays me; it alarms me. I'm possessed by it, so I defend myself by refusing it, fleeing like a thief from the occasions or situations proposing it to me. I don't know. it might be another case of Catholic conditioning, but music makes me melancholy. It fills me with remorse; it's a warning voice, a torment, because it speaks to you, reminding you of a dimension of harmony, of peace, of completeness from which you've been excluded, exiled. Music is cruel. It fills you with nostalgia and remorse, and when it finishes, you don't know where it goes; you know only that it's unreachable and this makes you sad.

COMMENT

The author has, must have, can't do without, total control. The only control I—worriedly—lack is the one on how much money the film makes. I believe I've always been outrageously robbed on the meager percentages I was supposed to get. I've never seen a lira on my percentage of the gross!

Moreover, I was never able to find out how much the film really cost. Everytime I ask, the cost is always higher than the preceding time. According to producers, a film never stops costing. Even the films I made thirty, forty years ago turn out to be continuously increasing in cost. I'll wager that right now, as we're having this conversation, you and I, the cost of my film has just gone up another couple of million dollars. When will it be possible then, to catch a glimpse of the profits? Films have no profits. Never.

Everything you see around producers—villas with swimming pools, personal jets, yachts, fazendas, small islands with airports, Picassos, oilwells—none of it exists. Or, at least it wasn't bought with the films' profits. Not only was that comfort not bought with film profits, but they lost money with your films, because you didn't want to change the ending and you didn't cut forty-five minutes projection time.

I'm joking, of course. Things really aren't like that at all. They're much worse.

Bryan Forbes

1. BACKGROUND?

I was born in the East End dock area of London—a true Cockney. When I left school, and before I entered the Army (1943 during WW II), I won a scholarship to the Royal Academy of Dramatic Art, which turned out to be a sexual finishing school—the ratio of heterosexual men to girls being roughly 1 to 140 at that time. After a year, I left there under a cloud [Ed. comment: that ratio, of course] and went into repertory [stock] theatre, eventually getting some West End jobs.

2. FIRST FILM JOB?

As an actor, my first feature film was for Michael Powell in *The Small Back Room* [1948]. I had been writing since age sixteen, publishing a turgid and immature novel when I was seventeen, and then having a decent collection of short stories published when 22, called *Truth Lies Sleeping*, which I am not ashamed of thirty years later. They seem to me rather good, even now, Sank without much trace, of course, and I didn't do any serious writing for another decade until Anthony Quinn and Akim Tamiroff asked me write an original screenplay for them—which I did.

It never got made, but this led to an introduction to Albert [Cubby] Broccoli, and in turn I was asked to write the famous *The Black Knight* [1954]. [Ed. note: This US/UK co-production was directed by Tay Garnett.] After that term on the chain gang, Cubby and Irving Allen gave me *Cockleshell Heroes* [1955] to rewrite, and this proved something of a modest success, and I got more and more screen-writing assignments.

I grew ever more disenchanted, however, with the way in which my writing was distorted out of all recognition by the time it reached the screen, and—in 1959—I joined forces with Richard Attenborough and we formed Beaver Films and made *The Angry Silence* [1960]. This got me an American Academy Award nomination, and won me the British equivalent, and more or less "launched" me, although, I believe, it was my 38th screenplay.

From screenwriting I stepped over the border to directing; *Whistle Down the Wind* [1961] being my first film as a director, which—again—I made for Beaver Films with Attenborough producing.

3. YOUR GOAL IN FILMMAKING?

I believe in two things: to tell a good story as well as I can, and to subordinate everything, in the last analysis, to the performances. This annoys people like Pauline Kael, etc. who prefer to write about the theory of film and neglect the performances whenever they can. But then, so much of film criticism is masturbation, written by people who have never progressed to the real thing.

I don't really have any _conscious_ philosophy when I start a new film—but I acknowledge that most, if not all, of my films are about aspects of love. Love interests me; sex, per se, I find boring, because—whereas the sexual act is, or should be, a private act if it is to have any significance at all—love is the most powerful of dramatic forces, and entirely legitimate to depict.

I abhor violence on the screen, and think that the media has a lot to answer for—especially television violence, where it is sold cynically like pet food and deodorants. We are reaping the whirlwind in the Western World by allowing our screens to be filled with spurious violence which makes no comment and is manufactured to provide the maximum returns. Don't tell me otherwise, because I have sat in on more script conferences, and read more dreadful scripts (most of which eventually reach the screen it seems) than most.

One of these days, the bright boys are going to turn the [Charles] Manson case into a musical, I kid you not. They must have thought about it, and are only waiting for the score.

I think films, as opposed to television films, are the supreme vehicle for taking people—the majority of people—out of their environment into a world that most of them will never see. I, personally, like looking at attractive rather than unattractive people, and I find that most of the porn is a great turn-off—I mean, who wants to see something that looks like a commercial for a meat packing company?

Films like _Last Tango in Paris_ [1972]— remember what Miss Kael said?—are artistic rip-offs. Take away the butter scene, the buggery and the four-letter words, and you are left with a piece of junk plot that most writers would throw out of the Ark. The trouble with films is that you _can_ fool most of the people most of the time.

4. IN WHAT GENRE DO YOU SEEK A STORY?

I don't mind. I have found stories in newspaper headlines, novels, plays—who cares as long as the final result stands up?

5. STORY SOURCE?

Basically the same answer as No. 4. I would like to see more originals for the screen; I would like to _write_ more originals for the screen, but the trouble is that those who run our industry hate to back a horse until it has gone past the winning post. Since there is little evidence to suggest that many of them can actually read, they prefer to have something in hard covers that they can, at least, weigh.

6. USE A SCRIPTWRITER OR DO IT YOURSELF?

I prefer to write my own screenplays, because—conceitedly—I think I am a better writer than most, and understand the medium I am writing for. Screenwriting in England is very impoverished, though there are many fine writers turning in brilliant stuff for British television; one of the troubles is that there is nobody to write for in England.

7. CLOSE COLLABORATION WITH THE SCREENWRITER?

Yes. There is no point in two people—i.e. the writer and the director—working in isolation. I obviously believe that the writer is all important, but writers in general want it both ways. They scream blue murder when they're rewritten, but they are not prepared to stay on the set from eight in the morning 'til eight at night, six days a week, for the entire shooting schedule. If something doesn't work, you have to rewrite it—otherwise every film would grind to a standstill.

I rewrite my own stuff constantly, sometimes I do nine or ten versions—but it's all got too bloody technical and, now, contracts stipulate how much rewriting, when etc—all nonsense and nothing to do with writing. Protect the innocent, by all means, but not those who command $100,000 and up. For that sort of money we ought to work ourselves to a standstill and be grateful. If you don't like the heat in the kitchen, etc. Write novels and take your $7,500 advance and nobody will alter a word, but don't take a king's ransom and then complain.

8. PREPLAN OR IMPROVISE?

No. I would throw a script across the room if it gave me camera movements. This is the bullshit of the amateur.

A script is the bare blueprint of the house—the director and the cinematographer add the plumbing. Any director has to be prepared to improvise—yes, compromise (unless he reaches the exalted status of a David Lean)—because you arrive on a location and nothing is right: the sun doesn't shine, the star has a big yellow spot on her chin, the house you chose two months earlier has been knocked down, etc.

What do you do with 120 technicians and four tons of equipment standing by on golden time? You have to shoot, and sometimes, you know, what started out as a disaster ends up a triumph, and you get praised for something you had never planned. Equally, you can plan the hell out of a schedule, and end up with crap. There are no rules.

9. MOST IMPORTANT COMPONENT OF YOUR FILM?

Undoubtedly the story/script. A good director can improve a bad script, but he can never lick it entirely. You need a great cameraman who can interpret your vision and add his dimension to it. Then, good actors to give life to it, and the others are in parallel.

10. WORK WITH A PRODUCER?

Yes and no. It depends on the deal. Some films come with a built-in producer, and some you hire.

I have worked with three great producers: Dickie Attenborough, the late Jimmy Woolf, and more recently, Stuart Lyons. All three had quite different qualities.

I expect a producer to service the set for me and get the bores off my back when I am actually shooting. With producers I like, I maintain that their word is law _off_ the set; _mine_ is law _on_ the set. If we have arguments, we do it in private, after shooting. It's too easy to become a producer, and some of them are total morons— subhuman.

11. USE A DIALOGUE DIRECTOR?

No never. I used one once to help an Italian actress learn her lines in English. But otherwise, no, and God save me from them. Another example of the industry's laziness and phoniness.

12. WRITER OR PRODUCER ON THE SET?

I don't mind who's on my set—everybody is welcome within reason. I hate rubberneckers, but interested people are never refused admission—that includes writers and producers.

13. WORK CLOSELY WITH THE CAMERAMAN?

As much as the budget allows. I have been lucky enough to work with some of the _great_ cameramen—in fact I have never worked with a dud. Arthur Ibbetson, Douggie Slocombe, Gerry Turpin (four times) Bernie Guffie (twice), Claude Renoir, Owen Roizman, and Tony Imi (twice).

I don't predetermine every camera angle—this would bore me to death and is, I think, counterproductive. I give the actors a vague shape and let them work within that. Inevitably they suggest better angles during the course of rehearsals.

The trick is the "conceal" art: conceal the camera movement (only critics like to _know_ that the camera is moving—it makes them believe they know what it is all about.)

What I do discuss in great detail with my cameraman is the _mood_ I want in any particular scene. Once we have got that right, I leave the rest to him, seldom interfering at all. Trust people with talent and let them get on with it.

14. SUPERVISION OF CASTING?

I cast everything—not from conceit—but from instinct. I have only tested two actors in my life, because all you really test is degrees of fear.

Casting directors perform a useful role in that they bring to a director's attention small part actors who might otherwise escape his notice. When I am in America, I pay great heed to my casting directors—especially for the smaller roles and I see anybody they suggest, but *I* make the final decisions.

15. PREFERENCE OF ACTING STYLE?

Well, tricky question—this. The best is when you get the accomplished technician who can also work from instinct. On balance I would vote for the instinctive actor any day.

My views on "The Method" is that it nearly destroyed a whole generation of American actors. (I am disregarding the greats like [Marlon] Brando, [Montgomery] Clift, etc. who would have made it with or without "The Method.")

When you have worked with a really great actress like Dame Edith Evans, you know that the rest is garbage. She despised "The Method," knowing it for what it was. The best method is to be able to act—and acting isn't being a tape recorder.

I particularly like the story told of Sir John Gielgud, who was rehearsing a Shakespearean production in New York and had a really dedicated "Method" actor playing the Duke of Buckingham or something. This joker was always holding up rehearsals endlessly and asking, "John, help me; I can't relate, I can't orientate, who am I, where have I come from?"

Sir John replied, "My dear chap, it's quite simple; you've just come *off* stage from whence you should never have strayed." That says it all.

16. PRECAMERA WORK WITH ACTOR?

No. I always say to an actor, "I don't mind by which route you reach my destination."

17. IMPORTANCE OF REHEARSALS?

I hate long rehearsals for *film*. They destroy the very essence that makes for excitement. By all means rehearse the moves well, and make sure that your actors know where they are, but don't push them over the top into stale performances.

18. ADHERENCE TO SCRIPT?

Unless the actor convinces me that he has a better alternative to the line I have written, he has to stick to the script. I am always grateful for the odd, brilliant lines that actors are capable of throwing in—after all, we get the credit, not them.

Business—well, one can't generalize; obviously, if a piece of business is vital to the plot, there is no sense in letting an actor change it.

19. EDITING SUPERVISION?

I stay with a film until the answer print is delivered. I enjoy the editing stage, because really it's like saying, "Well, I've mixed the paints, but I don't want to put brush to canvas,"—if you walk away from editing.

There are some directors—household names, some of them—who leave town the night they have finished shooting and never come near the cutting rooms. This, I will never comprehend. I enjoy going to rushes and I like the crew to come, too—it shows that they are involved. Bad crews never bother to show up, and I don't use them again.

I love handling film, experimenting with it—but I make my task easier by seldom printing more than two takes ever. I think this nonsense of printing two million feet of film to arrive at a two-hour film is self-indulgence to the point of madness, and merely betrays the fact that the director didn't know his own mind on the floor.

20. ROLE OF MUSICAL SCORE?

It's another and very important *emotional* layer to the film, and should, I think, underline the original emotion generated by the actors and the camera. Too much music is a killer—single instruments are great.

21. INVOLVEMENT IN PREPARATION OF MUSICAL SCORE?

Yes, and I think you can't start early enough. John Barry and I have worked on half-a-dozen films together, and I always try to get him involved before I start shooting so that he is thinking about themes and musical ideas.

The big snag—if you don't think about the music until much later in the day—is that it is such a hit and miss element. I mean, what happens if you turn up for the scoring session and hate the bloody thing? Too late. The musicians are all there, and the whole thing is costing a small fortune. I have often asked a composer to change things when I felt that his music was changing my film—the *feel* of the film, that is.

It is a gut reaction with me.

22. WHAT SCENES SHOULD HAVE MUSIC?

I work in close consultation with the composer to choose which scenes should have music.

23. SOUND EFFECTS?

Sound is, wrongly, the poor relation of films. I think this is sad—I hate those films when I can't hear the dialogue, and I am the first to take note when a sound effect grabs you. (Example: I remember the sound track on *Klute* [1971]: quite brilliant. Stunning, in fact. Chilling effects achieved with the minimum of noise.)

As with my cameramen I have enjoyed some great sound technicians working with me—the best of which, Bill Daniels, sadly died last year. They are very important people.

COMMENT

Finally, there is no book of rules for film directing. Film is a practical medium, not a theoretical medium. If you want to be a director, get yourself a camera, and beg, borrow or buy as much film as you can and go out and shoot things—people—life is all around you. Find out what you can do: cut the film yourself, get the feel of it, like fabric. Train your eye—use a 35mm camera which has roughly the same shape negative size, and compose shots.

Never, never humiliate an actor on the set. That's too easy and it is self-defeating. (Otto [Preminger], are you listening out there?)

And never say "Cut" until the actor has exited the frame.

Those are the only things the late, great Carol Reed said to me when I started, and I have never had cause to regret that I took his advice.

For the rest—dare! And good luck, because it's cold out there and eighty people out of a 100 are *willing* you to fail!

Milos Forman

1. BACKGROUND?

I remember, from my very early 'teen years, wanting to be involved in acting; I think everybody, at least once for a short time in his or her life, wants to be an actor. My only acting experience had been in high school productions. After that I wanted to enter theatre school to become a theatre director.

For different reasons, I was rejected from entering a theatre school, but was accepted to a film school where I studied screenwriting. Afterwards, when I finished the school in 1955—before I made my first film as a director in 1963—I worked in different fields.

For a short while, I was an anchorman on several television programs: announcing films that were shown, interviewing film directors on television. Then I wrote two or three screenplays which were directed by other directors, and I also worked as a director for a program called *Magic Lantern* [*Laterna Magica,* 1958], combining film and live action: a combination of ballet, theatre and still photography.

2. FIRST FILM JOB?

In the late 1950s, I wrote a screenplay which, again, was made by another filmmaker, and I was allowed to work as a first assistant director on the film. This was in Czechoslovakia. That experience just provoked in me a strong desire to direct my own screenplay. I realized, being on the set, that I would have done things differently. What I saw was a different interpretation of what I would have done as the director.

Because I was a screenwriter, it was very hard to get a start as a director. I did a film in 16mm and, thanks to the results of showing it to a studio, I was able to complete the film as a director professionally. That is how I started.

3. YOUR GOAL IN FILMMAKING?

I like to tell stories. I want the whole story, plus every little bit and part of a story, to be believed by an audience. I hope I succeed to be honest and true enough so that a message or philosophy comes across automatically. The philosophy of a story is not the prime concern for me. The prime concern is the story or characters.

4. IN WHAT GENRE DO YOU SEEK A STORY?

I look for happenings in real life—my own people, or those I know—stories that I've heard about, or literature. Usually my story is something based on a real event which happened that I witnessed, with the exception of two films that have been based on books: *Black Peter* [1964] and *One Flew Over The Cuckoo's Nest* [1975] All my films have been made like this.

5. STORY SOURCE?

I don't really mind where the source comes from, whether it's an original screenplay or from a book, or a treatment of a play. I know I will have to go through it and work on it—transform what's written so that I know what to do with it, so that it fits my capacity to do a film. I can't stand a page in a screenplay that I don't know what to do with.

6. USE A SCRIPTWRITER OR DO IT YOURSELF? /7. CLOSE COLLABORATION WITH THE SCREENWRITER?

Even when I was working originally as a writer, I didn't like to work alone. I don't know if it's lack of discipline, but I need a provocation. Even if I work for another director, I always liked either to work with him or with another partner, so that the work itself is a dialogue. What I'm doing now as a director is repeating this experience. I always like to work myself with a screenwriter. I like to work closely—word for word, line for line, action by action—together in the same room, discussing every line.

I'm not making any difference between screenplays and shooting scripts, because I like to describe actions in the screenplay, but I don't put in any angles or camera moves. I've not really prepared so-called "shooting scripts" from this point of view.

8. PREPLAN OR IMPROVISE?

I like to improvise, but I'm aware that about 90 percent of improvisation is very boring, and bad. I always have to have a very exact screenplay that I can go back to when improvisation fails me.

9. MOST IMPORTANT COMPONENT OF YOUR FILM?

To me the most important component of a film is what I'm doing at any specific time. When I'm working on a screenplay, it always seems to me to be the crucial stage; when I'm directing the film, I always feel that the writing was only the beginning, and now the directing is most important to me. Then, when I'm editing, that becomes the most important stage in filmmaking! It's like saying that spring-time is better than the winter, but the summer is better than autumn—it's all in a year, so who's to choose.

10. WORK WITH A PRODUCER?

I'd like a producer to be a partner in all aspects of filmmaking. The more I feel that a producer respects me and will give me the final word, the more I'm open to listening to him and all his opinions. I even seek his opinions.

My experience on *One Flew Over The Cuckoo's Nest* was unique. We developed a complete collaboration. No one felt shy of expressing his own opinions regardless of how different they would be. I consider this very stimulating to one's own creative potential.

11. USE A DIALOGUE DIRECTOR?

I never use a dialogue director. I somehow don't insist on actors knowing their lines by heart. I organize the shooting in such a way that it's within human capacity to learn lines in rehearsal.

12. WRITER OR PRODUCER ON THE SET?

It depends on who is the writer and who is the producer. If it's a man who has a good understanding—I prefer to have him or them on the set.

13. WORK CLOSELY WITH THE CAMERAMAN?

Prior to shooting, I work out with the cameraman the general and basic problems like choosing locations—what kind of tone and mood the film should have. That's about it. I don't go into the details of every scene.

When we start shooting, I like to work very closely with my cameraman. I'll tell him the general direction of the shot. I let him set up the camera and choose the lens and angle. Then I look through the camera and confront my feelings, sometimes going through arguments and fights with him. I try to find out the best possible solution. I feel that the relationship between the cameraman and director—there is always a bit of a conflict, which I think is very healthy for the final result of the film. I just don't like cameraman to be servants; I want very opinionated men.

14. SUPERVISION OF CASTING?

Well, with casting, I'm concentrating on the first very important and crucial part of the process of filmmaking, so I'm supervising castings very closely. I like to work with a casting director who has imagination, but I like to make the final decisions on the smallest of bit players.

15. PREFERENCE OF ACTING STYLE?

The ideal actors are the ones who work on instinct, but are still technicians. I'd rather choose an instinctive actor like Jack Nicholson, because they're more surprising.

There are so many methods. Method works for every individual differently. Somebody who is just seeking security, in learning method, can be destroyed; you can't learn security in art. You can't find anything that can safely be repeated with the same good results.

On the other hand, there are actors who can be helped by method to retain their intellectual control—which is necessary. In that case, it's fine, if he doesn't overshadow the instincts and impulses which are the source of great acting.

Method never made a good actor out of somebody who doesn't have talent, and has never destroyed a great actor who had talent. Method should be individual.

16. PRECAMERA WORK WITH ACTOR?

I don't like to discuss in depth with the actors the concept of the character or relationship before the shooting starts. I don't believe it's necessary, and I don't like it unless the actor needs it.

It's better to start from the surface and move to the depths. I like actors to surprise me with their own interpretations, so that we have something to start the discussion with. I like actors to work on a character from observation as opposed to analysis.

17. IMPORTANCE OF REHEARSALS?

I don't like to rehearse long, but it varies, because some scenes require longer rehearsal time. I like to block out scenes that are difficult in staging, but *that* is the only case for long rehearsals.

I like it when actors know their lines and situation for the first time. Film has one advantage over all media—that is to capture, within dramatic form, unrepeatable moments. Theatre can't do that. Only film has this capacity. So every way to capture this is welcome. The more you rehearse, the more you cut down on your chances of getting this.

18. ADHERENCE TO SCRIPT?

I never insist that an actor meticulously repeat his or her lines from the screenplay. However, when I feel that improvisation starts to hurt the rhythm and pace, I'll ask for a closer following of the screenplay. Yet, I still don't insist on word for word.

19. EDITING SUPERVISION?

It makes me very nervous to look at the film that has been shot. I always like to be together with my film editor, every time he touches the film. That doesn't mean I'm the editor. Again, I like editors with strong opinions.

20. ROLE OF MUSICAL SCORE?

The moment it comes to put in music, I feel it's most important, in certain ways, as important as the dialogue. The dialogue is carrying the story from an intellectual point of view, but the music is carrying the story from an emotional point of view.

I like to plan the music that I'll be using even before I start shooting.

21. INVOLVEMENT IN PREPARATION OF MUSICAL SCORE?

I guess I would be more deeply involved with the preparation and recording of the music, if I was much more a music man. My education in music is very limited. I don't dare interfere with composers. They are odd men, and it's good not to mess with them.

22. WHAT SCENES SHOULD HAVE MUSIC?

I like to have final control—which scenes—what kind of music will be used. When it comes to this decision, the director has already seen the film on the editing table so many times that you're losing objectivity and a fresh approach. I like to discuss this stage and use of music with the producer and, of course, the composer.

23. SOUND EFFECTS?

Sound effects are very important. You have to be careful about every detail so it's not phony. One little phony detail can undermine the believability of the whole thing, and sounds can damage the credibility of the picture. The audience should not be aware of film technique. The moment the audience is suddenly aware of technique, you're immediately caught revealing your tricks—it's like watching a bad magician: you've caught him in his trick.

I think good sound effects are a part of the magic film has.

Samuel Fuller

Mr. Fuller objected to answering a questionnaire, but graciously volunteered to write an essay, explaining his viewpoints and reporting his experiences.

-T.G.

An Essay on Film Directing Entitled "Headlines To Headshots"
by
Samuel Fuller

Weaned on New York's Park (Newspaper) Row, teamed with reporter Rhea Gore (John Huston's mother) on my first double-suicide, the eventual transition from newspaperman to filmmaker was the natural leap from dummy makeup to facial makeup.

Page One and the Screen are bedmates. Working in the morgue and shooting a movie trigger constant visions. A headline has the impact of a headshot, pulp and rawstock fight lineage and footage, a news lead is the opening of a film.

8-point Goudy, Widescreen Pica gauge, Moviola—reporter and film director spill blood on the same emotional battlefield of what is fit to print, and what is fit to film. The *thou cannot* and *thou must not* pendulum swings from black-and-white fact to Technicolor fancies.

The newspaper real, and movie imaginary, sharing bloodstained scissors, glue, proofs, cement, splicer, workprint give twin birth to the battle cry of rewrite, remake, retake, redub and matures with the press and projection machine.

Peddling the *Worcester Telegram, Boston Post, Boston American* in Worcester was my first contact with newspapers.

To New York at eleven, peddling papers at twelve at the 125th Street Ferry. In those days newsboys bought papers from the Circulation Department.

A love affair started with the *New York Evening Journal*, 238 William Street, off Park Row, a column away from the Bowery, across from the Newsboys' Home sponsored by Al Smith. One-eyed, half-deaf Tom Foley, foreman of the *Journal*'s Press Room, opened up Wonderland, showed me presses in action, linotypes singing in "composing," and finally gold itself: the City Room on the seventh floor.

The shouts of "Copy, boy!" with young men in late 'teens running, making "books," shooting copy through pneumatic tubes, was electrifying. The hell with peddling newspapers. Working on one became an obsession. Working on the *Journal*.

"Lie," managing editor Joseph V. Mulcahy said. "Tell 'em you're fourteen to get working papers. Then I'll put you on as a copy boy."

Running copy on the *Journal*, personal copy jumper for Arthur Brisbane, head copy boy (and *only* copy boy) on the *New York Evening Graphic*, police reporter on the *Graphic*, the *Journal*, the *San Diego Sun*, journeyman reporter on dailies, weeklies, bi-weeklies throughout the country slowly structured a stockpile of characters, events and conflicting emotions without thought of making a film.

First brush with Hollywood was when M-G-M's offer of $5,000 (to fictionize a solution to my bylined unsolved double-murder) was spurned because the City of New York offered $25,000 for a factual solution, naming names. The murders are still unsolved. The corpses were wealthy, white-bearded, miserly octogenerian Edward Ridley and his male secretary. My lead was *Who killed Santa Claus?* because Ridley loved foreclosing mortgages on Christmas. No regret turning down that $5,000. One day *Who Killed Santa Claus?* will be my film contribution of a case of murder that defies solution, yet maintains suspense to the empty end.

The question "Where do you get ideas for films?" isn't hard to answer.

Covering an execution....Told by a man who hacked his family to death with a meat cleaver on a Hudson River barge that he was sorry if he hurt them....Listening to a leaper's sex problem on a 30-foot ledge before he squashed a luckless passerby like a gnat....Extracting the identity of a blonde nude with paresis mounting a water hydrant singing the *Star Spangled Banner* because her name was Frances Key.... Watching reporters refuse to help Lindy swing the tail of his plane at Teterboro Airfield in Jersey, because they resented his reply to all their questions with "Is there anything else you want to ask?" Breaking Jeanne Eagles' death by discovering her corpse in Campbell's Funeral Parlor....Posing for a *Graphic* composite of French flyers Nungesser and Coli in their wrecked plane in the ill-fated Atlantic hop, only to baffle my mother who just couldn't understand if the photographer was that close why the flyers weren't saved....Accompanying a rookie cop from the 24th Precinct on a routine complaint to stumble over a slain body in a subterranean office....Successfully interviewing J. P. Morgan only to watch my copy destroyed by the City Editor, because he *knew* J. P. never granted interviews.... Hired, fired, rehired by the great Gene Fowler in the span of five hours while assigned to an Admiral's speech that erupted miles away in a Bowery bum's brutal murder near Lum Fong's restaurant in Chinatown....Phoning blow-by-blow from a Harlem cigar store during a race riot....Using Sunday editions as bedsheets and blankets riding the rods with Depression displaced persons....Taking footbaths with hoboes in troughs of condemned milk.... Drawing antichain market cartoons for a Rochester weekly while its editor and publisher ran for Governor of Minnesota to collect seven votes.... Making caricatures of Texas cattle kings dropping manure from boots on the thick red rug in the Scarborough Hotel in Midland.... Sketching whores in San Francisco while covering the General strike as soldiers shot strikers in front of the Ferry Building....

Every newspaperman has such a Hellbox to draw from.

Every newspaperman is a potential filmmaker.

All he or she has to do is to transfer real emotion to reel emotion and sprinkle with imagination.

This does not include critics. A newspaperman reports what happened, inwardly boiling with emotions that must remain personal. A critic outwardly reports what happened, writing what he liked or didn't like about what happened. Every story varies. A critic generally plays the same tune on his typewriter. A few have made it in films. Peter Bogdanovich stands out as one of that rare breed, but he was more than a critic. He analyzed films the way a reporter analyzes emotions. He lifted himself out of the well of observer to creator.

My only newspaper film *Park Row* [1952] was 1886 vintage, because a passion for that street made the film a must. Drunk on stories of newspaper Goliaths before my time, hanging around Doc Perry's pharmacy in the *World* building where once Pulitzer picked up his medicine, working where once those Goliaths worked, walked, ate, drank, dreamed, fought, laughed and wept, gave me selfish ejaculations when shooting the film on the stage replica of those paper-and-ink cobblestones.

Looking at the list of newspaper films to be screened, *Five Star Final* [1931] by Louis Weitzenkorn was based on Emile Gauvreau, editor of the *Graphic*. Gauvreau gave Winchell his break. Also on that pink tabloid were Jerry Wald [radio editor], Norma Krasna [drama critic], Artie Auerbach [photographer], who became funnyman "Mr. Kitzel" on the Jack Benny show, John Huston [reporter].

Weitzenkorn came from *The World* to replace Gauvreau who went to the *Mirror* to haunt Winchell who loathed him. The changing of the Czars was macabre. Gauvreau's exit with a twisted foot. Weitzenhorn's entrance with a twisted arm. Abandoning Pulitzer to hit pornographic bottom on Bernarr Macfadden's *Graphic*, Weitzenkorn struck playwright platinum: Gauvreau's exciting career.

Five Star Final's editor was factual. Gauvreau *did* updig an old murder, promised lurid revelations revealing the exonerated murderess' real name, terrified her. Result: the self-destruction of the woman and her husband. My role in that bulldog bouillabaisse was to season it with facts on the son of the suicides. In the film it is the daughter. Gauvreau always washed his hands after a distasteful story. So does Edward G. Robinson in the film expertly directed by Mervyn LeRoy.

Years later, when writing *Gangs of New York* [1938] it was ironic to run into Weitzenkorn who was writing a movie script called *King of the Newsboys*.

Seeing *The Front Page* play on opening night with Kermit Jaediker of the *New York Daily News* moved us because in Lee Tracy, we saw what we were not, but would like to be. It was thrilling. After the curtain came down it was back to the Press Room (a plumber's shop by day) across from the 47th Street Police Station, and to the grappling hook that finally brought up the body of a five-year-old boy from the garbage in the Hudson. The beads of water on the eyelashes of the dead boy made me think of the beads of sweat on the brow of the unfortunate bastard that was hidden in the desk in *The Front Page.*

There is a tale that when Howard Hughes decided to film *The Front Page* [1931], he said, "Get the man who's playing Hildy Johnson on the stage." Pat O'Brien was doing the role in Chicago. Hughes sent for him, believing he was sending for Lee Tracy. True or not, it's a good story and Lewis Milestone, who did a crackerjack job directing the film, is the man who can confirm or deny the tale.

His Girl Friday [1940] was a superb sex-switch of *The Front Page* with breathtaking, machine gun tempo. After World War II, the film became more personal because of Howard Hawks. My novel *The Dark Page* (purely a psychological study of an editor who commands a city-wide search for himself after murdering the wife he deserted twenty years ago) was written before World War II. The first draft was left with my mother who notified me in North Africa in the vicinity of Kasserine Pass that she spent the advance for the book she sold to publishers Duell, Sloan and Pearce. A hard cover of the book caught up with me in France near St. Lo, a Hollywood offer missed me in Mons, Belgium, and in Germany's Huertgen Forest, word was received that Howard Hawks bought the book for Bogart and Robinson for $15,000. He sold it to Columbia. It was filmed as *Scandal Sheet* [1952] with Broderick Crawford. That film is not *my* book.

Billy Wilder's *The Big Carnival* [*Ace in the Hole,* 1951] is the closest portrayal yet of a sonafabitch newspaperman. No punches pulled. Am eagerly looking forward to his version of *The Front Page* [1974].

What takes place in a newspaper has yet to be filmed.

A newspaper—like a church, whorehouse, DAR meeting, political convention, KKK gathering, synagogue, American Legion Hall, public library—is a living character replated hourly with highly charged controversial nuances in every man and woman on the paper.

To make a real newspaper film is as difficult as to make a real war film. The censor is not the only barrier. People who buy tickets and walk into a peacock temple to crack pop corn in soft chairs have been doped over the years with what war is like on the screen. They have been doped over the years with what a newspaper is like on the screen.

Doped, duped, deluded—they know what to expect and will not accept a war film with indifference to atrocities, with combat sacrificing wetnoses in a minefield, with the enjoyment of dehumanization, with the gall of brass referring to headless bodies as "my boys" while in the sack with women in the rear, with distorted battle reports to grab votes, make loot, wave flags, sell arms, deal over burned and bloated corpses in black market.

People will not accept a newspaper film with political atrocities and well-planned and paid-for character assassinations where names are accurate they will not accept the cunning of the Desk blindfolding a reporter through a fog because he's on the verge of exposing a President, hurt an advertiser, jail a Federal Judge, disrobe a Vice Squad. They will not accept the FBI involved in blackmail, because the FBI *is* the audience cracking popcorn. They will not accept publishers in theft tandem with politicians, publishers whoring with bankers, profiting with big business, running meaningless Op-Ed letters against financial backers.

Past films have dealt with fictional exposés.

One day films will use *living names* in exposure.

One hundred years ago, Washington politicians wouldn't give newspaper interviews unless they were paid. Today they pay ghosts to manufacture their autobiographies for a movie sale. Those autobiographies never give damaging facts. Until the turn of the 18th century, the Senate controlled newspaper exposés, thundering, "Secrecy is the enemy of democracy!"

Today, newspapers, *some* newspapers, publish Senatorial secrets that should be seen on the screen.

Trial by newspaper is still with us.

All the news that was unfit to print, all the scenes that were unfit to shoot, would make one hell of a newspaper film. It would have facts, legitimate characters, humor, shock, action. It would entertain and reveal. It would have the language of newspaper type spoken with flesh. It would show the passion of the printed word take on instant intimacy on film. It would go beyond the Bible, the newspaper, the stage. It would make words jump to life in shocking closeups. From Gutenberg to Griffith it would transfer from type to screen an accurate, shattering emotion of movement seen with eyes, heard with ears, and never forgotten with the brain.

The true story of J. Edgar Hoover and the FBI would make a hell of a movie today. Not the year 2000. But today.

To make such a newspaper film I would give my right Linotype. Perhaps one day...soon...at the moment I am delirious with a new edition, the *first* edition in the family. My beautiful wife, actress Christa Lan, gave birth to a beautiful girl named Samantha.

Right now Samantha is breast-fed.

Later she will be weaned on Mergenthaler and Films.

Tay Garnett

This chapter is being written under duress. Many people have urged me to express my own thinking in answer to my questionnaire, but I have consistently demurred: "How in the world can I proclaim myself a 'Master' director? My forté has always been comedy, but I have no intention of classing myself with the great men herein interviewed, and thereby evoking the biggest laugh of my career."

Then, suddenly, this guy came along...of course, I want it understood that my agreeing with him—when he said *I* should complete the questionnaire also—was in no way related to the fact that he is the publisher.

So....

1. BACKGROUND? / 2. FIRST FILM JOB?

Anyone interested in my answers to Questions 1 and 2, concerning my vocation prior to my advent into filmmaking, and the actual steps leading to my directing, will find all the pertinent facts in my autobiography, *Light Your Torches and Pull Up Your Tights*. It won't take long to read, if you skip the booze and the broads.

3. YOUR GOAL IN FILMMAKING?

This concerns itself with one's philosophy—one's aim or purpose in making a film. Like many of my contemporaries, my policy has always been to ENTERTAIN. However, I realize that anyone who has seen a lot of my films may turn in another verdict.

4. IN WHAT GENRE DO YOU SEEK A STORY?

This pertains to the specific genre in which one hopes to find his story material. I believe I've made pictures in every known category (barring pornos), but I insist that comedy is my thing.

In the "silent" days, we used a great deal of what we then referred to as comedy relief. This seems, in recent years, to have been relegated to the "obsolescent" file by many contemporary directors. Nevertheless, the practice is based on sound dramatic tried-and-true principles, and a great many of the ablest directors in the field are still using it. No doubt most of the film students are quite familiar with the method and purpose of comedy relief, but still it might be worthwhile for us to give ourselves a little refresher.

In developing a dramatic situation toward a climax, we devote every effort toward building suspense to the absolute ultimate—we wind it tighter and tighter.

Often we sense a moment when, unless we offer our audience something to relieve the pressure, there's a very real danger that they'll burst out with a great guffaw at some critical moment in our *drama*. If this happens, we can forget about trying to recapture that audience.

So, when we sense that the danger of our tension is going out of control, we try for a planned laugh—let them laugh with us rather than at us. Once the tension is relieved, we can start winding them up all over, right from where we left off. It is also worth remembering that it doesn't take too much of a joke to get the laugh under these conditions.

I believe comedy relief to be as essential to well-constructed drama as is counterpoint to musical composition.

5. STORY SOURCE?

As for my choice of source material, it's Story and Script Written Directly for the Screen, out in front by ten lengths and going away. Such stories are generally conceived and developed to take advantage of the many factors indigenous to the cinema, which are not enjoyed by either of the other media.

Of the other two forms—the novel (or short story) and the theatrical play—I much prefer the novel, as I consider it more closely related to film than film is to stage play. Theatrical productions are basically audio-oriented. One of the first things an actor must do, in the theatre, is to learn how to project his voice so that it is audible to the last row in the balcony.

Despite the opinion of an occasional egodolatrous ham, there is no known way in which one's visual image may be so projected without resorting to the use of an optical lens.

In my opinion, movies are just what the name implies: pictures in motion, with dialogue and sound effects as highly valued allies.

Of course, there have been many magnificent films made from beautifully written plays; however, the garrulous picture has never been my choice. I much prefer "action" pictures—comedy or drama. To me, that's what motion pictures are all about.

6. USE A SCRIPTWRITER OR DO IT YOURSELF?

Regarding the use of another writer on my shooting scripts: of course, to originate a story, then do a solo job on the shooting script is, obviously, a most gratifying ego trip. However, I have found that—for the good of the film—it is not to be recommended. A totally objective viewpoint of another writer is usually most valuable.

7. CLOSE COLLABORATION WITH THE SCREENWRITER?

One does not always have a choice as to whether or not he will use another writer as co-writer. In the days of the major studio dominance in Hollywood, one (being under contract) was handed a script which had been fully prepared. The only choice the director had at that point was whether or not he chose to make the picture. In any case, once he had agreed to do it, it was quite usual for the director to make whatever changes in the script he thought would improve the film.

Even in the case of a non-writing director, it was—I believe—a general practise that a director could ask for (and receive) the services of a writer of his choice to do whatever script changes he (the director) felt were indicated.

Today, with the growth of the independent production companies, these things are automatic. Everything having to do with the artistic aspect in the making of a film is under the control of the director, save in those relatively few cases in which the company is owned by a producer who does not direct. For the most part, this is the day of the director-producer.

8. PREPLAN OR IMPROVISE?

It does please me to have all the action and business worked out on paper before shooting, as far as is practical. I particularly want every idea my collaborator has, regarding the story, characters and movement, made graphic. I may not use all ideas precisely as he has suggested, but I have found that the suggestions are often very valuable.

Of course, action written for location sequences is often far wide of the limits imposed by actual physical conditions with which we are confronted. Nevertheless, the written ideas often supply guidelines for extemporization.

9. MOST IMPORTANT COMPONENT OF YOUR FILM?

The one specific comment which I regard as transcendent in the creation of a film is story/script/scriptwriter. Of course, stories are often selected as suitable vehicles for a particular star or stars, and the script prepared to best serve individual requirements. Nevertheless, the written material constitutes the cardinal factor from which the entire project evolves.

Once the shooting script is completed, then each of the other elements becomes, in turn, the *vital* component.

10. WORK WITH A PRODUCER?

Producers come in every imaginable size, color, volume and scent. I've tried every variety.

Occasionally a director hits the jackpot. I've been more fortunate than most in this regard. I've worked with some of the greats: Dick Jones, at Mack Sennetts's; Ralph Block, at Pathé-DeMille; Hal Wallis at Warner Bros.; Irving Thalberg, who built a legend called M-G-M. There were a number of other very talented producers with whom I worked; from all the good ones I got every aid that could be devised to ease my load. It was a genuine joy and privilege to work with those magnificently talented people.

Unfortunately, the no-talent characters far outnumbered the greats. Those inept, inarticulate—although highly vocal individuals—seemed dedicated to setting up obstacle courses for the already overburdened director, thus defying him to complete the course in top form.

Having worked with a number of problem producers, and also having functioned as director-producer on a good many projects, I can state that, for me, (unless I can get lucky enough to get the best) the job is a lot easier, and the results much more satisfying, if one can work in the dual capacity.

11. USE A DIALOGUE DIRECTOR?

Although I have tried a couple of times to work with a dialogue director, I have found it to be an impractical arrangement. Although I'm sure the people with whom I have tried this experiment were capable, and tried most seriously to give me what I wanted, there was always an undercurrent of friction that provided a serious hindrance to our work.

12. WRITER OR PRODUCER ON THE SET?

I like to have my writer on the set when I'm shooting, but not when I'm rehearsing. During rehearsal a writer is a serious nuisance; he simply cannot help but make suggestions as to the readings, etc.

I know how it is; as a writer, I was probably a lethal dose of audacity, before *I* started directing. When a director is shooting, the writer or writers always seem to know a better way. (I'm not too sure I always did.)

As for producer-dropper-inners, I don't mind as long as they do not discuss, with members of the cast or crew, anything to do with what we're shooting, or have shot. Most of the really good ones don't care about being on the set in any case.

I did have a serious go-round with Irving Thalberg on *China Seas* [1935]. He used to come on the set and discuss the previous day's work with [Clark] Gable and [Jean] Harlow. After he'd left, I'd wonder what had happened to my carefully planned and rehearsed characterizations. It happened two or three times before, one night—as we said in our early day silent titles—"Came the Dawn."

I went to Irving's house (on a Sunday) and we did a bit of verbal Indian-wrestling. After that, Irving's visits were purely social in nature. He'd seen my side of the problem, and always played it my way after that. Irving Thalberg was a lot of man.

13. WORK CLOSELY WITH THE CAMERAMAN?

I've always worked very closely with my cameraman, prior to, during, and after shooting. When you work with master cinematographers such as Joe Ruttenberg, Sid Wagner, Arthur Miller, and Leon Shamroy, you become aware very quickly that their interest is not limited to the photographic problems; they will have familiarized themselves with the script and anticipated many of the director's major problems.

Usually an experienced cameraman will prove to be the most knowledgeable man on the staff, and one with whom the director can discuss the difficulties that previous happenstance has taught him to anticipate. The greats among the cameramen are usually eager to help in this area if invited to do so.

Another vital member of the team is the lighting man. Unless the director has a man he knows he can trust all the way, he's in deep trouble.

14. SUPERVISION OF CASTING?

As in every other aspect of my filmmaking, I stay on top of the casting right down to the one-line "bits." Any one of these "bits," ineptly done, can throw your whole structure out of balance.

Because no other person can ever know precisely what you visualize in every part, you're not discounting a casting director's knowledge or judgment in exercising this vastly important prerogative.

15. PREFERENCE OF ACTING STYLE?

In casting actors, my preference is, by long odds, for the "instinctive" type.

Of course, technique is important, but technique alone is not enough. It has been my experience that the great technicians often come up empty in the "emotion" department. Even though every move and gesture, and each reading was performed according to specifications, there was often something missing—something vital.

Conversely, it seems to me that the instinctive actor, given enough hard work and experience, invariably develops a technique, and usually it's not as apparent as that of the pure technician.

As for the "method actor"—I'm forced to pass. The newly spawned method actor seems to fit neatly into the same pod in which all the other eager young "methodists" are bedded down so snugly. Of course, in time, most of them stop scratching and mumbling, and begin to learn their trade. But not on *my* time, thanks very much.

16. PRECAMERA WORK WITH ACTOR?

Having exercised the utmost care in casting the actor and—in most cases—having chosen him because of performances I've seen him give, it has been my practice to encourage him to bring his own best interpretation to the character.

In case that does not meet with my approval, it's time for in-depth discussion. However, if I've cast well, this doesn't happen too frequently.

17. IMPORTANCE OF REHEARSALS?

On a few occasions, I have rehearsed the entire show with the full cast before shooting. However, unless the piece is a one or two-set picture with a reasonably small cast, it's impractical.

In a more complicated picture, an actor may rehearse a scene several weeks before he is called upon to play it. Consequently, I prefer rehearsing on the set as fully as is required before each scene is shot, so that the actor goes right into it while he's "up." In that way I have discovered the areas in which I could be of most help to my actors.

In my opinion, that is probably one of the most important of all a director's duties.

18. ADHERENCE TO SCRIPT?

That an actor be required to adhere meticulously to the script—lines and business—is, in my book, ridiculous. (Unless we are doing Shakespeare, which—at this point—appears most unlikely.)

If the meaning of a line can be expressed in a manner that makes the actor more comfortable in the part –without distorting characterization or dramatic structure —I'm all for it. However, I must retain the right of decision as to the fitness of the alteration.

19. EDITING SUPERVISION?

Apparently there is nothing unique in my practice in editing my film. I sit beside my cutter in viewing each day's rushes. As they are run, I give him my thinking on the proper assembly (which is all I require of him at this point).

As soon as he has a sequence assembled, he lets me know and together, after the dailies are shown, we run the assembled sequence, and we plan a first rough cut of it. By using this method, we are able to view a first-cut version within 24 to 48 hours after shooting is concluded.

From that point we sweat it down, frame by frame, until I am convinced it is as good as I can get within the limits of all that lousy film I shot.

(There seems always to come a moment when most directors wonder why they didn't settle for selling neckties. With them one can, at least, choke himself to death.

(At one's first preview, aspirin is recommended. It is also deemed advisable to refrain from carrying strychnine capsules to a first preview, as the temptation to use them may prove too great to be refused by a budding director.)

20. ROLE OF MUSICAL SCORE?

In my opinion, a musical score is an integral part of any fully rounded dramatic or comedic film. Certainly there are spots in almost any picture that can be enhanced by the discreet use of music.

21. INVOLVEMENT IN PREPARATION OF MUSICAL SCORE?

Knowing little about music from a technical viewpoint, I can function only as a guide, trying to convey to the composer the effect I hope to achieve with music in each scene.

After he has completed his compositions, I hear them on the piano. As I said, I know nothing about music, but I do know, when I hear a passage, whether it says what I'm listening for or not.

22. WHAT SCENES SHOULD HAVE MUSIC?

Having had several unfortunate experiences, in which an over-ambitious composer flattened out the drama in a scene where no music should have been used, I became quite adamant as to which scenes should be played without score. I have a rule: when in doubt skip the music.

23. SOUND EFFECTS?

It is next to impossible to overestimate the importance of sound effects. It has been my practice to pay particular attention to both the recording and dubbing of the sound in my pictures. If there is the slightest doubt in anyone's mind as to the value of sound effects, let him run any violent action sequence—a chase, a rough-and-tumble fight or a shoot-out—without the track. It's likely to be pretty flat. Then let him run it with the track, and he'll probably leap up and shout, "See there! What did I tell you?"

COMMENT

Recent years have produced some major talents among the upcoming directors. However, it seems that, in their determination to bring something new and fresh to their films, there has been a tendency on the part of a gifted few, to turn their backs on one of the cardinal fundamentals of dramaturgy. They seem to cherish an absolute aversion to anything remotely resembling a storyline, having a beginning, a middle and an end.

In a couple of films I've seen, it would appear that the director had chosen to fade in on something that interested him. This was followed by an interminable series of apparently unrelated shots (sometimes with characters whom we had seen previously, but often with people we had never seen before).

Then, when in doubt, they have thrown in a couple of gory, violent scenes, or possibly some juicy sex exposure or sex deviation bits. Then, when the director appears to have run out of film, or money, or both, he had faded out.

A word of advice: if you're determined to go for the abstract in films, learn, first, how to make a good conventional film. Learn all the fundamentals so that, when you start to make up a shiny new set of laws just for yourself, you'll have some knowledge of what has gone before and how it was achieved.

That done, smash hell out of conventions if that's what you want to do. Bear in mind that most of our well-known abstract painters of today were fairly accomplished conventionalists before they decided to get rich quickly.

Howard Hawks

1. BACKGROUND?

After serving as a second lieutenant in the U.S. Army Air Corp during World War I, I became a professional race-car driver. I built several cars and airplanes.

2. FIRST FILM JOB?

My first job in the picture business was as property man with the Mary Pickford Company, during summer vacations. From the prop department at Famous Players-Lasky, I went to the editing department, and from there to the script department. Then, for some time, I was assistant to Marshall Neilan and Allan Dwan in 1922 and 1924. I was instrumental in setting up and producing independent films with both of these men.

From 1924 to early 1926, I was in charge of the story department at Paramount, where I wrote (or purchased) stories for over forty films. In 1926, I was signed by Fox where I directed my first feature length film (which I had also written), *The Road To Glory*.

3. YOUR GOAL IN FILMMAKING?

In making pictures, I've never gone for anything except entertainment. After I made my first picture, Sol Wurtzel, a very smart man and head of Fox, said, "Look, you've shown that you can direct. The critics like your work. But, for God's sake, make something that people will like to look at! Make entertainment!" So I wrote a story called *Fig Leaves* [1926] and made it, and it got its cost back in one theatre.

Since that time, I've had no sides to take. I'm not interested in trying to teach a lesson. I'm interested only in making pictures that people will enjoy and get fun out of watching. I am convinced that any director who tries to tell a message, is a damn fool.

I used to be a great fan of Frank Capra until he tried to deliver messages. That didn't work for him. I think he got off on the wrong foot.

4. IN WHAT GENRE DO YOU SEEK A STORY?

I probably like making comedies better than anything else—no matter from what source I get the story material. There's an obvious reason for this, beyond my natural fondness for the humorous. When you show a comedy to an audience, they will tell you very quickly—and very audibly—whether or not they think your picture is funny.

5. STORY SOURCE?

My primary choice in picking a story is, in a great many cases, based on personal experience—knowing the people I'm making a picture about. I've made a number of pictures on flying. I've made a number of pictures on the West, because I studied the West—I like horses, and had a horse ranch for awhile.

I try to do things that I've been through, about people I've known. I made one musical just for fun: *Gentlemen Prefer Blondes* [1953] with Marilyn Monroe and Jane Russell; I laughed all the way through it. It turned out to be, probably, the most popular musical made for Fox.

I buy three stories and wind up making one, because the other two just don't pan out. I've also made pictures to do someone a favor; I've told them I'm no good on that particular type of picture. They've begged me to make it anyhow, but it never turned out well. I have to tell stories about people I know.

I made *Land of The Pharoahs* [1955] with two writers; a friend of mine had a beautiful place near a lake in Italy. So we went there and worked. We developed a story to the point where we liked it, then wrote the screenplay.

I said, "You fellows can start writing—what do you want to start with?" Bill Faulkner said, "Wait a second, I don't know how a Pharoah talks. Can I write it as though he was from Kentucky?"

I said, "Go ahead."

Harry Kurnitz said, "Can I write it like King Lear?"

I said, "Damn it! Are you guys going to leave it up to me?"

They said "Yes."

I didn't know what a Pharoah talked like; I thought the picture was lousy. I thought the scenic part was great, but no good the rest of the way. When you write dialogue, you have to know the type of person who's going to be speaking it. The girls in my pictures were always outspoken and honest, because I happen to like that type of girl.

Strange thing happened: a man who is a very good critic and likes my work saw one picture I made and wrote: "Just when I thought Hawks would always be honest and stick to reality, he disappointed me in making *Only Angels Have Wings* [1939] and went far beyond reality."

I wrote him a letter and said everything in that picture is the absolute truth, so truth is stranger than fiction.

I got back a very nice letter from him.

Another example of the way I work: I'm going to do a comedy that takes place all over the world; it's a story about the scientists who work for oil companies. Wherever they smell oil, they go there. I have a good friend who has five of them working for him, and they're an amazing bunch of people.

I spent time with them and decided to base a story on the exploits of these fellows. They are a crazy bunch—they get about two or three hundred thousand dollars a year. They don't make good husbands, because they're away half of the time. So I'm doing an old-fashioned comedy—a wild, crazy story.

The Russians have asked me to make a picture in Russia; I hope to do it. It's taken me about a year to find a story that would be good for them. I'm going to use a second unit on the comedy, because it would cost too damn much to bring an entire cast. I'm using a fellow to shoot second unit work, while I make the Russian picture.

I knew Ernest Hemingway very well. I asked him if he wanted to get together with me and make a few pictures. He said he didn't want to go to Hollywood. I said he didn't have to; we could continue to hunt a fish and work on the story.

"No," he said. "I'm good at what I'm doing."

I said, "I can make a picture out of your worst story."

He bristled and asked, "What's my worst story."

I told him, "A piece of junk called *To Have and Have Not* [1944].

"Well," he said, "I need some money."

"That's why you should come and work with us—you always need money," I said.

He said, "How the hell can you make a picture out of *To Have and Have Not?*"

So we started to talk—not about his story, but about the two people in it, and how they came to meet.

I went back to Hollywood and bought the story. It was owned by someone who had paid $10,000 for it. I paid $80,000 for it. I made a deal with it, and made a hundred or two hundred thousand from it. The next time I saw Hemingway, I told him, he had made ten thousand out of it, then told him what I had made, and he didn't talk to me for six months.

I was lucky enough to know William Faulkner. I bought a short story from him and made it—we became friends. He helped me on a number of stories—he and a new girl, Leigh Brackett, worked on *The Big Sleep* [1946] by Raymond Chandler.

I told them, "Chandler is good; don't change a lot of things—just put it down." They wrote a scenario in eight days. Every time I got in trouble and couldn't solve something, I'd call Faulkner.

I never liked to work around the studio. I listened to too much stuff about their copying things—it's worst today than it was then—but I wanted to do things my own way.

Anyone who makes a successful picture—there are eight others who want to do the same thing. There was a producer at Warner Bros. who made *in*-expensive pictures. He said to me, "Howard, when I hear you're doing a picture, I start one about that same subject right away, because you always come out right."

I asked, "What did you do when I made a picture called *Tiger Shark* [1932]?

He said, "Oh, that was a bad one—I made a picture about the shrimp industry and it failed!"

Choosing a story is a strange thing. I was having lunch one day with a damn good director: Michael Curtiz. He said, "Howard, I'm not happy. I've got a story about the Tennessee Mountains. What do I know about the Tennessee Mountains?"

Then he said it was all about somebody named Sergeant York.

6. USE A SCRIPTWRITER OR DO IT YOURSELF? / 7. CLOSE COLLABORATION WITH THE SCREENWRITER?

When it comes to developing a story for a picture: I had John Huston working for me on *Sergeant York* [1941]. I told Jack Warner that I thought John would make a good director. Jack said, "Fine." I said I'd give Huston some help if I could.

John came to me and asked, "What shall I write?"

I told him, "For the first picture, don't write—it's hard enough just to direct—learn how to direct first." I added, "They own a picture over here called *The Maltese Falcon* [1941]."

John said, "They've made it twice already, Howard."

I said, "Nobody ever made it—they thought they could write better than [Dashiell] Hammett. He was one of the best writers in his field. You do it the way he wrote it."

Well, he made it, and he and I were up for Academy Awards that year.

I like to work with a good writer first. I always change the stuff afterward to suit my way of telling a story. I've worked with some very good writers: Ben Hecht, Charles MacArthur, Jules Furthman, William Faulkner, Dudley Nichols, Ernest Hemingway—and none of them ever fought over rewriting! What I do is adapt—I don't change their stuff—I adapt it to the style and way I like to make a story.

8. PREPLAN OR IMPROVISE?

In working on a script, I don't believe anybody can sit up in a room and develop action. I think that you have to get on the set for that. If I have a good speech for John Wayne coming into a room, and he stands up, reads the speech, then walks out—that's no good.

But, if he comes into a room and starts his speech, and does it in a walk or on the run, and carries it outside with him—then you have movement. If I've got a scene that I don't think is any good, I try to work out a moving solution for it.

9. MOST IMPORTANT COMPONENT OF YOUR FILM?

The importance changes with different pictures, let's say you've talked to Cary Grant about doing a comedy—you certainly know what to do with that. If you've talked to John Wayne about doing a picture—I can't think of anyone else with whom I'd like to do a Western, once I'd thought of Wayne. With stars of this calibre, there can be no doubt as to their transcendency.

The next important thing is the story. You can fall flat on your face with a badly chosen story. Sometimes, of course, the choice of story depends on who is going to be in it, as already mentioned.

So then, with star and story set, you start to think of cameramen. Who can do the best job with this particular star or story? Is your script one that calls for a lot of exteriors? Or is it played mainly in studio sets? If you don't pick the right cameraman you're not likely to get a good picture.

To sum it up, I'd have to say that, generally, the elements in order of their importance are cast, story, cameraman, and cutter, although there is no invariable rule.

10. WORK WITH A PRODUCER? / 12. WRITER OR PRODUCER ON THE SET?

Actually, I never had a producer on my set. Oh, one time at Warner Bros., I saw a producer who would kind of hide behind things so I wouldn't see him.

I liked working with Jack Warner. I made *To Have and Have Not*, with Jack. I never saw him or talked to him during the making of the picture. I got occasional reports from someone that Jack had seen all the stuff, and liked it.

Jack and I went to the preview together. I was particularly interested in seeing if the audience liked Bacall—if they laughed in all the right places. They did.

Riding back home afterward, Warner said, "We should make another picture with Bogart and Bacall. Got any ideas about a story?"

I said, "Sure. Raymond Chandler's *The Big Sleep*."

That way of working with a man is great for me. Jack Warner was a real showman.

I like to have my writers on my set. I once worked with Billy Wilder and Charles Brackett. I'd agreed to do a story they'd told me about. I went fishing in Florida with Hemmingway, and when I came back, they hadn't done any work on the story, saying they didn't know where to go with it.

I said, "That's easy—we do *Snow White and The Seven Dwarfs*—we use Barbara Stanwyck as Snow White and Gary Cooper as the prince. The gangsters will be the wolf, and all the professors will be the dwarfs."

They did it that way. The picture was *Ball of Fire* [1942]. They—Brackett and Wilder—were welcome on the set at all times.

14. SUPERVISION OF CASTING?

I've always done my own casting, except for one or two pictures. I've always been lucky. I made pictures with Gary Cooper—who was great in his own way. I made five pictures with Gary Grant—there's no one better. I made pictures with Bogart.

I usually know who's going to be in the picture before I start. I've always been in complete control now for thirty years.

Before that, I worked on a story for certain people acting in their first picture: [Carole] Lombard, [Rita] Hayworth, [Lauren] Bacall. (Garnett: "You gave Bacall that voice didn't you?")

I didn't give her that voice; I merely told her how one of the great actors achieved his great voice—by projecting.

She asked, "How do I project it?"

I said, "Get fifty yards away from a tree and read to the tree, or go read somewhere where they won't think you're a nut."

It took her a month, and she came in with this voice. She had worked so hard that I made a test of her, and decided to use her in the picture.

Incidentally, I've always worked with two scripts: one that I made the picture from, and one that I let the cast read. Too many people will steal your stuff. It takes a year to get a picture out and TV will have used it by then. If you make a picture today, and you have a script, within a week every agent in town knows about that script, and is talking to his clients about the story and why he wants them to make the picture.

I've used new people so often: Jimmy Caan, Duke Wayne in *Red River* [1948]... Monty Clift. Men are pretty easy to work with. Bogart never smiled in his pictures until we started a picture together. I asked, "Are you going to go through this picture with that sour face on all the time? Why don't you smile?"

He said, "I can't. My lip is kind of funny."

I said, "You were laughing and smiling at my house when we had a few drinks over dinner—can't you do that?"

Bogie said, "If you want, I'll do it for you."

A very good critic said it was the first picture in which Bogart had smiled. Bogie kept on using that smile—he liked it himself.

The reason I've enjoyed casting new women: women stars come to you and say, "The left side of my face is better than the right side," so they want you to photograph the left side. They're afraid to do anything new.

I worked with one girl who was awfully good. I said, "You're the first person I've worked with, whom—I feel—I didn't help at all. Someday you'll see the girl I wanted you to do, and how I wanted you to play the part. I hope it teaches you something."

One day I came home and she was waiting for me—car parked in my driveway—and she said, "I saw the girl you wanted me to play. I'll do any story you want me to."

"I said, "I'm very pleased, and would love to have you do another picture with me."

Once at a football game, this guy came up and said, "Why haven't you ever made a picture for me? Anything you want to do will be okay with me."

He left, and I asked someone, "Who the hell was that?"

I was told, "Harry Cohn, head of Columbia Pictures."

So I went to see Cohn, and told him I wanted to make *His Girl Friday* [1940].

He growled, "Hell, that's a remake." He shrugged. "But if that's what you want, make it."

So it was up to me to find another story, which turned out to be *Twentieth Century* [1934]. A cousin of mine—Carole Lombard—was in Hollywood. She had a marvelous personality, but she couldn't act. I asked Cohn to get Carole for me.

He yelled, "She can't act a lick!"

I said, "Okay, get me someone better."

So he got me Lombard.

I offered John Barrymore the male lead, saying, "It's a story of a great ham, Jack, and you're the greatest of hams."

He laughed and asked, "When do we start?"

I told him, "Monday morning."

During rehearsals Monday, Jack watched Carole dubiously. She was pretty bad. Finally, I told the crew to take a break, and I took Carole for a walk. I said, "You've worked very hard on this."

She said, "I'm glad it shows."

I added, "You're getting five thousand dollars for the picture. Right?"

When she nodded, I continued, "What would you do if you'd earned five grand, but you didn't get a cent of it, because someone told you what you could do to yourself?"

"I'd kick him in the balls," she said.

I said, "The Barrymore character practically said that to you. Why didn't you kick him?"

Quietly she asked, "You're serious, aren't you?"

I nodded. "Either that, or I'll have to fire you."

She said, "Let's go."

On the set I announced, "We'll try a take."

Barrymore said, "We aren't ready yet."

I asked, "Who's running this thing?"

Barrymore said, "You are."

"Remember—until four o'clock," I said.

They started reading their lines, and she made a kick at him. He put his hands in front of his balls—jumped backward—glared at her, and read his next lines. She started waving her arms around—they went through twelve pages of script, and he made his exit.

I said, "Cut, print."

He said, "That was great. I thought you were kidding me all this time."

Carole started crying and ran off the stage.

I explained the whole thing to Barrymore, and he said he thought she was just great. We made the entire picture in three weeks.

15. PREFERENCE OF ACTING STYLE?

It depends on the story. In making a picture like *Scarface* [*The Shame of a Nation*, 1932]—I saw [Paul] Muni in the theatre playing the part of a very old man. I told him about the story.

He said, "Mr. Hawks, I can't do a story like that. I can only do action."

I said, "Are you such a coward that you can't make a test?"

He said, "Since you put it that way, I'll make a test."

I made him look much bigger, much heavier; any time he began to worry about how it was going, I reassured him. We worked together very well.

I made *Tiger Shark* with Edward G. Robinson. It was made in 1930, and still runs in Europe.

Walter Huston was just fabulous. We made *Red River*; when Jack Ford saw it he said, "I didn't know that big son-of-a-bitch could act!" Jack cast him in two pictures, and within a couple of years Huston was one of the biggest actors around.

When Jack came down here to die (in Palm Springs), I played golf with him, and would have an occasional drink with him. One time he started to laugh heartily for no apparent reason. I asked, "What the hell are you laughing about?"

He said, "I'm just remembering all the things I've stolen from you."

We used to remember all the old times and remind one another of them. One day he said, "Howard, some time soon you're going to win an award."

I explained, "I've run up against some pretty popular pictures, very stiff competition, and all in all I've been lucky."

Within two months after that talk, I received a notice from the Academy that they would be honoring me with a special award that year.

16. PRECAMERA WORK WITH ACTOR?

I wait. I had a good actor awhile ago who asked, "What kind of part am I going to be playing?"

I said, "Comic."

He said, "Oh, good! All I've been playing is heavies,"

I had an associate producer, sort of a business manager, who said, "Mr. Hawks, you described a character that you want. I know someone—he's only an extra man, but he fits your description."

I said, "You get him up here and give him the scene—put him in costume, and save me all the trouble of seeing him."

The associate producer came in with the man. I looked at him and started to laugh. It was Walter Brennan. I said, "Mr. Brennan, did they give you your lines?"

He said, "Yes, they did."

"Are you ready to read them to me?"

He asked, "With or without?"

"With or without *what?*"

"Teeth," he said.

I started to laugh and said, "I'd like to hear you without your teeth."

So he took his teeth out there in my office, and started to read. He had been scheduled for a three-day part....I kept him for about a month, and he was nominated for an award. He won two awards with me, and he was nominated for every picture he made.

I thought he was very funny, so it was easy to think of things for him to do. In *Red River*, he had only one line written into the script. I called him and said, "Walter, I have a story I want you to do."

He said he'd be right over. He arrived, and I said, "I want to tell you this story...."

He said, "I want to sign the contract first."

"Okay, you s.o.b. sign the contract," I said.

He signed, then said, "Tell me the story."

I told him, "No, I don't have to, since you're already signed. You *read* it."

So he read it, and the next day he came in and said, "Gee, that's great story. What are we going to do?"

I told him, "Remember when you first came to see me, and you took out your teeth? I have an idea that you can lose your teeth to an Indian in a poker game and spend the rest of the picture getting the teeth back from him every time you have to eat."

He said, "We can't do that."

I said triumphantly, "You signed the contract—you didn't want to hear the story in advance—so that's what we're going to do," and I laughed. Of course, he was nominated for an award for that part. The film was *Red River*.

When you think of yourself as a storyteller, and you have someone in the cast that you can use in telling your story—you use that person. If you get somebody in the cast who's a disappointment, the actor can be dropped...*almost*...out of the story. I don't do that unless the actor doesn't do what I tell him.

18. ADHERENCE TO SCRIPT?

When it comes to dialogue, I listen to an actor. If he changes a line here or there, I don't care as long as it sounds good. I have always thought that I'd rather work with a personality rather than a trained actor.

That doesn't mean I didn't enjoy working with Paul Muni, Bogart, Robinson—they not only had training, but also personalities. I'm interested in personalities ... starting new people by starting them in a picture and developing that picture. I have no compunction about changing a scene—or cutting a scene—in order to tell the story I'm trying to tell.

19. EDITING SUPERVISION?

Editing is one of the most important of all things. You can make a damned good picture and spoil it by editing—you can make a bad picture and help it by a great deal of editing. I insist that the cutter come down on the set while we are beginning the rehearsal of the sequence, so that he knows what I'm trying to get, and hope to have in the thing. I want to see that the day after the rushes come back. On one occasion I didn't recognize one picture that I had shot—I fired the cutter immediately.

I try to hire a cutter that I know I have something in common with—someone who knows what it is I'm trying to do, because I think a reaction is far better than a flattering line. In almost all cases you get more out of it.

I like to tell people what I'm striving for; I trust them. If I'm at all worried that a scene is not going to be left the way I want it (if somebody is going to find a way of cutting it out), I don't shoot any close-ups that will allow them to cut it out.

20. ROLE OF MUSICAL SCORE?

Music can be quite a good thing, or it can be quite a bad thing. I put up with bad music for many years, because I didn't think I knew too much about it. About 25 years ago, I chose the composer I wanted to make the music, told him what I wanted beforehand, and became pretty successful doing that.

I made a picture called *Hatari!* [1962] When I returned from shooting in Africa, I brought back a lot of African musical instruments. I had recorded some chants. I had been using Dimitri Tiomkin, so I said, "Dimitri, I'm tired of those high-brow musical scores that go into pictures, and have been since I've been making them. Violins, woodwinds—I don't want you to use that stuff; it's all been pretty bad."

He said, "That's a great idea." He came in the next day and asked, "You were kidding me when you said all that about music, weren't you?"

I said, "You're fired unless you're delighted about doing it the way I'd like."

Meanwhile, I heard something on TV about a man getting some great sounds, some unusual rhythms—his name was Henry Mancini. I showed him the picture and told him what I wanted.

He said the next day, "I'm ready to record, and have a *violin*, but don't fire me until you come down and hear it."

So he had a fellow playing the violin with the strings on top, and the bow underneath.

I said, "That's a 'go,'" and he did a great job.

I would say that I have a lot to say about the scoring, although I don't know anything about music.

21. INVOLVEMENT IN PREPARATION OF MUSICAL SCORE?/22. WHAT SCENES SHOULD HAVE MUSIC?

I want to make a good picture; I'm not interested in who gets the credit. On one occasion, I had Hoagy Carmichael do some songs after I had talked over the film with him; with Mancini, I let him work on the thing, tell me what he's doing—we work that way.

23. SOUND EFFECTS?

In discussing sound, it comes down to the fact whether or not you think sound is important. I think *Hatari* was very good, also *Barbary Coast* [1935], which I did. I've seen pictures that were completely spoiled by sound—they warn the audience of what is coming. If I can't make a scene without sound, I haven't done a very good job of it.

But, if I can take that same scene and make it better by the use of sound, I think it's a damn good thing to use it.

George Roy Hill

1. BACKGROUND?

Basically, I wanted to be a musician. I majored in music, and studied classic composition under the German classic composer, Paul Hindemuth. My first interest was music, and it has remained very strong during my life. I am still an amateur musician, and I'm very much involved in things musical.

When I decided to enter the theatre, which was fairly late, I didn't do any directing until I was 33 years old. Up to that point I had tried acting and writing. It was through music into performing, acting and singing, then into writing that I finally became a director.

I made my first picture in 1962; there has been a lot of comment to the effect that I've gone like a rocket since that time. If that's true, it is because I had tremendous preparation for it. I had done a lot of live television, and I have done a great deal of stage work. I had worked for almost ten years in the New York theatre before I came to California, mainly as a director, although I started as an actor in New York.

I also sold a lot of my writing to television for hour drama. After that I started directing and doing my own writing; from that I started directing regularly. My foundation was solid, and it has certainly paid off. It's very important to get the right kind of a foundation—not necessarily music, but a comprehensive knowledge of almost any of the arts.

2. FIRST FILM JOB?

The first time I walked on a motion picture set to *direct* was the first time I've ever been on a motion picture set!

I did not even know, at the time, that an *operator* operated the camera, and the cameraman did *not* handle the camera. I was astonished when I saw the operator on the camera boom, and the cameraman sitting alongside, and I wondered what the heck he was doing.

I was experienced in live television at that time, but film was an entirely different technique. In live television, you do your own cutting as you go along—so it was good training from that point of view. It saved hours of time when I got into pictures. You can actually do a lot of cutting in the camera—at least, I do.

3. YOUR GOAL IN FILMMAKING?

I've never formulated a philosophy in my mind toward my films—at least I've never articulated it. I think there are certain subjects that I'm drawn to and certain general story lines that appeal to me, but I'm not conscious of saying, "I want to make films about losers." Or, "I want to make films about anti-heroes." My tastes are, I think, fairly wide; it just happens that a subject comes along now and then that appeals to me—that I want to write about, to make a film about.

It has been suggested that I like particularly to do things with a comedy slant. Actually, I don't think about it that way. Somebody once said that my films are a mixture of history and slapstick. It is true that if I take on any subject, I am inclined to see the slapstick side of it. I've always loved slapstick. I've always loved comedy, and whatever film I'm doing, I somehow find a space in it somewhere to go into fairly broad comedy.

4. IN WHAT GENRE DO YOU SEEK A STORY?

I have no particular area in which I seek material; I like dealing in _relationships_. I just don't believe a screen story can work without illuminating relationships.

Of course, I think films like the disaster pictures can have special effects and can be very successful.

But, normally I'm interested in human relationships that can be played out in any setting—it can be in ancient Greece, or it could be in sets anticipating the situation a hundred years from now. It is relationships of the people that will involve an audience, so that's really what I look for: relationships—good or bad—but relationships nonetheless.

As an example, there's a scene in _Waldo Pepper_ [1975] in which Waldo and the great German flier are facing each other just prior to getting into their planes, for the showdown. It is a silent scene with just those two faces intercut, but it says, louder than words, that this is to be the finish—to determine finally where lies the superiority in the air. In addition to that contest of skills there is a tacit, mutually admiring agreement that each has run out his string, and that this flight is for each man a salute, a consummation, and a finale. It played as an intense dramatic scene.

5. STORY SOURCE?

As to story source: somebody pointed out to me the other day that the two pictures I've had among the top ten grossers (due to get knocked out pretty soon) were written for the screen. All my others have been taken from other sources, so, naturally, my inclination is to use stuff that has been done originally for the screen, in preference to rehashing something else.

Now, that's not always the case; I've done things from material from plays, and I've done things taken from books. However, my preference is to try to do original stuff. I think it's more interesting, and more personally rewarding.

6. USE A SCRIPTWRITER OR DO IT YOURSELF?

I usually work very closely with whomever is working on the script. I think that the skills that make a novelist are not those that make a screenwriter. Of course, earlier in history, when some of the great novelists like [William] Faulkner and [F. Scott] Fitzgerald were working, they learned how to build screenplays. But, generally speaking, I believe novelists were not usually interested in making a screen play. They had *had* it.

It's like [Kurt] Vonnegut. When I did *Slaughterhouse Five* [1975], I was in awe of the book. I thought it was marvelous, and I asked him what I should do with it.

Kurt said, "Mess with it; there's nothing in this book that I think you can't lose."

He continued, and I'm quoting him, "I want you to make it your picture."

That was his attitude, and it's a marvelous attitude for a writer to have. It's a rare attitude and Vonnegut's a rare person.

7. CLOSE COLLABORATION WITH THE SCREENWRITER?

I have a theory about that. I think if you hire talent, you give talent a chance to work. For example, right now I'm working on material for a couple of movies that are coming up. I say this to the writers: "You go, and you write it. If you get into trouble and there are questions you want answered at this stage in the game, give me a call, but I prefer that you work it out yourself."

I believe that sort of creation should be a single job, and I think he should bring everything to bear on it without my putting my oar in. Eventually, of course, I will put my oar in, when it gets to the point where I think his concept is there. Then I try to serve that concept, and to bring what skills I have to move it to a further stage, but normally, I don't like to work with a writer to start with. I have script conferences with him, and I talk to him, but, then, I want him to go off and do it himself.

It's like dealing with an actor. If you hire an actor who has a great talent, you don't come in and tell him to put this foot here, to walk over there, or to give this inflection or that, because you let him use his talent. I always have a blueprint in my mind of what I want him to do, of course, but it's a director's job to provide the atmosphere in which the talent you've bought can flower to its utmost.

8. PREPLAN OR IMPROVISE?

I do both. I'm too cowardly not to do my homework. I can't walk into a place without having a specific notion of what I want. Once I have that security of knowing what I want, then I improvise.

I'm always hoping to find out something exciting that might come up, that I had overlooked, but—as I was saying a minute ago—I have every scene mapped out, where everybody is going to move, exactly, but done very, very carefully.

I never impose that upon the actors when I first come in. I spend two weeks on rehearsal, and during rehearsal we play it five different ways, because another and better way might come up—again you're dealing with talents—people who can and often do make a contribution. It's self-defeating to hire great talents and not let them perform and bring their talents to bear on what you're doing.

9. MOST IMPORTANT COMPONENT OF YOUR FILM?

I'd say the most important thing is the story. In fact, I'd go right down that list the way you have it. Without a story, I don't think you can succeed. There are exceptions, of course; there are mood things that are popular, or fad things that are popular, but, basically, I think you have to find a story.

Then you have to have it well written—that's the next important thing; then you have to have it well cast; if you have a good story, well written and well cast, your job as a director, I think, is about 75 percent over. The rest of it is just making it come to life, and that's fun. If you've got good scenes, with good actors in them, it's awfully hard to screw it up. On the other hand, if you've got a bad scene, with actors that are good, but miscast, nothing you can do is going to make that thing work! Even a good actor, properly cast, can't do much about helping a badly written or conceived scene. Nothing will make a bad scene work.

10. WORK WITH A PRODUCER?

Basically, I have worked with producers—all kinds. There are so many producers now in the business who are packagers; they can range from former agents who have no experience in film making, to somebody like David Selznick, who, as I understand it.... Well, when you did *his* film, you didn't do *your* film.

I think that, today, the power has moved more into the hands of the director; the producer has less and less function, and with the independence of the films, the director has more and more power.

I think that, nowadays, the director has to involve himself much more in the producing functions that he did in the old days when directors were simply assigned pictures and they would do a picture every four months or so. [John] Ford would do two or three pictures a year. No director now could do that, because he has become so involved with the production end of it. There's just not enough time. In the old days the producers would develop the story with a writer, a director would almost have the cast from the repertory company that each studio had, and the director's job was simply to direct. Now, I don't think directors can do that.

René Clair has been quoted as saying, "Let the producer raise the money, and from then on, stay out of my way." I think that is the same attitude that filmmakers are tending toward everywhere.

Incidentally, I don't like being called a "filmmaker." I prefer to be called a "moviemaker." It's *motion* that we're talking about.

11. USE A DIALOGUE DIRECTOR?

No, I don't use a dialogue director. That's my job, and that's my fun, and I don't want anyone else honing in on that. It's been my job for a long time. I can think of no way in which a dialogue director could enhance my operation; but the list of ways in which he might obstruct or hinder progress seems to me to be endless.

12. WRITER OR PRODUCER ON THE SET?

I don't like to have a producer there while I'm rehearsing. One way that a producer can be used, is to give you certain perspectives, and I do like to bring a producer around if, for example, there's a scene that puzzles me, or something that I'm unsure of. If I have respect for the producer I will bring him in and show him the problem, and get his opinion on it. But if he's there every day, and a part of the general work, then he will lose perspective too, so I like to keep him out.

I like to have writers present during the first two weeks of rehearsal. I have a particular way that I work: when we first start rehearsal, I say to the actors, "Nobody changes a line of his script for the first five days of rehearsal. After five days, if you want to talk about changing lines—if certain scenes are still uncomfortable, then we'll talk about it."

Actors are very nervous critters, and they will do anything to keep from acting. They will talk about the words, and if you declare open season on words, they're off and running. They'd much rather talk about the words than perform them, because they're so goddamned scared most of the time—just as scared as I am, mostly.

So, if you tell them they can't change the lines at that time, they often get used to lines that they wouldn't get used to ordinarily, and accept them eventually. Very often actors will want to talk about the lines the first day, but by the end of the fifth day, they've gotten the words—they're under their belt—so they no longer have any complaint about them.

By that time there may be scenes that simply are not working, so we sit down with the writers, and I let the actors come in on those sessions. I say, "Look, this scene is not working. Why? Let's rewrite it." However, this usually applies only to one or two scenes we've not been able to make come to life on the rehearsal stage.

13. WORK CLOSELY WITH THE CAMERAMAN?

Regarding a cameraman, my answer is the same as it is with the others. I begin by making damned sure we've got a top man to start with.

I bring my cameraman along with me during the location scouting where he can prove most valuable, and where we can see how things can be staged.

I work very closely with the cameraman as to the look of the picture—the physical style, the color and the mood. I will work with the cameraman and the art director to get a certain color—certain palate to the scene. I know exactly the color I want in a scene.

Again, the two weeks of rehearsal are very important, because I have the cameraman there, too; he does very little but just sit there, and watch the actors.

Then, if he comes up with an idea, he steps over and says, "Instead of having a dolly shot here, why don't we do this or that?"

Or he's sitting in his chair and he'll say, "You know, that's a helluva interesting scene, looking at it, from this point of view."

Again, it's a collaborative effort, and if you have a great cameraman like Bob Surtees, you let that talent have full sway.

14. SUPERVISION OF CASTING?

I cast 'em—down to the one-line bits...every single person...and I read 'em. I've worked with the same casting director for years. I worked with her on television; her name is Marion Daugherty, she's now executive producer for David Picker. In my opinion, she was the most skillful of casting directors in that she knew what I was looking for.

If you are casting at one of the major studios, and you explain you are looking for a certain type of actress, they'll send you a grocery list of twenty-five people for one particular role—and it'll include everybody from a Tallulah Bankhead to a Shirley Temple for the same part. The people in the department are covering themselves. I don't like that.

What I do like, is to sit and talk to a casting director like Marion Daugherty; she'll bring in maybe two people for the part. I'll read them, and I'll say, "Yes, that's the direction I want to go." Or I'll say, "No. Find me somebody with this quality."

She will find maybe two or three more, until I finally get what I want.

That goes right down to the smallest bit; I think the texture of a film has to go in depth. I mean, anybody who comes within fifteen-feet of a camera, makes an impression on that camera. So you've got to goddam well know who they are and what impression they're making, and I think that gives you the depth and dimension to your picture that you wouldn't get otherwise.

15. PREFERENCE OF ACTING STYLE?

Every actor works differently. Your job is to find out what his language is—what his dialogue is—how you can make him comfortable and secure, so he'll perform for you.

They all have different things that get to them, so you have to study them individually to be able to direct them properly.

There is the highly professional actor who has developed enormous techniques over the years. He's a joy to work with.

The instinctive non-professional is also a joy to work with, particularly if he or she is responsive, and has no bad habits.

The actors I have difficulty with are the ones in between—that have done just enough to have developed some bad habits of acting, but are not yet professional enough to have overcome their techniques, and to have become as natural as beginners are.

The great professionals have such simplicity about them—such economy about them—that they are almost like people who have never acted before.

Both ends of the spectrum are the ones I like to work with. It is those who have done fifty television shows and have developed certain tricks and certain mannerisms that you break your neck trying to get rid of that give a director trouble. So I like the extremes—not the middle section actors.

16. PRECAMERA WORK WITH ACTOR?

If I've done my job well in casting, I don't have to worry too much; I've already completed three-fourths of my job in directing the actor so that he can bring out his talents, or whatever talents he has, and—of course—I let him take off and go with it...unless I find him going in the wrong direction. Then, of course, I'll rein him in.

As to whether or not I talk to the actor in depth about my concept of the character, it depends upon how the particular actor in question likes to work. Some actors want to talk. Others don't. There are some actors whose security blanket is talking, and if they want to talk about the part, the director makes himself available to talk, because it's their way of getting into a character.

With other actors, you try to talk to them about a part, and they sort of glaze over, and they say, "Hell, I don't know what I'm doing. Let me get up there and try it, and see how it comes out."

It depends again upon the technique of the particular actor. You do what he wants to do, and you help him.

17. IMPORTANCE OF REHEARSALS?

I like rehearsals. A great deal of that is because I was trained on the stage, so I'm used to finding new things in rehearsal. There's a curious phenomenon that happens on the stage that I've never seen fail. You have maybe a month for rehearsal, and by the end of the first ten days you, all of a sudden, look around and say, "Well, I've got no more ideas. That's it. What do we need with any more rehearsals?"

From that point, everything starts to flatten out, so you have to be very careful to keep your actors a little off-balance. You have to hold back some of your own ideas, keep them to yourself, and introduce them later. If you're skillful about it, you can keep your actors fresh and interested.

Something else: the atmosphere of a sound stage is quite nerve-wracking, entirely different from working in a rehearsal hall where it's quiet and you can work on a scene. On a sound stage where there are fifty technicians standing by—all with hammers—you try to re-create your knowledge or vision of what a scene should be, and there's chaos. Previous rehearsals help you solidify what the scene was intended to convey.

I don't think, in most cases, that a scene or a show need flatten out. I think if you're skillful about adding a little seasoning, or putting a little something extra into it, that it will freshen up the actors, a new piece of business can work wonders. By that time, the actors are so solid in their characters that they can accept it easily. It will just lift them on to a better performance.

18. ADHERENCE TO SCRIPT?

As to adhering to lines, once again it depends on the type of actor you're working with. The think I dislike most heartily is the actor who comes in without his lines learned. That irritates me enormously.

Since I am a musician, I would say—as an analogy, that it would be like Rubenstein showing up for a concert without having memorized the notes, and saying, "I'll get it while rehearsing."

Well, you don't get the notes while rehearsing. That's not really the way it should be. On the other hand some actors are instinctively improvisational. If you see they're going in a certain direction that you like, you let loose of the reins a little bit and say, "Look, I like what you're doing. The lines in this particular scene are not that important—so go with it. Give me something like that," and they will do it.

But again, you must make up your mind—based on where you are at the moment. You don't do "To be or not to be," and let the actor improvise the lines, because the lines are too goddam important.

Yet, if you are doing an ad lib scene and there are certain built-in interruptions, and a give-and-take within the scene—lines talking over lines—and it's working— let it work.

It's all pragmatic: what's working, you go with; what's NOT working, you don't go with.

19. EDITING SUPERVISION?

Obviously you are speaking of John Ford, and I thoroughly subscribe to his thinking in regard to editing.

As I do with the fine experienced actor, when I have a really fine editor, I encourage him to use his skills and experience to the utmost.

When I've shown him the scenes at the rushes and told him the takes or angles I liked, I don't stand over his shoulder while he puts it together. I let him bring his talent and point of view to bear on the scene, because he's liable to find something in there that I didn't see.

Eventually, of course, I go over that picture frame by frame by frame, but why do that in the beginning when you're paying a lot of money for a real talent to help you?

20. ROLE OF MUSICAL SCORE?

Since I was trained in music, music is very important in my films. Usually, I have determined the style of the musical end of the film before I have started shooting. For example, in *The Sting* [1973], I knew I was going to use Scott Joplin music. I built certain montages and interludes around the Joplin music. I recorded it myself—played the piano—and did a sound track of my own piano playing to cut to, before I turned it over to Marvin Hamlisch.

I don't like underscoring. I don't like putting music under dramatic scenes. I've done it, but it has always seemed to me an admission of weak knees. The goddam scene isn't working so you throw in a few hundred violins, and you pump up a little emotion that has nothing whatsoever to do with the scenes, hoping you can fast-ball it back past the audience. Normally, I like to use the music as music, so that you can focus attention *on* the music.

21. INVOLVEMENT IN PREPARATION OF MUSICAL SCORE?

I score almost all of my films with records or my own piano-playing before I ever turn it over to a composer, so he can know exactly what I'm after.

Again, rather than resenting this, composers usually like it very much, because it gives them specific information of what I want; music is very hard to describe in philosophical terms, so as to be certain of what you're going to get. For that reason I use records and prerecordings.

I do not try to strangle the composer, but to give him some kind of guidelines. Here again, it's the same as with actors; if an actor comes up with something and says, "Hey, I don't think this is very good, so why don't we try this?" I listen.

But I'm there, always, in the recording stage, and quite often we write and rewrite cues on the recording stage. As I've said, one of my primary interests in film is music.

22. WHAT SCENES SHOULD HAVE MUSIC?

The determination of which scenes are to be scored, and which are to be played *a cappella*, must be mine on my films, absolutely; otherwise, they would not be truly my films. As I've said, I know where music is going to be, before I start the film. I've already laid in the music in my mind. I know specifically, exactly where it's going to be, and I can even budget it accordingly.

I had a small musical budget for *The Sting*, because I knew that it was going to be piano, basically. In *Slaughterhouse Five* I knew I was going to use Bach, so I dubbed the entrance into Dresden, knowing I was going to use the whole D Major Piano Concerto. I didn't know I was going to use the Brandenberg Fourth; that was Glenn Gould's idea. I had the E Flat Major Concerto in there, but he convinced me, and quite rightly, because with the fuguel entries of the Brandenberg Fourth, it worked beautifully with the montage of their coming in.

23. SOUND EFFECTS?

I'm involved from the very beginning. Sound effects are very much like music—it is important to have the proper sound effects at a specific time; I have all my sound effects prerecorded so that I can listen to them before we ever get on the stage. The sound men have all the material to work with as soon as the sound effects are finished. They do a lot of research.

In *Waldo Pepper* the sounds of those old rotary engines in the airplanes was terribly important to me. Sound men worked about a month-and-a-half, just getting the sounds of those rotaries in the Fokker and the Bamel in the last sequence. It's a specific sound. Very few people know the difference between the rotary engine and the sound of regular engines, but the few who do are going to get a kick out of it. And in the overall, whether or not the members of the audience know the difference, they will get a kick out of it. It's that sense of downright reality that the audience somehow senses or feels.

Jan Kadar

1. BACKGROUND?

Just before World War II started, a distinguished gentleman named Carlo Pleviska, famous as a photographer, had a film school in Bratislava. He organized a short course in filmmaking, which was very new at that time in Czechoslovakia. I enrolled in that course, but it was less than three months before war started.

2. FIRST FILM JOB?

When I came back from the war, I visited Carlo Pleviska. He told me, "Listen! Here in Prague is no place for you; so back to Slovakia. Probably it will be easier for you there."

So I went back; it was a funny situation I stepped into: all the bridges in the country were burned down or blown up, and it was necessary to make a detailed accounting for the Committee on War Reparations.

Among all the people who lived in Bratislava, nobody was willing to do the work. There was a cameraman who had come with me from Prague—because he had nothing to do—so *he* took the job, and I became, basically, his assistant. Mostly what I had to do was go with him, carry supplies, arrange accommodations at the hotel, and all this kind of business.

There was a funny thing about this man—he was used to having someone tell him what to do, so when we went through the bridges with a jeep (there were soldiers there with machine guns, but there was no security because the country was not consolidated) I, in a way, gave the orders. I told him, "Listen, don't put the camera there, put it here." I didn't know anything about the camera, but he was agreeable, because it was easier for him. That the photography turned out well was mostly luck with, perhaps, a little instinct.

When we finished the piece, which was basically for the archives, we sold the material. Somebody told me, "If you will film what happened with these bridges, you could put together a documentary."

So we went back and filmed one place—a very important area for communication and transportation—and showed how they built the bridge. We showed this material to an editor in Prague. I sat beside him, watching him put it together, and I was amazed at what was happening with our material. Next, I got a gentleman to write the narration, and a good actor to do the narrating. That is the way the first documentary film after the war was done! Everything, done after the war, was an achievement.

So, I started in the cinema pretty late. I was five years in a camp in Hungary, so I was 28 when I started to flirt with this business.

After I assisted in making two documentary shorts, I got the opportunity to work as an assistant to a director in Prague, where I assisted on two films.

Then I wrote a short story—a treatment for a comedy—and that was it! I started to make my first film. In that time, it was pretty easy, because the organization of the cinema in Czechoslovakia was very new, and everybody started there from scratch.

The Czech cinema had a pretty distinguished tradition before the war, but after the war, there was a time of lucky anarchy, so there was a lot of opportunity; there were dramas in that time; everybody felt that he was reborn, a new life was starting. It was a little bit of fantasy, because if you were alive, it was a gift. At such a time everybody was full of energy and hope and determination. I was thinking that if I had survived that damn war, at least I knew what I wanted to do, what I had dreamed to do all my life.

So that is why I got involved in this whole thing. The gentleman who helped me put it together was a man I worked with as partners for more than twenty-five years. He got me, first, a job as first assistant director on a feature. When he became a producer, he sent me to another director to be *his* assistant. With that director, I made another picture based on my own idea or treatment.

I started to make my first feature in 1949. Here is an interesting thing: the school in Prague was established at that time, and I intended to go to the school, but I realized that I was pretty old to go there for four years, so I dropped out, and that school later became one of the best in Europe.

I had a big respect for the school; what I didn't do at the school at that time, I am doing now at AFI [American Film Institute].

3. YOUR GOAL IN FILMMAKING?

That's a very complicated question. We could speak about this all day. How to make it short? Probably I should start with the answer that when I started to make films, it was in a completely different environment from what I found in the West.

Filmmaking at that time—especially in our country—had a special situation. I would say it is something you probably haven't heard from anyone else: the first industry internationalized in Czechoslovakia after the war was the film industry. Basically, it was initiated by the filmmakers themselves, during the war, because they believed that we could be free from any external pressure, so that film would become the media of the creators. It never happened that way, because we learned that the one who's paying, is the master anyway.

You know, the creators in that time, the directors and writers, were thinking that, once the money came for society, they would be able to do what was right. They didn't realize that the State had a different approach to the whole thing. The State's idea was that everything must be aimed at a particular political goal; they looked on film as a very important medium for the State ideology. The years that followed gave evidence of how much the State involvement and subsidizing film crippled any kind of creativity.

You know, we were always told that Lenin said once that film was the most important medium—the disciplined art—but in that time they did not have television. Now, television would be much more important.

I don't want to go into the complicated method of operating; we did it at the time, in a certain belief that we had to serve some purpose, that each film had to say something.

I still think that film has to say something. The question is, what to say? Therefore, I am still looking on film as kind of self-expression. I don't have the privilege of a painter or a musician—who doesn't need the complicated and expensive means that filmmaking requires. We are working with very expensive tools, and will always be limited in our freedom.

So, if you're asking my philosophy, it is to try to communicate, to bring some understanding, some joy from my own experience—to the audience. Certainly I'm looking for an audience, because it doesn't make sense—or money—to do a film for empty theatres.

The problem is only to make it so that people will come to see it, and all the effort is not in vain. It doesn't always happen that what you are doing will fulfill your hopes and ambitions, but if you succeed once or twice in your lifetime in doing something that will survive you, then the effort was worthwhile.

4. IN WHAT GENRE DO YOU SEEK A STORY?

It's hard to say exactly in what genre I hope to find story material. Those of us who come from Europe have a little different approach to filmmaking: we don't consider ourselves draftsmen; the craft is secondary. We are looking for material through which we can express ourselves best. Whatever the source of the material, I must find *myself* in it, in order to do it.

As for genre—what discipline attracts me most—it's hard to say, because my work is very different. As different as it is in style, it has the same idea that I am constantly pursuing: the relation between human beings, and the absurdity of this world.

I find myself at my best in the genre which we call "tragi-comedy." I don't believe that anything in life is totally tragic or entirely humorous. My life experience has taught me that the toughest situations I experience, has in them some kind of humor. From life in camp, I recall that the humorous things are those I remember; the tragic things I have managed to forget.

The Shop on Main Street [1965] was an unique film—which I didn't know at the time. I just realized later why this picture survived; it is about one of the darkest periods of mankind, and is based on a conflict of comedy.

I must conclude that my genre is definitely tragi-comedy. That doesn't mean I will always do only that kind of film; sometimes we have to do things which are not our closest thing, but we have to do them.

5. STORY SOURCE?

Very good question. I can respond to it briefly. I prefer screenplays written originally for film. I was surprised to discover—upon coming into this country—that some properties have to be successful in some other medium...whether it's a play, novel or whatever...to be put on film. It is my opinion that this is basically contrary to the spirit of cinema. If a piece of literature is really brilliant as literature, it cannot be equally successful in another medium. Nobody will ever do a film equal to *War and Peace*. It's been tried many times.

I don't know if you know this famous Czech writer, [Jaroslav] Hasek, who wrote *The Brave Soldier Schweik*—a humorous book. I've tried to convert it several times—never succeeded, because the beauty and the emotional values are in the words, in sentences, in literature.

Another mistake I'm seeing, in this eagerness to repeat successes is this: once a picture is successful, they make a lot of sequels which never can be as successful, even if they are better. To make a film is to make a prototype, as any piece of art is a prototype.

When I have to translate from another medium, I try to forget, right away, to be faithful to this. I take the idea, and try to transform it into my own medium. But I try never to do exactly what was done before.

6. USE A SCRIPTWRITER OR DO IT YOURSELF? / 7. CLOSE COLLABORATION WITH THE SCREENWRITER?

I'm not a writer, but I work on the script from the beginning with the writer. I consider working on the script one of the most important functions of the director—a good director is a nonwriting writer, just as a good writer is a nondirecting director.

If I'm doing a book, for instance, or a short story, I prefer to use the original writer; I don't care whether he has any previous experience in scriptwriting or not. No one knows the characters as well as the original writer does, and nobody could deal with them as freely. In *[The] Shop on Main Street*, the screenplay was written by a writer who had never written anything for the screen—and has never written anything afterward!

Certainly a collaboration between a writer and a director is like a marriage. To make it work one has to forget about egos, and see only the final goal. That happened with films I did in Czechoslovakia; once you are working with a writer closely together, by the time you've finished, you don't know who did what—and that's very important, and takes nothing from the writer.

I think egomania is responsible for many of our bad scripts and bad films. In the final analysis, I cannot make a film based on a script which is handed to me, just to go out and shot, I repeat, I'm not a writer, and I don't want to write, because I always think you should do what you do best. I can write dialogue or business, but why do it myself if somebody else is better?

Basically, it's a kind of collective effort, and you have to play the game. It's like playing with a ball, catching it and throwing it back. This way we achieve something of which neither he nor I was capable of originally. It is one of the most exciting parts of making a film.

However, I do oversee the whole thing. Working with the writer, as I do, by the time the script is finished, I know every phase of it; it has become part of my blood and my thinking. I'm in it, and I can direct the film the way a conductor conducts a symphony without looking at his notes.

8. PREPLAN OR IMPROVISE?

These are very good questions!

When I started to make films, I tried to have everything on paper so precisely that there was no room for the actors to create anything. Now, through time and experience, I am for improvisation, but not for anarchy!

I am for improvisation within the limits of my ultimate goal. I know exactly where I would like to go with a scene, and which way I'd prefer to go; However, some things cannot be preplanned completely, because I am working with human beings, not machines.

I made this mistake when I did my very first picture: out of insecurity, I asked my actors to do exactly what I had preplanned.

A colleague of mine, Elmer Klaus, older than I and very experienced, saw the rushes. He said, "Jan, it's all right, but you have fifty people behaving exactly like you. They made the same gestures, they spoke the same way—it is just awful."

By the time I gained a little self-confidence, I realized that I had to give freedom to the actors—to let them express themselves. Certainly, they must be guided, but I learned to be flexible on the set, and to be able to change and adjust.

Certain bits of business are important, because they are dramatically vital to the script, but dialoguewise or businesswise, the average script is not Shakespeare. The whole thing must be played freely.

There's one thing you have to know: to recognize when you achieve the right moment, what is good, what is right. It may not be perfect, but you have to realize what is the best you can get with the present set-up.

9. MOST IMPORTANT COMPONENT OF YOUR FILM?

You are making very intelligent questions; I really like that.

I would answer the following way: a director is usually as good as his story is. An actor is as good as the part, and the director is as good as the script. The others:

the cameraman, the editor, the musicians—all are as good and successful as the picture is. Usually, if a picture is good, everything in it is good. If a picture is lousy, everything is lousy.

In brief, it is impossible to make a good film from a bad story.

10. WORK WITH A PRODUCER?

This question is hard to answer in a short paragraph.

I was raised in a world where we didn't have producers, as you know them. For example, one man with whom I worked for a long time, Mr. Klaus, basically was a producer, which I only realized when I came to the U.S.

If you're asking me what is my relationship to the producer, that depends on who the producer is, and who is initiating the film. If the producer is initiating it, and you are entering solely as a director, you must create some kind of gentlemen's agreement with the producer as to what is your function in the film. Are you to execute the film on the level of the cameraman, or are you to function as a creative person who is taking the responsibility for the film?

I think the producer in the States is a very important person in case he's a creative individual. If he knows exactly, or if he has a dream or a vision, he should share it with the director. From then on, he should give to the director, full freedom. The director should be responsible enough not to abuse the confidence of the producer.

I was usually my own producer, which I didn't realize, because I only worked with a production manager who was responsible for the organization and the money. I was responsible for the money also, because all creative decisions were mine: casting, editing, script decisions, everything. That is the only way I can imagine a decent film being made.

It is difficult to define the proper function of a producer. He can be a deal maker; he can put together productions. It depends very much on the sensitivity of the producer. A good producer can be a big help, but if the producer starts telling me what kind of set-ups to make, or how to cut the film, I always say, "If you have to take out your appendix, do you do it yourself, or do you go to a good doctor? Then if you decide on a doctor, do you tell him how to do it? It is the same with me; I don't know why I should be told how to do my job!"

I have been here in the States for nine years all ready, and I'm still trying to find out the right function of the producer. The ideal director-producer relationship is a partnership. When I worked with my colleague in Czechoslovakia, he never interfered. We worked together on the script; we discussed everything in advance. When I directed on the set, he was always there, never interfering, but I had the feeling of a tightrope walker who is blindfolded, but must go through his act, yet always knowing somebody is down there to catch him in case he should fall.

And that, in my opinion, should be the producer.

11. USE A DIALOGUE DIRECTOR?

I don't use dialogue directors, but I will tell you a story. The first picture I made here was called *[The] Angel Levine* [1970]. It was a big flop, but I liked it; considered it one of my best. Actually, I did a European picture, instead of what I expected to do.

The producer was Harry Belafonte, and his partner was Zero Mostel, whom I really adore. Everybody says that Zero is difficult. I can tell you that Zero is a great talent. He has to respect a director; if he doesn't, he's a devil; if he respects, he is a pussycat.

I guess the producer was in a hurry when he hired me to do this picture, probably expecting me to repeat the success of *[The] Shop on Main Street*. If he had asked me, I would have told him that this thing could never be repeated.

Belafonte had a lady who was always with him, but I didn't understand what she was doing there. When we went on the set, she was always standing behind him, and he would look toward her to see whether she agreed or not. then, I realized she was there for this coaching; she was this dialogue director.

I didn't understand the language well at that time, because I didn't speak English. I felt like a captive animal. I didn't use an interpreter, so I didn't understand what they were saying exactly, but, somehow, I could feel whether it was right or wrong.

So I told him, "Listen, you are paying me a lot of money for doing this thing. If you have to have somebody telling you what is right, what is wrong, I can go at once away."

So this lady never came back onto the set. I think this episode speaks well of Belafonte. I had a very good time with him, and he was good in the picture.

So—you asked about a dialogue director: I didn't have a dialogue director, even when I didn't speak the language!

12. WRITER OR PRODUCER ON THE SET?

I like the producer to be on the set when I'm shooting, because, this way he is becoming part of the creative process. I also like very much if the writer is there, because for the first time he can hear his dialogue, whether it plays or not; he can make on-the-spot corrections.

For instance, in *Lies My Father Told Me* [1975], the writer was always on the set…unless he was bored. (Sometimes they get bored very quickly.)

If either the writer or the producer is bothering me, I ask him to leave, but I don't like to do it. I like them to be on the set only under the provision that they are not controlling me, but helping me.

13. WORK CLOSELY WITH THE CAMERAMAN?

No, I don't like to extemporize as far as camera work is concerned. I work with the cameraman before we begin to shoot; we go over the whole script to have a common understanding of the style of the film. I explain to him what I would like to achieve, then give him the freedom to achieve it.

As for choreography and the set-ups, I am saying specifically, because I know what meaning each set-up has to the whole. If the cameraman is an intelligent and cooperative one, not merely a good lighting cameraman, then he plays the game with me.

Once he has done it, I look again to be sure it's exactly what I had in mind. It means it is a kind of cooperative effort.

Most cameramen like it, but not all. Some prefer to be told. I never met a cameraman who opposed me, because I'm open to discussion, and if he comes up with an idea that's good...fine! If his idea doesn't fit into my conception, I have to oppose it.

14. SUPERVISION OF CASTING?

If I could, I would like to control my casting from top to bottom line. Casting, in my opinion, is sixty percent of the success of the picture. I think many pictures suffer from absolutely wrong casting. Casting is a question of instinct. It doesn't depend entirely on how good the actor is, but what kind of belief you have in this actor.

They didn't have casting directors in Czechoslovakia, because we knew everybody. Here, there are so many actors, nobody can know all of them. My casting director is usually my assistant with whom I cast the whole thing, but it is I who must feel that this guy fits into the mosaic which I am basically crafting.

That is the condition under which I am working now: I am doing a film for KNX [a Los Angeles TV station]—a three-hour show, and I use one of my AFI students, who is a theatrical director, for casting. He prepares everything for me, and I personally control exactly who will be in the film. I think to design the casting is as important as it is to work on the script.

15. PREFERENCE OF ACTING STYLE?

I have a very short answer regarding types of actors. I like to work with *good* actors, whoever they are, and regardless of the method they use. Sometimes, to put together seasoned actors and non-professionals is a very interesting experience. The method you are seeing then, you have to create yourself with the actors.

16. PRECAMERA WORK WITH ACTOR?

My approach to working with an actor is basically a two-way street. I like to work with actors just before I start shooting—to rehearse crucial sequences. In this rehearsing, I try to establish with the actor, the character he is playing.

Naturally, at this time, I am open to all suggestions from the actor. Often, he can bring something to it which will make the whole character richer.

Which brings me to what I believe to be a cardinal point in the actor-director relationship, and the director's responsibility. The actor, on the set, (even the most experienced actor) is alone and lonely. He has no audience. He has this machine, the camera, against him, the people around him; yet the only one who can give him support or a feeling of what is right or wrong is the director. That's what the director should recognize; his responsibility to give the actor this security. From the actor's viewpoint, at this moment, the director is replacing the audience—the millions of people who will ultimately see the picture; for the actor, the director *is* audience reaction.

There are certain directors who have a special method to not shoe the script to the actor; to use the actors basically as props. I don't agree with that, because once I have a human being on the set, he is the one who is most important.

I also allow and encourage actors to see the rushes. In the beginning, it is sometimes a shock to them, but they have to understand what I am doing, so we can discuss it. Basically, I believe in this kind of relationship with actors.

17. IMPORTANCE OF REHEARSALS?

Again, it's a two-way street. As I have said, I like to rehearse certain key sequences, to grab the character when rehearsing on the set. I rehearse up to a certain point, really not to exhaust the actor, but to leave a place for the happening of the miracle. When, finally, he is getting it, that is the miracle.

I don't want to wear out the actors, but to lead them up to a certain point before the shooting, so they can achieve the best in a certain moment. It's like a high-jumper who's not jumping his best, if he's exhausted, so he's saving his last effort for the Olympics.

If the actor, for instance, is intelligent in rehearsals, is grabbing the character, he could perform things which you would never expect, because he has *become* that person. That is necessary to achieve before the shooting, if I can.

18. ADHERENCE TO SCRIPT?

Basically, this is a continuation of my answer before.

It depends on the actor. Some actors are so close to the lines that they are unable to improvise. There are other actors who are so much into the character that they can behave freely within the limit of the character.

You have to adjust to the personality of the actor. If he is changing things, and it's believable, certainly I will let him do it, because the actor—for the sake of his creativity—needs as much freedom sometimes, as I have.

Actors are not puppets. You can give freedom to the actor in proportion to his ability as a performer.

19. EDITING SUPERVISION?

I shoot the picture in such a way that I am basically editing during the shooting, but in such a way that I am leaving myself enough freedom to work with the material. I am not shooting a lot of material, then—in the editing room—trying to find out what to do with it.

I know exactly what is hot, and how it relates—in my own vision.

Then, it depends on how good the editor is. If I have a good editor, I discuss what I had in mind by shooting this scene, then I leave him to do it for one reason: if I tell him exactly, "Now cut here, now cut there," I cannot expect anything creative from him.

I let him do the first rough cut, just to see whether what I had in mind works or not. The most important thing is that you have to shoot the material so it is flexible. Flexible, but not a mess. You can cut it three or four different ways, and it will always be the same, just better.

I had an experience with an editor in New York. Unfortunately, he is now dead. He was brilliant, his name: Karl Lerner. I was still shooting when I came to the editing room, and Karl showed me the first cut of the scene. I looked at it, and said it was fine, interesting, good.... As far as I was concerned, it was a finished product.

Next day, he told me, "Ah—listen, Jan. I recut it a little bit here and there."

I watched it, then told him, "It's really better. *That's* it."

Next day he told me, "Mmmmm...I made another change." He played the whole thing for me; he had found, in the material, things which I didn't realize were there!

Therefore, I can edit my own film, but I always like to have somebody who is a better editor than I am! The final shape of the film is what we essentially agreed on.

As with cameraman, as with editor, as with actor, as with musician, you have to trust your people; you have to select them rightly, then give them room for their own creative contributions.

20. ROLE OF MUSICAL SCORE?

With good music, you can enhance your film thirty to forty percent. With the wrong music, you can kill it. I worked with one musician through most of my pictures, and he taught me one very simple thing: you have to believe in the people with whom you work. You can have an understanding of music, but to write music is a completely different interpretation of the drama.

In working with a musician, I show him the film; I tell him what is my philosophy concerning the film, what I want to achieve with the film. Then I expect him to interpret the drama in his way, musically. not underlining, not pleasing *me!* A good musician takes the film and finds his own musical interpretation of the drama. If he's a good musician and a good musical dramatist, he will do it well. I hear a lot of music, but very little really good music.

21. INVOLVEMENT IN PREPARATION OF MUSICAL SCORE?

I think the musician should be responsible, not only for the musical score, but for the entire sound composition, including the effects.

Sometimes he will say, "Don't put this in those lousy naturalistic effects; I'll do it a different way, and it will be much more effective."

Then I usually give him a print to help him work on it. I don't ask him to play motifs or whatever; it's *His* business. Then if it is good, I can recognize it right away. If it's lousy, I stop the dubbing, because music is one of the most important components of the film. Usually it is difficult to know where to put music, but even more important to know where not to put music.

I am always present at the recording of the music; right away, I know whether we are on the right or wrong track. Before, I saw the picture; now, I would like to hear the picture. You can distinguish whether it is right or wrong only when you hear it.

You can discuss the performance, you can discuss the set-ups, you can discuss the costumes, you can discuss the lighting; you cannot discuss music. I have only one way to feel how the music is right or wrong. If I'm sitting at the recording, and suddenly I have tears in my eyes, or goose bumps on my back—then the music is right.

22. WHAT SCENES SHOULD HAVE MUSIC?

After I discuss the basic idea of the film with the musician, and he studies the material, we sit together and discuss where to put music, and where not. That is always agreed upon by us; if there is any kind of hesitation, then I leave it up to the musician. I never force the musician to use music where he doesn't feel it, or not use music where he feels music should be.

It's the kind of game you can play only with a good musician, because—if a musician is wrong—you cannot do a damn thing about it.

23. SOUND EFFECTS?

I discuss the sound effects, not with the soundmen, but with the musician. In my opinion, the musician is the one who is supervising and contributing to the sound composition of the film. I don't distinguish between the sound effects and the music. The sound can be music, and the music can be sound—both require someone who has creative vision for this component of the film. A director asks for the kind of sound effect he would like to have, and the sound man produces them. That, in my opinion, is a creative approach to the whole thing.

COMMENT

It is a privilege to be able to work in cinema. Once one realizes that, he must also realize that responsibility is forever wed to privilege. One cannot live without the other.

Elia Kazan

1. BACKGROUND?

I came off the New York stage where I worked as an actor and director. I think my first seven or eight films clearly show that this was my jumping off place. Only after these first efforts did I become more "cinematic," telling my story more by picture than by what was spoken.

2. FIRST FILM JOB?

I immediately made films as a director. I had to learn all the other crafts slowly, while I was trying to do the main job.

3. YOUR GOAL IN FILMMAKING?

I believe that if a subject and theme move me, they will move an audience. I think this is the unspoken premise we all work under. We must believe this. When it proves untrue, we are making special pictures for a limited group of people. This is all right, too. I have always believed that if I liked something a great deal, a large audience would too. Sometimes it has proved to be true, and sometimes not, but it is the only premise I have gone on and the only one on which I can go.

4. IN WHAT GENRE DO YOU SEEK A STORY?

In no particular genre. In fact I don't look for subject matter, or source material. It comes to me. I get enthusiastic about something and begin to see if I can make a film of it. Sometimes it's an event, *Wild River* [1980], other times a novel, *East of Eden* [1955], and other times a play , *[A] Streetcar [Named Desire,* 1951]. And sometimes it has been a "condition," or a social situation—*On The Waterfront* [1954].

5. STORY SOURCE?

See above. I have no particular preference, but more and more, as I evolved, I preferred writing directly for the screen. When I wrote my own screenplay [*America, America,* 1963] I felt I was on the track where I wanted to be.

6. USE A SCRIPTWRITER OR DO IT YOURSELF?

I choose now to do that work myself. But this, again, has certain drawbacks. It is not easy for me to be objective about my own work, so I've had some problems. But again, I feel I have no choice except to go my own way.

7. CLOSE COLLABORATION WITH THE SCREENWRITER?

When I have worked with other screenwriters (Paul Osborn, John Steinbeck, Tennessee Williams, Bill Inge) I have worked extremely closely with them, usually on a day to day basis, first the over-all concept, then on each scene. With Budd Schulberg, we—in effect—collaborated. He is very picturewise and knows that I will be telling the story in my way, as he tells it in his. I have the greatest respect for him, as he has for me, and we worked together on the agreed-upon story, and its progression, from our blending points of view.

8. PREPLAN OR IMPROVISE?

Neither. I go on the set with a firm idea of the basic movement and values in a scene. But I leave myself very open for developments as the rehearsals progress.

What is the value of having talented actors or technicians if we don't allow them to make their contributions? But the channel within which these suggestions and improvisations are made has to be chosen by the director. This is done by much conversation so that the actors and the director, as well as the other artists (cameraman, designers, cutters) are working to achieve the same intention. This basic goal has to be set clearly by the director. Once this is achieved, then these contributors can be allowed great scope and freedom for their contributions.

9. MOST IMPORTANT COMPONENT OF YOUR FILM?

No. They are all equally important. Every step is critical. The process of making a film is a total one—more so than any other art. A director needs to know a lot about each of the processes or crafts that make up "directing."

10. WORK WITH A PRODUCER?

I used to work with producers, and in some cases (particularly with Budd Lighton and Sam Spiegel) I got a great deal of help from them, especially in preparing a script. I now try to work as my own producer; this has advantages, but also certain drawbacks. But as I became more "personal" in my work, I had no choice except to work as my own producer.

11. USE A DIALOGUE DIRECTOR?

I don't like to use dialogue directors except to check on the lines—which the script girl can do as well.

How lines are read is terribly important to me—perhaps because of my stage background—and I want to determine this entirely myself.

12. WRITER OR PRODUCER ON THE SET?

It depends. Some, yes. I liked having Schulberg on the set. Others, less so. It depends on the script. If I think the writer can respond to what happens in a rehearsal in a creative way, bring more to the script than is there at the start, then by all means. But if the script already includes what, in my judgment, the writer has to offer, I'd prefer that he not be on the set.

13. WORK CLOSELY WITH THE CAMERAMAN?

I work very closely with my cameraman in both instances—basic intention clear and agreed upon. But both the cameraman and I have to be open and receptive to what is created in rehearsals, and what is told us by the set.

It is again a matter of having the values and effects clearly in mind, but of allowing everyone to work creatively within the basic framework. I've been fortunate in my cameramen. They have contributed a great deal to my films.

14. SUPERVISION OF CASTING?

I cast everything, carefully and meticulously. I take a long time to find the right person even for the smallest bits. I try out small part players all the time as I'm shooting the preceding scenes so as to make sure that every actor has what the scenes need.

15. PREFERENCE OF ACTING STYLE?

There is no reason why the two types (technician and instinctive) are mutually exclusive. Of the so-called "Method" actors, I demand precision and mechanical perfection. Of the others, the so-called technicians, I try to pull forth "realer" more personal feelings. The best actors have both emotionalism and mechanical precision. The division is a false one.

16. PRECAMERA WORK WITH ACTOR?

I talk the role over with my actors again and again, sometimes for days. I lay the basis in conversation, for what is to follow. By the time we get on the set, the actor will know what I want of him and why. And if I have been any good, he will want the same things I want.

Again, it is essential, as I see it, to have a harmony of goals established before the actual work of photographing scenes begins.

"Inhibition" of course is bad. But an erratic, willful performance is just as bad. It is, again, not an either-or matter.

17. IMPORTANCE OF REHEARSALS?

Rehearsals depend on the project. When the values involve subtleties of the play or of character, why then, rehearsals are important. When the action is simpler or more physical, then spontaneity is important. The danger of "flattening out" is a real one. It has to be guarded against in working, but it's a danger that has to be risked sometimes. I have worked both ways and must say again that no general rule is valid here. It depends on the problems you face. These considerations also concern the actors. You soon get a sense of how your leading performers work best and produce most. You go with that.

18. ADHERENCE TO SCRIPT?

I do not insist on mechanical and rigid reproduction of lines and business. A creative person who is an actor will have much to contribute. Some actors I've worked with often, once having agreed on the basic contribution a scene should make, have brought more to the scene than I imagine possible. You have to leave an opening for this possibility. There is nothing more gratifying to a director.

19. EDITING SUPERVISION?

I see the rushes with the cutter and tell her or him what I had in mind, what I hoped to get out of the scene and where, in each day's work, I think I may have caught what I wanted. I tell him or her how I thought the scene should go and what the mechanical aspects of it are, pace, rhythm and climax. Then I turn away and go about my business, giving the cutter a chance to contribute and again hoping that the artists will perhaps see more in the scene and each day's rushes than I did. You always hope for little miracles.

But it is fundamentally important that, in each sequence, the main goals be the ones you believe will build the film to the result you want. Again great freedom within a firm path.

20. ROLE OF MUSICAL SCORE?

Sometimes I believe the musical score to be very vital; Other times not so. I have done films with almost no music. I have done films where the music has been a great contribution for which I was most grateful.

Again, here it is important either way: that you talk to your composer before his work starts, and at length, so that your goals are synchronized. I do not believe in throwing the cut in his lap, saying "Here, give me music." Like all aspects of film, it is a collaborative work.

21. INVOLVEMENT IN PREPARATION OF MUSICAL SCORE?

Yes, I am deeply involved in preparing the musical score, as in everything. I like to consider the themes the composer suggests and make choices with him. I like to be in on everything and at every stage.

22. WHAT SCENES SHOULD HAVE MUSIC? / 23. SOUND EFFECTS?

I exercise complete control. Sound effects are critically important. They can be a nuisance if overstressed. On the other hand, not only can they provide authenticity and realism, but also drama as well.

I often plan these—as I did the music—at an early stage. Sometimes I shoot a scene with the knowledge that there will be music behind it, or a persisting sound effect, so not knitting the dialogue too tightly, and at the same time relying on the music or sound effects to help the scene work as I want it to.

It's all one: directing; everything is a part of the vocabulary and the means of the director. Nothing is irrelevant, nothing can be slighted.

Henry King

1. BACKGROUND?

I had a brief experience in the theatre—as an actor—with repertory companies—one night stands—some vaudeville. Directed some plays in summer stock—with road shows—managed the stage—in addition to playing a part. When the show would arrive in a town, I would go to the theatre and carefully examine backstage and evaluate the scenery—many times find scenery that had never been used—and greatly enhance the production value for the play.

2. FIRST FILM JOB?

In New York I was negotiating with a theatrical company for a good part in a play, when I accidently met a motion picture producer from California and, for some reason, he wanted me to go into motion pictures. I told him I had blue eyes—they do not photograph well. He laughed, said we have solved that problem years ago—He made me a definite offer, with as much salary as I was receiving in the theatre and 52 weeks a year: *That did it*—I came to California as a motion picture leading man. My most difficult task was *waiting*. In the theatre you work: in silent pictures—you wait. Sometimes I would work an hour in the morning and have nothing to do until three or four o'clock in the afternoon. This I could not tolerate. I put a desk in my dressing room and wrote screenplays. Some were good, some not so good; several were produced into fairly good and entertaining pictures.

In almost every motion picture there was a fight between the hero and the villian. Most of them were all alike—we had a story with a fight. I prevailed upon the director to make the fight different from the others—he said how? I asked him to allow me to write it out for him. I had in mind a fight that I saw between two men when I was eight years old:—the following day the company was on location doing scenes in which I did not appear. I wrote the fight sequence in *detail*. The director read it, said it was good, but could not be photographed—too many cuts—too many short flashes. In my eagerness to explain to him how to do it, he decided for me to direct it—that was the beginning of my hobby…that has lasted fifty-odd years.

3. YOUR GOAL IN FILMMAKING?

First, the purpose of a good motion picture is Entertainment—knowing the great influence a good, well told, motion picture has upon an audience should make us very careful what we tell. A few things we should avoid are brutality just for brutality's sake, vulgarity, profanity, just for profanity's sake, and out of character. Audiences copy many things from the screen. For instance, Cecil B. DeMille changed the architecture of the bathroom all over the world by the pictures he made. Motion pictures can be a great influence for good—for better dress—better appearance, better manners—at home and abroad. I was present when the late Mr. Kruschev, then premier of Russia, said: "Give me control of all the motion pictures for ten years and I will control the world." Need I say more about the power of the motion picture.

4. IN WHAT GENRE DO YOU SEEK A STORY?

The first thing I look for storywise is a story worth telling, and that can come from any source—book—play—original for the screen. One story I enjoyed doing very much was adapted from the Bible—*David and Bathsheba* [1951].

5. STORY SOURCE?

I have no preference as to the source of story material. I have done many original stories written for the screen—as I have said previously—a story worth telling is what I look for.

6. USE A SCRIPTWRITER OR DO IT YOURSELF?

I prefer that a dramatist do the first draft of a screenplay, regardless of the source of the story. If it is an original, he has already done that—should it be a book or stage play—we have several conferences—many authors will want to discuss sequences as they come along. I am always available to give him all the time and the benefit of any idea I have.

7. CLOSE COLLABORATION WITH THE SCREENWRITER?

I am not a writer—as you must have learned by now—I can't spell—and in silent pictures that doesn't show. I consider it a great privilege to work with a real pro—like Nunnally Johnson, Philip Dunne, or Casey Robinson—these men are not only top craftsmen, but great writers—scholars. Reading a screenplay written by man of this calibre is a great inspiration.

8. PREPLAN OR IMPROVISE?

Regardless of how much of the action is written out in the screenplay, the director must improvise on the set and make a translation from screenplay to film.

9. MOST IMPORTANT COMPONENT OF YOUR FILM?

The director is a storyteller—it is his responsibility to tell the story we start out to tell. That story must be on the motion picture screen—regardless who writes, photographs, edits et cetera. All must work closely with the director, or else you will have different interpretations, technically perfect—and telling nothing. No one person makes the picture—many people contribute. But all contribute together—with one interpretation. The director must set the pace—the tempo—visualize the characters—create the atmosphere around them. He must create on the motion picture screen what the author puts in a book.

10. WORK WITH A PRODUCER?

Yes and No—there are good and efficient producers—and others. A good producer that has his story will seek the director that he knows will do the best job of storytelling—and then assist him in every way he can.

11. USE A DIALOGUE DIRECTOR?

No, I do not use a dialogue director—my script girl or man makes sure the players know their lines before they come on the set for rehearsal. We must not have two different interpretations of the subject.

12. WRITER OR PRODUCER ON THE SET?

Tay, I am surprised that you ask the question—regarding the producer coming on the set. I am sure you know that no experienced producer would want to come on the set. He is interested in quality and cost—and by coming on the set he would interfere with both.

13. WORK CLOSELY WITH THE CAMERAMAN?

The cameraman is the director's right arm. I make long scenes five to ten pages of script—this requires long rehearsal. The cameraman follows me continuously during the planning for camera movement and rehearsal—it is not uncommon for me to rehearse half of the day on one scene.

This gives him the spirit and mood of the scene. When rehearsal is finished we clear the set of the players and, with the second team—"stand-ins"—he does his lighting. When he has completed this, I go in for one or two good rehearsals—with the players. By now everyone is ready for the scene—I generally print the first take—make a second take just for insurance, in the event of a negative scratch—or something unforeseen.

I make very few individual "close-ups." My reason for this is: I try to use the individual "close-up" in a motion picture as a writer would use punctuation in a written paragraph.

14. SUPERVISION OF CASTING?

While I do believe the director, producer, writer, casting head all work together making suggestions and agreeing upon the cast, it is my opinion the director must interview and discuss with each one, right down to "one line" bits. I have always followed this policy to get on closer terms with the player, and to help him adapt himself to what will be done—and the way I hope to do it.

15. PREFERENCE OF ACTING STYLE?

Personally I love to work with excellent actors—not "technicians." By excellent actor I mean an actor who has the instinct to feel and become the part rather than just act like it. The technician is the one who is always technically right—but seldom gets under the skin of the audience. You ask what I think of "The Method Actor"—I have not had the privilege.

Please do not get the impression that I am always looking for actors of long experience—for I have given newcomers the opportunity to show their ability more than anyone. I have always taken great pride in giving a worthwhile newcomer his or her first opportunity for a feature part. To name a few—the late Ronald Colman, had his first part with me in *The White Sister* [1923]. He was from the New York stage. I made extensive tests to overcome his fear that he would not be good. Gary Cooper had his first part with me in *The Winning of Barbara Worth* [1926]. I moved him up from the extra ranks.

Tyrone Power had his first part in *Lloyd's of London* [1936]—that made him a star. In all I did nine pictures with him. Don Ameche in *Ramona* [1936]—he had done one small part prior to *Ramona*—Jennifer Jones in the *[The] Song of Bernadette* [1943]—she won the Academy aware for that performance. [Ed. note: Ronald Colman, Tyrone Power, and Jennifer Jones had all appeared in films prior to working for Henry King.] Jean Peters in *Captain from Castile* [1947]—and many more—all that I mention here had that great ability to listen—understand—and visualize what they were doing.

I had the privilege of doing four pictures with Gregory Peck—whom I consider one of the finest actors of all time—and the most sensitive player I have ever known, and Lionel Barrymore—another of the greats—my career has been interesting; I have loved doing every picture that I have ever made.

16. PRECAMERA WORK WITH ACTOR?

Prior to rehearsal I like to discuss the play with each player—many times, when possible, have the entire cast together—and each one read him or her part. In so doing they understand what I am reaching for—also I get some valuable ideas from them. I have never engaged actors or actresses for their weight—or height—but for what they are able to contribute.

17. IMPORTANCE OF REHEARSALS? / 18. ADHERENCE TO SCRIPT?

My experience with players has taught me that they are as anxious for excellency in the film as I am and when they come forward with a change of dialogue that I feel is an improvement, I accept it gratefully. I change dialogue each and every day—for many reasons. When we are on the set rehearsing, and seeing the play or scene come to life, any defect shows quickly and the change of a few words—or a speech here and there—make a great difference. The character is imbedded in the dialogue—the expression of the character—no two characters in a play speak alike—if they do, you have no character. I prefer to eliminate dialogue, rather than add it—we're making a motion picture, not a phonograph record. This is an endless subject.

19. EDITING SUPERVISION?

I control the editing of the film—from assembly to final cut. Film must be assembled as it was intended when the director made it. Otherwise, it may tell a different story.

20. ROLE OF MUSICAL SCORE?

The musical score for a picture greatly depends upon the picture—some need music, others do not.

21. INVOLVEMENT IN PREPARATION OF MUSICAL SCORE?

A great composer and conductor like the late Alfred Newman always made an important contribution to a picture. For instance, when I made the ending scene for *Love is a Many-Splendored Thing* [1955] I did it with Al Newman in mind—I went to him and told him: "I made that scene for you Al. It is silent, you do the dialogue in your music." And he did that and more, because he loved doing it—and humbly thanked me for doing the scene that gave him the opportunity to make music say *something*.

22. WHAT SCENES SHOULD HAVE MUSIC?

Regarding the scoring of a picture—there can be no fixed rule—we always make a dupe print for the composer conductor. He studies it carefully, then we discuss it—I have great respect for composers who seem to have the ability to come up with an idea—music in a picture that the audience is not conscious of—yet it's there.

23. SOUND EFFECTS?

Sound effects are important but can easily be overdone—do not do sound just to have sound. The sound effect can have the same dramatic effect as the right dialogue. It has the same importance, of course, depending on the situation and scene. Therefore, I am always present in re-recording to see that the above is carried out. I remember a motion picture when a man stepped on a peanut in the hallway of a hotel—three o'clock in the morning—most exciting scene in a good picture!

COMMENT

Directing a motion picture is a job of endless responsibility—and unless the director realizes this and assumes this great responsibility, he is apt to wonder why his picture is not meeting the public demand: while good in some values—misfire in others. A confusing problem to say the least. It is so easy to overlook simplicity and become complicated—and overtell the story by embellishment with ingredients it does not need. Many of these so-called ingredients destroy the story value because they are out of character and out of place.

Audiences love to participate in the picture—become deeply engrossed in the tale—and live with characters, forgetting they are in the theatre.

Here I will quote from the late Cardinal Bonzono: "A drop of poison put into the thinking of a person is a far greater crime than poison put in his drink."

Stanley Kramer

1. BACKGROUND?

I have never had any vocation besides film. I came to California immediately after graduation from a university.

2. FIRST FILM JOB?

My first position in the movie business was as an apprentice writer. I have been, at various times, a film editor, researcher, story editor, assistant to producers, a producer and then finally a director.

I always wanted to be a director, but after World War II, I became an independent producer because in those days the producer was the absolute boss…and one had to be the boss to choose the subject, edit the films, etc., etc.

3. YOUR GOAL IN FILMMAKING?

The philosophy behind the making of film runs the danger of pretension… because the aim, as in all art, must be to satisfy first, *oneself*—and then to *capture* an audience.

I have dealt mostly with film which takes a point of view and tries not to reflect, but to establish a premise on the future with a somewhat controversial point of view. Entertainment has so many different definitions.

If the job is done well, it *is* entertainment.

4. IN WHAT GENRE DO YOU SEEK A STORY?

I do not seek any particular genre in the search for a story.

5. STORY SOURCE?

My preference is for a story and script written directly for the screen. I have had greater success and a lot more enjoyment working with original material of this kind.

6. USE A SCRIPTWRITER OR DO IT YOURSELF?

I prefer to work with a screen dramatist in the preparation of the shooting script. It is a close collaboration—but the perspective retained by a collaboration, rather than a solo job is worth a great deal.

I started as a writer—the temptation for solo credit and independence of anyone else is often tempting, but not for long. Today, I'm a better editor and constructionist for the collaboration.

7. CLOSE COLLABORATION WITH THE SCREENWRITER?

I work very closely with the scriptwriter but not as a co-writer—I certainly want him to have freedom—but I like to go on the set with the script representing our total agreement.

8. PREPLAN OR IMPROVISE?

I might prefer all the action worked out fully on paper before shooting, but I believe it to be impossible. The location—particularly on action sequences—dictates many of the setups and moves.

9. MOST IMPORTANT COMPONENT OF YOUR FILM?

I think there can be no doubt that the story and script are of primary importance in the creation of a film.

10. WORK WITH A PRODUCER?

I do not work with a producer, because I am a producer-director.

11. USE A DIALOGUE DIRECTOR?

I have used a dialogue director and a competent person can save a good deal of time for the director in reviewing dialogue. I prefer that the dialogue director does not participate in any way in the styling of the scene.

12. WRITER OR PRODUCER ON THE SET?

I *am* a producer-director, and I *do* like to have the writer on the set. There are exceptions, but this would be due to personality differences.

13. WORK CLOSELY WITH THE CAMERAMAN?

I work very closely with the cameraman prior to shooting—on everything possible down to the smallest detail. We study production design sketches together whenever possible.

14. SUPERVISION OF CASTING?

I maintain rigid control on selecting the entire cast.

15. PREFERENCE OF ACTING STYLE?

I personally set no rules for actors—whatever their methods or instincts. There is a relationship that must be established between director and actor, and this is a personal thing—it has to do with respect and patience and sometimes downright mutual affection.

16. PRECAMERA WORK WITH ACTOR?

I really insist that each actor bring everything he can to the role—free from inhibition of any kind. I am prepared to discuss, change, even argue. But it has never seemed to reach a crisis when the climate is warm and creative.

17. IMPORTANCE OF REHEARSALS?

Rehearsals can be governed by the subject matter. Total long rehearsals are invaluable on some scripts. For *Ship of Fools* [1965], we were never on shipboard, always on the stage, and rehearsed for two full weeks with great benefit to all.

On *It's a Mad, Mad, Mad, Mad World* [1963]—it was all location, and could take only rehearsal on the spot before shooting—and not very much on the action.

18. ADHERENCE TO SCRIPT?

Since I worked closely with the writer, I represent him very carefully in the change of lines, because I represent myself. The writer has written and rewritten and it has meant a lot to both of us to write "Finis" to a screenplay.

I want to be as true to my responsibility to the writer as I can be, in regard to outside pressures. If I make the change, it is as though *we* make the change. Certainly change is permitted if this will accomplish our purpose and make the actor more comfortable.

19. EDITING SUPERVISION?

I supervise the editing on every film frame for frame. I think it is a vital, basic part of picture making and it is the responsibility of every director worthy of the name.

20. ROLE OF MUSICAL SCORE?

I think the musical score can be fantastically important. It has been for me in my films. *High Noon* [1952] made it a large part of the way on the singing ballad being used as a bridge throughout the film. *The Wild One* [1954] used "bop" as a character. In *The Defiant Ones* [1958], a sheriff's pocket radio was used as a chase menace and character study. Certainly "Waltzing Mathilda" helped *On The Beach* [1959], and "The Glory of Love" didn't hurt *Guess Who's Coming To Dinner* [1967].

21. INVOLVEMENT IN PREPARATION OF MUSICAL SCORE?

It is part of the job to be deeply involved in the discussions, cues, themes, and to be present at the recordings of the score.

22. WHAT SCENES SHOULD HAVE MUSIC?

The cues are the result of the creative cooperation of the director and com-poser—just as close and just as important as the relationship of director and writer.

23. SOUND EFFECTS?

I cannot recall ever having missed one minute of the dubbing sessions of any of the films with which I have been associated.

COMMENT

Many young filmmakers use as their credo the search for truth. In a complex society, *the truth* is often obscured—difficult to find. We find, instead, half-truths—and on half-truths some of the greatest lies in the history of the world have been built. Better to rest on one's own truth—and a willingness to accept some compro-mise toward its achievement—just so long as the basic principle on which it rests is itself never compromised.

Alberto Lattuada

1. BACKGROUND?

After I finished high school, I entered the School of Architecture at the University of Milan, a five-year course. Those years of study, which covered mathematics, together with ornate drawing and the specific science of construction—forty exams were involved—allowed me to cultivate my vocation for my career in cinema.

In 1940, together with Mario Ferrari and Luigi Comencini, I founded the Italian Film Library (of which I am still President) and wrote critical essays and articles on cinema, as well as short stories for daily newspapers and literary magazines.

In those times, I used to go to the movies as often as three times a day! I didn't pick up any particular show in advance; I simply watched everything, curious about every aspect of the cinema, spectacular or theoretical, commercial, experimental or *avant-garde*. Even today, I am an ideal audience. I sit in the dark, ready to witness the miracle of the screen, open to suggestion, like naive child.

My critical faculties and all my technical and aesthetic knowledge intervene only at the end, to pass a negative or a positive judgment on the show. I hate those conceited judges who claim to classify a movie during its showing and whisper their comments to the person sitting next to them. The so-called "private showings" for critics are usually poisonous places where—for the most part—people create legends based on errors and on prejudices (ideologic or aesthetic) which bear no resemblance to a serene and historically valid appraisal.

My father was a composer; opera was his *metier.* One of his operas, chosen by Toscanini to premiere at La Scala of Milan, had great success both in Italy and in the rest of the world. It was also staged at the Metropolitan of New York. It was entitles *Les Precieuses Ridicules* [*Ridiculous Affectations*], based on the Molière play. My father also wrote a lot of symphonic music, and musical scores for motion pictures.

When I was a child, I was lucky enough to fall asleep with the sound of the piano, and to wake up in the same harmonic atmosphere, so that, even then, my fantasies were greatly stimulated by the "bath" of musical notes.

(Later, I was able to fill the "generation gap" when my father wrote the musical score for several of my films.)

At home we always discussed art (music, literature, painting, cinema) with great eagerness and passion. We ended up shouting our arguments in order to overcome each other with quotations and names of the great masters. The moment in which the family gathered for the main meal had turned from an oasis of peace into a battleground. Finally, my mother ruled that every member of the family had the right to take the floor for five times only, trying to condense his or her thoughts in a clear form. Once one's five turns of questions and answers were exhausted, he had to become completely quiet until the end of the meal. By applying the above rules, we avoided the consequences of bad indigestion, ergo: ulcers!

Another important habit of my family was that vacation didn't mean to turn away from each other, as it often happens today. After deciding where to go, whether to the mountains, by the lake or by the sea, the family enjoyed the free time with sporting competition between father and children.

We all participated in physical activities, during which we enjoyed the beauty of nature, which my father loved passionately. In the afternoon, my father, mother, sister and I were busy selecting a picnic site. We used oil paints to draw our favorite subjects. The four of us would work in silent concentration, then compare the results with great joyous laughter, or ironic critical observation. The family atmosphere was generally happy and filled with love of nature.

I experienced the miracle of my "vocation" when I was introduced to the secret passages of the Teatro della Scala where my father was busy staging his operas. The rising and falling of the painted backgrounds, the colored lights that, in imperceptible crescendos and diminuendos, turned night into day and the sun into a fabulous tempest, the coming and going of wigs, beards, costumes, the technique of the workmen who controlled the amazing movement of the stage, the powerful sound that rose from the orchestra, all blended together to enchant me. All this gave me the mad desire to create from nothing, a fantasy of gigantic proportions with which I could touch and capture the eye and heart of the audience.

At that time, we were at the eve of World War II, and I was writing for two antifascist newspapers, *Walking* and *Tide*.

2. FIRST FILM JOB?

I took my first step into the motion picture world as movie critic of *Domus,* a magazine on literature and architecture. Following college, I was signed as co-writer and first assistant director for the film *Piccolo Mondo Antico* [*Small Old World,* 1941], directed by Mario Soldati.

I worked so hard—I would almost say "frantically"—at this assignment that the producers decided to give me a chance at directing. In 1941, I wrote and directed my first film, entitled *Giacomo l'Idealista* [*James, the Idealist.*]

This motion picture represented a challenge to the great movie industry, because it defied the idea that you must have a big name star in order to achieve success. While I made my debut as a director, Marina Berti, then seventeen-years-old, made hers as an actress; Carlo Nebiolo was director of photography, and Carlo Ponti was producer. The picture was quite a success, but the war and our flight after the Nazi occupation of Italy scattered our group.

On the day following the liberation of Rome, I was already writing my first neo-realistic film, entitled _The Bandit_ [_Il Bandito_, 1946].

3. YOUR GOAL IN FILMMAKING?

To me, the making of a motion picture means to communicate to the audience what I believe is the truth, or a portion of the truth. Obviously, in this work, I do not presume to undertake the solution of problems that plague human life. As a mater of fact, through perusal of history, we can easily see that man, in a carefully dull way, continues to repeat the same errors that have been pointed out to him by history itself.

The adage "historia magistra" should be corrected to the more authentic "historia non est magistra." Man does not learn anything from the events that mark his coming and going along a path which is always the same, even if under a different sky. The above mentioned "portion of truth" is, therefore nearly always condensed in the ending of my pictures where man, after various ups and downs, finds himself in utter solitude. The condition of solitude is not to be considered defeat.

I think the fight for what we might call "good" against what we feel is "evil," is to be accepted, even without the consensus of the masses. This is, therefore, an active, fighting solitude, and not a loneliness made of skepticism and sacrifice.

This theme is contained in almost all my pictures, whether costume films [_The Tempest/La Tempesta_, 1958] or contemporary pictures [_Mafioso_, 1962]; whether the picture has a positive hero, or is a provocative film with an anti-hero.

Naturally, in order that this particle of truth may reach as many people as possible, I always strive to make shows which will appeal to a large audience. If a thought contained in a motion picture is important, but its presentation doesn't reach the audience, the work is a failure. Rather than to misuse a motion picture as means of communication, it is better to write a philosophical essay.

At times, the instantaneous success of a picture gives rise to misunderstandings. Television, by resuming the showing of the best work of the past has often devaluated films that had enjoyed undeserved success, or—in other cases—has re-evaluated films which were severely denounced by critics as wholly unworthy.

My favorite adage is "Nihil humani a me alienum puto." [Terence, 190-159 B.C.: "I am a man; nothing human is alien to me."] Weaknesses, errors, illusions, achievements, sins and purifications characterize my own disorder, and nourish my sincere effort toward synthesis of experience and confession.

Incidentally, a thing called "Progress" fails to enchant me. If, after having admired the technical wonders of the astronauts walking on the moon, you may look over your shoulder, only to discover that the cave man has surprisingly survived to raise his murderous club over your fragile head.

4. IN WHAT GENRE DO YOU SEEK A STORY?

Considering that it takes approximately nine to twelve months to make a film, the director must be completely enthusiastic about the value of the story. We cannot throw away twelve months of our lives without justification.

What I seek, above all, is a logical examination of the human condition, and the endless errors that men make through the centuries. Progress is a very slow and patient process, which history fights in a cycle of destruction and reconstruction. Even in an intimate story involving only two characters, one can always contribute to the analysis of errors and the proposal of remedies. Even a costume picture can help the audience to understand today's life, the historic moment in which we live.

5. STORY SOURCE?

When looking for a story, it is impossible to follow a definite pattern. There must, rather, be a constant position of sincerity on the part of the director, who must express something he has at heart.

Two different lines of work characterize my motion pictures: the first concerns films based on an original idea of mine, or on material from a current event. The second concerns movies based on a book freely adapted for the screen, which—above all—must originate in indignation, mixed with a longing to remedy injustice reigning for centuries.

I have made a list of the so-called "original" movies, and a second list of those deriving from a literary subject. The first list includes _The Bandit_ [_Il Bandito_], _No Mercy_ [_Senza Pietà,_ 1948], _Vaudeville Lights_ [_Luci dei Varietà,_ 1951], _The Italians Look Back_ [_Gli Italiani Si Voltano,_ 1953], _The Girl Friend_ [_L'Amica,_ 1969], _The Overcoat_ [_Il Cappotto,_ 1952], and many others.

When I select a literary text, I plan to abide by the inner meaning of the original work, yet I consider myself completely free from the written material. In other words, while giving the audience the message conveyed by the book, we must feel free from the pedantic nature of the text. One single line may become a sequence; on the other hand, a hundred pages can be summarized in a scene of a few frames. Let's say that I consider the literary text a libretto of an opera. The movie is the music that springs up and grows freely from this libretto, bringing out its most hidden, poetic truths.

6. USE A SCRIPTWRITER OR DO IT YOURSELF?

Since my very first movie, I have been assisted by screenwriters or even by writers who had no experience in screenwriting, but who were familiar with show business in general. At any rate, even though absorbing all the good ideas from my collaborators, I always wrote my scenarios myself.

7. CLOSE COLLABORATION WITH THE SCREENWRITER?

Nearly always I work with the writer (who is seldom a woman) as follows: first we discuss at length (sometimes even for a month) the structure of the movie, based on a synopsis or treatment, summarized in five or six pages.

When that phase of work is satisfactorily completed, I tell the story, following the treatment's outline. Later, the work proceeds separately. The writer, who acts as the devil's advocate by mainly objecting to my ideas, writes some scenes, or parts of scenes. I do the same. Upon reading both texts, I improve and give the finishing touch to the screenplay by myself.

At times, in order to have the feeling of the final edited footage, I read the screenplay, timing it with a stopwatch. I re-enact the whole movie and fill the gaps of action sequences (fights, car races, walks outdoors, etc.) with the help of a sort of vocalization and gestures to approximate as much as possible the length of the silent scenes. This system has proved to be good, and the timing is always very close to the final screening.

8. PREPLAN OR IMPROVISE?

I always considered the script as a narrative guideline. The size of shots, various scenes and reverse angles were never written in the script, but were improvised by me while shooting. I never enforced the stupid rule of counting the close-ups of the female star so that they would match in number the ones given to the male lead. When I became a director, the stardom syndrome was already fading. During the period of neo-realism in particular, a motion picture was no longer referred to as a "Paramount Picture," or an "M-G-M Film" (as during the times of the old American films) but as a "De Sica movie" or a "Visconti movie."

My screen plays were written as books, without indications of shots or camera movements. However, the dialogue is written as accurately as possible. Once shooting starts, I might change both action and dialogue with full liberty and taking all responsibilities toward the producer.

In other words, I don't hesitate to make drastic changes if, while shooting the film, I feel that action and dialogue do not have the necessary natural quality. In the morning during the first hour of work, I jot down the entire sequence as it should be cut, with all the various sizes of shots and camera movements, pans and dolly shots included. Usually at the end of the day, all material—in complete detail—has been shot exactly according to schedule.

9. MOST IMPORTANT COMPONENT OF YOUR FILM?

The story is the only important element you need to decide whether to make the picture.

After that comes the selection of writers, actors, editor, art director, director of photography, musicians, etc. The theme of the story is the only decisive element that drives me to the creation of a film. All the other elements are like instruments of an orchestra that the director conducts with absolute control. To avoid the danger that mannerism might take strength from the initial theme of the film, none of those instruments must intrude on the others.

A film cannot be a vehicle for a great performance by an art director, a director of photography, an actor or an editor. All must humbly be at the service of the original idea, and they must all follow the director's instructions thoroughly.

This is the only way a film (which is the product of the work of many and therefore is not pure) can approach the stylistic unity which is characteristic of a work of art.

10. WORK WITH A PRODUCER?

In the beginning, I usually worked with a producer. In the course of my career, I worked alternatively with [Carlo] Ponti, Dino De Laurentis, and Goffredo Lombardo. At times, the "producer" was a group of people wishing to finance a motion picture of a certain artistic value, as happened with *The Overcoat* [*Il Cappotto*]. In that instance, my sister, Bianca Lattuada, and I acted as sole executive producers.

During my association with Ponti or De Laurentis, they only discussed the weak points in the script and analyzed the production schedule from a financial point of view. Once shooting started, I never allowed the producer on the set, and I never discussed my work with the producer during the making of the picture. Only when editing was almost completed, would we discuss some cuts or changes. I never discussed the choice of the composer, the taping of sound effects, etc.

Today, I am my own producer, in collaboration with my sister, Bianca Lattuada. When the two of us make a decision, nobody can butt in.

I think that the present good fortune of the American cinema is due exactly to the fact that authors are given all responsibilities. Their personalities can produce astonishing results, each one different from the other, thus betting on many winning numbers on the roulette wheel of the artistic and commercial success of a motion picture.

11. USE A DIALOGUE DIRECTOR?

Usually, the first assistant director (and not the dialogue director) is in charge to make sure that all actors know their parts. However, I don't require a painstaking preparation, because—in case of changes in the dialogue—the actors would not feel comfortable. At any rate, I have complete control over all the acting.

12. WRITER OR PRODUCER ON THE SET?

Only the technicians and my assistants must be on the set, never the writer or the producer. Should a phase of the picture be discussed or analyzed, I interrupt the shooting and call a private meeting with the writer or the producer.

13. WORK CLOSELY WITH THE CAMERAMAN?

I am very particular in giving my cameraman all camera positions and movements, as well as light effects. In the past ten years I have used up to three cameras at the same time. Only one camera has to follow the movements and the set-ups previously established. The other two receive vague instructions, so that the second and third cameramen, while following one actor or the other, are able to steal expressions and gestures that retain the freshness of actions which were not prearranged. The material so obtained has always two or three moments of extreme spontaneity and vitality that can well be used in the editing, in addition to the takes of the main camera.

14. SUPERVISION OF CASTING?

Casting takes a long time during the technical preparation of my pictures (which follows the delivery of the final screenplay).

I not only give famous actors screen tests in order to check makeup or other details of the characters they are going to portray, but I test almost everybody that will be in the picture, even if that actor has only one word of dialogue.

At times, a character that makes a very brief appearance may be just the key to the dramatic situation of a particular sequence, thus making the choice of casting very difficult. The search for such a necessary character may delay preparation work until the face that reflects the ideal image in my mind can be found.

15. PREFERENCE OF ACTING STYLE?

An actor of great and subtle technique must never lose the quality of spontaneity. I try to work with actors who have both sufficient technique and richness of instinct. However, should I find myself in the dilemma of choosing between the two qualities, I would pick instinct, because I know I can take all responsibility with regard to technical devices.

Many young actresses, between sixteen and eighteen years of age, have made their debut as leads in my pictures. Among the most well-known, I can cite Guilietta Masina, Catherine Spaak, Jacqueline Sassard, Eva Aulin, May Britt, Carla Gravina and last, Therese Ann Savoy. With the exception of Guilietta Massina, who had theatrical experience, all these young women became actresses overnight.

There is not a specific method in dealing with actors. Human nature has different aspects and the director must study his actors and apply various methods: (a) persuasion by words (b) love, familiarity and charm, (c) moral humiliation, (d) whispered instructions, (e) shouting, (f) persuasion by touch, as when petting a dog or a horse before a race.

16. PRECAMERA WORK WITH ACTOR?

I wish the actor/actress to read the whole screenplay with particular care as to his or her role. Afterward, I like to discuss briefly with him or her, the value of the character in connection with the picture in its entirety. If the actor/actress is very intelligent, I hardly point out anything in particular, and I let him or her run at "full gallop," correcting and controlling his or her excesses, but always with lots of love. I don't believe in the "cruel" director's method.

I am also against long rehearsals prior to the shooting of the picture. Too many rehearsals may result in mannerism and in mechanical acting.

I hardly rehearse dialogue, but I thoroughly rehearse business, positions and movements. Therefore, I am in favor of "shooting the rehearsal." I often repeat a scene without making any corrections, trying to convey my message to the actors and to get the most out of them without warping their spontaneity with my words. If I don't reach perfect results this way, then I start again by giving detailed instructions.

18. ADHERENCE TO SCRIPT?

If the lead is a great actor/actress, I am willing to accept all small changes he or she may suggest with regard to both lines and pieces of business. It is rare to find an actor who has the gift of creativity, namely who can add a meaningful touch of real, rich color to the director's instructions. However, when this happens, it is indeed a gift that must not be rejected.

19. EDITING SUPERVISION?

As for editing, I proceed the following way: in the morning, I screen one or two rolls of film with my editor, while the secretary takes new notes. In case of a long close-up of an actor/actress, showing a series of various looks and expressions, I comment without exactly specifying the shots that I wish to keep.

After this preliminary work I let the editor cut the scenes as he best pleases, asking him to show me the result of his work at the end of the day. When I screen this first projection, I only make some general comments. After two or three rolls of film are cut this way, I view them at the moviola, where I can make all my remarks in particular, and even mark the frames at the exact point where they should be cut.

Sequences particularly difficult to cut, such as big battle scenes, require more extensive work, which is done at the moviola, following precise written instructions.

Finally, the film is viewed on the big screen. It was just while editing the battle scenes of two of my films [*The Tempest* and *Fraulein Doktor,* 1969] that I had to disown my own work and start all over again. I even had *reprinted* the scenes I wanted to examine, so that I could have them under my eyes in their original form.

When reaching the final editing of a film, it is my practice to leave everything alone for about twenty days. Then, together with my editor, I screen the picture.

The two of us pretend to be part of the audience, and not people who know the film by heart. This is the only way faults can be easily noticed.

At times, producers hurry to release a motion picture in order to save a little money, without realizing that a rushed editing may mean the movie's death sentence.

20. ROLE OF MUSICAL SCORE? / 21. INVOLVEMENT IN PREPARATION OF MUSICAL SCORE?

The score is certainly an element of great importance in obtaining emotional effects. In my films I do not want the music to substitute for any lack of emotions that MUST derive from the image. If anything, the music must enhance the image's effectiveness.

22. WHAT SCENES SHOULD HAVE MUSIC? / 23. SOUND EFFECTS?

More than music, I greatly value the use of sound effects: gunshots, brakes, doors, trains, footsteps.

When well applied, I think that sound effects represent fifty percent of the emotion, both amplified—thanks to the most modern technical devices—and extremely delicate, imperceptible almost, as the noise of a woodworm at work.

On one occasion, during the final phase of mixing, I was impelled to interrupt the work and start again to put together the sound track, correcting the shortcomings that came out only after words, music and sound effects had been put together.

It is obvious that I am the one to decide which scenes must be accompanied with music. If a composer has some suggestions, I listen to him very carefully, and—in many cases—I follow his choice.

I select the music only by instinctive feeling and never by cold reasoning or prejudice. I control all recordings, with a dubbing of dialogue or sound effects as well as the musical score, even during arrangement prior to mixing; even when we work for particular balance in sounds of various types of instruments, recorded on channels at the moment of execution.

J. Lee Thompson

1. BACKGROUND?

I was first an actor, and not a very good one. Since I wasn't getting many parts, I wrote a play which had a part about the length of *King Lear.* I took this to a management company, and they said, "I hope you're not thinking of playing the lead part yourself?"

I said, "No. I'm not."

At which point they became interested in producing my play!

When I got outside the theatre, I thought to myself, if I lacked the guts to say "Yes" after having written that part for myself, I have no business being an actor. I am a writer.

The play was produced; it had a moderate success. I was young at the time—eighteen, I believe—and for the West End of London, this was looked upon as quite a good thing, so I received some critical acclaim.

Shortly afterward, a film company came along and asked if I would like to write a screenplay for them. I said "Yes," and that is how I became a film writer. Now, I was in the film business, and that's how it began for me.

2. FIRST FILM JOB?

Having become a film writer, my first work was to devise a screenplay of my own play. It was a film called *Double Error.* I wrote a script which I thought was pretty faithful to the play. It was given to Walter Summers, who had a good reputation as a war film director.

I'll never understand why they gave him this little thriller to make. I went to see him shooting, and was stunned, because what he was doing bore no resemblance to anything I had written.

Somehow I was forgiven for this bomb that was created out of my play. I'm not saying it would have been any better if they had stuck to the original play!

Now the war came along, and I went into the air force. I went back to writing plays, and wrote one called *Murder Without Crime.* This play was highly successful, running two years in London and one year on Broadway. This, again, was brought to a film company. After the war was over, they not only asked me to write the screenplay, but also they asked me to direct the film. It was around 1950. I directed my first feature film: I had everything going for me yet the film was not a success.

Again, everything looked very bleak. I had discovered that I enjoyed directing and wanted to continue.

Two years later I was offered another film which is one of my favorites: *The Yellow Balloon* [1952]. It was a small film, and became a success. This now meant that I was pretty solid, and I began to think of myself as a director. It had all evolved. I had been a dialogue director with Alfred Hitchcock on two pictures, and having seen him work, I thought one day I might have the opportunity to become a film director. However, it fell into my lap through writing plays. That's how I became a director.

3. YOUR GOAL IN FILMMAKING?

In the early days (I suppose this happens mostly to directors in Europe), my philosophy was to make films that had a message. I did take it all very seriously, not that you don't take filmmaking seriously all through life. Yet I didn't pay attention to the box office; I was not interested in my films making money. Originally, I wanted to make films with a theme of some importance.

I'd like to think that one of my films called *Yield To The Night* [1956], which was against capital punishment (at a time when England was considering whether or not to abolish it) had a message. The film was shown in the Houses of Parliament, and I'd like to think that, if it swayed one person in the "House," it was worth making. So I took this type of thing seriously, and always looked for films with a social theme.

It has been said that I was one of the first directors to make what is known as "kitchen sink dramas." I did that with *A Woman In a Dressing Gown* [1957], and *No Trees in the Street* [1959], which were social documents. I prided myself on this until I got a rude shock, and found that I was looked upon as a noncommercial director.

Subjects were beginning to arrive less and less on my desk. I suddenly seemed to wake up, and say to myself, "I must make some commercial films." I had found that it's not a good thing to make films just for yourself in order to please a handful of critics.

Now my philosophy is: you damn well should make films that entertain the public. They pay hard-earned money to see something to be entertained. If you can make an entertaining film that also has social comment, it's marvelous. They are hard to find. Primarily, now, I seek to entertain.

4. IN WHAT GENRE DO YOU SEEK A STORY?

Now I hope to find it in the thriller-adventure. I would like to find stories like *The Parallax View* [1974]. The recent film I did, *The White Buffalo* [1977] is a fine adventure story. This is what I, personally, look for.

5. STORY SOURCE?

What I would prefer, but it's hard to find, is the original screen story. An idea that you take to a screenwriter that you feel you can work with, and you knock it around, and from that evolves a pure film. It was created as a film idea, and is pure film.

The one way, strangely enough, that I don't like is the play. The play is such a different thing. It really is confined. Very few good plays lend themselves to film. I think that the good plays need to remain photographed stage plays, therefore they are not so interesting for the filmmaker, and—in the long run—not so interesting for the audience.

Novels are much nearer to it. They can breathe. By taking a novel, you have so much material that you have to cut it down. Again, it becomes a process of trying to manufacture from another article.

The best thing is to try to get an original idea.

6. USE A SCRIPTWRITER OR DO IT YOURSELF?

I would prefer to get hold of a good screen dramatist. Although I'm basically a writer, I don't consider myself a natural writer. I find it very difficult to write, so I might have taken the easy way out by directing. I need a screenwriter who can produce quickly.

7. CLOSE COLLABORATION WITH THE SCREENWRITER?

There really isn't a set answer to that. If it's your idea to begin with, and you bring in a screenwriter, I personally like to work closely with that screenwriter. I wouldn't work in collaboration with him; I would simply hope to see each scene that he's written and then discuss it. But that might throw him. It depends on the man you're working with. If the writer says, "Leave me alone to write each scene myself, then let me show it to you," I understand that. What I like to do is be able to go twice a week and see what he has written.

8. PREPLAN OR IMPROVISE?

I prefer to work it out: every shot very fully, and all the action that goes with that shot. I draw it out myself, so I can go onto the floor knowing that if something goes wrong, I have a solid way of shooting that film, and that day's work. It gives me security: it's my security blanket.

I have always, since I started directing film, been prepared fully. That means I can throw away and improvise, because I'm secure. If something goes wrong with the improvisation, I can go back to my drawings, knowing that will work. We can shoot that, and it will make a good picture. But, maybe in rehearsals, you find that it's much better to do something in a different way, and I think you should try things. You shouldn't come onto the floor and say, "This is the way it's going to be."

I tried that once with Gregory Peck and Anthony Quinn in *The Guns of Navarone* [1961]. I happened to put my script down on a table where they were sitting. Greg happened to look at my script, and saw my drawings. He said, "Lee, you're treating us like puppets. You have it all worked out, so we can't do anything creative."

I closed my script and said, "Let's play around with the scene, and please feel free to try whatever you'd like." Nowadays, I never leave my script around for anyone to see. It's a good thing, once you get onto the floor, to see if you can't do a better scene than you imagined. Obviously, you really do stick to what you've worked out, because that was your first visual look at the film. There is no reason, however, why you shouldn't try to improve certain scenes that you've worked out.

9. MOST IMPORTANT COMPONENT OF YOUR FILM?

Through the years, I've learned that no matter how many brilliant people you surround yourself with, it really doesn't matter if the story is hopeless. If the script isn't good, you're fighting a losing battle right from the start. For years, I would read a script, and if there was something in that script—say a good scene perhaps—I would try to make myself believe that the rest of the script was good, when it wasn't. I've made too many films like that. We've all had bad scripts. I will say, without doubt, the chief thing in making a film is the story or script.

10. WORK WITH A PRODUCER?

It really depends on what producer you're working with. The majority of producers I've worked with through the years were utterly useless. Today, producers no longer get the money for the pictures. Today they may be ex-agents or anyone who puts a package together. The majority of those people are uncreative, they don't know anything about the process of making a film. They have no visual ability, and have no idea as to what the creators are feeling.

Now, I must qualify that by saying that I have worked with some very good producers. When you do manage to work with a good producer, then you feel that you always have someone there who cares, and who understands all the difficulties of making a film. You should treasure the good producer, because he is someone you can bring your troubles to; he will take those burdens off your back. That's what a good producer should do. A good producer should support you to the hilt. This doesn't mean that the producer must compliment the director on everything he does. If he's a creative man, he may have suggestions for you, and be right. It's a wonderful partnership that can be formed.

In fact, Pancho Kohner, who is producing *The White Buffalo* is very young and is the perfect example of the ideal producer. A bad producer is one who makes himself an enemy of the director. I have been fortunate, and can't really complain. I'm only bitter for a few bad moments, and to see the way my colleagues are treated.

11. USE A DIALOGUE DIRECTOR?

One of my first jobs was being a dialogue director in the industry, when a dialogue director was what he was supposed to be. This means, a director who could come up with different lines when an artist didn't like a line he or she was saying. The director would turn to the dialogue director and say, "Give us another line."

I was always sweating, because it would generally take me a week to come up with a line. My life as a dialogue director was confusion. I honestly think that a dialogue director can't really add anything. An actor, these days, comes prepared.

12. WRITER OR PRODUCER ON THE SET?

I very much would like to have the writer on the set with me. It's a way of life in the theatre that a writer is almost always present, so that the director can turn to him. That's a wonderful partnership in the theatre; it doesn't happen that often in film.

In the case of *The White Buffalo,* Richard Sale was not always on the set, but I would call him and ask him to join me. It was a lovely feeling to have him on the set; sometimes he'd even give me lines over the telephone.

I'm afraid the economics of film is such that writers, today, are invariably writing another film for someone, and can't see their work through. Some directors, I understand, resent having the writer on the set with them. I welcome the writer.

As for producers, I'll have to refer you to my previous answer.

13. WORK CLOSELY WITH THE CAMERAMAN?

Before a film starts, I thoroughly discuss the look of the picture—which is terribly important. Either you decide on a kind of muted look, or perhaps a garish look. I even do tests with my cameraman in trying to get exactly what I'm seeking, so that the whole picture has a style. It might be a lush forties type of style, or a muted, very quiet style. All that ycu discuss ahead of time. The "look" of the film must first come from the director. Naturally, the cameraman will have his own ideas and will discuss them, showing you certain things which you may or may not like, and so you can choose accordingly. The actual details of the set-ups, I will work out and "storyboard." I don't inflict my ideas on the cameraman until we're on the set. He really doesn't want to know too much ahead of time and probably wouldn't listen anyway.

14. SUPERVISION OF CASTING?

I like to keep control of the entire casting; it's very important. The casting director is important, too, because if he's good, he will introduce you to actors you've never heard of before. I don't enjoy casting sessions, because you have to turn down actors. Having been an actor myself once, I feel as though I would like to take on everyone, but I can't.

It's not enjoyable when I have to interview twenty people for a bit part, and turn nineteen of those people down. Choosing the right person, even though the other nineteen actors are talented, is part of putting the mosaic together. That, I do enjoy—getting the whole chemistry of casting correct.

15. PREFERENCE OF ACTING STYLE?

Actors are so different! If I had to make a choice, I would prefer to work with the technician, the highly professional actor. I'm not even sure why I say that myself. I'm not sure where the technician ends and the "method actor" begins.

Once Tony Quinn came to me and expressed how he wanted to play a specific scene. I thought his idea was dreadful, but since I don't believe in being cruel to an actor, I just said, "Tony, I'll have to think about your idea."

He could tell right off that I disliked his suggestion. He said, "There's no reason to get upset, Lee. I'm a bargain basement, and I bring my wares to you so that you can choose."

That, I consider a very great technician. Charles Bronson is another. They all have their tricks and know what works. Marlon Brando is on to himself. He's so clever that I think his entire bag of tricks, the whole of cinema, is likely to bore him; He'll go out there and do outrageous things just not to be bored.

I'd rather work with the technician than the "method actor" who, although he may bring moments of brilliance to your film, will cause you difficulties later. You have to make something that will appeal to audiences, and you have to control your product. I'm not sure if we can afford to have films made by a lot of "method actors."

16. PRECAMERA WORK WITH ACTOR?

I think what happens is that the director (and I can only speak for myself) had a concept of the entire film, and of the character that the star is going to play. What I do is have a meeting with the star and talk the film through with him. Some actors will be very willing to discuss every scene if you'd like, and other actors may be reserved. Perhaps the reserved actors haven't yet zeroed in on the way they will be playing their character. There most be a collaboration between star and director. Very rarely has an actor come on the set and suddenly become a bad surprise. You know what you're getting.

Recently, in a film I made called, *St. Ives* [1976], I called upon Charles Bronson to be more relaxed. Now, I think that one of his greatest assets is his smile. I would ask Charlie to smile, and he would say, "You're treating me like a commodity. You say 'Smile' and I smile." He knew the right moments to smile.

Bronson is so highly professional, that—when you talk to him beforehand—he gives the impression that he knows little about what is going on. However, if I'm disappointed with the way he approaches doing a scene, even before I say a word, Charlie will stop and say, "Let's do that again." It's either my look, or the way I said "Cut" that is an indication that we have to do the scene again.

In brief, with certain actors you discuss the scene fully; with others you don't.

17. IMPORTANCE OF REHEARSALS?

It all depends on who you're working with. Some actors like very meticulous rehearsals, and others don't. My own preference is not to have long rehearsals. If you map everything out, and have very long rehearsals, you can't always be right. If an actor is uncomfortable, then something is wrong. This I found to be true since my earliest days of directing. You must see what has made them uncomfortable and try to correct it.

In my early days, I would become very upset over this, and thought perhaps I was a very bad director. Now, if someone feels uncomfortable, I'm the first to get up and say, "Let's work this out." The majority of actors I'm working with today like the read-through method.

18. ADHERENCE TO SCRIPT?

Never in a thousand years would I insist that an actor adhere meticulously to the script. In fact, when you employ an actor, you hope that he brings creativity to his part. I would be very upset if an actor spoke word for word from the script he was given. It would mean that he has no ideas to offer. You can always improve by rethinking or rephrasing; I'm not afraid of saying that this or that could be better. A director should not set himself up as a dictator. That was the old days of Europe when a director was God Almighty. I would never ask an actor to adhere to the script.

19. EDITING SUPERVISION?

I feel that editing is probably the most important phase of filmmaking. I love to edit my own films, and I can't imagine not editing them. I will give the editor notes on exactly how I see the film cut, right down to even cutting on a word. In the notes, for example, I'll put "No. 33—I'd like close-up of girl, close-up of man, overlay the word 'you.'" My notes are very carefully worked out, that I see the cut frame by frame.

Now I say to my editor, "If you use those notes like a Bible, you're fired." I now expect the editor to improve on the way I see the scene cut. He will cut the scene, then I'll take a look at it, perhaps give it some polish, and we will work together.

Editing is the most enjoyable part of filmmaking for me—those actors cannot talk back to you, and you can take out lines if you see fit and if the actor refused to drop it on the floor.

Too many studio executives think that you can cut a big picture in a couple of weeks: they don't understand that one sequence, say perhaps a battle or adventure scene, can be cut in a lot of different ways. Cutting is something that should be taken more seriously; it seems to be brushed aside by those studio executives. If you have a so-so picture, you can make it a good picture in the editing room; if you have a good picture, it's worth its weight in gold, the time you spend in the editing room.

20. ROLE OF MUSICAL SCORE?

I consider the musical score to be very vital. I think that some musical scores have made average pictures into above average pictures. On the other side of the coin, I think that some bad musical scores have made good pictures seem poor. A director should do everything possible to get a good score for his film.

Now this is something that is really a roulette wheel. You have a musician who will write a score for you; he can't really play you that score; he might be able to play you a theme tune on the piano, and certainly that's what I ask for him to do.

The general presentation only comes along when he has his full orchestra there, and has the whole score orchestrated. That costs a lot of money. You can't get up in the middle of a scoring session and say, "Scrap it; I don't like it." There is a little too much chance in the scoring of a film.

Speaking personally, I have not been over-lucky in the scores I've had for my pictures. I have learned that you should take more care than seems necessary, because it's vital to get a good score.

21. INVOLVEMENT IN PREPARATION OF MUSICAL SCORE?

I am deeply involved; I ask the musician to play whatever he can of the score for me. I go to all the scoring sessions, and sometimes give my advice by saying, "Perhaps you can alter this by making it less dramatic," etc.

22. WHAT SCENES SHOULD HAVE MUSIC?

I do exercise final control on which scenes are to be scored, and which are not. Again, if you have a good musician with you, a good producer, it's a matter of collaboration. I say, "I don't think we need music there", and both the musician and the producer think that music belongs there, I'm not going to be dogmatic. I'll say, "Write it."

Since I have control of my first two previews, I can decide whether to use it or not. After the first two previews, the studio can do what they like with the film.

I do exercise final control on where the music should be. There is never any fixed rule for me where the music should be. Sometimes when you're shooting a scene, you think there might be thunderous music here, but then you see your first rough cut, you find that it's playing better with natural sounds.

You must be very careful about music not competing against the scene; it should be an adjunct; it must help the scene.

23. SOUND EFFECTS?

I always go through the dubbing of my films. The editing, scoring and dubbing are key factors that make or break a film. I would be miserable if could not dub my films. If the picture is simply a comedy of manners, and is simply dialogue—then all you're striving for is a good presentation of the dialogue. Mostly, films are dependent on other sound effects. You shouldn't overload your film with sound effects, but get as many of the best as you can. Dubbing is getting the right effects presented correctly so they enhance your film, and bring some added attraction to the film.

COMMENT

I'm lucky as a director in that when I make a film, I do have my first and second preview cuts. That means that the film is mine right up to the second preview.

There are many directors who are not given this courtesy. I consider it a case today, in the industry, that a director—in the final analysis—can have his picture taken away from him by an unsympathetic studio or an unsympathetic producer. A director can have his picture cut to ribbons and manhandled by people who are uncreative, and who do not know the film process. After all, the picture belongs to the director, it is his concept. He has created what's on the screen, and for a bunch of people who are not fit to stand on a studio floor to ruin his work is a curse we have to live with in this industry.

Fortunately, there are studio bosses like Mike Medavoy, who understand the creativity of the director.

Claude Lelouch

1. BACKGROUND?

I went to high school but during this time I was always very much interested in film. I was making amateur films, my father too: He had a camera to shoot his family, to shoot the dog, to shoot the maid. So I used his camera to make my first amateur film. On my free time, I was taking his camera and I was shooting my friends. So I have always made movies, then little by little I made more and more but I started by doing all the jobs, because in amateur film you have to be electrician, gaffer, cameraman, soundman, etc....In fact I learnt how to make movies maybe like it should be learnt, at least for me. I did not go to any film school. I met people from whom I have learnt certain things. I saw a lot of movies, thousands and thousands. Since I was eight years old, I used to go two or three times a day to the movies until I was 22 or 23. Now I just go once a day.

So I learned how to make movies in the most simple way: amateurism.

2. FIRST FILM JOB?

Once I knew how to shoot with an amateur camera, I bought a 16mm camera. It was in 1956. And I started to make newsreels all over the world on topics that interested me. I wanted to be a newsreel cameraman and because I did not have any professional references, I could not get into TV or into the newsreel business. All the doors were closed for me because I did not have any diploma. So I decided to shoot things that do not exist, then people will buy them; it was a means of making me known. I went through the world, to shoot the big events that were happening here and there. I went alone with my camera and I shot the Budapest events in 1956 [the Soviet invasion of Hungary], the Suez Canal, I went into Moscow by myself, without any authorization. I went to the United States, and I was selling my films by myself, independently. Since the beginning, I have been the producer of my own films because I did not have any professional references to enter the movie business

I have been a newsman for two years, and then I got tired of it very quickly, because news is always the same. It is always people who answer to interviews, it is always war, it is always people that don't like each other, that hate each other. It is always for the same reasons. In fact, when one has filmed around the world for one year, one discovers that the next year it is exactly the same, it is always the same catastrophe, if only a change of location.

So I decided I wanted to tell stories, because the stories I was filming seemed alike. I began to write stories while I was continuing to make newsreels. Then little by little, I became interested in writing, in directing, in everything that makes the business. What I want to say is that I came to directing progressively, nothing was premeditated. At the start, I wanted to be a cameraman.

Then I went to do my military service and I was in the cinematographic department. This allowed me for 28 months to make films for the army. So I was able to learn a lot. In fact, the school I have followed is the film school of the army.

3. YOUR GOAL IN FILMMAKING?

My only aim is to make the people not bored. It is the only one. I don't expect to make them learn anything, neither to tell them anything (to give them any message). I always hated teachers. I have always been a bad pupil because I always hated the people that wanted to learn something. I have always learnt what I wanted. I think that every human being, at a certain time in his existence, has the need to know certain things. It is at the time he needs them that he has to learn them. And I think that there is nothing worse than to have them learn something when you are not in the mood. One learns well what one wants to learn. I am a filmmaker and I don't want to give any lessons to anybody. Even if I knew things they don't know—which is not certain.

But to entertain them, I can do it. Now, if in my entertaining, sometimes, there is something else, if they find some intention from my part, if they learn something, then I am very happy. But at the start it is not my aim. I don't want to play that game. I like to entertain.

For me, the most important thing on earth is pleasure. I think that any human being is running after it. What one calls happiness. What I mean is a certain way of expressing oneself. The only pleasure that I can give to the public is that during two hours, I can entertain them, when it is a success, or I can bore them and then I am very unhappy. I don't have any other ambition. I try to make it as entertaining as possible by putting everything I know in the film.

As soon as you begin to talk about yourself, you stop to make a show. I speak only of the things I know, and the things I know the best are the things that happen to me. I try to have a life as full as possible. Then by having a lot of things happening to me, I have a little to tell about.

But I never start a film by saying "I want to say that." I don't have any political ambition.

4. IN WHAT GENRE DO YOU SEEK A STORY?

I like to find stories that deal with the reality or deal with facts that could happen. All the things that are true touch me very deeply. It comes certainly from my newsreel background. I like what is real. So when I tell stories I try, if it is not true, to make it seem that it was possible.

5. STORY SOURCE? / 6. USE A SCRIPTWRITER OR DO IT YOURSELF?

I prefer scripts written especially for movies. I practically wrote all the scripts of my films, and I try to write for the film. I don't feel like adapting a book or a play. I think that film is rich enough in itself to be able to write especially for it. I write so it will become a film and not a novel or a literary masterpiece. Most of the scripts are very often very pleasing to read and look more like a book than like what could become a film. My scripts are really impossible to read. They are more like notes so I will not loose my memory. I write dialogues, sentences, camera movements, lighting: I take notes of a lot of elements that put together will make a movie. But I don't write my script to be read. First because I don't let people read them. Even when I work for a producer or with a co-producer, I'll tell the story, in their office. If it pleases him, we do the film together. If not, we talk of something else. But I don't want to make him read a script because I think that everybody is a director, and when one is reading a book, one cannot avoid to have images in his mind. When I read *Gone with the Wind,* I cannot help images and put them together as if I were directing it. Then I go to see the movies. If the director is more talented than me, I find that the film is better than the book. If he is less talented I prefer the book.

I think that film is a popular art, that can be very simple, accessible for everyone, which is for me the most important thing. So I work with this idea and no other way.

7. CLOSE COLLABORATION WITH THE SCREENWRITER?

I work alone at the level of the script, I mean at the level of the construction of the drama. At the level of the dialogue, I very often ask people to work with me, because I think that for dialogue it is better to get several viewpoints, but not for the script itself.

When I do dialogue for a film, I ask people that I like very much to come to my house and we begin to speak like we were in the film. We speak for an hour. I record it. Then I usually take the thirty or forty seconds that I think are interesting, when something happens. I do this with different people that look like the characters of my films. I work very often with the actors. But also with anybody. I am fascinated by dialogue and I can do it in many different ways. But the script itself, the story I do it on my own.

8. PREPLAN OR IMPROVISE?

When I begin a film, everything is ready. I have it all written down. Then I improvise. But I would never improvise if everything was not ready before. In my film there is ten percent of improvisation and ninety percent of things that are written from the start.

9. MOST IMPORTANT COMPONENT OF YOUR FILM?

I think that the most important element is the story and the person that will film the story. So the two most important persons on a film are the screenwriter and the director. And when it is the same man, it is for the best. Then there is the cameraman. This is the reason I am my own cameraman. Because I think then that there is a certain unity.

10. WORK WITH A PRODUCER?

For some films, I work with a producer, for others I don't. When the film is easy to produce, I do it myself. When the production is more complex, I take a co-producer. Then I am expecting this producer to be on the set permanently to solve the problems and not to be a businessman, somebody that one never sees and who only makes comments and criticizes the day the film is shown for the first time. A producer must help so that the director is free and happy to work. When I have an easy film like *A Man and a Woman* [*Un Homme et une Femme,* 1966] I produce it myself. In fact there is no general rule. It is the script that makes me decide whether I need a producer or not. When a producer is doing his job well, he is a very important person.

11. USE A DIALOGUE DIRECTOR?

Certainly not. The last thing to do is this. I am against rehearsal. In theatre, it is very important, but not in film. Because in film, spontaneity is a very important thing that one must preserve as much as possible. And rehearsals kill spontaneity. But it is my point of view. Some people can think differently. I like and respect all kinds of films, when they are a success the means used are of no importance. I am telling you my way of trying to succeed sometimes. But it does not mean that everybody must do it the same way.

12. WRITER OR PRODUCER ON THE SET? / 13. WORK CLOSELY WITH THE CAMERAMAN?

I prepare in relation to what is going to happen during the shooting. As I am my own cameraman, I don't rehearse. Each time I arrive on the set, I light it at 360 degrees, so the actors can feel free to move wherever they feel comfortable. At the time of the shooting, most of the crew leave the set. The lighting is good from any angle, and the actors can go anywhere. I try to follow them with the camera. So I don't rehearse any camera movement. My camera will move with the actor. And for each take, I want the actor to move in different positions. This is one of the reasons I am my own cameraman. Because there would not be any possible rehearsal. Everything is prepared in advance (lights, shots), but with a lot of different possibilities, so the actor can be on the set wherever he feels comfortable, where he would like to be in real life. I don't want to disturb my actors with technical considerations. Together I prepare very well everything and I can in two seconds, if an idea arrives on the set, forget everything that has been planned and apply the new idea. The last idea is always the best. I work with one of my assistant cameramen for the lighting. And I have a crew that knows how I like to work. They are always ready. It is like hunting; they wander to where the rabbit is going to appear this time. So they wait and watch. When I shoot, my crew is like a little football team. I mean I have them all around me. I have the ball and they protect me. And we shoot like this. This is the reason why I shoot my films very rapidly, because there is on the set a lot of tension that could not last twenty weeks.

14. SUPERVISION OF CASTING?

I attach importance to every role. There is no secondary role in a film. I choose the main character. For the others, because I don't have the time to go and see all the films and plays, I have an assistant who is doing that all through the year, who spends her life seeing films and plays. And she tells me what she thinks could be interesting. Then I see the actor. I think one should go and see everything that happens.

15. PREFERENCE OF ACTING STYLE?

I want to work with intelligent people. This is most important. Instinctive or professional is the same for me. What is important for me is to work with actors that I respect in real life as men and women. I mean that when they have stopped acting, they are capable of having a personality of their own and with whom one wants to talk, to spend an evening. I like to work with friends, with people I like. So I choose people that are not only actors. Because there are a lot of actors that I would not like as friends. Those, I work with them. All my friends act in my films. For instance, all my crew have a part in my film. My producer sometimes. As soon as I like somebody I think I can direct him. Because to film somebody is everytime a little love story. And one films what one likes. So I try to film people I like. I have discovered that the people I liked were generally talented.

16. PRECAMERA WORK WITH ACTOR?

In general I use actors that are very near the character of the film. There are enough good actors in the world. I am not very fond of synthetic actors. I mean I don't like a woman to play the role of a man. It is exaggerated and "campy," but it is common in the Japanese theatre. I like the actor to resemble the character. Then one has only to adjust everything. I like to talk with the actor for a long time about the script, the story, the location. So he can enter more easily into his character. It happens also that I write while thinking of an actor, which makes things much more easy.

17. IMPORTANCE OF REHEARSALS? / 18. ADHERENCE TO SCRIPT?

It is a kind of democracy of the set. I think that an actor who has a character to play for a certain time has the same rights as the author of the film, because to live for eight weeks in a character can give ideas. And it is stupid to refuse this idea. I always give attention to ideas proposed by the actor and if I can use them, I always do it. What is important for me when an actor plays is not that he says it word for word, but that the idea that I want to transmit can appear through what he is saying. And if he needs more or less time, it is not important. And what is important is that it is working.

19. EDITING SUPERVISION?

I think that while making a film, one can foresee most of the editing. I shoot and think about the editing. But very often during the screening, I realize that some scenes are in the wrong place. I think that the editing is the last step that permits the director to correct what one was not able to see during the shooting. I am not capable of foreseeing everything before the editing process, unlike people like [John] Ford and [Alfred] Hitchcock who say they are. They are much more talented than me. I think that I can foresee a maximum of things for the shooting. But the editing is a rhythm which is dealing with the interest of the public with the story. A story well told must have a certain amount of information which must arrive in a certain order. Thanks to the editing one can change this order to find the best way to tell the story. I think that the editing is a second film. I mean that there is the film that one has foreseen to start, that one can edit the way it has been foreseen or that one can change in the construction. I think it is a second very different step in the making of a movie. Once I have shot my film, I always look to see if there is a better way to edit it than the one I had in mind at the beginning.

20. ROLE OF MUSICAL SCORE?

Music has several advantages. It is an accelerator. I think that a musical effect which arrives at a good time in a film can increase a feeling. Very often with music, one can advance the emotional content, one can prepare the viewer so that when the "denouement" arrives, he is prepared for it. Music has a wonderful power to change the mood. In a film there are several different moods. And music permits a segue from one to another. I am using music especially to change the rhythm and personality of characters. It is this kind of music that I like in film. But I don't like when the music accompanies an image to the extent that it overwhelms it.

21. INVOLVEMENT IN PREPARATION OF MUSICAL SCORE? / 22. WHAT SCENES SHOULD HAVE MUSIC?

I work a lot on it. Usually I record all the music of my film before the shooting. Because it can help to find ideas. So I work very hard with the musician who makes me listen to the melodies he found. I work very hard with the music arranger. In fact, there are no rules. In every film, it is different. But let me say that music is an element over which I take much care. In my last films, there is a little less music than in my previous. Maybe because I succeed better in changing the rhythm without the help of the music. But there is still music. I did not succeed in making a film without music. There are certainly films made without music: [Robert] Bresson's films for instance. But they are not the ones from which one gets much entertainment. Why not use music which is a wonderful emotional element. In a popular art like film, it is stupid not to use any music. What one should be careful of is not to overuse it.

23. SOUND EFFECTS?

The soundtrack of a film is very important. A sound effect can completely change the meaning of an image. A silent image has a meaning. Silent films were asking more of the imagination of the public than talkies. The more an image is realistic, the less it makes the imagination of the public work. It depends on the film. If you want the viewer to work his imagination, you take out the sound. If you don't want his imagination to work, you should put in a lot of sound.

You have a lot of directors that deal only with the imagination of the public. Those that are called intellectual. And it is easy to work the imagination of the public, since you make the problem more complicated. I think after the twenty films I have made that the most difficult thing is to stay simple: it is to be clear. It is to not leave everything in the dark. But this is my own feeling. I don't enjoy a film very much when I don't understand it. I get bored very quickly. I can work my imagination in a film which is clear. I am free to dream. When you have had a film where you have had the elements of the plot, then you can solve the plot. Very often in films, they don't provide all the elements. It is like a teacher who does not give the right elements of the problem to his pupils. There is a good chance the student will not be able to solve the problem. If the problem is well presented, it is already half solved. Then you just have to deal with your intelligence and some references. I am very unhappy when in my film, people say, "I did not understand that." Then I have the feeling I have missed the point. Now when I hide some things, sometimes I want it. Sometimes it happens.

COMMENT

To students the only advice I can give is don't listen too much to your teacher, and go and see as many films as possible. Go also to a maximum of shootings. They are doing visual work. They have to go and see as much as possible about the job.

I will advise them also to do amateur film, because I think it is the best film school because it forces you to know everything. So buy a camera, a little film and have fun with your friends.

Mervyn LeRoy

1. BACKGROUND?

My personal background can be covered quite briefly: I didn't graduate from any school. I had to get out and work hard all my life. In my early days, I worked at every sort of job that I could get—anything a kid of my age could do. Before I went into the movie business, I was a vaudevillian with an act called "LeRoy and Cooper—Two Kids and a Piano." We played that act on the Pantages circuit, on the coast, and Keith Time in the east. We even played Gus Sun Time. We did the act for over two years, all over the United States.

I guess I was really hooked on show business when I was six months old, and my mother let me play the papoose in *The Squaw Man* at the Alcazar Theatre in San Francisco; however, those two years in vaudeville undoubtedly turned me on permanently.

2. FIRST FILM JOB?

My first position in the movie business was in the wardrobe department at the old Lasky Studios on Vine Street in Hollywood. I was folding "North" and "South" uniforms for a picture called *Secret Service* [1919] starring Robert Warwick, and directed by Hugh Ford.

From that job I was transferred to the laboratory. In those days there was no color of any kind in our movies, although I believe it was around that era when a few pictures were made in France. They were photographed in black-and-white, then were hand colored by artists. Working with magnification, they painstakingly colored each frame in a semblance of realism. I recall seeing one such film, and it seemed to me that the color crawled disturbingly like an itch under the skin.

With us it was different. We had to daub the film in a blue wash if we wanted a night effect; a sort of pink wash if we wanted sunlight, and a sort of amber wash if we wanted nightfall. I used to come home at night with one arm blue and one arm amber, and my fingernails pink. Then I was taught to be a second cameraman. Cecil B. DeMille always said that I invented the soft focus, because everything I shot was out of focus.

The steps which led to my directing: I was set as a gagman with director Alfred E. Green at First National Pictures. I hated the name "gagman," and—at least for my own use—changed it to "comedy constructor."

Al Green and Colleen Moore were directly responsible for my future. They really went to the front for me. As a result, I was set to direct Colleen in a movie called *When Irish Eyes Are Smiling* [*Smiling Irish Eyes*, 1929]. Just as I was about to start, John McCormick, Colleen's husband and production head of First National Pictures was fired, and my bright prospects stormed out the front gate with him.

But Colleen hung in there. She fought like a tigress for me, and finally came up winner. She got me set to do a picture called *No Place To Go* [1927], which I made with Lloyd Hughes and Mary Astor.

3. YOUR GOAL IN FILMMAKING?

My aim regarding my films is to make pictures that have a great rooting interest, so that I can be sure that they never become monotonous.

If I read you correctly regarding " . . . an underlying objective," I have no aim other than to entertain—to make honest entertainment through a direct appeal to the deeper emotions—human interest—heart appeal.

I have no political messages to deliver, nor am I interested in proselytizing any cause or creed. I have found it to be an all-consuming job to make movies that are consistently entertaining and stimulating.

4. IN WHAT GENRE DO YOU SEEK A STORY?

As I have always said, "Give me stories with lots of 'heart' and I've got it made." I guess I'm talking about human interest. I have no particular leaning toward a specific period or background, just so the emotional content is there. As for the period, human emotions, basically, have undergone no changes since the beginning of recorded time.

I guess it's an accident that the majority of my films have been laid in modern times. I say "accident" because I'll jump at any good solid entertaining story, regardless of the period in which it plays or, for that matter, regardless of its genre.

5. STORY SOURCE?

I have no choice as to where my story comes from. I have made pictures from stageplays, books and originals.

To name a few of the stageplays from which I have made very successful films: *Too Young To Marry* [1931], from the play *Broken Dishes*, starring Loretta Young and Grant Withers, for First National Pictures, Warner Bros.; *Five Star Final* [1931], with Edward G. Robinson and Aline MacMahon for First National, Warner Bros.; *Three Men On a Horse* [1936], with Joan Blondell, Frank MacHugh, and Sam Levine for Warner Bros.; *Mister Roberts* [1955], with Henry Fonda, Jack Lemmon, James Cagney, and William Powell; *Rose Marie* [1954], with Howard Keel and Kathryn Grayson for M-G-M.

Among others, the novels include: *Little Caesar* [1931], starring Edward G. Robinson, with Douglas Fairbanks, Jr., and Glenda Farrell and written by W. R.

Burnett; *I am a Fugitive From a Chain Gang* [1932], with Paul Muni, Edward Ellis, and Helen Vincent, for Warner Bros. It was written by Robert E. Burns; *Oil For the Lamps of China* [1936], by Alice Teasdale Hobart, with Pat O'Brien and Josephine Hutchinson, for First National; *Anthony Adverse* [1936], with Fredric March, Anita Louise, Olivia de Havilland and Claude Rains for Warner Bros.; *The Wizard of Oz* [1939], by L. Frank Baum (produced by me and directed by the great Victor Fleming) with Judy Garland, Ray Bolger, Bert Lahr, Jack Haley, and Frank Morgan, for M-G-M; *Blossoms In The Dust* [1941], starring Greer Garson and Walter Pidgeon for M-G-M, written by Ralph Wheelwright; and *Quo Vadis* [1951], by Henryk Sienkiewicz, with Robert Taylor and Deborah Kerr, Peter Ustinoff and thousands of others for M-G-M.

Of course there have been a lot of excellent pictures made from "Originals" written directly for the screen. To name a few: *Tugboat Annie* [1933], by Norman Reilly Raine, with Wallace Beery and Marie Dressler, for M-G-M. *Three on a Match* [1932], written by Kubec Glasmon and John Bright, starring Bette Davis, was another.

It all adds up to one thing for me: I'm an audience when I read a story property, touch my heart and you've got me. And time has proven that audiences like the things I like. The point I'm making is that each man (director) must, ultimately, trust his own judgment and instincts implicitly. Everything he does is built on that. The source of the material is relatively unimportant.

The source is never photographed.

6. USE A SCRIPTWRITER OR DO IT YOURSELF?

I do not write scripts myself, so—certainly—I would want to use a screen dramatist. I am not credit-hungry.

Actually, I've always felt it to be a very healthy setup if I could have another point of view on the story to counter-balance my own. I particularly like working with the author of the story. Obviously, he knows more about it than anyone else.

Naturally, every time you go to work on a new story, you try to milk it for every value there is in it. That's your responsibility. But a good and experienced screen dramatist is less apt to try to improve a good story into a flop.

7. CLOSE COLLABORATION WITH THE SCREENWRITER?

Yes, I like to work very closely with the writer, him or her, *not* to be a co-writer, but to polish the script with the writer so I can be sure that the script represents exactly the way I feel that specific story should be told.

After all, when the chips are down, it's the director who's holding the bag, good or bad, when the picture is released. I've never heard anyone in an audience say, "Man, that was a badly written scene." But if you blow it, you can be sure you'll hear a lot of people who'll say, "Man, the director really loused that one up!"

In my opinion, the difference between success and failure lies in the director's unceasing vigilance in every step of the preparation of a picture. Joe E. Lewis said it best, in discussing wealth and poverty: "I've been rich and I've been poor, and believe me, rich is better." The same goes for success and failure.

8. PREPLAN OR IMPROVISE?

Yes, I do love to have everything worked out in the script most of the time. Of course, I do make changes and adjustments if need be, as the changes are indicated when rehearsals start on the set. Often, certain emotional values are attainable through an added bit of business—a move or a simple gesture may prove to be most eloquent.

Actually, I believe in infinite attention to the most minute detail in preparation—every phase of it. Obviously, I must exercise no less detailed concentration when shooting starts.

9. MOST IMPORTANT COMPONENT OF YOUR FILM?

I always say, the play's the thing—and Shakespeare agrees with me. Seriously, it seems pretty obvious that, granting that you have an excellent story, you need a fine adaptation and script from a top screenwriter. Of course, it helps too, if you are working with a Broadway hit play or a best seller novel. Anything that is pre-tested packs a lot of insurance.

After that, the best cast you can get becomes a matter of major importance. (Generally, some people have a star or stars in mind before they start the script.) Not me. I get the script first.

Each of the things you've listed becomes vitally important as you come around to it in its turn.

10. WORK WITH A PRODUCER?

Yes, I have worked with a few producers.

As to what I expect from a producer: first of all, I expect him to have a good creative mind, and to know his business. I mean motion picture business!

Next, I expect him to organize and prepare everything for me—to anticipate the things I'll need and have them ready for me when my need arises. Once I'm shooting, I expect him to keep things off my back—things which could disrupt my concentration at a crucial point in the shooting.

Of course, for the last ten or fifteen years I have directed and produced my own pictures.

11. USE A DIALOGUE DIRECTOR?

No, I do not use a dialogue director. The words are among the most important of the actors' tools. For a professional actor to show up without knowing his lines, is comparable to a carpenter reporting on a job without a hammer and saw.

As for the dialogue director bringing out other values in the lines: if I don't know the values in the lines, I shouldn't be a director.

12. WRITER OR PRODUCER ON THE SET?

I like to have my writer on my set any time, and if he is not actually on the set, I certainly like for him to be available to me, so that I can send for him if I find that a scene does not play as we had anticipated. Note: this can be due to a single actor or actress or to all the actors involved in the particular scene we are working on, or it may be due to a calculated risk—a thing we felt would be great if we could bring it off—only to discover, on the set that it wouldn't play.

As far as the producer goes: naturally, I like to produce and direct *myself,* which I have done with most of my best pictures. However, when I have been working with another producer, I have felt that he did not belong on my set. If something really important came up, making appearance on the set necessary, I expected him to be as brief as possible. The finest producers I have known have been men who felt the same way about it.

13. WORK CLOSELY WITH THE CAMERAMAN?

Yes, I work very closely with my cameraman prior to shooting. Not to determine every camera set-up in advance, certainly, because I believe that you get your best set-up and composition after you have rehearsed the scene thoroughly with the first string players. I never give a camera set-up until I feel that the action is smooth and set.

Of course, the key lighting is planned from the start.

Camera movements too, are subject to final selection, only after rehearsals have indicated clearly where such movements can enhance the dramatic values of a scene, either through pace or impact.

14. SUPERVISION OF CASTING?

I pay particular attention to the casting in all of my pictures, even down to the smallest bit because it is very dangerous if even a bit-part actor speaks his lines without feeling or a full understanding of how that bit relates to the story or the scene of which it is a part.

There is no such thing, in my pictures, as an unimportant part, and that's the way I approach every department of picture making.

15. PREFERENCE OF ACTING STYLE?

In answering this, I can only say, "Give me a pro anything."

If an actor is a real pro, he'll have all the right instincts. He was born with them. With experience, he has developed a definite technique, with or without the knowledge that he has it. Such technique is as vital to the fully founded actor as a technique is to a ballet dancer or a pianist. However, a truly fine technique is completely unobtrusive, and to the lay eye, utterly undiscernible.

Which brings me to the "Method Actor." My views toward the "Method Actor" are, I'm afraid, very bad. I don't like "Method Actors." Actors are born, as I said; not made through some trick method or technique. Most of the "Method Actors" I've seen, regardless of the character they are portraying, give me the feeling that they are all alike—all playing a "Method Actor" giving studied imitations of the characters they are playing. In watching one of them, I am always more conscious of the "Method" than I am of the character he's trying to portray. I could write a book about "Method" actors—but it wouldn't be very flattering.

16. PRECAMERA WORK WITH ACTOR?

I always go over my script, or have a reading with the whole cast before I start a picture. At such readings, in my office or on a sound stage, I like to have the writer with me. The main purpose of such readings is to find out the thinking of the various cast members, each regarding his own part.

Almost invariably, some of them will come up with fresh ideas that are important to me and invaluable to the picture ultimately. If my stars or actors come up with any suggestions, believe me I'm happy to listen to them, and—if they coincide with my concept—you may be sure that I latch onto them.

Naturally, the final decision must be mine. The director is the one who says, "Print it!"

17. IMPORTANCE OF REHEARSALS?

I am definitely one of those directors who believes in long rehearsals. However, when I start shooting, if the first take is perfect and not mechanical, believe me, that's it!

I am never worried about "leaving the player's best performance on the rehearsal-hall floor." I feel that the director, when he says, "Roll the cameras," should feel that he is the audience, and—if a scene does not ring true to him—it will not ring true to an audience. And, believe me, if it's not right, it will be shot over and over again until each performance in the scene equals the best that I feel these actors can give me.

This does not mean that I subscribe to the multiple-take system, where a director figures that if he reshoots a scene long enough, he's bound to come up with a perfect scene. I only mean to imply that I do believe in shooting until I am convinced we have got the best we can get out of that scene.

18. ADHERENCE TO SCRIPT?

Yes, I do insist that an actor adhere to the script. This is not to say that the words are inviolate, because there are some very able actors who could, and often do, come up with a really valuable suggestion. My only concern, in this area, is that a suggested change might effect my storyline. Under no conditions must I allow anything to upset the dramatic structure or a storyline.

19. EDITING SUPERVISION?

First of all, I would not like to have a film editor who did not have a story-mind, and a sharp sense of dramatic values. I also like to have my film editor come around my set frequently, while I am shooting, so that he can get the "feel" of what is going on.

In the evenings, after we have run the dailies (often two or three times), I stay and talk with him about how I feel these scenes should be cut. In the next day or so, he's rough cut the scene that way, and we look at it. I really don't feel there is a rule for working with an editor (there are rarely any serious personality problems) once you and he have reached a complete understanding as to the story and character development, values, involved.

20. ROLE OF MUSICAL SCORE?

Every picture is different. One will make rather extensive demands on music, to stress emotional values. Another picture may be so constituted that its musical requirements are minimal. In comedy dialogue especially, music can be disastrous. As a matter of fact, except as it is used very faintly—remotely—it is dangerous in a dialogue sequence. Of course, every one of the top musicians scoring pictures today is as acutely aware of these hazards as we could possibly be. Of course, the above does not apply to the occasional use of musical trick effects such as are used to italicize a comic value. However, having worked with most of the greats in the musical field, I have learned that, here again as with the fine film editor, once the composer and I have reached a complete understanding as to the dramatic values toward which I am striving, there is very little likelihood that he will do anything but help the picture. If, at a preview, we find that music hurts rather than helps a certain sequence, the composer is usually as quick to see the error as I am. The removal of the offending bit is a simple matter.

21. INVOLVEMENT IN PREPARATION OF MUSICAL SCORE?

Yes, I do like to be involved with the composer who is scoring my picture. Particularly, prior to his starting to compose the score. It is through these early meetings that I am able to make sure the composer and I are viewing everything in the picture eye-to-eye. Once this is achieved, I'm home free.

As concerns my involvement in the recording: I like to attend the recording sessions, because I can visualize the effect this music will have on my film, as it's recorded. However, I am not a musician, and beyond the uplift my enthusiastic approval may provide the composer, my attendance is of no particular value.

22. WHAT SCENES SHOULD HAVE MUSIC?

As I mentioned above, I do not exercise final control immediately: not until I have heard the score previewed, and found out from the preview audience, whether I needed more or less music.

Yes, I do have a fixed rule by which I determine this. That is to listen to the audience reaction. After all, they are the ones who infallibly give you the right answer. As I have indicated before, the fine composers with whom I have been privileged to work have been as sensitive to these audience reactions as I have—possibly even more so.

23. SOUND EFFECTS?

No, we who have directed many silent pictures, and who have been raised in show business as I have, do not overestimate the importance of sound effects. I am convinced that sound effects are as essential to the complete motion picture as any other single element. Particularly this is true in "action" sequences.

As in every other phase of making my films, I certainly do participate in the recording and dubbing of the sound effects. After all, as my father once said, "A fish smells from the head," so—if it's your picture—you'd better stick with it all the way.

Louis Malle

1. BACKGROUND?

I was lucky enough to be able to play with an 8mm camera when I was twelve. Since then, I have never considered any vocation other that the making of film. If film did not exist, I would perhaps be an architect or a musician. Certainly not a writer, because I like to work with a team. I have been at the University for a while (political and economic studies), and I began to work in film professionally at twenty.

2. FIRST FILM JOB

I started as an underwater cameraman with Jacques Cousteau. Cousteau trusted me immediately, and I was responsible for all cinematographic activities of his organization for three years which taught me all the technical aspects of film—photography, editing, sound and music recording, working with the laboratory, etc.

When I left Cousteau, after [The] Silent World [Le Monde du Silence, 1956], which I co-directed with him, and which was a great international success, I was ready; none of the different technicians of a shooting team could fool me. I think that it is necessary for a director to be able, for instance, to discuss the sound equipment with the sound engineer.

After Cousteau, I was an assistant director with Robert Bresson and soon after (at age 24) I begun as a director of a film called Ascenseur Pour L'echafaud [Frankie, 1958].

The only area in which I was incompetent was the direction of actors, which was quite obvious in my first films. Now, directing actors has become my specialty, whereas in the beginning it was my heaviest handicap.

3. YOUR GOAL IN FILMMAKING?

I don't have any preconceived philosophical ideas when I begin a film. Film is for me, a means of investigation, and each film makes me learn something about myself and about the world which surrounds me.

Let's say that each new film is, for me, a way to satisfy my curiosity. I don't particularly try to entertain the public, but to make them individually do a bit of soul-searching with me. For me a good film must be a surprise for the one who does it, as well as for the one who sees it.

4. IN WHAT GENRE DO YOU SEEK A STORY?

I don't look for a story. I try to define what interests me the most at the precise moment where I am. Once the choice of subject is made, the script comes by itself, sometimes very quickly, like *Murmur of the Heart* [*Le Souffle au Coeur,* 1971]—the first draft of which I wrote in four days; or it may come very slowly like *Lacombe Lucien* [1973]. The main idea or theme of the latter was first conceived as happening in a Mexican background, next it was transferred to Algeria during the Colonial War, etc. Sometimes I am unable to treat what I feel as a fiction story; then I make a documentary like *Phantom India* [*L'Inde Fantôme,* 1969]

In short, there is no precise "genre" that I prefer. I am completely eclectic.

5. STORY SOURCE? / 6. USE A SCRIPTWRITER OR DO IT YOURSELF?

Ordinarily I write my own stuff. Occasionally I have started from a book written by somebody else, but it is always about a theme or characters which obsess me at the time.

For instance, I made an adaptation of [*Le*] *Feu Follet* [*The Fire Within,* 1963], a novel by Drieu la Rochelle, which is the story of the last 24 hours of a man who is going to commit suicide. In fact, I was actually writing an original script on this theme when I discovered this novel which seemed to me to be laid in a better background for the film than the one I had planned to use in my own script.

I always choose a subject I want, whether it is in an original script or a book already published. Before beginning to write, I discuss it with Chislain Uhry, for instance, who is my casting director, or with Jean-Claude Carrière, an excellent screenwriter and one of my best friends. Then I work alone, going as far as possible, even to a shooting script unless further discussion becomes necessary.

In such case, I choose my writer—depending upon the topic involved and his compatibility with me. For instance, for *Lacombe Lucien,* I was working with Patrick Modiano, a young novelist who had never lived during the period of the story, but whose imagination had been fascinated by the situation and the characters. It was a happy choice, and the film owes him a lot.

I must add that I once shot a film, the topic of which was not mine, but which was proposed by a producer. The result was total disaster.

7. CLOSE COLLABORATION WITH THE SCREENWRITER? / 8. PREPLAN OR IMPROVISE?

I will never allow a writer to do a script as a solo. I have done that twice, and twice I have found myself holding a script which was totally foreign to me. In both cases I refused to shoot the film.

When I work with a writer, we discuss each scene fully, and we write progressively. If it is a dialogue scene, he writes it alone. If it is an action scene, I do it. Then we reread the text and modify it together.

If I choose to work with somebody, it means that I trust him, and his opinion is as important as mine. We have a detailed discussion covering every aspect, but at the end, I write the shooting script. In my shooting script, there are not a lot of technical indications, I rarely write in a closeup or a dolly shot. I describe just enough so that my technical collaborators can prepare the work and understand what I must do.

I rarely give psychological indications to the actors, because I prefer first to hear their views. I like my script to be as "open" as possible, because I like to improvise during shooting.

9. MOST IMPORTANT COMPONENT OF YOUR FILM?

Each aspect of the film is important. To make a film is like building a house. In the choosing of each artisan who is to work on it, it is vital that the director regard the contribution of each as essential. If the bricklayer is very good, and the plumber very bad, the house will not be habitable.

I lay claim to the fatherhood of my work, and assume full responsibility for the result, but during the shooting, I regard myself more as a supervisor of a collective enterprise to which everybody contributes the best of his talent. I humbly admit that an important part of the qualities of my films emanates from the talent of my team-mates, and that's why I choose them with the utmost care. For instance, I often change my cameraman from film to film, depending on the type of lighting I want to obtain.

Another example: I mistrust stars, and I use them less and less. They are often a threat to the cohesion of the team, and make my job unnecessarily difficult. There are, of course, stars with whom it is very nice to work, but today there are a lot of stars who conduct themselves as *prima donnas.*

The problem is, that in many cases, the star has accepted as *reality,* the mythical image of himself which has been created by his past film roles, and this self-concept is superimposed on every character he is now called on to play. The result is a confusing, undefined characterization.

I had an experience like that with Jean Paul Belmondo in a film called in French *Le Voleur* [1967] and in English, stupidly, *The Thief of Paris.* He was perfect, as to appearance, but the film character did not correspond to his self-image of a sympathetic loafer—popular, amusing—which is the essence of most of the roles he has been playing for ten years. Result: the public had been deceived, and they did not accept him in this unfamiliar character. I am sure that if *Le Voleur* had been his first role in films, critics and the public would have been enthusiastic.

10. WORK WITH A PRODUCER?

I prefer to be my own producer every time it is possible. I don't like producers, anyhow in France, because they don't have the money themselves, and are simply intermediaries between the money and the filmmaker. They are, at best, parasites, and at the worst, pimps.

Of course, I gladly share responsibility for the film with an executive producer, who is a friend, and who is part of the team.

11. USE A DIALOGUE DIRECTOR?

I have never used a dialogue director because the part I enjoy most during shooting is to work with the actors, and I would not like to let someone else do the job.

12. WRITER OR PRODUCER ON THE SET?

The screenwriter comes to visit us sometimes, but to really participate in the shooting, one must be present 24 hours a day, and that is not the job of the writer. Whenever I have a problem, or want to change a scene, I turn to him for assistance if it is necessary.

13. WORK CLOSELY WITH THE CAMERAMAN?

I confer with the cameraman a long time before shooting, and I often like to shoot some test footage in advance.

For my recent film, *Black Moon* [1975], Sven Nykvist and I spent a week with an Arriflex on location to try all kinds of things, like filter, lenses and lighting effects. Then, having made our choices—but not rigid choices—we still modified certain things during the shooting.

Camera movements and set-up I discuss every morning before shooting time. After I have explained to the cameraman how I see the day's work.

14. SUPERVISION OF CASTING?

The casting of a film is an essential part of my work, and I deal with it personally until the smallest part is set. If you make an error in casting, you can be the best director in the world, but the mistake will still be evident on the screen.

That is why on the *Lacombe Lucien* film, for instance, I spent three months doing the casting which was composed only of amateurs or actors who had never worked in film before. I was very proud of the whole cast, with a couple of exceptions, but it was an enormous job. We actually shot miles of video tape.

15. PREFERENCE OF ACTING STYLE?

I don't like "technical" actors. They are, of course, easier to work with, but they are completely predictable, and I prefer actors who surprise me. When I am in front of a too technical actor, I try very often to break his technique, so that he is forced to open himself—to denude himself in front of the camera, instead of hiding himself behind a technique. For instance, at times I even change his dialogue at the last minute.

About "method" acting: I will say that it is a good preparation by itself, a discipline which can be very useful, but I don't like it to become a mystique, or only technique. One thing is certain: the "method" has a very disastrous effect on mediocre actors! I really prefer the instinctive actors.

Then there are those actors who do not automatically assume a character, but who constantly present themselves exactly as they are personally—often completely unaware of it. Obviously, one must help these people a lot more than the others.

16. PRECAMERA WORK WITH ACTOR?

I don't have any rigid technique for preparing an actor for his role. Some are so anxious that they need to be reassured and the discussions often produce fresh ideas which prove to be valuable when we start shooting.

Other people prefer to arrive at shooting time with a sort of virginity, thinking that everything goes better within the mood of the moment and with mutual trust between actor and director.

(Jeanne Moreau is like this: she does not learn her lines in advance, as she feels that to do so must wear out the spontaneity.)

17. IMPORTANCE OF REHEARSALS?

Regarding rehearsals: I like to read the script with my actors several times before shooting to study their reactions and to uncover the difficulties and to find out if a scene or a line works. This gives me an opportunity to make changes if they are necessary. This is comparable to trying on a coat: the actor puts on his character and one sees immediately the things that tend to make him uncomfortable—the things one must adjust.

Before the shooting of *Murmur of the Heart,* while rehearsing with the boys who played the three brothers, I modified a lot of the lines with their collaboration. What I had written—memories of my own childhood—were often expressed in words that were difficult for the boys, and they usually had substitute words to offer which expressed the thought and felt more normal to them.

18. ADHERENCE TO SCRIPT?

The actor is the most important thing in a motion picture. Actors are on the film, not directors. When you say "action" they are alone in front of the camera; that is why many are so nervous and self-conscious. Consequently, we must like them and help them.

I am always ready to change a light, the camera movement or line, if I feel that I can help the actor to be more relaxed, and, therefore, better in the scene. It is unimportant to me if an actor changes the text, and I definitely like it if they improvise, on the condition, of course, that they stay in the mood of the film, and that their interpretation enriches the change.

Of course, it does not always work that way, and one must be careful. Actors very often are mistaken as to what they are projecting. They sometimes try to color a character in a way that satisfies their ego, but which is out of character for the film.

I don't like the too intellectual approach to an actor's work. I believe that an actor has more to say with his body, his bearing, and his facial expression than with his intellect.

19. EDITING SUPERVISION?

I don't supervise the editing of my films. I do it entirely with Suzanne Baran, my editor, who is my oldest and closest collaborator, beside me, in front of a moviola.

Each cut is the result of thoughtful analysis and discussion. I don't like to edit during shooting. I look at my rushes only to be sure that I have covered everything. We make a first choice, and Suzanne edits a rough cut to see if there are any problems. I don't even look at any of the assembled stuff until shooting is completed. At that time we remake final choices after having reviewed all of the stuff. This provides us with our first full view of the film.

The editing is my passion. It is a time when one can experiment the most—where one can really think, and where one can analyze every aspect of the film. One can look forty times at an actor executing a movement, and try to understand why this movement irritates you, and what he should have done or said that he did not do. During the shooting, everything goes very quickly, and it is better to trust instinct. The editing is the time for reflection, and also the time for the truth. It is during the editing that one really learns to make film, but one learns seriously only by editing one's own film.

I saw India better during the editing of _Phantom India_ than during the shooting. In editing, one analyzes his work thoroughly. It is sometimes discouraging, because it is too late to shoot anything else. But, by the time a film is ready for sound-mixing, I can say with Suzanne that "We have exhausted the field of the possible," as André Gide expressed it.

Some fine directors, like Luis Buñuel, whom I admire greatly, do not interest themselves in the editing. Buñuel shoots in a definitive way, so that nothing can be changed afterward. The editing of a Buñuel film takes one week. I have not yet progressed to that point, but I shall never cease trying.

The first week of shooting I make several takes of each set-up, each at a different rhythm. This way, the first day's rushes determine the tempo.

20. ROLE OF MUSICAL SCORE? / 21. INVOLVEMENT IN PREPARATION OF MUSICAL SCORE? / 22. WHAT SCENES SHOULD HAVE MUSIC?

The more I progress, the less I am inclined to want to compensate for the weakness of the drama. Music is often used to give rhythm where there is not enough emotion. I sincerely believe that a film perfectly directed and acted, does not need any music, unless it is integrated in the story.

In the first sequence of *Murmur of the Heart* one sees a young boy—the hero of the film—stealing a record in a shop—a record of the great jazzman Charlie Parker. The boy is very fond of music, and one hears Charlie Parker on the sound track of the film four or five times, which is a natural consequence of the situation in the script.

I rarely ask for original music. On the occasions when I have made that request, I have not been satisfied with the result. On the other hand, when I write a script, I listen to a lot of mood music which reflects itself in the work I am doing. Naturally, after the shooting is completed, I use the same music as an integral part of the film. This was the case with the sextet of Brahms for *The Lovers* [*Les Amants,* 1958], or the "Gnossiennes" of Erik Satie for *Le Feu Follet* [*The Fire Within,* 1953].

In *Black Moon,* the only music used was "Tristan et Isolde" by Richard Wagner, which the protagonists sing at different moments in the film. I anticipated one other musical accompaniment, percussion to intervene under formal sequences. However, repetition of the mixture persuaded me that the percussion was unnecessary, so I decided to omit it.

As for music, and in other things, I consult specialists, but always I make the final decisions. I consider it part of my work, and I do it with pleasure because of the great role music has played in my life.

23. SOUND EFFECTS?

I attach great importance to sound effects, considering them highly useful in substituting for music.

In *Black Moon* we totally reconstructed the soundtrack studying the film. We combined a series of special sounds exactly as if we were putting together a musical score. To accomplish that, the question was doing an elaborate job in which I collaborated with the sound engineer. We tried a number of effects before choosing one which satisfied us completely.

Lewis Milestone

1. BACKGROUND?

I had all sorts of jobs unrelated to the motion picture business; yet incidents that happened on every job contributed very materially to the future. I constantly review everything I've done, and very often I've recalled a situation or a piece of business which, dramatized, would fill the bill.

2. FIRST FILM JOB?

Assistant cutter with J.D. Hampton, an independent producer. As a New Yorker, bred if not born, I took a taxicab to the studio every morning. This resulted in a mixture of awe, bewilderment and annoyance among my fellow workers, who were strictly streetcar-oriented in Los Angeles in those days.

"Who does this guy think he is—coming to work in a taxicab?"

"Aw, he's just an assistant cutter."

"Well, how the hell can he afford a taxicab every day?"

That was the dialogue.

It wasn't long before the head cutter called me on the carpet. "Look," he said, "you're getting a quick twenty bucks a week, yet you arrive in a taxi every morning. You're a big puzzle that everybody's trying to solve—and that takes up too much time. So—if you want this job—don't come to work in a cab."

"I don't buy that," I said. "If I want to ride in a taxicab, you're not going to tell me I can't do it."

That was one battle I lost with no trouble at all.

But, the next day, my lucky star saved me. Henry King stepped out on the porch where the assistants usually hung around for their cigarette break. He spotted me. "I've heard a lot about you, and you intrigue me very much. Would you like to work with me?" he asked.

"Yes. I'd like to work with you," I said.

He smiled. "Okay," he said. "I'll fix it with the front office."

And that's the way I started. Henry King was the first man to show me how to break down film for assembly, and to patch film and so forth. Everything he had to give, I took, with great appreciation. Assisting Henry was my first significant step.

3. YOUR GOAL IN FILMMAKING?

If I find a story, or an idea for one, that I feel will make a good picture, and if it contains a "message" with which I agree, that fact will not only NOT deter me from making it, but could very easily become the main reason for making.

4. IN WHAT GENRE DO YOU SEEK A STORY?

I never look for a story in any particular genre. If you start looking for a specific type story, you're in trouble, because you've already set up a lot of obstacles for yourself. If I tell a literary agent that I'm looking for a story, he will know what type of story I would like.

There have been occasions when I've had only a very slender idea to start with. For example, *Two Arabian Knights* [1927], for which I won my first Academy Award. The magazine story on which it was based contained one good situation: two men trying to break out of a German military prison. They busted out, and the rest of the picture dealt with their adventures on the road to God-Knows-Where.

Now, *A Walk in the Sun* [1946], was about an Army outfit that lost its lieutenant, then its sergeant. It was really leaderless when a buck private took over. Their mission was to take "A WALK IN THE SUN" six miles down the road to reconnoiter a certain farmhouse. If it was not held by the enemy, they were to occupy it and hold it. That was the story. Of course, the drama came out of what happened on the way, and how the buck private leader met each situation. The idea you walked out with, after seeing the picture, was that any man in the outfit could have taken over just as successfully as our buck private did. So, how are you going to lick a multiheaded outfit?

The Mack Sennett Comedy companies had a unique way of finding stories. They'd go to Westlake Park (now MacArthur Park) and sit on a bench until one of them came up with an idea, usually triggered by some little incident that happened in the park a minute ago. The director would say, "That's a pretty good idea. We'll start with that." From then on, they'd keep going until someone said. "Hey! We've got enough—more than enough—for a two-reeler."

Automatically, they'd go into the chase.

5. STORY SOURCE?

I have no preference among the things you listed. I don't care *where* a story comes from, if it has an idea in it, and the idea appeals to me, I do it. I remember an instance: I was under contract to Paramount. I recall sitting in the office of Ernst Lubitsch, then head of the studio.

I said, "Ernst, I've been here a long time without an assignment, and you've been paying me a lot of money. The next thing you know, somebody is going to look at the total they've paid me, and find out that, if I start right now, I'll still be the most expensive director they've had in a long time, and that's no good for either of us. So what about an assignment?"

He sighed. "I wish I had one. I don't even have an assignment for myself."

While he was talking I noticed a big, fat manuscript on his desk in front of him. From my angle it was upside down, so I couldn't read the title. Finally, in desperation, I pointed at it and said, "What about that thing? Its thickness intrigues me."

He shrugged and said wearily, "You don't want that. It's headed for the pulps."

I said, "I don't care where it's headed. Look, Ernst, you make one type of picture and I make another, so let me decide if there's anything in this bulky story I can use."

He sighed, "Okay. But I'm warning you, it's junk! But you read it, and good luck to you."

So I took it, and read it. The name of this thing was *The General Died at Dawn* [1936]. It was pulp all right. It had enough incidents for twenty pictures, yet I felt the manuscript lacked something. "A message!" an inner voice insisted. "The kind of dramatic message that Clifford Odets would write. Get Clifford Odets," the voice insisted. "Get Odets."

By that time I had been assigned to a producer by the name of William Le Baron, a wonderful guy; I liked him very much. I laid out my story plan to him: "The idea is, we put two new characters in it. One will be a sympathetic Joe like Gary Cooper, and he'll represent Democracy. The other guy is a General, a Fascist, the kind of guy that springs up with a military junta now all over the world."

Le Baron asked, "Is this all original?"

I told him, "The two characters are original, but we'll need this pulp material. It's loaded with good incidents."

He said, "All right. Got a writer in mind?"

I was ready for that one. "I'd like to have Clifford Odets. I don't know him, but I saw two of his plays in New York, and he's what I need."

Le Baron considered, then nodded, "Okay."

I asked the studio to locate Odets for me, but the next day I ran into him at a party in Beverly Hills. After I had introduced myself, I told him that if he had come to Hollywood to work, I had a story I would like him to read. "I have a lot of apologies for some of the material in it," I admitted, "but I have an idea that will make it worth your while to read it, so plow through it, then call me."

He spent that night reading it.

The next day I had a studio limousine pick up Odets and bring him to the studio. I asked him what he thought of the material.

He replied, "Well, as you said, it's pulp, but it's crammed with good incidents. But what's this big idea of yours?"

I told him about the lead representing Democracy. He was listening, so I went on, "Opposing him will be the military guy—a Chinese warlord." I looked at him questioningly.

He didn't keep me in suspense, "I'm nuts about it!" he announced.

Next morning, early, I was in Le Baron's office. "Bill, we're in luck. My writer loves it; we're going to have a helluva script!

Deadpan, Bill asked, "Who is this guy again?"

I repeated Odets' name.

Bill said, "But you said he'd never written a script."

I answered cold and flat, "Right. But he's written a lot of Broadway plays, and I sure will help him with motion picture technique."

I got my writer. The result was *The General Died at Dawn.*

6. USE A SCRIPTWRITER OR DO IT YOURSELF?

I never work without a writer. I get the best writer I can lay my hands on. The thing I insist on is that he accept me as a collaborator. I never ask for credit.

After the writer has gotten over the fact that I am a director, I say politely, "Look, you'll find me very useful. Now, if you find that I am of no use at all, then two things can happen: either I fire you and get myself another writer, or you get used to me and learn to appreciate me."

So, I offer them a choice, and most of them wind up wondering why they ever objected to working with me.

I hate it when a producer says, "Hell, he's a director, let him direct, and a writer should write."

7. CLOSE COLLABORATION WITH THE SCREENWRITER?

That is a very important point. Now, how much time does he take to write this thing? He wants to express all his ideas, then let me have a look at it.

Very often, the time he spends by himself is a total loss. In the meantime, I've spent weeks—only to come up empty.

Well, after this has happened to you a few times, you try to explain to a new writer, way up front, that you can't afford to give him this time alone, because you have eighteen people sitting on your neck, demanding, "When are you gonna start *shooting?*"

So, when a writer says to you, "Look. I'll call you when the script is finished," duck!

8. PREPLAN OR IMPROVISE?

Improvisation is wonderful, but in my opinion, that should be done only after you've fortified yourself with a solid script you are ready to shoot. If you are not solidly prepared, and an emergency hits you, it's a day lost, because you don't know where to put the camera or what to tell the actors.

Rehearsals were created for one reason: during rehearsals you learn everything you need to now about your scene. Often, even in the best prepared script, there's a bit here, or a line there that needs some work. *That's the time of improvisation.*

I just can't buy the idea that rehearsals rob you of spontaneity, inspiration or whatever. Through rehearsal, running it over and over, you give yourself, the actors, everyone a chance to catch something that's very valuable. If you don't probe deeply, you're liable to wind up with a surface thing. However, you'll never dig down deep without finding something that you could only discover through painful work.

Of course, no amount of preplanning can supplant that, but it can provide a solid launch-pad from which your improvisation can be airborne most effectively.

9. MOST IMPORTANT COMPONENT OF YOUR FILM?

All the things you're enumerated are vitally important. I don't think any one of them is more important than the next. They will all come out in front, each in its own time; when you are constructing a script, or when you are constructing the production.

The story, of course, is the backbone of the whole thing....what you start with. If the story's not good, you'd better not start.

10. WORK WITH A PRODUCER?

If I'm offered a story to do, and I like it, I say, "I think I can live with it." My next question is, "Who's the producer? Can I live with *him?*"

So, you're told who's going to be the producer, and—unless you have serious objections—you accept it.

Once you're set, the producer has you sit in on everything. It's a series of conferences, and pretty soon you learn to live with the guy.

However, much later in my career, I didn't have any producers. It was stated from the beginning that I would produce and direct.

11. USE A DIALOGUE DIRECTOR?

I have used a dialogue director on several occasions. My reason for using one has always been the same: that I have run across some exceptionally bright young man who, I was convinced, really had something special. I knew I wanted this particular character to be my personal assistant, so that I could talk with him, and he'd be my sounding-board.

Now, because of the complexity of major studio business structure, it's a big production to get this guy on salary—what do you tell the management about why you need him? They've already given you a complete crew, and now you come along and want this Joe Blow. Then, even if you get the deal past the production office, which is unlikely because they never heard of a guy being used as a sounding-board, you'll still never get past the guilds and unions.

If, in the first place, you'd say, "Dialogue director," you'd have been home free. They still wouldn't have understood, but it's a nondescript profession, and this guy is a faceless character; therefore you can use him.

12. WRITER OR PRODUCER ON THE SET?

That's a question with which I am very familiar. A lot of writers ask me if I'd like to have them on my set while I'm shooting, in case I should need a line change or something.

They always add, "Besides, it will help me if I'm allowed to come. I'll get the idea of how pictures are made, and it'll be a big help for me on my next script."

I have a pat answer: "You're always welcome on my set, and I'm flattered that you feel you can learn something there, but I want to warn you that when you do that, you must come in the morning when we start shooting, and you don't leave until we finish. Nine to six are the hours, and there's no pay. The management would never understand why they had to pay you to stand around and learn something."

As I said, the request comes very often from writers. Usually they show up once, then they get lost.

As for producers: there's an anecdote involving Jack Ford which illustrates how most directors feel about producer visitors: Jack was doing a picture for 20th Century-Fox. Darryl Zanuck was Mr. Big at the studio at that time.

One day, the assistant director came up to Jack, just as he was about to make a take. The A.D. announced, "Mr. Zanuck is outside, and wants to know if it's all right for him to come in."

Jack said, "Of course. Show him in."

Zanuck came in and Jack, personally, placed a chair for The Boss beside his own. Jack treated him as a *very* VIP guest. They chewed the rag for quite a while about one thing and another—until Zanuck became conscious of the expenditure of time. He said, "Jack, I'm sorry, but aren't you shooting?"

Jack said, "How can I? You're my guest and I can't be rude to you. I certainly can't start shooting a scene while you're still here."

Zanuck jumped to his feet, snapping, "I'm gone!"

He didn't even get out of earshot before Jack was shooting. Darryl never again paid a visit to Jack's set.

13. WORK CLOSELY WITH THE CAMERAMAN?

I don't really believe in extemporizing in advance on anything. I believe the more preparation before shooting, the better. I can't emphasize that too much!

I think I can show you an example of how strongly I feel on this point by telling you how we prepared *Of Mice and Men* [1940]. My cameraman was Norbert Brodine and Duncan Mansfield was my film editor. Our location was the Agoura Ranch. I showed Brodine every intended setup. After I had laid out the whole thing with Brodine, Duncan followed me around the location with a sketch artist, who illustrated in sketches everything we had worked out. After the sketches were complete, I walked Brodine through again, showing him the drawing for each setup, and asking the same question for each: "What time do you want to shoot this one? What's the best light?"

He'd tell me, "We should shoot that particular scene the first thing in the morning." About another, he might say, "Early afternoon—right after lunch for that one."

We wrote down the ideal light time for every scene in the book, so that my assistant could lay out each day's work ahead, when we started shooting. He was able to say, "I think you can shoot twenty scenes today." And that's the way we shot it.

Because everyone knew exactly what he was supposed to do, I never had to answer a question. All the answers were on that sketch-board, and it was like a silent drill: all I had to do was to concentrate on the performances.

There's another thing I've done on my pictures, involving preplanning with my cameraman. We go on a set as soon as it's available. We have some extra actors, present. We hand them a script and tell them the dialogue runs from there to there, and have them walk through it. This is a great help in predetermining lighting problems and camera movements, before we bring in the first-string actors.

14. SUPERVISION OF CASTING?

I supervise the casting of my films as closely as possible, and it pays off, and saves us a lot of time and wear and tear in the long run. If you're forced to stop shooting at any time on a picture because some "bit" actor can't cut it, you've got a lot of expensive problems on your hands.

Even though I do exercise this rigid control right down to the smallest bits, the casting director has a list of suggestions. Naturally, I take advantage of any good suggestion, whenever or wherever I receive it, be it from a propman, a grip, an electrician, an actor, a cameraman...or a casting director!

If the idea is right, then—regardless of who suggested it—I grab it.

15. PREFERENCE OF ACTING STYLE?

To answer a question like that, I can only say, "The test of the pudding is in the eating." It's really the individual and his approach to his craft that's important.

Very often you don't know whether a particular actor is going to prove to be "instinctive" or decidedly a technician. I know some marvelous actors, and there's one particular situation I've experienced with many of them.

Let's say I've just done a scene with one of these guys, and he's done it wonderfully, but—for some reason—someone blows a line. Let's never forget that there are other actors in the scene with him.

Now, I wouldn't put it past any actor, who didn't like the way he was coming off in a scene, to blow his lines hoping that maybe in the next take the other guy isn't going to be so good. He believes that would be better for him.

I recall a scene between Marlon Brando and Trevor Howard. Brando didn't like the way it was going, so he'd blow his dialogue, maybe even on the last speech in the scene. So we had to do the scene over—again and again and again. I'll bet we had to do that scene a hundred times, and it was always the same.

Finally, Brando had to give up, and really play the scene, and that take was exactly like Take Number One, except that it played straight through the way it should. You see, Brando was up against a champ. Trevor Howard is a consummate "technician," but he is also magnificently "instinctive."

As for the "Method Actor," I've never met a good actor who didn't have a method—*his own method!* They all have some kind of a method, but when some member of a "select group" tells you proudly, that—to him—the Stanislavsky method is the Holy Bible, that defeats the whole purpose right there. When an actor delivers a method rather than a characterization, he's in deep trouble.

16. PRECAMERA WORK WITH ACTOR?

Let's review the first contact you have with that actor; when you're casting, and his agent brings him in, and you have to tell him something about the part to find out if he wants to do it. Naturally, you describe the character. Of course, you're doing a selling job, because you think this guy might be great for the part, so you extend yourself so he'll say "Yes."

Actually, all the time you've been selling him, you're throwing your concept of the character at him, so that he's bound to latch onto what you see in it.

Now, you don't make any appointments with him for the specific purpose of discussing the part in depth, but every time you contact the man—when he comes in to discuss wardrobe—you discuss everything else besides wardrobe, always slanting everything toward that character.

He may say, "Why do I wear these boots?"

That is the type of question you've been hoping for. You answer, "Well, I think the guy would wear them....would dress like that." Then, in explaining why you feel that way, you're once more giving him a pretty complete picture of the character as you see it.

Every time he comes in there is more general discussion of the character, and very soon he's asking a lot of questions. By that time, you're actually telling him a lot more about your concept than he realizes. In many instances there have been such huddles when the guy would, unconsciously, play back to me something I'd fed to him earlier.

17. IMPORTANCE OF REHEARSALS ?

I don't believe there is any rule for this. I believe that any director who knows his business will rehearse a scene over and over, as long as he feels that there is something in the way his people are doing a scene that can be improved.

Certainly rehearsals are necessary—full rehearsals. During rehearsals, the actors find interesting bits of business; they come to understand what they're doing; each actor begins to make the dialogue his own. The only way he can really do that is by doing the words over and over again with the other people in the scene. Then there comes a time when, if you were to ask him, "Is that line in the script, or is it your own?" he wouldn't be able to answer. That's when you're beginning to cook right.

I recall an anecdote that will point up the value of rehearsals—lots of them. It concerns that magnificent actor, Pat O'Brien. I saw Pat on the stage, giving a performance, and *what* a performance!

In one spot, he had a very important and sentimental speech. He delivered that speech in a flat, dead voice—completely unemotional. It tore the audience apart.

I couldn't wait to get backstage with the big question: "Where did you get the idea of using that terrible voice?"

"In rehearsals. Where else? Worked okay, didn't it?"

I nodded, and he went on, "Well, you know I'm an emotional guy."

I gave him the Christmas Tiger.

Pat grinned. "Racial, I guess. Anyway, during rehearsals I got so involved with this character that I'd break up every time I got near that speech. I'd crack up long before the emotional impact could possible reach an audience. I was a dead duck. I knew my only out was to de-dramatize that speech. That God-awful voice was my solution. I'd have loused up that scene if I hadn't found that answer—I wouldn't have been able to play that scene at all."

A propos of that: I'm reminded of the many times one of the new actors has popped up with a tragic pan, after a take or a rehearsal, and said, "I didn't feel it!"

My answer is always the same: "Fine. Let's keep it that way. Just make me feel it—make the audience feel it."

18. ADHERENCE TO SCRIPT?

My answer to this would depend on the piece we were doing. If you were doing a Shakespearian play, I don't think you'd want the actors to fool around with the dialogue. You'll sometimes get the argument: what's the difference if you use this word or that word? The difference is that if Shakespeare had wanted another word, he'd have used it.

It doesn't necessarily have to be Shakespeare. Any dialogue that comes from a successful Broadway or London West End play has been reviewed and approved by everybody.

On the other hand if it's an "original" written specifically for the screen, you watch and listen very carefully when you take the scene. If the writer wrote the scene well and it plays right, but the script-girl comes up to you and says, "He changed two or three words," and she shows you what the words were, you weigh it carefully. If you are convinced that the change has in no way altered the intent or mood of the scene, there's no sense in your doing it over.

If, however, your scene doesn't play well on that first take, you probably say something like, "Once more, please. And this time, let's try it the way the author wrote it."

19. EDITING SUPERVISION?

Of course, you're referring to John Ford. His attitude about not looking at his stuff depended on conditions—for and with whom he was making a picture.

I asked him about that many times, and his answer was always the same: "Look—you've got a producer, and he has the right to pick the 'takes.' So, if he picks one and you pick another, he'll use the one he picked. Why should I waste time looking at the damned thing?"

But when Jack was making a picture with someone whom he liked and with whom he had a harmonious relationship—where he had complete freedom—he was present at the rushes as often as anyone else.

As for the extent to which I supervise the cutting: to a great extent, I "camera-cut." I wouldn't know how to shoot a picture if I didn't know how the different angles would fit together. People who don't have our kind of training do it with lots of extra angles for "protection," but that's very costly.

Personally, I don't trust the people in whose hands the film may wind up. The more film I give them, the more chance they have to screw it up. I've often had producers say, "You don't give me enough film to play with."

My answer has been, "Oh, you want to play with the film? I can buy you toys that are much more amusing to play with." I continue, "Doing it my way, you don't have much film to throw away. I shoot what I think you need. When you go to a store and buy a jigsaw picture puzzle, they give you a box full of little pieces. Now—do you ask them to give you a lot of extra pieces to 'play with?'" That stops them.

20. ROLE OF MUSICAL SCORE?

It depends so much on the particular show you're doing. In some pictures, music is essential to underline emotional or dramatic values. This applies particularly to melodramatic or sentimental type stories. Also, a great deal depends on the man who is doing the scoring. You run the picture with him, then listen to what he has to say. Those first reactions are important. This man has ideas or you wouldn't have him. If he impresses you as being not only a fine musician, but a man who knows exactly what he's talking about, you relax because you know your scoring is in good hands. This guy just looked at your picture, and you liked his response to it, so you tell him any ideas you've got about it, and let him translate them into musical terms. From then on, he's got the ball.

21. INVOLVEMENT IN PREPARATION OF MUSICAL SCORE?

I am not a musician, consequently I do not become "deeply involved" in the preparation of the score. I don't have any preconceived notions about these things, but I do make very sure that the composer sees the same values in every scene in the picture exactly as I see them—the precise points to accent and emphasize. How he gets the effect he is after, is a complete mystery to me, but when I hear the score and visualize each scene for which it was intended, I know damned well whether it does its job or not.

Some of our directors are very knowledgeable along musical lines: there's Rouben Mamoulian with a fine operatic background, and Vincente Minnelli, with his musical comedy know-how.

Despite the danger of being redundant, however, I must repeat: if you don't really know music, you'd better feel your way with great caution in anything involving it.

22. WHAT SCENES SHOULD HAVE MUSIC?

In so far as it is possible, I do exercise final control as to which scenes are to be played *a cappella.* Unfortunately, this is not always feasible. Then, too, there are occasions when—in spite of my most diligent efforts—things seem to contrive to get of hand. Let me illustrate that.

In *Of Mice and Men,* there was this one scene in which the old man had to shoot his dog. That dog meant everything in the world to the old man, and everybody knew it. So when he walked the dog out, the guys left behind tried hard to make conversation, but it was no good—nothing worked—they were all waiting for the sound of that shot.

There must not be any music in that scene!

Well, when the music department got hold of the thing, they slipped in a track that had been written for the spot, but with instructions that it was *not* to be used, except as "protection," if—at a preview—the scene failed to play.

That "protection" cost us very dearly, because somebody made a mistake and put it in, and it was in all the release prints before I knew about it. To take it out would have been prohibitively expensive.

We never did get rid of it. It was a stupid mistake, see? Nobody wanted to do it, but it slipped in. It just killed one of the best suspense moments in the show.

Of course, music in comedy is infinitely more dangerous than in other types of entertainment. Eighty percent of the time music kills comedy dialogue. In one of the major studios here, the studio head was crazy for music, and you couldn't get it loud enough to please him. He murdered a lot of comedies that way.

23. SOUND EFFECTS?

In my opinion, it is impossible to overestimate the importance of judiciously used sound effects, not only in "action" films, but in every type of picture.

An example: in a room where music and raucous laughter have filled the air, the abrupt cessation of all sound can deliver a startlingly dramatic effect.

Whether or not we've ever made silent pictures, all directors have seen chases projected without the sound track. By comparison with the sound-and-sight projection of the same chase, the silent running is flat, unexciting and wholly unreal.

The same can be said of rough-and-tumble fighting or an armed combat sequence, a storm at sea, or in desert wilderness, or the cry of a wolf on a silent, frozen night.

Naturally, as in every other phase of my business, I supervise the sound-dubbing very rigidly.

Satyajit Ray

1. BACKGROUND?

Before I took up filmmaking, I was, for twelve years, a graphic designer with a British-owned advertising agency. I was also, at the same time, designing book jackets and doing illustrations and typography for an Indian publisher.

2. FIRST FILM JOB?

I still had my advertising job when I scripted and directed my first feature film, *Pather Panchali* [1955]. The film was shot largely on weekends and holidays, and took two-and-a-half years to complete. I worked with an amateur cast and a 22-year-old cameraman who had never handled a movie camera before. My art director had assisted Eugene Lourie on Renior's *The River,* and my editor had worked on a couple of independent assignments after serving as an assistant over a number of years.

Even as an advertising man I had become seriously interested in movies. I founded the first film club in Calcutta (and one of the first in India) for the study of the cinema as an art form. I also started writing screenplays as a pastime.

In 1950, half a dozen meetings with Jean Renoir when he came to Calcutta to shoot *The River* left a deep impression on me. In 1951, I wrote the first treatment of *Pather Panchali.* For a whole year, I tried unsuccessfully to find a producer for it. Eventually, we decided to start shooting with our own small funds, buying ten reels of Kodak Plus X negative, and hiring an old Mitchell camera!

It took us a whole year to produce a rough cut of about four reels; but still, no backers. The project was then abandoned. Eventually the Government of West Bengal took over the film and provided the money to complete it.

After the international success of *Pather Panchali,* I gave up advertising and took up filmmaking as a fulltime profession.

3. YOUR GOAL IN FILMMAKING? / 4. IN WHAT GENRE DO YOU SEEK A STORY?

My primary aim in making a film is self-expression, but I have realized more and more that a film lives and breathes only in the presence of an audience. Full satisfaction is only possible when there is adequate response from a discerning audience.

I had to contend with a relatively backward audience in India when I started. But I avoided trying to cater to the lowest common denominator. Some of my early films were better received abroad than at home. But, over the years, due largely to the spread of the film society movement, a more discerning audience has emerged in India; an audience that takes the cinema seriously and is not daunted by the off-beat.

Apart from the Trilogy [*Pather Panchali, Aparajito,* 1956], and *The World of Apu* [1959]—which I now regard as a single film—I have tried to avoid repeating myself thematically and stylistically. I have tried various genres: comedy, satire, fantasy, adventure, intimate psychological drama. I have dealt with our feudal past, with rural poverty, as well as with the problems of the urban middle class.

In the process of making films, I have come to know my country and my people better. I have tried to discover universal traits in human behavior, emotions and relationships within the orbit of my own culture and society. This continues to be my quest. I believe human beings are basically the same all over the world, and I try to prove it through my films.

5. STORY SOURCE?

Three of my 23 films have been based on my own original screenplays. The others have been adaptations of novels—long and short—and short stories. Often the adaptations have been fairly free, while retaining those elements which drew me to the sources in the first place. My experience is that the long short-story is ideal for the two-hour span of an average feature film. One can treat the material in depth; whereas with a full-fledged novel, one is more worried about what to include and what to leave out.

When writing an original screenplay, I prefer to deal with milieus I am familiar with. I have avoided plays because of their excessive dependence on words, but I can see that a play can be very well suited to an intimate medium like TV where a concentration on close-ups and on performance can be turned to aesthetic advantage. (One thinks of some of the recent Bergman films.)

6. USE A SCRIPTWRITER OR DO IT YOURSELF? / 7. CLOSE COLLABORATION WITH THE SCREENWRITER?

I always write my own screenplays, dialogue, and shooting scripts.

8. PREPLAN OR IMPROVISE?

I try to work out the action as closely as possible in the script, particularly when a film is to be shot largely in the studio.

When one is working on location, one has to leave some room for improvisation. Often a change in weather, whether for better or worse, necessitates a modification of the original shooting plan. This is fine as long as the overall structure, the master plan, is not affected.

I do not improvise, and I am suspicious of directors who claim to have improvised their films. I believe it is possible to achieve a relaxed, free-flowing quality in the finished product even if one adheres closely to a well-worked-out script.

Also, improvisation sounds like an expensive process. Where I work, one has to teach oneself to be economical. My shooting ratio has never exceeded four to one. Planning goes a long way toward cutting down costs. In any case, I have a classical turn of mind; I like my films well-shaped and my stories well and coherently told.

9. MOST IMPORTANT COMPONENT OF YOUR FILM?

I believe in the primacy of the screenplay, and find it hard to believe that a satisfying film can be made from an indifferent screenplay. But the other aspects, too, are not to be belittled. In fact, a harmonious blending of all the elements is a *sine qua non* of an artistically satisfying film.

10. WORK WITH A PRODUCER?

Barring two early films, I have always worked with a producer. In my case, a producer has been the person who provides the money—as well as complete freedom—to do just as I please. I could not work in any condition other than that of total control over every aspect of the film. Given this freedom, I find filmmaking enormously exciting in all its stages. Deprived of it, filmmaking for me would turn into a chore.

11. USE A DIALOGUE DIRECTOR?

I do not use a dialogue director. The leading actors are provided with copies of the finished script well before the shooting starts. This is usually preceded by a session when I read out the screenplay to all the main actors, acting out all the parts myself. This serves as a guideline for the kind of performance I expect from my actors.

12. WRITER OR PRODUCER ON THE SET?

I do not "like" to have my producer on the set while I'm working, but I have never gone to the extent of barring him. It really makes very little difference to me, one way or the other.

13. WORK CLOSELY WITH THE CAMERAMAN?

Since my shooting scripts are in a visual form—all the setups being sketched out—my cameraman usually knows what I am after. Although I have a lighting cameraman, I compose the shots and operate the camera myself. I discuss the mood of a scene beforehand with the lighting cameraman. Like everything else that goes into the film, the lighting has to have my approval. By and large the aim is towards realism. We have been using a system of diffused lighting in the studio for day scenes ever since my second film [1956], long before it came into vogue in other parts of the world.

Camera set-ups and movements are, on occasion, improvised. In other words, a scene originally conceived in three shots may be taken in one, and vice versa.

14. SUPERVISION OF CASTING?

I do all the casting myself, down to the smallest bit player.

15. PREFERENCE OF ACTING STYLE?

In my first film I worked with amateurs facing the camera for the first time. I have continued to do this from time to time, but now, more and more, I find myself mixing pros and non-pros, with very good results.

If Brando, Jack Nicholson, Jane Fonda, et al. are prime exponents of "Method" acting, I am full of admiration for it, but there are scores of other actors and actresses who are not identified with the "Method," who have yet given superb performances, although the extent to which a director contributes to a satisfactory performance in a film remains a closed book to all except those connected with the making of the film.

16. PRECAMERA WORK WITH ACTOR?

If an actor wants an in-depth discussion of his part, I am willing to oblige him. I am always ready to accept intelligent suggestions from actors regarding details of performance, *provided* they do not run counter to the basic conception of the character. After all, it is the director, not the actor, who has full sweep of the film in his head.

With a professional actor, I usually let him act a scene in his own way, first. Often I find this adequate for my purpose. If not, I guide him until I am satisfied.

17. IMPORTANCE OF REHEARSALS?

I can only rehearse on a finished set with all the props in place, or on a location which has been finally selected as the right one. This usually boils down to three or four rehearsals before the actual take. Since I have found this a satisfactory method, I see no point in considering alternative ones. If I am satisfied with the first take, I never go for a second one.

18. ADHERENCE TO SCRIPT?

Even an amateur can do things which, while departing from the letter of the script, nevertheless provide something which enhances a scene. I am always grateful for such surprises.

19. EDITING SUPERVISION?

I sit with my editor at every stage of the cutting. I feel editing to be one of the most vital and exciting aspects of filmmaking.

Although my films are largely cut in the camera, there is still a lot of room left for refinements, especially in scenes of dialogue involving cutting back and forth between actors. Often a scene like this would be cut and re-cut several times until a final, satisfactory form has been achieved. Even after 25 years of filmmaking, I can truthfully say that I learn something new about the nature of cinema every time I cut a film with my editor.

20. ROLE OF MUSICAL SCORE? / 21. INVOLVEMENT IN PREPARATION OF MUSICAL SCORE? / 22. WHAT SCENES SHOULD HAVE MUSIC?

I have been my own composer since my seventh film [*Two Daughters,* 1960]. As in everything else I do in films, I am an auto-didact.

I sometimes wish one could dispense with background music altogether. The images ought to be telling enough. Still, I find myself writing bits and pieces in the hope that they will serve to underline some emotional or dramatic point.

This may be due to a lack of confidence, because—having written the music and put it on the track—I often find myself dropping it at the time of mixing—later regretting the decision when watching the film with an audience.

23. SOUND EFFECTS?

I have often personally recorded sound effects for use in my films. For instance, one particular story takes place in a train travelling from Calcutta to Delhi. I made a preliminary trip (800 miles) just to record all the various sound effects (running train, station noises, etc.) which later went into the film.

COMMENT

As the above answers indicate, I am a director who enjoys an extraordinary degree of freedom, and exercises full control over every aspect of production.

It is difficult to imagine many directors being in the same position.

I am, therefore, a little doubtful whether my methods can be applied by directors who will be working—or forced to work—in conditions normally found in Europe and USA.

Jean Renoir

1. BACKGROUND?

I was born in a milieu of artists. My father was the painter Pierre Auguste Renoir. My background certainly helped me to understand the basic visual problems of the film medium. My first trade was ceramics.

2. FIRST FILM JOB?

I started all at once as a producer, director and, alas, as moneyman! My first pictures were merely a demonstration of my technical preoccupations!

3. YOUR GOAL IN FILMMAKING?

I don't believe that I had any secret purpose in shooting my pictures. I was trying to provide good entertainment. I discovered the "deep" meaning of the film while shooting it, and even more *after* shooting it.

4. IN WHAT GENRE DO YOU SEEK A STORY?

I tried to make films beyond categorization. My ambition was, and still is, to succeed with a mixture of comedy and drama.

5. STORY SOURCE?

I have no preference as to source material. The ideal combination, obviously, is to have the author telling his own story: Chaplin is the most brilliant example of this. But it costs time. A story or a stage play or a murder related in the papers may be an excellent springboard, but this springboard must remain a springboard and nothing more. The real creation must be found in the work of the director.

6. USE A SCRIPTWRITER OR DO IT YOURSELF?

I believe that the author should tell his own story; he must not only prepare the dialogue but also the shooting script. Let's not forget that my ideas concerning the shooting of a picture are based on my belief that the author is center of the operation.

7. CLOSE COLLABORATION WITH THE SCREENWRITER?

I prefer to work closely with the writer.

8. PREPLAN OR IMPROVISE?

I do prefer to improvise.

9. MOST IMPORTANT COMPONENT OF YOUR FILM?

No. Everything and everyone is important.

10. WORK WITH A PRODUCER?

The author of a film is the equivalent of the author of a book. The book should reflect his personality. A work of art is nothing but a conversation with the author. The function of the producer is to maintain the artistic and technical unity around the author. It is also to provide the money—and that is certainly not the least of his functions. The producer must also fight savagely for a good release with a good publicity campaign.

11. USE A DIALOGUE DIRECTOR?

In my opinion, the work of a dialogue director is a menace against the personality of the author-director, let us call him a "filmmaker."

12. WRITER OR PRODUCER ON THE SET?

Who does?

13. WORK CLOSELY WITH THE CAMERAMAN?

I like to play an active part in all the technical phases. I like to be in close touch with the technicians way before the first day of shooting. I like to have discussed each set-up of the camera; I like to rehearse with the actors; I like to check each prop with the property man; to check the make-up of every actor. But I also like to improvise on the set. The best shots in a picture were often conceived and executed at the last minute. A good preparation is indispensable, but when you are caught in the spell of shooting, you discover things you had not seen before.

14. SUPERVISION OF CASTING?

Nothing is unimportant in filmmaking. During the shooting, you must dedicate as much attention to the "bit" actor during the one minute you're with him as to the star of the picture during the shooting of one of her close-ups.

A bad make-up, even for a character who will last a few seconds on the screen, may ruin the scene. Let's not forget that in many productions, it is the actor who chooses the director, and not vice-versa.

Personally, without the actor, I would have done very few pictures. Many actors liked my work, and demanded of the producer that I should direct them.

15. PREFERENCE OF ACTING STYLE?

The trouble with some professional actors is that they repeat themselves during their whole life. In the beginning of their career, they had been successful with a certain skeptical smile, and so they will repeat that same expression their whole life long. The public is delighted, so are the producer and the director. I am not.

A long illness forbids me to go to the movies, so I have no opinion on a matter that I ignore. According to what I heard of "Method" actors, they are playing a big part in the Renaissance of American movies.

16. PRECAMERA WORK WITH ACTOR?

I prefer to discuss *my* conception of the part with the actor long before the shooting.

17. IMPORTANCE OF REHEARSALS?

I am not in favor of too many rehearsals. It is essential to keep as much freshness as possible. The actors should give the impression that they see the lines for the first time in their lives. I believe firmly in rehearsals the Italian style—that means to sit down around the director who forbids the actors to give any expression; the reading of the lines must be as monotonous as would be the reading of a telephone directory. After several sessions of this exercise, there are good chances that one of the actors will give a little sparkle which is the hope for a great performance. The danger, by allowing the actors to give expressions before getting acquainted with the physical part of the role is to fall into cliché. Innocence is an important part of genius.

18. ADHERENCE TO SCRIPT?

I accept gladly the suggestions of actors. My job is to maintain those suggestions within the frame of my own conception of the subject.

19. EDITING SUPERVISION?

I consider the cutting of a picture as one powerful tool given to the director to express himself. The director must have discussed the cutting with the cutter almost frame by frame. The ideas I am expressing here were supposed to be strange when I was producing actively. Today, these ideas are considered common sense. Even the word "director" is slowly but surely replaced by the term "filmmaker" which seems more appropriate.

20. ROLE OF MUSICAL SCORE?

To me, a musical score underling the acting suggests that those actors are incapable of playing their parts with talent alone and must be helped by the musical score, the lighting of the cameraman, the setting and by all the technical means that they are surrounded by. A real actor must have the power to express himself, as well as the character he is portraying. Good actors do not need too many props; they do not need a musical score either.

21. INVOLVEMENT IN PREPARATION OF MUSICAL SCORE?

I remain in close touch with the composer. A big part of the music is the result of friendly discussions around the piano.

22. WHAT SCENES SHOULD HAVE MUSIC?

I believe that in case we cannot do without a musical score, it is preferable to base it on the "counterpoint" system.

23. SOUND EFFECTS?

Sound effects are of primary importance and should be treated very realistically. Clumsy sound effects may ruin a good sequence.

Alain Resnais

1. BACKGROUND?

I first wanted to be a bookseller, because I felt that this job would allow me a lot of spare time. Later, I wanted to become an actor. The atmosphere of the theatrical-cinema world completely fascinated me. Everybody was so warm. But I considered myself an actor with an unpredictable future. So, to keep in touch in one way or another with these people, I decided to become—and eventually became—a film editor.

2. FIRST FILM JOB?

I have been an extra in some films, especially in *Les Visiteurs Du Soir* [*The Devil's Envoys,* 1942] by Marcel Carné. After that I was engaged as an assistant to Nicole Védrès for *Paris 1900* [1947].

And then I made my first short film, *Van Gogh* [1948] in collaboration with C. Diehl and R. Herseus. I have previously shot little private films which were never commercially released.

3. YOUR GOAL IN FILMMAKING?

Film, for me first of all, is a profession, a pleasant way of earning one's livelihood. I never have had, consciously, the intention of expressing—through a film—a particular message. I've always tried to present a kind of controversial issue to the viewers, hoping to make them a little more open, more tolerant toward the other man's ideas. I hate violence, which fact I hope I have made clear in most of my films. I work in this way wherever it is possible, of course, because not every topic allows such development.

4. IN WHAT GENRE DO YOU SEEK A STORY?

Rather than seek a story, I looked for a screenwriter who wanted to work with me, and with whom I would like to work. The "genre," the topic, does not matter. It is the friendship in the collaboration which is important.

5. STORY SOURCE?

My preference goes to the script written especially for film. In adapting a novel or play, I have always had the feeling that one is inevitably faced with restrictions implicit in the perfection of the book or drama, so any changes may alter the whole structure. I am speaking for myself, of course, because it is obvious that there are very good films which are based on a book.

The other advantage that I see in the original screenplay method is that the screen writer's position is one of complete personal involvement. In writing the script and the dialogue he is functioning under his own responsibility and with complete artistic freedom.

6. USE A SCRIPTWRITER OR DO IT YOURSELF?

I never could imagine a director not working on the script.

7. CLOSE COLLABORATION WITH THE SCREENWRITER?

I have always worked with a single screenwriter to whom I would give complete liberty. However, I reserve the right to criticize his work. Only reluctantly will I accept the intrusion of a third person between us, to write the dialogue. To me unity is the all-important thing.

8. PREPLAN OR IMPROVISE?

By preparing in minute detail beforehand, I allow myself complete freedom for improvisation when shooting starts. It is easier to change when one knows where one is going. Faced with scant preparation, one is forced to overextend oneself, resulting in a poor job. On the other hand, the more we work on the preparation of the script, the better we are equipped to improvise when that becomes necessary. It is verified, especially when working with actors! I like to rehearse with them one or two weeks before (whenever it is possible) because it saves time and gives us, during the shooting, a wider freedom of action.

9. MOST IMPORTANT COMPONENT OF YOUR FILM?

I dislike very much to do this kind of classifying. I would have a tendency, however, because just appreciation of his talent is often neglected, to name the screenwriter.

10. WORK WITH A PRODUCER?

I always work with a producer. Here, once more, it is more a matter of friendly collaboration than financial relations. Of course, the producer is the one who finds the money for the film, but from my point of view, the money angle is of secondary consideration.

Actually, he is the one who renders it possible for me to make the film I want to do, and I am always deeply grateful. I have never had serious trouble with my producers. They have never raged at me. On the contrary, up to this point I have been very lucky, meaning the producers have shown complete confidence in me.

11. USE A DIALOGUE DIRECTOR?

Actors in France are supposed to know their text. There is no dialogue director.

12. WRITER OR PRODUCER ON THE SET?

I work with the screenwriter until the day before the shooting. From that point on, it is understood that he will not interfere in any way until the editing. It is vitally important to me that he has a fresh point of view when we run the first rough cut. Eventually, we make the corrections jointly.

13. WORK CLOSELY WITH THE CAMERAMAN?

I try to work, naturally, very much with the cinematographer and his assistant. Here again, I am able to go into the most minute detail without being hesitant about making changes as they become necessary.

14. SUPERVISION OF CASTING?

I care a lot about the casting of a film and especially the voice of the actor. I compare it to the formation of an orchestra. Like the conductor, in filmmaking the final decision is the director's prerogative. It is often said that a film, well-cast, is already half completed.

It is important, on the other hand, that actors (at least the leading parts) know their script very well, and are able to discuss it with the director. The actor is not only a performer; he is also a creator.

15. PREFERENCE OF ACTING STYLE?

I don't have any preference. The important thing is that we understand the depth of the individual actor's sensibilities. The director must adapt himself to take full advantage of each actor's approach to his craft. Anyway, the frontier between instinct and technique is very difficult to define. According to the day, the mood, the scene, the same actor can use either or both—use technique if instinct fails.

About the "Method," I think it is a very fertile basis for discussion which makes a lot of things easier. I am very happy to work with actors who have practiced the "Method" a little. It is not a panacea, obviously, but the more dangerous is *still* the lack of method!

16. PRECAMERA WORK WITH ACTOR?

I like to have discussions with the actors before shooting them, and analyze with them the motivations of such repartee of accompanying action or business, so that everything is clear between us regarding the way we conceive the film.

17. IMPORTANCE OF REHEARSALS?

In conducting too many rehearsals before the take, we encourage the danger of losing the spontaneity for which we are always striving. Better it is to rehearse the scene "cold," and if possible several days before it is scheduled for shooting.

It is necessary, during the few rehearsals before the take, to be in readiness for shooting—lighting, set-up, etc., in case the first take proves to be a perfect one, which happens frequently. To make the actor completely relax, during a very emotional scene, I have a tendency to promise him that we will shoot the scene as much as necessary, so that he must have no doubt about it. I average four or five takes, rarely more than twelve takes. Very often I have been satisfied by the first one.

18. ADHERENCE TO SCRIPT?

We always try to agree before the shooting, which avoids last minute discussions. If there is any real difference of opinion between the actor and myself, I suggest we shoot the scene both ways and then we choose the better one at the editing.

19. EDITING SUPERVISION?

I choose the good take with the editor. I go every day to the editing room, and we discuss. I don't have any theory. Everything is solved during this daily conference.

For myself, I think that most of the editing is done during the shooting. The camera set-up, the angle of shooting, the time of the scene, imply the place where the cut will be. As I always shoot with a single camera, and as I foresee for each set-up only *one* proper placement, the editing opportunities are limited.

20. ROLE OF MUSICAL SCORE?

Music, for me, is not an *accompaniment* for the film. It is an integral part of the film. I do not believe that music should be used to increase the emotion or to decrease it, but to say a certain number of things that neither the image nor the actor can say.

Music is present to complete the structure of the editing, for instance, to make the audience realize that the sequence being viewed is in the present, or in the past; or, sometimes to supplant pages of dialogue. In no case can music be used as padding.

I give the same importance to the choice of the musician as of the actor or the cameraman. Also, I know—during the editing—exactly when the music must occur.

21. INVOLVEMENT IN PREPARATION OF MUSICAL SCORE?

I am, of course, present during all the mixing and the recording. It is current, in France, to do so.

22. WHAT SCENES SHOULD HAVE MUSIC?

I don't have any fixed rules. I just follow my instinct.

23. SOUND EFFECTS?

I try, whenever it is possible, to have a soundtrack as smooth and as silent as possible. I mean to eliminate all parasitic sound: steps, door slams, etc.

I choose with the technicians the sound that I *want* to minimize, and—on the contrary—the sound that I want to emphasize.

Tony Richardson

1. BACKGROUND? / 2. FIRST FILM JOB?

In some ways, entering the movie business was very easy for me, because I never thought about doing anything else. I've been seeing movies since I've been about six years old; I was taken to all the matinées in the north of England. My father was a pharmacist. In fact, no one in my family had anything to do with show business. There was never any choice for me wanting to do anything else. I started by directing plays with local groups, and then did more at the university I attended. I made my first film on an amateur basis in collaboration with director Karel Reisz.

3. YOUR GOAL IN FILMMAKING?

Film, primarily, should entertain—but you ask: what is entertainment? Entertainment cannot be just a few laughs. Entertainment, I think, on its best level, reflects an attitude toward life. It raises questions about society, and questions about human beings. It's absolutely essential that you give people a good time while you're doing it, though. They're going to the cinema to get some type of pleasure. Whatever the movie, it must give some pleasure in some way to everyone. On the other hand, the most important thing for me is to present human beings, and create human characters, and to create life as I perceive it to be. You must have the right basis or it really can't be entertaining. I'm not interested in fantasy. I'm interested in giving people a good time based on an understanding of life as I see it, and I hope an audience sees it.

4. IN WHAT GENRE DO YOU SEEK A STORY?

It's very hard to say why you choose a story. You choose them for all different reasons. I certainly don't look to any one genre. It's perfectly true sometimes that, after you do one genre, you run away and try to find something as different as possible. When I made *Tom Jones* [1963], I didn't really want to make another period piece for a long time. I think what appeals to you is exactly like a love affair: it's an inexplicable attraction. Sometimes it might be a paragraph in the newspaper, it might be a book you like, or a character that fascinates you. There isn't any real way of knowing, it's just accident or chance.

5. STORY SOURCE?

The dream is always to have a script written directly for the screen, and it's an original idea. It's quite difficult to do and to find writers. I think that is one of the most difficult problems of anything to do with film. I think the best contemporary writers really don't like writing for the movies, although they like the money. They don't like rewriting, and few really like collaboration. I feel this is why one often looks for material in stuff that already exists. Usually, I think that novels are a better source than plays. Plays are like pouring jelly into a mold, it's already set. To really tell the same story on the screen, you must dissolve it all again and start from scratch.

6. USE A SCRIPTWRITER OR DO IT YOURSELF?

In the same way, I will always work on the script very closely with the writer. I do like working with writers, because I find that writing is too lonely a business for me. I like to shape the script with the writer, and to bounce ideas off someone else. I like feedback. I've never really found the ideal collaborator. When I worked with the screenwriter of *Mademoiselle* [1966]—after he had written the film script years before it was actually made—I finally found it and wanted to make it.

He was living in England, and I went to see him, saying, "Let's work together."

He agreed to this, and we worked for about two weeks. He was more meticulous than any other screenwriter I had ever worked with. After completing about two weeks work on the script, I made a great mistake. I said to him, "I've never worked with anyone as professional as you." After that day, I never saw him again. He was someone who could not stand any type of compliment. That was the end of collaboration.

7. CLOSE COLLABORATION WITH THE SCREENWRITER?

When I'm working with a writer on a draft, I do a treatment or outline of the basic question of the story and how it's going to be approached. Once I've worked out this basic approach with the writer, I feel that the writer should be left alone to get on with it; he takes it on from that period of time. Inevitably a lot of the script will change when you start to shoot. It would be a dream to have a script that you didn't have to revise on the floor. I don't find it happens too often.

8. PREPLAN OR IMPROVISE?

I don't have anything worked out before I go on the floor. I know that there are schools of directors who do plan every shot. I can't, because I'm too dumb. I have to go onto the set, and get the ideas when I see the scenery and the actors. This becomes terrifying when you have a very complicated scene with hundreds of people, and there are a lot of elements that you have to integrate.

Joseph Andrews [1977] is a film that opens with a scene of a May Day, and it's enormously complex, because it introduces the principal characters as well as setting the mood and style of the whole film. Although it was a scene which I discussed and rehearsed, when the moment came to be on the set, sometimes you're there without an idea. Then, perhaps about an hour later the ideas start to pour out and it all starts to work.

I'm a total improviser. The only thing that I always do know is what purpose the scene should serve. I have a strong sense of what the atmosphere of the scene is. I also try to have a sense of time in the scene. I don't mean how long the scene should play. I'll explain. In my second film with Larry Olivier, *The Entertainer* [1960], Larry said a thing that still shocks me even today. He said you must work out the time of every shot, because if you don't, it won't be *your* timing. It will be ours.

As a result, I've always been very conscious of timing—whether a scene should be slow in mood, or fast. One of the things that is really a sign of a great director, is when they have a marvelous sense of rhythm and time. This is just as important often as the images.

9. MOST IMPORTANT COMPONENT OF YOUR FILM?

The most important thing for me is always the story. Everything else is incidental, because if you don't have the right story, there is nothing you can do. After that, the most important element is casting the film properly. Film is so much bound up with the human face and the human body; there are many talented actors who just don't work on film. There is some kind of curious empathy, some kind of thing that happens between the lens and the film that however gifted an actor may be, he doesn't communicate to the camera in the way he can in the theatre. If you don't have that one thing that makes an audience like, or dislike, you as a character, then film just doesn't work for you.

10. WORK WITH A PRODUCER?

My concept of a producer is someone who gets the film together, and makes the thing work, keeping the unit happy. If he can suggest things, that's fine. I think the producer's first job is to create the conditions for the director to create in. I don't feel he should ever be in a controlling position. The producer should be filling up the aquarium for the fish to swim in.

11. USE A DIALOGUE DIRECTOR?

I rarely use a dialogue director, because I think that's one of the director's jobs. You should be working closely with actors. The only times I've used a dialogue director has been when it's been a question of foreign language, or learning an accent of some type. Again, in *Joseph Andrews,* Ann-Margret played an English lady with a British accent. The dialogue director first worked with Ann on the accent, but it's the director who works on the performances.

12. WRITER OR PRODUCER ON THE SET?

I don't mind having a writer or a producer on the set, but it depends. On the whole, I think that the writers are better kept away, because their work is done at that point. Most of the time it is quite boring, and they can be off working on another project. They really can't add that much anyway.

13. WORK CLOSELY WITH THE CAMERAMAN?

I don't work anything out with my cameramen before I start to shoot. I choose my cameramen very carefully, because I absolutely adore working with them. It's important to make the distinction between the director of photography and the camera operators. Although the look of the picture is the responsibility of the director of photography, the day to day work is created by the operators. I think this is especially true in Europe. It's important that I always work out the basic approach to the style of the film with the director of photography. We also discuss the possibility of using any special lenses or special processes. If the script calls for scenes that are slightly different in style from the rest of the story, then we will talk about the ideas to realize that. Beyond a general approach, I don't work out anything. The only other times I work something out is if there are special technical problems. I'll work out the kinds of equipment and the kinds of shots, but after that I entirely extemporize.

14. SUPERVISION OF CASTING?

I cast everyone of my films totally myself. I even try to cast the extras. I don't think that one can ever be too meticulous about casting. It's fine to have a casting director who can suggest new people to you, but I do everything myself. I like to see a lot of people for the same part.

15. PREFERENCE OF ACTING STYLE?

Good actors are good actors, and that's it. It's a great pleasure if you have a good actress who has a good understanding of the camera. Some actors have a rather superficial attitude towards film technique. They feel that they'll provide the acting and the technicians can provide the shots. It doesn't matter how great the acting is unless you get the right shots, the most expressive shots. Actors will be just that much better if they understand and appreciate the technical problems.

However, I don't choose people for those reasons. Now, I think "method acting" is what acting is all about. I know there are bad actors who indulge in a lot of mannerisms that people call "method acting."

In my opinion, the greatest actress I have ever worked with is Kim Stanley. A lot of people call her a "method actor," but to me she is just a very great actress.

16. PRECAMERA WORK WITH ACTOR?

I like to have discussions with actors beforehand. Again, it depends on the nature of the subject and of the style. I have done films for which I've rehearsed at least two weeks, yet I prefer to have as little rehearsal time as possible. It is a great thing when an actor can use that type of freshness.

I remember working with Kate Hepburn in *A Delicate Balance* [1973]. When we got on the set for the first day of shooting, I started to give directions on where she should move and Kate said, "Let me show you what we actors can do."

It's a good thing to let the actors have a chance to try to do what they want from that very first day when you come on the set. The more the director and actor can have an understanding of the character, the easier the practical work will go.

17. IMPORTANCE OF REHEARSALS?

A lot will happen when you get on the set, and not too much should be done before then. Everything changes; it changes with the weather; it changes with the mood everyone is in. These are very important factors. This is the difference between theatre and film. Theatre acting is a process of a long period of reflection, deliberation, building and carefully considering a character. Often, there's a certain amount of spontaneity that goes out of it.

The great thing about film acting is that an actor can use his or her first impulses. He can change, try things he would never dare to in the theatre. Often some accidental thing will happen that an actor can use on film, and increase its effectiveness because of the accident.

18. ADHERENCE TO SCRIPT?

I don't believe that an actor should stick to the script. When they do want to change something in the script, I want them to have a good idea of why they're making that change.

Again, it depends on the type of material you have. If it's well written, then I feel that noting should be changed. If it is a bit too sketchy, there is nothing wrong with a little rewriting. There are actors who can mess about, or fiddle with the text, and feel that inserting pauses will give the impression that it's spontaneous. I think that is just bad acting.

However, there are no rules on this. It also depends on the sensitivity of the actor. Some actors, by changing things, can create out of their experience and knowledge tremendous new effects. Obviously, one hopes that one has dialogue that doesn't need changing. An actor should first approach it: how do I make this work? Not: how can I change this to make it work for me?

19. EDITING SUPERVISION?

I do supervise the editing for my films totally and completely. I can see why you say that some directors like to have the editor make the first rough cut, but I've found that's a waste of time.

I have a very clear idea, when I've done a scene, about how I think it should be edited. I usually prefer to get the editor to put it together roughly in the way I intended it. When I see the first assembly, it's more or less the way it was meant to be when it was shot. Then, if the editor has his ideas, I'm willing to look at his ideas. They may be better. He may have a lot of ideas. Then I completely throw away my original conceptions, but I like to see them done once.

Film is a living, breathing thing that has a life of its own. It's no use imagining what the original intention was, because you've either achieved it clearly, or you haven't. You have to live with what you've caught hold of. If anything, I've always found that editors tend to be more conservative than directors, and they stick to their original concepts when they've been superseded long ago by the reality of what you've actually shot.

20. ROLE OF MUSICAL SCORE?

Music is just a marvelous thing. I love what you can do with music. I don't like it when music is matched to the image. Instead, I try to have the music as a different element of its own. For instance, you might feel that the musical style can be a comic approach, and you have a serious scene. With the music, you can totally change what the picture is. If you have a very romantic film, it's much better to have a serious theme which can be played over certain scenes, but which aren't related absolutely to every detail of the action and of the shot, the mood. Music can also cover up all your mistakes.

21. INVOLVEMENT IN PREPARATION OF MUSICAL SCORE?

I talk to the composer about what the music's role in the film is. Then we try to specify certain themes and certain basic approaches to it. That done, he goes off and writes the music. Every few days he'll play a bit of what he has written for me on the piano. We will discuss it in relationship to the overall conception. Orchestration is really the whole style of the movie, and is most important. For *Joseph Andrews,* we used some very old musical instruments.

22. WHAT SCENES SHOULD HAVE MUSIC?

I think I have answered this question in the previous none. I plan everything with the composer. Together, we discuss it in detail...everything to the last cut of the film.

23. SOUND EFFECTS?

I don't think it's possible to overestimate the importance of sound effects. They're absolutely vital. I've been very lucky with most of the sound recorders I've worked with over the years. I think it's smart to cover yourself during the actual shooting with as many things as you can, and as many sound effects as you think you might want.

After that, I don't actually supervise all the recording of the sound effects. I know exactly what I want. Unless it's a particularly strange effect, I leave the sound people to get on with the normal sort of doors opening, and footsteps and so on. I watch things very carefully in the mixing, and if I don't like the work that's being done, I will redo it.

Dino Risi

1. BACKGROUND?

I studied medicine and graduated with a degree. However, by the time I had completed the course, I realized for a certainty that I had no true inclination toward the practice. As a matter of fact, I believe that, right then, I knew exactly what I really wanted to be—a filmmaker.

2. FIRST FILM JOB?

I was fortunate enough to get a job as an assistant director, in which position I served for two pictures. These were followed by thirty documentaries. By the time these were finished I felt that I was ready to move up to my major objective—actual filmmaking. Apparently, some producers agreed with me, because soon after that I started my first directorial job.

3. YOUR GOAL IN FILMMAKING?

My primary motivation, beyond providing entertainment, is the pleasure I get, personally, out of telling stories.

As for a philosophy? There might be one behind my burning passion to learn; the desire to know myself. I felt this should emerge inevitably from a growing accumulation of my films, which in total, must be regarded as an expression of my true inner self.

4. IN WHAT GENRE DO YOU SEEK A STORY?

The type of stories with which I feel most comfortable and at ease, are comedies—grotesque perhaps—films depicting the ways of life.

Of late, however, this trend has changed materially. As of today, I am also—and above all—intensely interested in dramatic stories.

5. STORY SOURCE?

I have no preference as to source of story material. All sources are good with the one exception of the theatrically oriented play.

However, I have—nearly always—worked with original and modern stories written directly for the screen. This does not imply that, were I to see a book or short story which intrigued me, I would not be delighted to develop it for a film.

6. USE A SCRIPTWRITER OR DO IT YOURSELF?

I nearly always use a collaborator—sometimes even two. The objective viewpoint of other cinematic professionals is of the utmost value in my method of filmmaking.

7. CLOSE COLLABORATION WITH THE SCREENWRITER?

Usually, to begin with, I discuss the idea on which we are basing our screenplay with my writer (or writers). This joint effort continues right on through the treatment stage. At that point, I step aside, so that by the time the script is completed, I am able to judge it from a truly objective point of view.

8. PREPLAN OR IMPROVISE?

Through experience I have found that it is far better for me to have a solid basis—a well and fully developed script—on which to work during shooting. From that point on, I depend a lot on improvisation.

9. MOST IMPORTANT COMPONENT OF YOUR FILM?

Even more important than the story—which is a matter of prime importance—is the basic idea from which the story is born. Certainly, each of those other components listed, is of major consequence. Any one of these functions, improperly executed, may well become a determining factor in the final quality of your film.

10. WORK WITH A PRODUCER?

According to my experience, the producer helps only to find the money with which to make the picture—he has no other function.

11. USE A DIALOGUE DIRECTOR?

I never use a dialogue director. Such a function would, in my opinion, be a redundance—an encroachment on my personal work and responsibility.

12. WRITER OR PRODUCER ON THE SET?

I can see no possible good resulting from having either the writer or the producer on my set during rehearsal or shooting. Certainly the writer, and probably the producer as well, have their own visualization of how the story should be done. The chance of the visualization of either coinciding with mine is most remote.

A criticism, from either, of the way in which I am handling a line, a scene, or a bit of action, can only cause confusion and irritating delay of my operation. Still, either man, if allowed to watch the action, would be unable to restrain himself from voicing his opinion of any bit with which he disagreed.

13. WORK CLOSELY WITH THE CAMERAMAN?

I like to work impromptu. At times, I walk on the set without even knowing which scene I am going to do next. This seems to be the only way in which I can avoid becoming completely disenchanted with a picture after a few weeks of work.

14. SUPERVISION OF CASTING?

Sometimes, production requirements—such as the need to use a specific star or player who is under contract—determines the selection of the principal roles. Aside from that, I cast all parts, down to the last extra. I do not use a casting director.

15. PREFERENCE OF ACTING STYLE?

I have, of course, worked with both types of actors—the technician and the instinctive type. I much prefer the spontaneous type player.

16. PRECAMERA WORK WITH ACTOR?

My theory in respect to "discussing in depth" with an actor before shooting has begun, is that it should not be necessary. Rule Number One is: the right person for the right part. However, there are exceptions.

17. IMPORTANCE OF REHEARSALS?

I rehearse as little as is possible. And, at every rehearsal, I introduce a little novelty, maybe by shooting the same scene two or three times with some changes. Work must be pleasant, never too repetitive or monotonous. If we are bored on the set, most likely the picture will come out boring. The "human" climate created by the director among the members of the cast and crew, is very important. Everyone will produce more, and better, when working in a good "atmosphere."

18. ADHERENCE TO SCRIPT?

I agree fully with the actors you mention. *Good* actors are creative people and should be allowed the freedom to function creatively. Furthermore, the script is not the Bible. (Even the Bible can be amended, and has been).

19. EDITING SUPERVISION?

I also hate to watch dailies. Usually I screen them at the end of the first week to check photography, makeup, costumes, etc. Then I put off those agonizing hours in the projection room sometimes until the end of shooting. However, I personally follow all operations from editing to mixing. I also see, personally, to the sound effects.

20. ROLE OF MUSICAL SCORE?

Music, as well as camera movements, should not be noticed. This applies to music of "emotion." However, music must play an essential part, or even a leading role, in a particular kind of motion picture, such as thrillers and action films. Many films owe a great part of their success to the music! Just think of Carol Reed's [*The*] *Third Man* [1949], John Ford's *Stagecoach* [1939], or the works of Fellini!

21. INVOLVEMENT IN PREPARATION OF MUSICAL SCORE?

As stated above, I think that music is very important, even though I've not always been too lucky with the scores of my films. I consider the scoring phase of a picture the most pleasant moment of the whole production.

22. WHAT SCENES SHOULD HAVE MUSIC? / 23. SOUND EFFECTS?

I consider sound effects to be very important and, as I said before, I attend to them personally and completely. Obviously, their importance varies according to the type of picture.

John Schlesinger

1. BACKGROUND?

I was brought up in the 1930s in England. My father was a doctor, and my mother a musician. We lived in a very protected middle-class life. I was always encouraged to do things. Going to the theatre or the cinema was always a special occasion. It wasn't until I was sent to boarding school that I saw films on a regular basis.

2. FIRST FILM JOB?

I started as an actor and a still photographer. Since the time I was a kid, I was always attracted to pictures, and that led to my having my first camera and making my own short films. Later, I made 16mm films when I was in the army.

When I was at Oxford University, I made a short called *Black Legend*. I went around showing my film to various film companies, or—wherever I could, really. I couldn't afford a soundtrack so I had twin turntables.

The film was an enormous success. I guess this was really the first time I was bitten by the bug, and wanted to get into the film business. I finished my studies in 1950, and acted for a living. I soon got the chance to make commercials; eventually made short films for the BBC in England. that's when things really started for me.

3. YOUR GOAL IN FILMMAKING?

I think it really depends on how one defines the word "entertainment." For me it isn't necessarily escapism. Entertainment means engaging the attention. I do, though, somewhat agree with Goldwyn, who said, "If you want to send a message—send it by Western Union."

In making a film there are always things you want to say other than just providing entertainment; you can move, excite, disturb, and amuse an audience, or expose them to certain things that, perhaps, they've never been exposed to before. A film should be entertaining, but it's also there to pose questions, and to give an audience—above all—a special experience.

4. IN WHAT GENRE DO YOU SEEK A STORY?

I always look for something about human beings and human relations that will affect my emotions. I've made eight films at this time, and all, in a sense, have the same theme: the problems of trying to face compromise in one's life and relationships.

Even in *Marathon Man* [1976], which was my first attempt at a thriller, the fear of the student, surrounded by complications and having a need to confront them, was the theme. There was this kind of emotional thing at the core of the character that really interested me.

5. STORY SOURCE?

Obviously the best material is the original screenplay. You can get a story really from any source, but it's best to start from scratch. It's sometimes difficult to get the original off the ground. The front office is usually so frightened of trying anything that hasn't been proved in another medium. Best sellers or hit plays have a much better chance of seeing the light of day as films. I have only done two original films. I tend to stay away from plays, because they're too scene bound and I'm not really interested in them anyway as films.

6. USE A SCRIPTWRITER OR DO IT YOURSELF?

I've found that if someone has written a novel, he sees it in a certain way; therefore, it isn't always the answer to get the writer of the original novel to write the screenplay. It *can* work, though. I worked with William Goldman on *Marathon Man.* He wrote the novel as well as the screenplay.

I think there comes a point in time when the novelist-screenwriter finds that he's run out of ideas. I find that it's good to have a writer that comes fresh to a subject, if it's existed in a different form. I always work closely with the writer myself.

We will discuss a subject, and then I'll let him go out to battle himself. After he delivers the first draft script, that's when I really start to get to work with that writer. We may go through three or four drafts, and even alter them constantly while I'm shooting.

7. CLOSE COLLABORATION WITH THE SCREENWRITER?

I think I've already answered this. It's a very long process. The screenplay must be flexible, because you shoot, certain things change, and it has to have a life of its own.

8. PREPLAN OR IMPROVISE?

I always do my preparation the night before. If it's a big sequence, I'll have it storyboarded. I think it's very important to be organized. However, it's no use not allowing yourself to be flexible, if, when you get on the floor, something happens during rehearsal that's good, perhaps you will want to change things. If you've worked things out too tightly, you're in an inflexible position as a director. You have to allow for things to happen which can still be accommodated in your master plan.

9. MOST IMPORTANT COMPONENT OF YOUR FILM?

I think all of the components are important. Film is a collaboration among a lot of people. I believe it's a directors' medium, because the director has the final deciding vote on how something is going to work. It's he who is going to make the selections as to how he's going to shoot a particular scene, or make a cut. In the selection of what to emphasize, and how to emphasize what an audience looks at, lies what directing is all about.

The choice of the story is a personal thing from the director's point of view. The script is of paramount importance. I've always felt that it's the writer who is the first man out of the trenches. Actors are not puppets and you must give them space to create. In the initial stages, the writer is most important.

10. WORK WITH A PRODUCER?

Yes, I do work with a producer. I don't fancy producing my own films. I don't want the headaches of dealing with a front office on a daily basis. I've been lucky to have worked with producers who I consider to be highly creative individuals, people who align themselves with me, and protect me. The film that we are making becomes the child of both of us. That's what I expect. The producer can be protective, and give an objective opinion when you need one.

11. USE A DIALOGUE DIRECTOR?

No. I've never used a dialogue director and quite honestly never really understood their function. It seems to be an invention of Hollywood.

12. WRITER OR PRODUCER ON THE SET?

I don't think the producer can really do much good on the set. He's most helpful at, perhaps, script sessions, or when you start to edit. The writer can be very helpful, particularly if the scene isn't going well.

13. WORK CLOSELY WITH THE CAMERAMAN?

I like to work with a cameraman very closely, particularly in the question of style. When we did _The Day of the Locust_ [1975], we intentionally gave it a glamorized romantic look at the seamier side of Hollywood life. Conrad Hall and I did endless tests with different filters and lens to give us what we wanted. Often, I'll bring in the production designer who can have a great influence on the way the film can look.

I think the use of color must go hand in hand with the photography. It's the vital key to the style of the film. In fact, draining it of color can be used for dramatic purposes. Primary colors like red photograph very brightly if set against things that are intentionally designed in a muted fashion. This is something that a cameraman designer, and I work very closely on. Again, you must allow yourself to be flexible for changes.

14. SUPERVISION OF CASTING?

I think casting is of such importance that I'm involved in the entire process. Casting is balance. Balance between the principals and the minor parts. I take a great many photographs and post them on a cork board in my office, so that I'm able to study them for balance.

Interviewing actors at casting sessions can be very valuable in that you're working on a screenplay as you cast. You may go with a fixed idea of how certain people are to look, or who they are to be. As you go through the process of interviewing, you can alter your own ideas. Someone may come in who would make the part different. If you're aware of that, it can be helpful.

It's interesting to look back on the casting for *Midnight Cowboy* [1969]. Jerome Hellman and I had considered Jon Voight as "The Cowboy," and completely rejected the idea, because he didn't fit in with our ideas of how the cowboy should look. It was really the casting director who insisted we look at Jon.

In *Marathon Man* we had Dustin Hoffman and Larry Olivier—from totally different schools. They worked great together out of respect for each other's background. Olivier is a man who's much more used to being rigid, and Hoffman forever wants to improvise. It was, needless to say, very interesting working with both of them.

15. PREFERENCE OF ACTING STYLE?

Everybody is a method actor in a way. I do like the more instinctive actors. I sometimes like the unknowns, who are truly instinctive.

16. PRECAMERA WORK WITH ACTOR?

I think it's a mixture of all these. If a director has worked a great deal on the screenplay, he obviously has a set idea on how he wants something to play. A screenplay isn't just for actors. It's about atmosphere, and how certain scenes are put together, in some of which the actor has no part at all.

17. IMPORTANCE OF REHEARSALS?

There comes a time when you can over rehearse a thing. I don't mind a lot of rehearsals, if the actors aren't too sure of their lines. That can sometimes produce an emotion which may not be intended by the actor, but which is exciting on the screen.

Rehearsal period is the only time you can discover things, and experiment. I try to get as many people from the cast as I can for a reading. Very often it's not so much the scene, but what led up to that scene that's important. In *Sunday Bloody*

Sunday [1971] one knew, going in, that the young man was going to leave his lovers. Very early in rehearsal, we found it helpful to go back in time to find what it was like when they were at the height of their affair. Those are the kind of things for which I use the rehearsal period.

18. ADHERENCE TO SCRIPT?

The script is a blueprint. Very often an actor can improve something. It's entirely up to the director. Sometimes the lines are perfect and don't need rewriting. You have to realize when that's so.

19. EDITING SUPERVISION?

I work very closely with the editor. It's very similar to working with the writer. While I'm shooting, the editor will be on the set as much as possible, so he sees what is happening. I give him notes, and I always go away for a break at the end of shooting.

During this time the editor can complete his first assembly. Then I come back and look at his cut. At this time an intense collaboration begins. I've worked with the same editor for years.

20. ROLE OF MUSICAL SCORE?

I believe the score to be enormously important. The whole sound portion of the film is important. I think of the music in conjunction with the sound effects. Music should be used sparingly, and always for a specific purpose.

21. INVOLVEMENT IN PREPARATION OF MUSICAL SCORE?

Again, I am deeply involved. I had a certain musical upbringing, and learned to play the piano. I can, at a pinch, halfway find my way around a score. This way, I am not a complete dummy when it comes time for scoring sessions. I love those sessions, because it's the first time—after many months of work—that a new element is added. I think a director should be very much a part of hearing it, and using it in certain ways. It can also be very helpful if one knows what instruments are being played, so as to help the composer.

22. WHAT SCENES SHOULD HAVE MUSIC?

Yes, I exercise full control as to which scenes are to be scored. Again, a producer can be very helpful here. You will all discuss where music is to come from, months before. Then when you come to the mix, the producer may say "Try it without music." You weed out certain things in the final dub.

23. SOUND EFFECTS?

In the editing of the sound and music, we all group around the moviola and kind of sing the film as we go through as to what sound we want at any given moment. For instance, *Marathon Man* sounds were used for immense dramatic impact.

Martin Scorsese

1. BACKGROUND? / 2. FIRST FILM JOB? / 3. YOUR GOAL IN FILMMAKING?

The school of filmmaking I came out of seemed most concerned with what we had to *say* in the film. I should rephrase that: I was a film student at a time when there were a lot of new things happening in film—1959-1961. There was the French new wave, all these new filmmakers coming in, plus the resurgence of the appreciation of the American film.

In the 1950s nobody paid critical attention to directors, except when Lindsay Anderson in *Sight & Sound* magazine, in 1956, wrote an article on John Ford. Then other writers started writing about other directors, and took a new look at the American cinema.

I had grown up on American films—I didn't discover foreign films until the late fifties, early sixties. By the time I was at NYU, I was more interested in expressing myself on film; I wasn't thinking of entertainment, although the first short films I made were pure entertainment.

When I made my first feature in 1965, it was to get something out of my system, and everytime I'm making a film now, it has to do with something strongly related to my own feelings. They wind up being expressions of my own state of mind. At the same time, I'm trying to reach a mass audience.

When I first tried with a film called *Who's That Knocking At My Door?* in 1965—I think it was finally released in 1969—it took three years to make and was sort of the first part of *Mean Streets* [1973]. It dealt with the same characters, only eight years earlier. When I first tried with that film, I had no audience in mind. I did it for myself totally. That's what happened, too—nobody went to see it.

I shot one sequence of it in 1967, another in 1965, and then shot a nude sequence in 1968, in order to get the film released because of the new rating system. Luckily, it worked, but I had to shoot the nude scene in Amsterdam, Holland, and make it look like New York.

I made that film to get something out of my system. It had to do with my first real relationship with a woman—a woman whom I eventually married. That's what the film was about: those feelings. What *Taxi Driver* [1976] and *Mean Streets* are about, too, in terms of trying to find out how you shake off those things you were brought up with: the religion, the concepts and codes of it, the idea of women being either goddesses or whores.

The main character was played by Harvey Keitel, who was supposed to be me.

He also played me in *Mean Streets* in 1966, right after I finished shooting the first part of *Who's That Knocking?* That film was not right; we shot it in 35mm and 16mm, blown up to 35mm sections.

Everything that wasn't in that film went into *Mean Streets* when it was made in 1972. It dealt with all those feelings of rejection—wanting to make movies and not really being accepted; the idea of having a goal and not getting to it. The idea of wanting to be recognized, but having nothing to show for your work.

We made *Mean Streets* in an allegorical way by setting it in the neighborhood which is really where I'm from—the Italian-American section in the lower East side of New York. The lead wants to make it in the high ranks of the gangsters, but he doesn't really have the guts, he's not made that way. All those complexes, all those feelings are in the film. When I made the film, I never thought it would be released; I just thanked God I'd had the chance to make it.

I had just finished *Boxcar Bertha* [1972] when I met Jonathan Taplin over dinner and he said he wanted to produce a movie. A week later I gave him a script of *Season of the Witch* which became *Mean Streets.* He liked it; he saw *Boxcar Bertha* and liked that. He said he could raise the money and make the film for $150,000. That's what we started with. The rest was deferred. Did it very quickly in 24 days. *Boxcar Bertha* was made in 24 days, too. For me that's fast.

I never set out to entertain. I just hope that somehow the film hits both levels. When I read *Alice Doesn't Live Here Anymore* [1975], I found that it dealt pretty much with the same problems I was having with women. I tried to identify with that, believing that I could learn something if I made the film. It had more of an entertainment purpose, yet there was still that personal draw.

In fact, we improvised a lot and worked on it. *Taxi Driver* is a film that is highly personal. It was a "do or die" situation. My producers felt it was going to make money, but I felt it wouldn't. Actually, it's making more money than any picture I've done to date.

I had asthma so my parents wouldn't let me engage in sports. When I was three years old, my father took me to the movies a great deal; about the only place I could go was to movies. My whole life revolved around movies and the church. I went to Catholic school and intended to become a priest. Even when I was making my first short films at NYU, I still had intentions of becoming a priest. Then, everything changed after 1963-1964.

By the time I got to college, the university was set up like a ministudio situation, so that you would write a script and if the head professor like it, you would direct it. There were some kids who went directly into writing, others went into photography. I guess I started as a director.

When I got out of school, I thought I'd get a job easily, but it didn't work that way. I had a hell of a time from 1966-1971. I took editing jobs, editing low budget features in New York. I also took a teaching position in 1969. I went back to my old classes and aided them in their scripts, editing, etc.

I organized film festivals—movies in the park type of thing. Then I got involved in a movie called *Woodstock*. Eventually I was called to Hollywood in 1971. Warner Bros. had a problem with a movie called *Medicine Ball Caravan* [1971]. They had a nine hour rough cut, and didn't know what to do with it. It took me nine months to cut *Medicine Ball Caravan*.

Next, William Morris Agency arranged a meeting between Roger Corman and me; Roger wanted to know if I would be interested in directing the sequel to *Bloody Mama*. I said sure.

He said he'd have a script in six or seven months! I didn't believe him, because I had met my share of those guys who made promises on which they never delivered.

Meanwhile I worked with John Cassavetes doing sound on one of his pictures; I had finished that job when Roger Corman came through with the promised script. I became a member of the Directors Guild—made the film in Arkansas in 24 days and edited it. Next, I edited another for Corman called *The Holy Rollers*. Then I edited *Elvis on Tour* for M-G-M [1972].

At about this time I met Jonathan Taplin, who wanted me to do a script, but I was advised to avoid making another picture like *Boxcar Bertha,* so I passed up that opportunity and went to work on *Mean Streets;* the rest of that story has already been reported.

4. IN WHAT GENRE DO YOU SEEK A STORY?

I prefer to get back to writing my own scripts—or with a screenwriter, or even with the actor who has a good sense of story telling. I love all the genres of the movies. If I had my pick, I'd like to do all approaches to film, but always dealing with things I know, and I did in *Mean Streets, Taxi Driver,* and *New York, New York* [1977] which is about the 1940s and deals with problems we have. It will look like a musical, but I want to have a different character.

5. STORY SOURCE?

I really have no preference. I don't think I'd ever want to make a film version of a play. Personally, I'd go right for a novel. One of the problems with *New York, New York* is that the script is 165 pages—it's more like a novel. The writer is a novelist and has never written a script before; he's 23, and quite good.

6. USE A SCRIPTWRITER OR DO IT YOURSELF?

We work together. I get the script from them—his or her ideas—then we work together changing it. Then I usually wind up polishing it myself with perhaps another writer. On *Alice Doesn't Live Here Anymore* everyone was giving ideas and it was just too much. The first cut of that film was three hours and twenty minutes!

7. CLOSE COLLABORATION WITH THE SCREENWRITER?

On *New York, New York* the writer doesn't like to work in my office—there's too much craziness. He likes to work alone. I tell him what I'd like—he brings in pages the next day. I trim them and cut them.

8. PREPLAN OR IMPROVISE?

In the actual shooting script, I sometimes don't read the descriptions! Sometimes I visualize a scene from the dialogue a different way, so I like to storyboard everything. As a kid, my first thoughts about movies were that I would draw them. I like doing the storyboards, so the cameraman and everyone will know what's going on. I prefer to have it worked out: I storyboard so that it serves as a blueprint—a security basis from which to improvise.

10. WORK WITH A PRODUCER?

I never work without a producer. In New York, the producer simply raised the money. On the West Coast, things are different. I want a producer to keep the studio people away from me; that's his job, and I want him to do it. We had a lot of heavy interference on *Taxi Driver.* It was supposed to be a low budget film, 1.8 million, and we had started with 1.3 million dollars. We went over, and studio people were on us every three seconds. I just asked my producer to tell them that everything would be all right. They told me to print fewer takes!

I also expect a producer to get me what I want within the budget, and leave us alone artistically. I'll take ideas from anyone, but I don't want them to be forced on me.

11. USE A DIALOGUE DIRECTOR?

I never use a a dialogue director (I don't even know what it is). On *Boxcar Bertha* I had a friend who made sure everyone knew their lines. I don't really think we need one now. I guess we're working with a different group of actors today.

12. WRITER OR PRODUCER ON THE SET?

Only one of my producers has been on the set: Michael Phillips on *Taxi Driver,* but I felt OK with him, because we were fighting the common enemy—the studio. He was a lot of fun. Paul Schrader, the writer of *Taxi Driver* was on the set a few times, but he trusted me.

13. WORK CLOSELY WITH THE CAMERAMAN?

Again—storyboarding. I really have long conferences with my cameraman as to the look of the film. In *Alice* it never stops moving—it was purely experimental—seeing how far I could go.

14. SUPERVISION OF CASTING?

I control all the casting, down to and including silent bits. It's the only way.

15. PREFERENCE OF ACTING STYLE?

I really prefer the instinctive actor. In fact, I'll get people who are not actors, and use them. My friend, Steve Prince, who was the gun salesman in *Taxi Driver,* was really like that at one time. I talk to actors a long time. I work very closely with them. They speak of "Method"—I never took acting classes, so I really don't know what "Method" means. In *Mean Streets* Bobby De Niro put a hat on and said, "This is much more the character I'm playing," and that touch was perfect. I doubt that was "Method" as much as sense of dramatic value.

16. PRECAMERA WORK WITH ACTOR?

I like a combination of both ideas. We talk, but I don't push concepts on him unless he or she needs it. Usually I like situations when actors and I are in tune with one another. Ellen Burstyn asked me to direct *Alice* and we both hit it off as to what we wanted to say. We trusted each other in our choices. De Niro asked me what type of animal the character he was playing is. I said, "Well, how about a tiger?" Bobby said, "No. I think he's much more like a wolf—always looking around—waiting." So he went to the zoo and watched the wolves. I appreciated that, because I expect the actors to bring me something.

17. IMPORTANCE OF REHEARSALS?

I don't like to rehearse that much. I take the major scenes and rehearse them. Two weeks at the most. With too much rehearsal, I'm worried about losing something. I've been lucky, because the actors I've worked with really prefer short rehearsals.

18. ADHERENCE TO SCRIPT?

Yes, I do insist that an actor sticks completely to the scriptlines and business.

19. EDITING SUPERVISION?

Editing, for me, is the favorite part of the film. I usually like to watch rushes alone—I don't let certain actors look at their work. I make notes into a tape recorder as to what takes I like—give them to an editor; this way, they're working with takes I've given them. Even if it doesn't cut, I want to see it. I used to have time to cut my own pictures. now I don't. Any editor who works for me knows that I control the cutting. On *Taxi Driver* we had three editors, because we had a fast release date. I would go from one room to another, editing.

I edited *Mean Streets* myself. With *Alice,* I did a lot of the cutting myself, but worked with someone else. It was good, because I had another point of view. It would be ideal to have five or six months alone to be able to cut a picture, but that's impossible for me.

20. ROLE OF MUSICAL SCORE?

Music is most important. I don't like music that emphasizes what has already been seen on the screen. I like it to counterpoint against it. In all my films except *Taxi Driver* I've used what's known as "tracking"—records. rock 'n roll groups like "The Rolling Stones."

The two songs we used in *Mean Streets* cost us $150,000. I chose that music because that was a way of life. *Alice* used rock 'n roll music. "Where or When" is a song of remembrance of the past. Each song had to be carefully chosen to give it kind of an oblique look. *Taxi Driver*'s character was completely alienated, so I thought it was perfect for a score. We had Bernard Hermann do an original for us. That was actually the first time I had sat down with a composer. *New York, New York* will have the authentic music of the 1940s.

21. INVOLVEMENT IN PREPARATION OF MUSICAL SCORE?

Yes. I am deeply involved in all aspects.

22. WHAT SCENES SHOULD HAVE MUSIC?

I think I covered that. I've used records pretty much the same way you use a music score.

23. SOUND EFFECTS?

Sometimes watching a rough cut of a picture, I get very much involved in seeing sequences without sound effects. Very often I get married to certain sound effects on the production track—I really like them.

You'll have a sound effects editor come in and say, "Make that cleaner."

"I'll say, "No, leave that in."

Then we work from there and I ask for other things. The biggest job of sound effects for me was with the ending of *Taxi Driver.* It was done really in three parts: the firing of the gun, the overall sound and whatever it was hitting, and it was all edited together. We often let the music come up and take over. I find it interesting to look at old films, especially at the beginning of the sound era. Some of the action shots were taken silently, I assume, because the people were moving at a slightly rapid speed. I work very closely with the editor and also the title sequence people.

Don Siegel

1. BACKGROUND?

I'm not exactly sure I understand this question. Obviously I went to school. I traveled a great deal both here in America and in Europe. When I lived in Paris I made it very obvious to anyone who saw me that I was an artist, because I had paint stains all over my suit. I developed an *avant garde* manner of speech concerning my efforts in painting, but in actuality, I couldn't draw a straight line.

2. FIRST FILM JOB?

I started in 1934 at Warner Bros. as an assistant in the film library. This meant that I would correlate and keep a record of the stock shots that could be used in other pictures. I found this job interesting in that I ran many movies, making notes for possible stock shots, and I began to work with film. Not very well, I might add. I remember cutting sunsets which became sunrises as I couldn't tell where the frame line was. Even so, I became an assistant editor.

I started to understand what editing was really all about, and got an opportunity to become head of the insert department. This was an enormous advance for me, because I had at my disposal a camera crew from an operator on down, a grip and an occasional electrician. I would shoot "inserts," that is, close shots of newspapers or of anything such as a book of matches. I had to examine with great care the film into which the insert was going to be cut, so gradually I began to learn how to match action, etc. I became somewhat bored with the restrictions placed on the size of the shots that I was making. I would go to a director and say, "Why not let me shoot the star getting out of the car and pan her into the building?"

I pointed out to the director that it would save him a lot of time. Remember, I had this crew at my disposal. So, within a short space of time, Tenny Wright—who was the production manager at Warner Bros.—started making cracks to the effect that any shots the director was too lazy to make, automatically became an insert.

Of course I didn't know it at the time, but what I was going was starting to direct second unit.

The next step was probably the most important in developing my skills at directing. I started the montage department. Before I did this, montages were handled at Warner Bros. in this way: the editor of a particular film would assemble a lot of stock shots and material that the director of the picture had shot, and let the optical printer put it all together without any particular discipline or instructions. That would become a montage. Almost inevitably there was a great deal of super-imposition.

In developing the Montage department, I wrote in great detail what the montage was supposed to get over, like a passage of time, and I would list all of the shots I was going to make. I literally began directing.

Montage is unusual in one aspect that it does give the audience credit for intelligence...by using symbolism, forcing the audience to think. One learns the value of film footage, because one has to tell this particular segment of the picture as briefly, concisely, and clearly as possible.

Consequently, again without my knowing it, I began to develop a certain taut style from doing hundreds and hundreds of montages.

Next, I started doing second unit work. In general, second unit does the violent parts of the movie...car chases, run-away horses, etc. etc., scenes that the director of the film wouldn't have to spend his time on. I worked completely as a separate unit. The next stage was the implement of sound. I discovered that I could do the montage better, and in many instances the second unit, with the implement of sound. It was a major victory as the studio, at that time, felt that montages and second unit work didn't necessitate using sound.

3. YOUR GOAL IN FILMMAKING?

I believe in making films primarily for entertainment. That, to me, is the name of the game...to make something that will satisfy the paying customers. Hopefully, not in a particular genre; hopefully, not with an obvious message. I don't have any underlying objective other than the need to earn a living. I can do that by making successful films.

4. IN WHAT GENRE DO YOU SEEK A STORY?

Unfortunately, having done so much second unit, I became known as a director of violent scenes. Many of the fights that I staged, like that in _Saratoga Trunk_ [1965], etc., got me going in a genre that I wish hadn't happened. Hence, most of my films are in the genre of crime movies or violent movies. That includes, of course, Westerns.

But in your question you ask, "In what particular genre do you hope to find it?" I hope to find a film that I can do one day that is a simple love story or a comedy. The difficulty there is that the studio doesn't like to get off a winning horse; inasmuch as I have achieved a certain success in doing action pictures, I am finding it difficult to change the genre of my films.

5. STORY SOURCE?

I don't have any particular preference as to the source of my story material. Generally speaking, if you're lucky enough to find a good novel, at least the characters are well delineated and, in general, a plot structure is there. On the other hand, if I am lucky enough to find a script that is useable, I am that much ahead.

6. USE A SCRIPTWRITER OR DO IT YOURSELF?

I have had varying success with working with screenwriters. Some of them have been stimulating, and have given me the essential details to make a picture. At best, I believe an excellent screen play is the blueprint for the director to make the picture. However, on any script, I involve myself in it. Not so much with the actual writing, but in hopefully giving the writer encouragement, directing him into channels of thought that possibly he might not have come up with. Certainly doing a great deal of editing. Frequently giving the writer a step outline for the new structure that I feel the story needs, etc. Once in a great while, I might take pen in hand and do a scene but I am basically not an author. I wish I had that talent. I am an *auteur.*

7. CLOSE COLLABORATION WITH THE SCREENWRITER?

I'm afraid I work differently with different writers. In some instances, I work very closely with the screenwriter. That seems to be the best modus operandi for me. I always try to encourage the writer to express his views as fully and freely as possible and although I may go into a final script polish, I try to involve him, too. However, there are some instances where I can't communicate with the writer and I'm forced to do the final polish, more or less myself, which is not particularly healthy.

8. PREPLAN OR IMPROVISE?

I don't care if the writer of the screenplay has not worked out the action (business) fully on paper, because the script would become much, much too long. However, I work it out very fully in *my* script before I step on the stage. But having done that doesn't mean if something better comes along, I won't improvise. I'm fairly disciplined in my shooting, but still try to work loose.

I don't even let the actors know that I have worked out the staging. I let them stumble around a bit, and then suggest something here and there, and then I more or less have it as I envisioned it on paper. However, if the actor, or anyone on the set for that matter, has a better idea, I will steal it. I'm the worst thief in the business.

9. MOST IMPORTANT COMPONENT OF YOUR FILM?

Obviously, the most important part of a film is the script, and as an auteur director I work very hard on the script. I feel *that* section of the making of a motion picture is the most important part. Of course, the cast (not only the stars) is another important section. I don't feel that a director, no matter how much control he has over the picture, is the only person responsible for that picture. I am involved very closely in the editing of the film, and obviously I work very closely with the art director and the cameraman. I don't lean on them, but I'm very appreciative of their help.

10. WORK WITH A PRODUCER?

Generally, I produce and direct. The reason for that is the name "producer" is a misnomer. It used to be that the producer was the gentleman who gave you the wherewithall to make the picture. Now, he works for a salary, as do I, or has a piece of the picture, as do I. He doesn't put up any actual money for the picture. Neither do I. I respect a producer, if he is a good producer.

Malheursement, I don't truthfully feel there are many good producers, I expect a good producer not to be too worried about protecting his prerogatives as a producer, but instead to encourage the creativity of the people who are working for him. I have found producers like that, and when I do, it is a joy to work with them. They relieve me of many duties; boring details at which I am no good anyway. They protect me—God bless them.

11. USE A DIALOGUE DIRECTOR?

Dialogue directors are very dangerous. The worst mistake you can make is to have a dialogue director that you don't trust, one who starts directing the actors before you have a chance to work with them. I always fire those dialogue directors immediately. Most dialogue directors are frustrated directors.

I have been particularly fortunate in the last fifteen years in working with one dialogue director who has been of enormous help to me. He not only saves me a great deal of time in making sure that all the actors know their lines, he also warns me about certain problems that I may have to face: unprepared actors, actors who want dialogue changes, etc.

In addition, my dialogue director is of more help probably than anyone else with the actual shooting script. I lean on my dialogue director more than anyone else in the company. He is my sounding board. I bounce things off him. Obviously you can't do that unless you have a very superior dialogue director, otherwise you will find yourself in serious trouble. I'm very lucky in that my dialogue director and I work well together.

12. WRITER OR PRODUCER ON THE SET?

I don't particularly mind whether the writer or the producer is on the set when I'm rehearsing or shooting, although I don't encourage it. If I should become self-conscious, then I would simply ask the writer or producer to leave.

A great deal depends on the relationship that one has with one's writer or producer. The important thing is to get the scene shot as well as it is possible for you to do it. Now, if the writer or the producer's presence has a negative effect, then I must remove him from the set.

13. WORK CLOSELY WITH THE CAMERAMAN?

Of course I block out everything with my cameraman and tell him what I want. I'm not interested in the cameraman giving me set ups. I feel that I want that to be my province. However, I do want his enthusiastic support, and I want him to do his job as quickly as possible so that I will have more time to work on the scene. I repeat, I don't lean on my cameraman. I respect him. I don't expect him to do more than photograph the scene.

14. SUPERVISION OF CASTING?

I work very closely on the casting of all my films. Most of the suggestions as to who should play the leading roles, and a great many of the minor roles, come from me. Certainly I check out any and all suggestions. It is only with regard to the financial limitations that I will give in to the studio, and use someone that I feel is not as good as someone else, yet I fight very hard to get my way as far as casting is concerned.

15. PREFERENCE OF ACTING STYLE?

I don't care whether the actor is a "seasoned" or an "instinctive" type. All I am interested in is whether he can do the part. I am not interested in whether he is a Stanislavsky actor or whether it is purely experience in an entirely different school of acting that he employs. It so happens that I studied Stanslavsky, so in that area I am able to communicate with actors who use the Stanislavsky method, but I wouldn't say they were better actors because of it.

16. PRECAMERA WORK WITH ACTOR?

I don't exactly know how to answer this question. Of course, in talking to the actor about the part, I go into it as carefully as I can, and in as much detail as I think necessary. I try to work out the differences, possibly, in his interpretation of the role as against my interpretation of the role. On the one hand, I don't want him to be a robot, yet, on the other, I certainly want him to be uninhibited, and to bring to the characterization a plus which might be entirely his own. Then it will be up to me to decide whether or not I like his interpretation.

Certainly, there's no pride of ownership. I am only interested in doing the best job possible. If I feel that the actor is making the character more vivid, more interesting, in doing it his own particular way, then I'm grateful to him. If, on the other hand, I feel that the actor, possibly, is overacting, ... using strange mannerisms, etc.—I won't allow it.

17. IMPORTANCE OF REHEARSALS?

If one has an opportunity to rehearse one's cast, obviously it would be a mistake not to take advantage of the rehearsal period. A great amount of information can be learned both by the actors and the director during this rehearsal period. Unfortunately, my pictures are generally done on a short schedule and bounce about so much as far as locations are concerned that a serious rehearsal is impractical. It would be much too costly for the budgets that I am allowed.

However, there is one thing I always try to do. I call up each of the actors, and ask if he can come to my house or to a rehearsal hall and simply sit around a table and read the script. It is definitely not a rehearsal, but it is extraordinary how much help it is, particularly for me.

The reason I call up these actors is that it is unofficial; therefore they are not put on salary. The actors know this, and always most enthusiastically agree to this "reading time."

18. ADHERENCE TO SCRIPT?

Of course I don't want the actor to adhere meticulously to the script. If he can improve it...again, I'm very grateful. Certain lines, for example, that Clint Eastwood would read could not be read by an actor like Michael Caine. They have an entirely different approach to the part they are playing, and words that might sound marvelous for Clint Eastwood wouldn't sound at all correct for Michael, and vice versa. I cannot stress too much that making a film is not a contest of will between the actor and the director. It is a team in which, because of the actor's talent and, hopefully, the intelligent guidance of the director, a film role can be made better.

19. EDITING SUPERVISION?

As a former editor, obviously, I supervise the final editing of the film very closely. I don't understand your reference to "one of the all time greats" who loathed viewing his own rushes. To me, it is of paramount importance that I see all the rushes. Having seen them, I know whether or not they will go together; whether or not I am getting what I want out of my actors; whether or not the photography etc. is what I want.

At the start, depending on the editor, I let the editor alone. He only comes to me when he feels he is in or that *I* am in trouble. For example, he might suggest an added close-up. I may or may not agree. I like the editor to take the film...work on it...in many instances his approach is somewhat different from mine, and I find the result stimulating. On the other hand, generally speaking, through no fault of the editor, the first rough cut is always long because I want to see all of the film.

The result depresses me. I not only hate the film, but also I hate myself. After viewing it, perhaps once more, the following day, I will then start working on the film with the editor. That period is very important, as is the rest of the post-production work. It is difficult for me to understand directors who aren't responsible for the final cut of the film.

The result depresses me. I not only hate the film, but I hate myself. After viewing it, perhaps once more, the following day, I will then start working on the film with the editor. That period is very important, as is the rest of the post-production work. It is difficult for me to understand directors who aren't responsible for the final cut of the film.

20. ROLE OF MUSICAL SCORE?

If a musical score is done really well...in a sense it defeats its case. One will not be aware of the music that is a perfect adjunct to the picture. If the music is too flamboyant...too much of it, etc....although it does attract attention, it may not be helping the picture.

Obviously the purpose of the musical score is to, in every way, reinforce the mood of the picture. I have been very lucky in working with intelligent, extremely talented composers whose contributions to my pictures have been outstanding.

21. INVOLVEMENT IN PREPARATION OF MUSICAL SCORE?

I don't believe that I should become too deeply involved in the actual notes that are being written for the score, because of my lack of knowledge. I am not equal to it. However, with the composer, I do run the picture very closely many times, and express what I feel is needed to help the picture. Frequently I will tell the composer that I don't like my work, and I need help in sequence work. If I had directed it better, I might not have needed any music. I might also add that most pictures are overscored.

22. WHAT SCENES SHOULD HAVE MUSIC?

Yes, indeed, I do exercise final control as to which scenes are to be scored. I spot the music very carefully. Frequently, in the final dubbing, I will not only eliminate music, I will transpose music written for a particular sequence, and use it somewhere else. This, of course, is always done with the enthusiastic permission of the composer.

23. SOUND EFFECTS?

The importance of sound effects can't be over-emphasized. Great care must be taken not only in the obvious instances in "action" sequences, but throughout the entire film. It will make the picture more realistic. I am particularly finicky about sound effects. When they are well done they greatly help the picture.

COMMENT

There is one thing that occurred to me which all directors must face: at varying times throughout a career, they are under the controlled influence ... dictates ... of the various people they are working with. Of course, a director, particularly a young one, should listen to all the diverse counseling, admonitions, threats that he receives, but in the end *he* must make the decision.

That decision should be based on truth. The director must make the film for himself. He doesn't make it for the executives, and he doesn't make it for the Gold Star Mothers. He doesn't make it for the censoring board, and he doesn't make it for the Jews nor the Poles. He doesn't make it for the aged, and he doesn't make it for the young.

He makes each picture for himself. If you try to outguess a particular group, or more specifically your own boss, you're dead.

Steven Spielberg

1. BACKGROUND?

I've always been movie-oriented. I served food in the college cafeteria (working my way through, and catching films), and I whitewashed citrus trees in Scottsdale, Arizona (again for bread and circuses).

2. FIRST FILM JOB?

Many of my friends think I've had it too easy since I began as a director under term contract with Universal Studios in 1968-69. I was 21 when Sidney J. Sheinberg said, "Today you are a director," and threw me Joan Crawford, and a Rod Serling pilot script, to cut my teeth on.

Few knew about my ambitious beginnings nine years earlier, when the Boy Scouts of America began offering merit badges in photography, and I grabbed a 8mm Kodak rather than a 35mm Roliflex, and made a sweeping adventure—three minutes long.

That's when I started paying my dues. I was financier, director, cinematographer, actor, set director, editor, writer, and even composed original scores using the elementary school band. Insufferable? I sure was, but there wasn't much to do while growing up in Arizona. I felt old and experienced when the time came to "go pro."

3. YOUR GOAL IN FILMMAKING?

Having only directed a few feature motion pictures, I haven't really had much of a chance to demonstrate a general philosophy through my work. If someone gave me an opportunity to make a film that would magically change the world, I wouldn't know what to do. I am so scattered in my tastes that I doubt whether a vivid social consciousness will be evident in films I choose for a while longer. A few years from now, if I'm still lucky enough to continue making the movies I want to make, a body of work might show me what I'm about. Right now, though, whisking an audience off its feet and into a two dimensional world of fourth dimensional ideas is enough to keep me going.

4. IN WHAT GENRE DO YOU SEEK A STORY?

I wouldn't want to look in just one place for an idea. I've tried to be open-minded and find unfamiliar genres interesting rather than make films only about what I am interested in.

5. STORY SOURCE?

I'll go any route for a good idea in short story form, treatment, original notion, the ad section, or a Superman comic, or the unpublished great American novel.

6. USE A SCRIPTWRITER OR DO IT YOURSELF?

I find it hard to work with a Smith-Corona Super 12 Electric typewriter. It only hums back at you when you're trying ideas on. I enjoy collaborating with new writers. Pitching sessions are sometimes more fun that getting out there, and shooting the actual scene half a year later. Ultimately it gets down to my asking, "Who am I trying to entertain? Three writers locked in a hotel room at four in the morning, or myself?"

I will usually do a draft of my own, before sessions providing outside help. On *Jaws* [1975] I never really stopped writing, but chose to bring in Howard Sackler, Carl Gottlieb and John Milius before returning to my own gut level instincts, dating back to the first impression I had, after reading the unpublished *Jaws* galleys. My films will get better, once I start accepting my gut feelings, which usually are my first impressions. Until then, most of my movies will share ideas with a minimum of three script doctors, and we'll split the screen credits.

7. CLOSE COLLABORATION WITH THE SCREENWRITER?

I would prefer to write my own scripts, but sometimes this is impossible. Inherent in Peter Benchley's *Jaws* deal, was his right to a first draft with a set of revisions. On *Close Encounters Of The Third Kind* [1977], whereas the original idea was mine, I was so preoccupied with pre-production on *Jaws* that I hired another writer to do a draft before taking over the writing entirely on my own. [*The*] *Sugarland Express* [1974] was also an original notion based on a factual newspaper account, but in that case I had met a couple of writers, Hal Barwood and Matthew Robbins, whose talent was undeniable, and whose participation, I felt, was as important to the realization of the idea in screenplay form, as the actual idea itself was.

With the exception of *Sugarland Express,* I found myself ultimately doing the lion's share of work behind the typewriter, for better or worse. *Jaws* and *Close Encounters* express my feelings as filmmaker. As I expressed to you, Tay, I find that working with two or three outside writers increases my own objectivity and gives me a fresh look at an idea that can easily become stale during the year it takes to develop, and the next six months of principal photography.

8. PREPLAN OR IMPROVISE?

If I don't have all the "plays" worked out ahead of time, I can't face the day. I am lost. But if I stick with the plays to the letter, I am bored. I feel like a garage mechanic assembling a Volkswagon the only way it can be assembled. Simply knowing that a game plan exists, gives me the confidence and courage to deviate and improvise and discover new ways to go. Without a plan, I will worry about how to make the scene function in the most elementary way. That will preoccupy all of my thinking. With a plan, I can look at all possibilities, and pick the most compelling.

9. MOST IMPORTANT COMPONENT OF YOUR FILM?

As dozens of movies prove every year...without a good story this director is "up a creek without his paddle."

10. WORK WITH A PRODUCER?

This is a question I am often asked, and one that I find the hardest to answer. The best criterion would be asking yourself, "Could I have made the last picture without the producer?"

Without Richard Zanuck and David Brown, *Jaws* might not have been made at Universal. United Artists, Warners, maybe Columbia were next in line.

Aside from that it's silly to say I *couldn't* have done it without them. But *with* them, I felt less pressure from the studio, when the production spilled over schedule and over budget. They absorbed the studio slack. They believed in me, and gave me more self-confidence than I would have had at that time in my life. I respected them and let them talk me out of a couple of rotten ideas I wanted to try on for size. They are a formidable team, and their names are almost as famous as the title of Peter Benchley's book. They supplied a lot of good public relations.

It was nice to know I had producers ready to fight the bureaucrats so I could make the kind of movie I wanted to make, in an atmosphere of absolute freedom and total comfort.

11. USE A DIALOGUE DIRECTOR?

I've never used a dialogue director. Maybe this is due to the fact that—up until now—I've only made action pictures.

12. WRITER OR PRODUCER ON THE SET?

This really depends on the people in question. Carl Gottlieb spent the first eight weeks of our 32 week shoot, standing by to help me make sense of the constant pitching sessions the actors would have at my house after filming each day. I never liked the first two acts of my own last draft, and was open to any good new ideas on *Jaws*.

On *Sugarland Express* I didn't invite Hal Barwood and Matt Robbins onto the Texas location. They are enormously talented, highly opinionated, and had a strong influence over me. This was my first feature, and—win or lose—I wanted the filming to be reflective of my own tastes and judgments. I guess I didn't want to share that. Plus, I was very sanguine about our screenplay, and pretty much shot it verbatim.

On *Close Encounter Of the Third Kind,* the writer was on the set every day. I wish I could have stopped him from visits.... Although, half of me coming to work every day wouldn't look right!

I never had a producer on the set with me, so I don't know if I'd like it or not. On *Jaws,* Dick Zanuck only appeared when special effects were about to be set off ...or when an executive decision involving schedule or money arose. Otherwise, he monitored activities on a little five watt walkie-talkie in his Vineyard home.

Dick was much more involved in *The Sugarland Express.* That was his real baby ...including his son, Harrison, who played Baby Langston. Dick did everything on that one from baby-sitting to teamster work, to set construction, to bandaging a few hurt actor egos. In all cases, his presence was always felt by me, and gave me a lot of confidence.

13. WORK CLOSELY WITH THE CAMERAMAN?

When I first started making film, I never unduly concerned myself with the written words. I'd always allow the camera to tell the story. Recently I have tried to let the story tell the camera what to do. Everything is predetermined.

One of my first visual impressions after reading the book *Jaws* was: All water shots should be eyewitness angled...i.e. where the camera is eye level with the waterline, bringing the water right up to the viewer's chin. The story told the camera what to do.

I hired a studio sketch artist to follow me around for eight weeks. Through him I planned the camera placement, composition and cutting sequences for the entire last sixty minutes of *Jaws.* Overall there were two hundred and fifty master concept shots sketched and boarded. When the ordeal of making the movie was over, every sketch had been committed to film. In many cases, however, some of the sketches were improved upon via a creative working relationship with the cinematographer, Bill Butler, and the production designer, Joe Alves.

I played it looser with the on-shore drama. I choreographed the "scenes with the actors"...rehearsed it...then walked the set and in twenty minutes predetermined all of my set-ups for that particular sequence. But I'm the sort of director who enjoys riding around on moviola dollies and Chapman cranes with one eye glued to the eye-piece. Determining camera placement on a set is like being the arranger of a complicated musical variation on a main theme. To this extent I am somewhat autocratic as to where the camera goes.

As to how the people are lit, I leave that to the cinematographer. I cast Vilmos Zsigmond to photograph *Sugarland Express* not because I liked his compositions, but because I thought the textures he brought out through his lighting and exposure gave the film a period identity and created a mood that made a simple story more thought-provoking.

14. SUPERVISION OF CASTING?

I collaborate with the producer on the major roles to be cast. In these star-conscious days, the studio has a few things to say, too.

Nobody has ever been forced upon me. I brought Richard Dreyfuss and Roy Scheider to Richard Zanuck and David Brown for their approval. David Brown wanted Robert Shaw to play Quint. I resisted at first, until I'd looked at six Shaw films, then kicked myself for not thinking of Shaw earlier.

Shari Rhodes is a casting person I met in Texas. She was assisting the casting director, Mike Fenton, on *Sugarland Express* and had such a good nose for ferreting out natural actors from regular street folk that I hired her again for *Jaws,* and again for *Close Encounters.* I trust Shari enough to let her sift through hundreds of possibilities until she brings me her top ten choices for each of the smaller roles.

15. PREFERENCE OF ACTING STYLE?

I like working with any actor who isn't bound by a set of rules. Actors who are intuitive about a part, and open to sudden changes in the relationships are vital to the way I work. I like actors who can view a role from two sides: how they relate that particular character to parts of themselves to bring out the best of both, and how they see the character they are playing from a totally objective audience point of view.

If the actor I hire is conscious of the people he is performing to, he automatically becomes his own worst critic, and his own best re-writer.

I think the term "method actor" is a dangerous one. Its meaning is lost in ridicule. If an actor is confused and doesn't know why he is being ordered to say a certain line in a certain way, the inarticulate director will sometimes save face by muttering to the camera crew, behind the actor's back... "method actor." They should strike the term from common usage. There are too many ways it can be improperly interpreted.

16. PRECAMERA WORK WITH ACTOR?

The minute an actor reads a part that is being offered, an impression is intuitively etched in his mind. I don't think it can be helped. More and more, I find myself trying to undo preconceived images about a character by the actor playing it.

Sometimes, especially when I use local talent, that is all I want. But at certain times, as with Goldie Hawn playing gun-snapping Lou Jean Joplin in *Sugarland Express,* I had a prototype in mind that was a hundred miles from the person I thought was Goldie. The emotional moments originated, of course, deep inside

Goldie herself. But the look of Lou Jean, that walk, that voice, and all of the affectations, were conceived by me and written by Barwood and Robbins.

As a director, I use the rehearsal time to watch quietly, and make choices. I hate to talk a part to death. Some actors are only satisfied when they think of their role in perfect planar balance with the cosmos. You can't hire an astrologist to do a reading on a fictitious part, born from the prismatic imagination of two, maybe three, different writers. Characters in movies have no place in the universe; I would never ask a character in a script, "What's your rising sign?"

17. IMPORTANCE OF REHEARSALS?

Goldie Hawn, Bill Atherton and Michael Sacks got together with me in Houston for a rehearsal one week before our first shooting day on *Sugarland Express.* We read through the entire screenplay. This was the first time I had done anything like that and it was worth it. We could tell the strong scenes from the weak ones. We could hear what played, and what just sort of crawled into a corner to die. I could feel where the energy centered, where the excitement occurred, as well as those scenes that functioned as bare scaffolding, holding up the story, but lacking color.

It gave me time to fix things before the meter started running. All the in-fighting between the principal actors about their parts, and each other was resolved on the floor of the hotel with room service and clean "johns."

On the first day of shooting all the actors were happy, and had no questions. But a week later the movie began to take on a life of its own, and all the problems we thought were solved in the air-conditioned hotel took on greater dimensions, and caused bigger problems.

In rehearsals, we speculated how the characters would feel toward each other. In the harsh light of a shooting day, Goldie's spontaneity, Bill Atherton's polished precision, and Michael Sacks' sense of humor took the movie in another direction away from all our profound scheming.

The human importance of the events remained. But the nature of the relationships in the car became more fun-loving, naive, and soulful...like a big Chuck Jones "Road-Runner Cartoon."

I now think reading through a script is vital, and rehearsing just to try things on for size is great. But locking oneself in a hotel room in order to lock in the parts, is the worst mistake one could make. You know that saying, "Today is the first day of the rest of your life?" That is how I am beginning to look at a movie in the making. Every day is a new deal. Every day, anything is try-on-able. Spontaneity is everything.

18. ADHERENCE TO SCRIPT?

There are instances when a piece of business or an isolated line is crucial to having the story work, or the plot make sense. If an actor wants to change one of those, that's a fight I have to win.

Or, take the case of a joke. There aren't many ways to make a joke work, except the right way. That's another battle.

Then there are favorite selfish moments. Maybe it's a speech that I can't envision any other way, or a piece of business like the sight gag in *Jaws* in which Quint demonstrates his machoism by inhaling a whole can of beer, then crushing the can with one hand...which Richard Dreyfuss counters by imitating Robert Shaw's every action—with a styrofoam cup!

There are instances when a point must be communicated to the audience in no uncertain terms. It might be an obvious overstatement, but anything more subtle could be lost forever. An actor who has too often performed Kafka or Pinter might object to those lead-pipe lines.

On the other hand, whole scenes sometimes require a good fleshing out. In *Jaws,* I budgeted for three, as yet, unwritten scenes that I felt were critical to three specific sections of the film. One of them turned out to be the final plea for help to the Mayor of Amity Island, just before the 4th of July tragedy.

Weeks after principal photography commenced, I could better see the direction each character was taking. That scene was written after extensive improvisational gestalt one day before I shot it. Most of the dialogue was supplied by the actors. So far, in the films I've made, I find myself depending on the actors' good judgment as much as they depend on mine. As Lee J. Cobb said in *On The Waterfront*— "Every-body works."

19. EDITING SUPERVISION?

I think that I am more at home in an editing room than on a sound stage. When photography on a film wraps, I simply transfer locations. The cast and crew go home, and I go to the editing room until I am happy with my movie. I've always taken editing as seriously as I do a good story, and a successful shoot. Editing is no more, and no less than one added extension of the directorial process, so it mystifies me when I hear of directors who actually waive their first cutting rights or allow the film editor to assemble the rough cut without the director being in the room, working the brake, cut for cut, frame for frame until the total outcome complies as idealistically as can be with that director's first vision.

Certain directors I know seem to feel that their job is over on the last day of shooting when they say, "Cut—print" and the A.D. yells, "It's a wrap."

Apparently it doesn't disturb those directors to think of the film editor as a sort of relief pitcher, who carries the ball until the picture jives with that editor's belated vision, yet this happens time and time again. Mainly in television, but too many times with big feature films.

That it happens in television is semi-understandable. Journeyman "grunt" directors go from episode to episode so fast that they sometimes forget that the *Marcus Welby* they are watching on TV is one of their own!

In television, I would drive the editors up a wall. I wouldn't leave their editing rooms. I cut my one and only _Marcus Welby_ over Dick Wray's shoulder as if it were _Citizen Kane._

Ed Abroms, who edited my first professional assignment in 1968, threw me bodily out of his cutting room, and called the producer to complain. I think he threw something heavy at me, too, but missed.

When I directed a "Movie of the Week" entitled _Duel_ in 1971, the network decided they wanted it to air one month after I completed my last day of shooting. George Eckstein, the producer, and I went to Dick Belding (the editorial supervisor), and hired five editors. Sort of "on roller skates" I glided from room to room for _fourteen_ days of twelve hours each, selecting takes, determining the length of each cut, creating all the pacing and rhythm, and creating moments that were never shot. When the film was all together, there was no apparent division of labor or style. The film was a continuation of what I do as a director in interpreting—in this case—Richard Matheson's original vision into film, the film I wanted to make of it.

I find it hard to work with a lot of film editors who consider themselves sort of postproduction directors. A few editors have turned me down—refused to work for me. Recently, three extremely successful editors simply came out and said, "I must be alone when I work on your film."

I said to them, "I know you think you're going into surgery, but I gotta be there too...I'm the _patient._"

Verna Fields, who cut _Jaws_ with me, was a special case. She cannot work on a film _without_ the director. She plays well as the devil's advocate and becomes a good sounding board. She adds fizz to the creative juices, much as Lee Strasberg functions in his acting classes. Part of it is her personality, and part of it is the difference in our ages. After all, she was cutting sound effects on some of my favorite Saturday afternoon shows when I was around seven years old.

I really don't know what Verna would do if [Peter] Bogdanovich or [George] Lucas or I said to her, "Don't talk to me. Here's eighty thousand feet of my selected takes. Make me a movie!" Verna's not a quitter, but I suspect that would push her close to the brink. She is one of the few cutters who understand that editing is the continuation of the directorial process. In an era in which everybody wants to be the star, that sort of folks are hard to find in the A.C.E. [American Cinema Editors]

20. ROLE OF MUSICAL SCORE?

Because I'm a "moviegoer," I've been conditioned to accept the musical score as the familiar sidekick that heightens the reality of the experience. Nothing seems more natural than some haunting theme as Lawrence of Arabia walks out of his tent to confront the night. Everybody who has ever seen a movie has been conditioned _not_ to wonder why a large orchestra is playing so near the Arabian bivouac area.

For me, especially in a fast-paced action sequence, music can literally hide the cutting. It can make a sloppily cut-together sequence look like camera magic.

An even better example is in *The Bridge On The River Kwai* [1957], David Lean recorded mass whistling of the Colonel Bogey March, which sounded *verité* enough until he slowly introduced Malcolm Arnold's music with the London Symphony Orchestra, and created a crescendo of excitement that made me feel British and heroic. I've mentioned Lean a lot in conjunction with movie music, because next to Hitchcock—I think he is the most skilled in his knowledge and use of film music in perfect unison with the nature of his work.

21. INVOLVEMENT IN PREPARATION OF MUSICAL SCORE?

I get as involved in the preparation of the music as the composer will allow. I feel that my creative contribution has ended after I choose the composer, run the picture with him, spot sections of the film where I feel music is essential, and have a few rap sessions about genres and textures.

I would never hang around the place where a composer composes, and hum things into his ear. I admit this is one area between cutting and dubbing where the directorial continuum is suspended. All the director can do is pray you've met the right man, and said the right things. Very little can be done if the score isn't up to expectations, but I've been lucky with the only two composers I have been associated with: Billy Goldenberg and John Williams. Both of them are aces.

The net result of the total effectiveness of *Jaws* as a horror suspense thriller is, in large part, due to John Williams' original contributions to the sound track.

(There is no one else with whom I can share that, with the possible exception of Joe Alves and Bob Mattey, the production designer and the special effects engineer.)

22. WHAT SCENES SHOULD HAVE MUSIC?

When I first ran *Jaws* for John Williams, I stayed away.

John ran the film again and called me. He was really excited and had some strong initial impressions that he quickly wrote down. He saw a full orchestra and a real colorful movie-movie score. Not a score that would copy or mock other genres, but a nongimmick (meaning nonelectronic) classical sound in the best traditions of Steiner and Stravinsky. A real sea symphony. A week later, I ran *Jaws* with John, and I suggested a lot of places where music should go. John had ideas of his own, and we figured that it's better to have too much than not enough.

As I was putting *Jaws* together with Verna, I used certain "cue" tracks from other movies to give the cutting a musical rhythm. John never heard those "cue" tracks because Verna took them all out before we showed him anything. However, I did borrow the music from one of John's scores, *Images* [1972], to create textures beyond what was on the film during the cutting process. At least this gave me a definite idea as to where I felt music would heighten what was already there.

Some scenes, I felt, played without music altogether, like the July 4th beach panic. I wanted whole sequences without music, because of the sounds of seagulls, kids innocently playing near the water, splashing, radios and general summer sounds which were orchestration enough. John agreed with this concept immediately, feeling that a lot of ominous natural things would be the best introduction for his famous *Jaws* cue telling you... here it comes again!

John felt strongly about putting music under the first moonlight victim. I really objected. I wanted to open the film as naturally as a Fred Wiseman documentary. But John had this instinct, and I trusted him. It worked, *Jaws* was not a Fred Wiseman documentary.

I also felt the sequence in which the three men in the Orca chase the one barrel dragging through the water behind the shark was strictly an effects sequence. I wanted the engine sounds and the sounds of water against the prow to carry it through.

When Verna and I assembled the scene, Verna—on her own—had cut in great sound effects that served as music. We paced the scene according to engine pitch and the volume of water washing over the barrel. It sounded like anything added would make noise out of our inventiveness; however, John composed a scherzo that was totally against the grain of the scene, and it worked like gangbusters.

It united the three characters as they shared a kind of insane American blood sport. This frolicking pirate music made allies of three desperate types, and for the first time allowed them a temporary upper hand against the shark. Music can sure turn things around.

Leopoldo Torre Nilsson

1. BACKGROUND?

I don't recall any vocation before entering cinema. My father was a cinema director and I started to walk around the sets at fifteen, rather disliking the world of actors and technicians. I wanted to be a writer; it was some time before I started to believe in cinema.

2. FIRST FILM JOB?

I was an assistant director and developed into a scriptwriter under very uncertain conditions, because Argentine cinema always provided a very uncertain future.

3. YOUR GOAL IN FILMMAKING?

I always understood cinema as a way of talking about my ghosts, or my people, or my country; the pitiable errors of society as it is, the possible beauty of mankind under better conditions of life. But I am very unhappy if I feel a lack of technical knowledge to express those things.

4. IN WHAT GENRE DO YOU SEEK A STORY?

As to the particular genre in which I hope to find material for a film, literature is very close to life; so it is to life or literature that I look.

5. STORY SOURCE?

I feel that I am open-minded to different reasons which provoke a film. Sometimes I find an idea, and I fight for years, trying to search for financing.

Sometimes, rarely, financing comes first and one has to force himself into loving something. The essence, I believe, is to love filmmaking, and second, to have true inspiration.

6. USE A SCRIPTWRITER OR DO IT YOURSELF?

I like to be surrounded by collaborators wise enough to enrich my ideas, but not so wise as to contradict me too much. Alone, I am a bit lazy.

7. CLOSE COLLABORATION WITH THE SCREENWRITER?

It is difficult for me to assimilate others' ideas; I need to remake everything myself, and in my own proper, mistaken, talented or foolish way. The only long, big, beautiful dream I have never conquered 100 percent is absolute freedom of operation.

8. PREPLAN OR IMPROVISE?

I like to have everything put down on paper and thoroughly prepared. So, the inevitable improvisation afterward is a pleasure and not an obligation.

9. MOST IMPORTANT COMPONENT OF YOUR FILM?

Every part, human and technical, is definitely important; you can kill a film with a bad line, a mistaken sound, a wrong face or an inadequate lens. I respect all collaborators. Naturally, depending on the film, some come to be more important than others.

10. WORK WITH A PRODUCER?

A producer is another collaborator that I prefer to have for discussing, financing, cast, launching and other peripheral components of the film.

11. USE A DIALOGUE DIRECTOR?

I don't believe in a director of dialogue, because making, or helping, or provoking the actors to say their lines is one of the most important "mementos" of the cinematic creation.

12. WRITER OR PRODUCER ON THE SET?

I don't really mind who is there, because in heart and conscience I'm absolutely alone with my collaborators; if one of my collaborators feels intimidated by or shy of any presence, then I shall ask my mother or even the president of the republic to leave the place. (This is not always the safe thing to do, however!)

13. WORK CLOSELY WITH THE CAMERAMAN?

I like to talk and plan before, but I believe much more in the magical moment of shooting. Actors and camera facing each other in a set have, for me, the earthly strength of a couple in love.

14. SUPERVISION OF CASTING?

In casting, as in every other phase of filmmaking, I don't understand any director losing control of a single moment, colour, bit part, casual line or sound. He may have collaborators who suggest, but the decision is always that of the director.

15. PREFERENCE OF ACTING STYLE?

Every character in a film can give birth through spontaneous or elaborated acting. You must have the instinct of what you want for your souls: a trained actor is easier, but many times can give less. A director is always a director of actors and should know all the terms: Grotowsky, Stanislavsky, Bergman, Fellini, Wyler. All elicited great performances using, I am sure, different techniques.

16. PRECAMERA WORK WITH ACTOR?

I like creative collaborators, actors with a world inside, technicians with ideas. I never like to kill an idea.

17. IMPORTANCE OF REHEARSALS?

I don't like rehearsals for cinema: I believe in the magic moment of shooting. Rehearsals are necessary for theatrical reasons, or to economize time, but they make you lose the engrossing moment of shooting.

18. ADHERENCE TO SCRIPT?

I believe I've already answered this question.

19. EDITING SUPERVISION?

I supervise editing, but I shoot editing—"camera-cutting," I believe you call it. Sometimes I leave possibilities to the editor; sometimes I tie him down with my shooting. Editing, then, is rhythm, and I keep close to it.

20. ROLE OF MUSICAL SCORE?

I believe in sound and music as a part of image.

21. INVOLVEMENT IN PREPARATION OF MUSICAL SCORE?

I would like to be able to compose my own music, or the sounds coming from nature. Every image requires an adequate sound, to its own motivation. Music is the easiest way to solve the problem.

22. WHAT SCENES SHOULD HAVE MUSIC?

In my films, I am simultaneously concerned for *every image and every sound*— that can be voice, nature or score.

23. SOUND EFFECTS?

I select, with sound editor, musician and editor, every sound which is going to be played in the film; I supervise the prerecording, mix and final cut.

François Truffaut

1. BACKGROUND?

Before entering film, I worked as a delivery boy, runner at the Stock Exchange, welder, projectionist for the Ministry of Agriculture, and as a journalist.

2. FIRST FILM JOB?

During 1950, I MC'd a "Cine-Club" during which I met André Bazin, who had been the leading French critic from 1945 and continued until his death in 1958. I was lucky to work with Bazin, who directed the cinematographic section of a popular cultural association called "Travail et Culture" [Industry and Education].

After 1953, I became a professional film critic for monthly magazines such as *Les Cahiers du Cinéma, La Parisienne;* for weekly magazines like *Le Bulletin de Paris, Radio—Cinéma, Arts-Spectacles,* as well as for a daily paper, *Le Temps de Paris.*

For two years I was assistant to Roberto Rossellini, preparing films which were never shot. I shot a first silent film in 16mm, *Une Visite,* the only copy of which has, happily, disappeared. Then I wrote my first script *A Bout de Souffle* [*Breathless,* 1959] that I couldn't sell, but that I later gave to Jean-Luc Godard, who improved it considerably and used it as his first feature film: *Breathless.*

I obtained, at this time, a contract as "second assistant" on Max Ophül's film *Lola Montès* [1955]. After trouble with the executive producer, the deal fell through and I went to shoot two short 35mm films: *Histoire d'eau* [1959] (working with Jean-Luc Godard), and *Les Mistons* [*The Mischief Makers,* 1958] with five children in the south of France. Then, at the end of 1958, I began to work on *The 400 Blows* [*Les Quatre Cents Comps,* 1959].

3. YOUR GOAL IN FILMMAKING?

To make a film is an intellectual action, because it implies total dedication, after one has made a decision as to subject matter. It is also an artistic action because our taste dictates those choices and decisions. It is also an emotional action, because our sensitivity and our intuition play a role.

I believe it is an error to think that a filmmaker is somebody who has "something to say." A film of ninety minutes says fewer things than a newspaper article of 3,000 words.

On the other hand, the making of a film lasts eight weeks during which one only records two or three minutes of useable film each day. Because of the slowness of execution of the film medium, the man who would only like to deliver an "urgent message" will rapidly come to understand that it is more effective for him to resort directly to a social or a political action, or to use journalism.

One must not delude oneself that the one who makes a film behaves like a child with his construction game: the director detaches himself from the immediate world, and builds another one as he sees it.

When directing, surrounded by thirty or more people, one car pursued by another, a man running into an elevator, the faces of two lovers as they approach each other, a director becomes a child (even if he is making a film for adults). He must be animated during his work by his childhood feelings that, in all probability, he has never lost.

On the other hand, the conception, the realization and the finishing of a film usually occupy nine months of the director's life. One can compare it with pregnancy followed by birth. I admit that is a cliché, nevertheless, I am convinced of the truth of this cliché anyhow for myself. I, personally, make film to experience the emotions of maternity and the inner fullness those emotions produce.

I should add that, during my youth, the cinema was a sort of refuge. Because of this, I bring to film a love bordering on the religious. I cannot evoke the same interest for politicians as for the filmmakers. I admire, and I sincerely believe that, in the history of England in the Twentieth Century, Charlie Chaplin was more important than Winston Churchill.

In conclusion, I make films in order to feel good, and—when they are a success—they can eventually bring a good feeling to others, which is ideal, because selfishness and narcissism attached to an activity are a source of guilt and anxiety for the creator.

4. IN WHAT GENRE DO YOU SEEK A STORY?

I never feel that I am looking for a film idea, because each time I choose a topic it means that I put aside two or three others—life is so short—*too* short. In my choices I put aside pure drama because life is not so tragic; I refuse pure comedies because life is not so funny; I put aside gangster stories, because I don't like such people: I put aside police stories for the same reason. I try to film neither boats nor horses, because they scare me, nor people in uniform, because they bore me. I rarely show people swimming, skiing, or dancing, because I don't know how to swim, nor to ski, nor to dance. I don't understand anything about sports.

Thus, to choose my subjects, proceeding by elimination, I work with what is left: love stories and children stories. If a film director can compare himself to a captain on a sinking ship, I adopt this very well-known slogan, "the women and the children first."

5. STORY SOURCE?

Like every filmmaker, I meet a lot of difficulties and problems each time I attempt the adaptation of a large novel. I work better with factual stories or original scripts, but we need audacity to start with nothing; it means facing a blank white sheet of paper, and I don't always have this courage.

6. USE A SCRIPTWRITER OR DO IT YOURSELF?

I have been very lucky in finding my collaborators like Marcel Moussy, Jean Grualt, Claude de Givrary, Bernard Revon, Jean-Louis Richard, and Jean-Loup Dabadie. They are writers, professional or amateur. They are especially friends, because I think—like Jean Renoir—that a film must be prepared like a big heist: surrounding oneself with *good accomplices.*

7. CLOSE COLLABORATION WITH THE SCREENWRITER?

If the scriptwriter I have chosen happens to be very talkative, I prefer him to work far away from me, then permit me to modify his text, and continue our collaboration by mail. If the scriptwriter is somebody quiet and organized, then we lock ourselves together and work that way—which does not keep us from amusing ourselves, because in the world of spectacles, it is very important to amuse oneself while working.

8. PREPLAN OR IMPROVISE?

Sometimes the way to direct a scene emerges at the conception of the scene. Often it becomes obvious only at shooting time. Planned studio shooting makes it easier to anticipate directorial requirements than day-location shooting. I am often disappointed by the realization of scenes I have carefully preplanned. On the other hand, I am often pleasantly surprised by scenes that caused me trouble until the last minute.

9. MOST IMPORTANT COMPONENT OF YOUR FILM?

The only thing which counts for a director is that he makes his work interesting to other people in order to make them look at him, and listen to him. The script of a film is important, but it is not always the *most* important thing. The eyes of an actress like Gene Tierney always said more extraordinary things than the dialogue she was asked to speak. The strong point of Orson Welles is the poesy. The strong point of Lubitsch is the charm. The style of a director is very important. If you give the script of *Psycho* to Daniel Mann, you will obtain a very bad film.

In conclusion, everything is important at the beginning, but when the film is finished, one often discovers that the *star* was not the actor, but rather the dialogue, or the set, or the music, or the harmonious mixing of elements united by chance.

We must accept the idea that the success of a film is mysterious; a lot of intelligence, energy and taste will not certainly make a good film if the mixing of those elements is not harmonious. The quality of the result is not proportional either to the money spent, or to the work done. Luck plays a big role, too.

10. WORK WITH A PRODUCER?

I usually produce my own films. The function of a producer is more clearly defined and important in America than in France.

11. USE A DIALOGUE DIRECTOR?

The need for a dialogue coach does not exist in France.

12. WRITER OR PRODUCER ON THE SET?

When he is shooting, the director is like a school boy during play time. He is happy in his private world; he does not want to see his parents intrude in this world of friends. For the director, it is not the parents he hopes to avoid, but his wife and the scriptwriter.

13. WORK CLOSELY WITH THE CAMERAMAN?

I wasn't interested enough in photography while shooting my first feature films. Black-and-white enabled me to discover a sort of poetic translation that suited me.

When it became necessary to shoot in color, I realized that an "ugliness" had entered the image. I am speaking of the ugliness of walls, objects, sky, streets, and I decided then to pay more attention to the plastic aspects of my films. I think I have a long way to go in this area.

To summarize: I can say that black-and-white film reinforced "fiction" while color leads the film towards the "documentary." If our purpose of storyteller forces us to fight against the documentary, it means that we must fight now against color, because a copy of reality separates us from art.

14. SUPERVISION OF CASTING?

There are no casting directors in France, but shooting a film in London, I was able to appreciate the value of the casting director, Myriam Breekman.

15. PREFERENCE OF ACTING STYLE?

For some roles, I like to use well-known actors, for others, unknown actors, and for others, amateur actors. Personally, I would prefer the instinctive over the technicians, but it is not a rule. In any case, actresses like Jeanne Moreau or Julie Christie seem to me both very technical and very instinctive.

The casting of a film is very important, because when one looks at an old film one has shot, one can forget the mistakes of directing, but the bad choice of an inadequate actor will always be a stain on the film.

Today, in 1976, the filmmakers who stress plausibility and credibility have taken on a growing importance. For instance, if one shoots a story in which the imaginary character is already known to the public (from a best-seller), or a film showing real characters (Victor Hugo or Edgar Allan Poe), I think it is better to take unknown actors, because it is hard today to superimpose two celebrities on the same character.

I do not mean that the day of the star is finished. It will never end, but *for stars,* it is better to write original stories. I don't hide the fact that this viewpoint is very French. One does not think this way in Cinecitta or in Hollywood, and still I can't keep myself from thinking that *The Birdman of Alcatraz* would have been a better film if the hero had been played by somebody who had never been seen before.

16. PRECAMERA WORK WITH ACTOR?

I plead guilty, because I don't treat any actor very scientifically. (1) I give him the script to read, and I ask him if he wants to play the role. (2) When he accepts, I avoid meeting him until the first day of shooting (as if it were a *rendezvous* to which one does not go before the exact time). (3) When we begin to shoot, I let him play according to his own ideas. (4) If he acts well, I say, "Cut, not bad." (5) If he plays badly, I take the actor into a corner, and we rehearse the dialogue quietly. (6) If he still plays badly, I change the dialogue and the setting. (7) If it is still bad, I ask my assistant to come and work with me in the evening, and we change the script. Happily, problems rarely go as far as No. 6.

17. IMPORTANCE OF REHEARSALS?

I can do, individually, face to face rehearsals with this or that actor before casting him, or during the shooting, but I hate the principle of the total and complete rehearsal in a group. I don't say that it is bad, for I am sure that there are many very good films which have been made like this. But I hate it *for me,* and that's why I have never accepted an offer to direct in the theatre.

I think that film is an art a lot more intimate than the theatre and because of this, the method of work itself must be intimate. The whole team and the other actors don't need to hear what I murmur to an actor to make him modify something.

Here is an example: I have a scene which deals with a boy and girl of eighteen, to be played by two inexperienced, but eager young actors. I let them act out the scene and they give me a performance full of sensitivity, but which lacks vitality. I take the boy aside and I whisper to him: *"You are eighteen, but I want you to act in this scene as if you were twenty-five. After all, this girl is only a child. You are a man, and you must make it felt in your acting."*

Then I ask for the girl, and I tell her, *"You must act in this scene, not like a young girl, but like a woman. This guy is still a child; he doesn't know life. You DO. O.K. let's go."*

The shooting begins and I obtain a wonderfully acted scene—much better acted than if I had given these directions collectively, and in a loud voice.

Once more, I don't pretend it is the only method, simply that it is mine and I like it. One can say that this way looks like manipulation. It is true, but it is effective manipulation—okay for everyone.

The difference between a conversation and a lecture rests entirely in the idea of manipulation which imposes itself on the second situation: that is, a film looks more like lecture than like a conversation, because its purpose is to make people look at you, and hear you without being interrupted. Obviously, when a lecture film can give the illusion of a conversation film, it presents an effect of sympathy and warmth for the benefit of everybody. But we must remember that it is still an illusion.

18. ADHERENCE TO SCRIPT?

One cannot *oblige* an actor to do anything. I don't like the idea of compulsion applied to a job which must be a constant pleasure for everybody. The cinema is *intensive,* not only for the audience, but also at the level of the shooting. A team during shooting means at least thirty people who, together, are infinitely better than themselves individually.

To return to the actors, there are a thousand ways to help them, to put them on the right track. One can utilize literary comparisons, musical or animal. There are wonderful actor-technicians who need a lot of help, because they don't see themselves act. There are less accomplished actors (even nonprofessional, but instinctive) who can direct themselves very well.

When I give direction to an actress, I never ask her to behave like another actress; perhaps I will speak to her of Charles Laughton or Michel Simon. One must never publicly compare actors of the same sex.

Some actors bring a lot of personal invention to a character; others only lend their face or their profile, and it is not important to know if theirs is one superior to others. Everything depends on what one seeks to obtain. The area of acting being one of special cases and exceptions, I've no generalities to express in this area. The things I've said must not be regarded as inviolable.

19. EDITING SUPERVISION?

For my first films, I spent a long time in the editing room, because the shooting was not very professional. In my present films, the editing is foreseen at the time of shooting except when there is a lyrical or musical scene requiring a lot of takes.

I don't approve the method which consists of covering a scene by filming it from all conceivable angles. The man who does this is not a director, but a recorder, and the real director is the editor. Each take of a film can only have one good angle and a proper duration. It is the cinema of Hitchcock, Bergman, Bresson, Rohmer, Kurosawa, Buñuel, Hawks, Lubitsch, Dreyer, Milos Forman. It is *film.*

20. ROLE OF MUSICAL SCORE?

Since 1930 there has been too much music in film. Nearly all the films of Warner Bros. from 1940 to 1950 are good, but if they are dated, it is because they had eighty minutes of music on ninety minutes of image.

I don't like the utilization of music like jazz or rock or any music that is not melodic, because it falsifies the duration of a scene, and makes it seem to last three minutes, when in actuality it lasts only one minute. In the screening of a film, unrolling like a ribbon ("A ribbon of Dreams" said Orson Welles), music must also be a ribbon. It should not be pleonastic, but a music that accompanies the film like color. It must be *more* lyrical than the image, but must find a level that corresponds well with it. One can nearly say that cinema is a flat art to which music adds a feeling of depth.

21. INVOLVEMENT IN PREPARATION OF MUSICAL SCORE?

I am deeply involved in the preparation and recording of the musical score for my films.

22. WHAT SCENES SHOULD HAVE MUSIC?

Yes, alone or together with the musicians, I choose the musical moments. No fixed rules except this one: never put music in a dialogue scene that is supposed to be in the present, because it tends to kill the effect that it is happening now, by putting the scene back in the past or making it repetitive. The music has a lot to do with grammar. We can imagine the sentence of a novel: "Then, as you don't want to make love with me, I am going to take the boat to Europe." No need of music over this dialogue.

Now, the novel continues narratively. "She traveled to forget her love. She knew the melancholy of the steamship." Here, good mood music is necessary.

My second rule is to reject the instrumental solo that is too easy to identify—like the piano or the harp—because I am afraid that the public will be inclined to superimpose in his mind—over the film's image—the nimble fingers of the pianist or the harpist.

23. SOUND EFFECTS?

Unhappily, the sound in France is not as good as in America, or even as in England. I admire the sound of *Birds, French Connection, Chinatown.* I think the soundtrack of *Monsieur Arkadin* [*Confidential Report*] is one of the most beautiful there is.

King Vidor

1. BACKGROUND?

I started becoming interested in film so early in life that I didn't have any vocation in life before filmmaking. I worked in jobs connected with film—taking tickets at a theatre or running a projector, but it was all directed toward being a filmmaker. The only other job I can remember having is selling automobiles, which I didn't do for very long. The rest of my 'teens was directed toward filmmaking.

2. FIRST FILM JOB?

The first movie work I did was with a camera as a newsreel cameraman, and the first films I made were short films, from fifteen minutes to half-an-hour.

The first film I made starred me in the leading role. I also directed. I was not the cameraman, but an actor and the director.

Later, I became a writer, sold scripts, and accepted writing jobs of various kind in Hollywood. Universal Studios hired me as a writer, and in silent picture days I did my own film editing, and I had jobs from time to time as a cameraman. The only job connected with films that I haven't done, is that I have never been an agent.

3. YOUR GOAL IN FILMMAKING?

When I started, very young in life, thinking about making films and directing, I remember distinctly one aim I had, and that was to make the films seem real. At that time, most of the films were overacted and overdramatized and they had a very *unreal* feeling about them. Even the actress used too much makeup, which made them look like actors and not like people, and their gestures were all so broad and exaggerated that one could never feel one was watching something happening in life. It was always a movie with a feeling of distance.

I remember thinking, before making my first picture, Wouldn't it be good to at least make the films *look* real?

This doesn't mean that I was tied down to documentary-type films. I want to emphasize the fact that they should *look* real, and not necessarily be restricted by what some people think is the way it is done.

The other distinct feeling I had was that I should always have something to say in my films, and this took different forms. Principally, you might say that in many of my films, the leading character expresses a kind of search for truth. This is not to say that in all my films the leading character was searching for truth, but certainly the first film I made and many thereafter had this quality.

We must divide filmmaking into two categories: making films that come from one's *gut,* and making films for money, to keep working, to be active. I have to say that the word "entertainment" always was a big question-mark for me. I never really knew what it meant, unless it applied to a musical, or some sort of violence. The only answer I have is that if it is entertaining to you (the director), you might have a pretty good chance of making it entertaining for an audience.

4. IN WHAT GENRE DO YOU SEEK A STORY?

I have made two types of film: the one that just had to come out of my insides, and the one that was just a good story from a play or a novel, or that somebody else had bought.

Whenever I searched for a story, I didn't use any criterion other than whether is interested me. If it interested me sufficiently to keep me enthused for six, nine months or a year, I felt I could convey that enthusiasm to an audience. I didn't limit myself to any particular type story—just whether it interested me.

I stayed away from the fool-proof type of story unless it especially intrigued me. I was considered for *Gone With the Wind* for about four days; when I was told that they'd secured Victor Fleming for it, I was very pleased not to have to do it.

I also was asked to do the first and second version for *Ben-Hur,* but, frankly, I turned them both down; they were just a little too surefire and melodramatic. I was glad that I didn't have to do either one of them.

I found my likes going to a more human type of story, one with which an audience could identify without such a far-reach of the imagination. I remember giving interviews, in the very earliest part of my career, saying that if something happened to my Aunt Bessie or my sister Kate, it was much closer and more understandable and real, than if something happened to a bunch of people in Afghanistan.

5. STORY SOURCE?

It is difficult to determine a preference for the source of story material, however, I am inclined to favor a story or script written directly for the screen—in a screen story—the technique of motion pictures is very much in mind in the original inspiration of the story.

In the designing of a story for the theatre, the fewer the sets, the better—preferably not over three settings. A novel can ramble all over the place, backtrack, and do all sorts of things that may not be effective in motion pictures. Therefore, always I am inclined to favor material written directly for the screen.

6. USE A SCRIPTWRITER OR DO IT YOURSELF?

I prefer to secure the services of a very sympathetic (that is, sympathetic to the idea) scriptwriter, and then I like to work closely with him. It's actually a collaboration.

The reason is that in this sort of working arrangement, I usually lay out the sequences ahead of time, and after a day or less of discussion, the scriptwriter goes away and works on it.

Now, when he brings it back, I am free to criticize or make demands, because I don't have to do specific work myself. If I were doing it myself, I could not lay down the top demands that I do when I am in the position of a producer-director in addition to being a collaborator on the script.

I'm a tougher taskmaster and I can think freer and set my sights higher than I could if I were faced with having to do every bit of the actual work myself; I think if you write the whole script yourself, you're inclined to narrow it down.

7. CLOSE COLLABORATION WITH THE SCREENWRITER?

I've answered part of this in the preceding comment, but to elaborate a little further, I'm very much against a writer going away and writing a whole script and then turning it in.

Some producers do that, but I have never done it, and wouldn't do it, because the writer can be way off on a track, and he has to do a whole, complete script before you say, "No, this isn't the way I see it." My method assures that he can't go wrong (differ from my viewpoint) for more than a couple of days, because I would catch it in every sequence.

I've had experiences with producers who wanted writers to be let absolutely alone. In one instance, the producer would not permit me to have anything to do with the writer; he was a television writer, and had never written a motion picture script. The producer kept us apart, and the writer wrote three scripts, all of which I refused. I think the producer himself would have refused to do them.

The end result was that this picture was never made by that producer; it was made by another producer for television, and it was a big success, but I never saw any of the scripts until they were finished, and then I said I wouldn't do it, even though I was very enthused about the story; in fact, I had optioned the story myself and the producer took it over.

8. PREPLAN OR IMPROVISE?

I think that as much as possible, that is practical, of the action or business should be worked out on paper before starting to shoot. However, you still leave room for improvisation, because no matter how detailed the script is, when you have actors go through it, you want to take advantage of what the actors will contribute, what the set director and the cameraman will contribute. You must allow for a certain amount of improvisation.

Still, I think it's essential, when a writer and director are working, for them to develop action as fully as is practical; their quiet collaboration promotes freer thinking, during which they can put in a lot of things that might be difficult to concentrate on in the midst of the mechanics and confusion of production.

9. MOST IMPORTANT COMPONENT OF YOUR FILM?

Considering most of my filmmaking activities from the viewpoint of a director, and being thoroughly aware of the director's contribution, and the essential contributions of all others which go to make up a film, I must automatically believe that the director is transcendent in importance.

Looking over your question, I'm surprised to find that you have omitted the director; maybe you mean, "Who are the others among those listed who assist the director most?"

Of course, in that case I would have to say, the leading actors or the script, and of course the cameraman. I don't entirely agree with William Shakespeare who says that the play is the thing. It's probably true of the theatre, but it is not true of movies and moviemaking.

I think that any brilliant director can take practically no story, no script at all, or very *little* material, and turn it into a brilliant film. Observe Ingmar Bergman or Antonioni, Hitchcock, probably Fellini—the story is not the thing; the script is not the thing. It's how and what the director does with it. All the others that you mentioned make terrific contributions—I'd almost put the cameraman second to the director, because beautiful photography can carry the thing along itself.

10. WORK WITH A PRODUCER?

I have worked, in my career, very much with producers. Basically, there are two kinds of producers: those who contribute nothing, and those who contribute a lot to the making of a film.

The main contribution I like from a producer is to do all the promotion. In the early days we didn't need promotion, but we needed help in getting the materials to work with, getting the cast and getting stars. [Irving] Thalberg was good at this, and it was certainly true of David Selznick.

But, today, I think there's a new and specific purpose in working with a producer who attends to the money and the distribution and does all the things for which the director, let's say, has no talent.

To mention Irving Thalberg again: he paved the way, but didn't interfere; he was too busy supervising too many films—the studio was turning out fifty films a year, so he didn't have time to get in your hair at all; he looked at the rushes but you never really talked to him until the picture was over.

11. USE A DIALOGUE DIRECTOR?

Of course, it's good sense to have someone checking on the actors knowing their lines. However, if a dialogue director should go on too much, saying how they should read their lines, beyond an intelligent interpretation, that would be out of the question.

In the early days of sound pictures, I used several dialogue directors: Laura Hope-Crews on *Street Scene* [1931], and Lionel Barrymore on *Hallelujah* [1929]. I had to take them both off, because they were going too far with the dialogue direction; they were almost staging the scenes. After two or three days, that was the end of that.

12. WRITER OR PRODUCER ON THE SET?

No. I do not like to have the producer on the set while I am rehearsing scenes or shooting. I'm not against the writer being there, but I think the writer can function much better if he's in an office, but available to do rewriting if it is found necessary, which often is the case. But as to having producer and writer on the set as part of the direction: no, it is too late for that.

I wouldn't object to showing what we are doing, after the rehearsals are all organized, as we did on *Street Scene*. We rehearsed one week and on Saturday I showed the whole film, in rehearsal, to the producer and some of his guests, including Helen Hayes.

This was an unusual example, made possible only because the street set was standing, and we didn't have to leave the one set; also all the actors were on salary and available.

13. WORK CLOSELY WITH THE CAMERAMAN?

Both methods are used. I don't believe in getting so frozen on any one way of operation as to exclude the benefits that might come from the other. I try to have my cameraman as far ahead of actual shooting as possible. In a few instances, I've been able to have them for several weeks, or at least during selection of locations and even in set-design conferences. It gives the cameraman a chance to think over all the possibilities that he can contribute.

Of course, there is usually difficulty in getting the cameraman early enough, because, number one, the company doesn't want to put him on salary before he's absolutely necessary, and number two, he may be finishing another picture and want a few days rest before starting a new one.

However, it's absolutely invaluable to have him there and to bring him in on the creative side well in advance. Camera movements and compositions cannot be completed until actual rehearsals are begun, because your actors are part of the composition.

In some instances, a continuity sketch can give composition, but here again we have to extemporize.

14. SUPERVISION OF CASTING?

As to casting one of my films, I think that I would be very lax in my job if I didn't cast all the parts, including the extra people. I think the term "casting director" is rather a misnomer, because he doesn't direct the casting. He brings people to the director for his approval, and he learns what is wanted by the director's rejection or acceptance of actors for specific parts.

I think, as far as the stars go, a producer can be of great assistance in securing certain stars for certain roles, but I can't see myself neglecting any part in the casting of a film, no matter how small the one-line "bits."

15. PREFERENCE OF ACTING STYLE?

Again, it is impossible to make a hard and fast rule. It's a question of taste and intelligence between the seasoned technician and the equally experienced instinctive type. However, when the technician's technique begins to show, you'd better get somebody more instinctive, so the audience will be unable to watch the wheels go round, a condition that can exist with some of our pure technicians.

As far as the "method actor" goes, I don't know exactly yet what defines a "method actor." I believe "the method" is supposed to come from complete absorption with the facets of the character—the more the actor understands and knows about who the character is, the better performance he can give.

This is nothing new; this has (or should have) been done for a long time. I remember in *War and Peace* [1956] I used to refer to the book before each day's work, and read all that Tolstoy had to say about the characters. I would transfer this, whenever possible, to members of the cast—at least the principals—and try to give them a deep feeling of the characters that would help their performances. I notice it when an actor doesn't seem to have a complete knowledge, in depth, of the character he is playing.

16. PRECAMERA WORK WITH ACTOR?

If an actor comes on the set with his first thoughts about the character he is going to play, it seems to me to be a little late. Discussions should be held even in the director's office about the character in the first interview or two.

As for any question as to whether one lets the actor play his own interpretation, or makes him completely fulfill the director's ideas, it is, again, a combination of both.

The director would be very foolish to exclude any benefits the actor may bring to the part. I learned very early in my career not to make the actors conform entirely to my preconceived ideas; they are much too individual, and they've become prominent based on this individuality. It would be stupid to try to obliterate the individuality that caused you to select them in the first place. In the early D. W. Griffith films, all the people used to look very much the same because they were doing everything the way Griffith saw it. Let's take as an example of a highly individualized performer: Gary Cooper. I was aware of his unique individuality in the two films I made with him, particularly in *The Fountainhead* [1949]. He had to play it as Gary Cooper. If I'd had, say, James Cagney, it would have been done in a much different way.

The director must use his intelligence to know exactly what part—what sections of what part to sway toward his own way, or what parts to give in to the actor.

When I cast a film, I think, looking at the actor, I'm giving you the script, the story, the role—what are you going to give me? I've always thought the answer was a two-way street, a 50/50 deal.

17. IMPORTANCE OF REHEARSALS?

I'm very much on the side of the director who doesn't want to leave the best performance on the rehearsal floor. I've always stopped rehearsals before they seemed to be perfect with the thought in mind that we would photograph the best, spontaneous performances, and it invariably worked out that way.

I know of cases in rehearsals where actresses and actors gave performances that they never seemed to be able to recapture. I remember Margaret Sullivan in a picture I made called *So Red The Rose* [1935]. In rehearsal, she read a letter from her brother at the battle front, and everyone on the set had tears in their eyes, listening to her read it. When it came time to shoot it, it was just not as spontaneous or moving, it had flattened out, so that's something that should be carefully guarded against—permitting everything to flatten out.

18. ADHERENCE TO SCRIPT?

Again, no hard and fast rules, but generally speaking, I feel the script is usually right. It has been given much consideration and study, and the actor can be guilty of avoiding some situation; his reason may be a psychological cover-up of some sort, or a problem of security. It's happened time and again for an actor to say, "I can't read that line," although it would be some simple line that could be read easily.

Well, I don't think an actor has a very good grasp of his character if he lets one line throw him. I have even set up systems that would make it difficult to change the lines just as a protection against actors wanting to make alterations.

In the case of *The Fountainhead,* Ayn Rand, the author, worked on the script without pay for an agreement that no lines would be changed without letting her know. I encouraged this, because—by the time we let her know and she drove over to the studio—a couple of hours would have passed. Generally, by that time, the actor would have changed his mind when he found how difficult it was going to be to make a change. He'd go ahead and read the line as it was originally written, and read it well.

However, here again one cannot make a frozen rule about this. Consider the theatre and how often changes are made for the benefit of the play. In any case, it's something to be guarded against and watched carefully.

19. EDITING SUPERVISION?

I believe in the director shooting the scenes with a definite assembly plan in mind, then commenting upon them during the running of the rushes. I usually ran the rushes twice, and talked about the intent with the editor—particularly on the second running. That accomplished, I believe in the editor going ahead and assembling the film as I've outlined it. In that way, work can be carried on while the director is shooting.

When a sequence is assembled, the editor runs it for the director, again getting his ideas. It's a close cooperation between director and editor, with the director making the final decisions.

It's good to have a picture more or less put together by the time shooting is finished. In any case, the shooting should not be so slipshod that it can be cut very many ways. I think a film should be shot so it can be cut only one way, except in the case of a battle scene where many, many angles are shot, and much, much footage exposed. In such instances, the editor can do a wonderfully creative job.

20. ROLE OF MUSICAL SCORE?

Concerning the music score, my feelings about it go back to the big orchestras and organ accompaniment that went along with the large films of the twenties and the thirties: D. W. Griffith's *Hearts of the World, The Birth of Nation, Intolerance,* etc. They used hundred-piece orchestras, and their emotional impact was fantastic!

Ever since, I've always worked closely with the composer, and I've had strong feelings that my sequences or scenes would be enhanced or spoiled by whatever the musician did.

I think very much in terms of music, both from the standpoint of melodic content, rhythm, pace, and even to the details of orchestration such as in *The Big Parade* [1925] when we used simply a bass drum and stopped the musical line.

Again, I think the association of director and composer is a 50/50 deal. Although I don't think music is 50 percent of the film, it's 25 to 30 percent of the total impact.

21. INVOLVEMENT IN PREPARATION OF MUSICAL SCORE?

Except in one or two instances (one of them being *Street Scene* with Alfred Newman writing the score) the composer doesn't come in until after the picture is cut and edited. At that time, I sit down with him and listen to his suggestions, and his contribution. We mark exact places where music is to start and stop, and he goes away and only works on those places. He may call me up, or come back and say, "I think you should do this, cut it off sooner, or lengthen it a little bit."

Generally, however, this is decided after we have a final print and can knock off a dupe for it—a black-and-white—for the composer's fixed rule.

In the instance I've mentioned earlier, the composer was available throughout the making of the film, so we were discussing it scene for scene all during the shooting of the film; the composer spent much time on the set and in the rushes; he was very much a part of the decision making.

Again, no hard and fast rule applies; cooperation to get the best results from the contributor to achieve the best possible final effect is the goal.

22. WHAT SCENES SHOULD HAVE MUSIC?

I believe I've answered this pretty fully in the two preceding questions. I can only stress that, as in all other matters concerning my films, it is a general practice to exercise complete final control.

Usually the composer is in full agreement with my decisions, so there is no opposition.

23. SOUND EFFECTS?

The sound effects are, to me, just as important as the music. The wrong sound can spoil the scene—spoil what the director intended—or can enhance it greatly. Sound effects are so vital that I think a director is walking out on his job if he doesn't work closely with the sound effects, which can add as much to a scene as the photography, the acting or what have you.

The whole strength of a film is unification, and the individuality of the man who's making it; the great mistake in filmmaking is to fragment it. There is only one fellow who can answer all the questions correctly, who pulls it all together, and that's the director.

All films cannot be made this way, but when we talk about the best way, the right way, to make a film, it's the director who comes up with the answers, and he's the fellow who can say "Yes," or "No," about everything.

If he *feels* what he's doing, and it's important to him, he certainly should think unity. Sound effects are part of that unity.

I sit in on dubbing and recording, saying how much should be played up, or played down; how much the music should take over, and how much it should be sacrificed for dialogue.

Generally, I feel the dialogue is more important, and if music interferes with understanding the dialogue, it should be pushed down. Since the advent of sound, I've always been much in favor of *few* instruments, instead of big orchestras, so that you can push it down without losing too much. If you suppress the sound of a big orchestra, you're losing very, very much; with just a few instruments, you don't necessarily lose so much. The composers should be aware that perhaps their score and recording will be suppressed for the dialogue to be understandable, and they should orchestrate accordingly.

In summation, I can only repeat that the making of a film is an expression of an individual. At least, it should be—just as a novel or a painting, or any work of art is the expression of one individual.

I've known instances in which a set dresser (as an example) worked on a picture—maybe halfway through the picture—before he was sure of the period in which the story was laid. Many artisans work on so many pictures, they haven't time to study any one film.

For that reason, every important decision should be the work of one man, and unless that man is convinced and secure, and his judgments final—not subject to debate-the picture is likely to come out a complete hodgepodge.

Obviously, I'm all for the *Auteur* theory—always have been. That seems to be the answer to most of the questions asked about filmmaking.

Raoul Walsh

1. BACKGROUND?

Fascinated by the sea, I signed on with a four-masted schooner, out of New York, bound for Havana. In the Caribbean, we were caught up in a hurricane and my love of the sea was somewhat dimmed. By the time we limped into a small Mexican port for major repairs, I'd had it.

From a Mexican Indian, I learned to ride and rope—"Western style." Then, as a working cowhand, I made my way across Mexico to Texas. This experience gave me a wealth of first-hand knowledge in preparation for the "Westerns" I was to make later. Making a movie is a tough job, physically as well as mentally and emotionally, but those days at sea, and the subsequent rough life of a working cowpoke and bronco-buster prepared me as few things could have done.

In addition to the benefits I derived from the range work, my time on that four-master paid off beautifully when I made *Captain Horatio Hornblower* [1951]. Of course, a bit of my experience as a working cowboy rubbed off on every one of the "Westerns" I made; of that I'm sure.

2. FIRST FILM JOB?

I was an assistant director and an actor with D. W. Griffith. After acting in some fifteen or more one- and two-reelers, during which time I assisted Mr. Griffith and studied filmmaking, the great master gave me an opportunity to direct. Incidentally, I starred in the first several short subjects directed under the Griffith banner.

3. YOUR GOAL IN FILMMAKING?

My prime purpose was, always. to entertain. Many directors have chosen to devote themselves to some one particular theme or category within which to make their pictures—as witness Alfred Hitchcock with his consistently excellent suspense-thrillers, or George Roy Hill's lusty comedies, or Francis Ford Coppola's sagas of violence.

I, on the other hand, in pursuit of that nebulous something which would intrigue moviegoers, have done every type of film imaginable, from World War I's *What Price Glory* [1926], to Mexico, to ride with Pancho Villa for the filming of *Life of Villa* [1914], and later to London to film *Captain Horatio Hornblower.*

Anything, anywhere, to get a film I believed would please audiences. I was never reluctant to tackle any job I believed in, no matter how tough it was, or where it might take me.

4. IN WHAT GENRE DO YOU SEEK A STORY?

I have never looked for material in any specific category. I always sought material—regardless of theme or background—which, after careful study, convinced me that it had real dramatic potential. Having chosen a property, I looked to myself to supply enough action to keep the story moving and to fulfill my entertainment quotient. There is probably no moment in picturemaking that is more acutely essential to a director's success than the instant of his choice of story material. For the director, that is the moment of conception.

5. STORY SOURCE?

My only point of discrimination in seeking a yarn from which to make a picture lies not in the source or form of the story, but rather in the content of the tale, or the theme itself; is it entertaining? Do its entertainment values lend themselves readily to adaptation to the film medium? If it qualifies in all these areas, the source is relatively unimportant.

I have done many successful films from almost every known source. From the Lawrence Stallings' play, for instance, I did *What Price Glory. In Old Arizona* [1929] was adapted from an O. Henry story called "The Caballero's Way." *The Thief of Bagdad* [1924] followed, loosely, the theme of *A Thousand and One Nights,* but I've always regarded it as an original, "suggested" by the book.

Gentleman Jim [1942] was an original screenplay, based on the life of James J. Corbett, and his winning of the world heavyweight championship from John L. Sullivan. Probably over half the stories I've done on film were based on originals written directly for the screen. But it all boils down to will it make a film that will please and entertain audiences?

6. USE A SCRIPTWRITER OR DO IT YOURSELF?

I prefer doing that work myself. Even in the unlikely case of my being handed a completed script, it was my habit to go through the entire script myself, rewriting everything in it that did not coincide with my thinking about the over-all finished picture. This must not be taken to mean that I believed I was a better writer than the fellow who did the first go-around, by any means. My thinking in this area was guided completely by the fact that no one else could possibly know exactly what I intended to do with the story—where I wanted to lay the emphasis, where I wanted to hit it hard, and where I planned to tread most lightly. Even though my writing, as such, may not be equalled in quality by that of the first scriptwriter, it sufficed, and it coincided in every way with *my* concept of the finished film.

7. CLOSE COLLABORATION WITH THE SCREENWRITER?

When conditions permitted, I found it beneficial to work very closely with the writer (provided he had anything on the ball). However, there have been many occasions when I've been handed a so-called finished shooting script—which I felt needed a lot of work without my ever having seen the scriptwriter. In such circumstance, if the writer was available, I like to have him with me to do the heavy lifting under my guidance, after I had filled him in on my visualization of how the whole thing should go.

In the early days, when I was young and eager, I tried to do it all. It took me a long time to learn to use whatever help was offered me to the fullest, for whatever it was worth. Even with all the help he can get, a director's job is a brutally demanding one, requiring assiduous attention to every detail of the production. So, if help is offered from any quarter, a director should latch onto it gratefully. After all is said, it's *your* name that goes up there as the director who made the picture. No one demands that every idea in it be your brainchild. If you are smart enough to grab every good idea that comes along, and it results in a great picture, no one would care who sired the ideas. It's your triumph, and believe me, it's worth shooting for!

8. PREPLAN OR IMPROVISE?

I much preferred to start shooting with a finished script—finished in detail. However, if things bogged down—certain scenes wouldn't play, for instance—then it was improvisation—time down south. But, certainly, the finished script clued actors and staff as to what we were trying to do.

It is inevitable, I believe, in most pictures, that "action" sequences, as written, can only be very sketchy diagrams for what is required at that juncture in the story. It is obviously impossible for any writer to write action that will fit into the location, or to meet local conditions which he has never seen. This is the point at which the director is pretty much on his own. Usually, from the instant I decided on a location—before shooting ever got under way—I had started dreaming up action that would work smoothly in that location, and under the prevailing conditions.

9. MOST IMPORTANT COMPONENT OF YOUR FILM?

In order to answer that question, I'm impelled to lump two of your listed components into one: story and script are inseparable, from my viewpoint. As Shakespeare said, "the play's the thing."

In pictures, the story/script is, or should be, the fundamental reason for your wanting to make the picture in the first place. If your screenplay is not sound, the greatest stars in the world, plus the most capable and artistic cameraman and the most lavish production, can never make a sound movie from it. An inept script can make good actors look pretty bad. It is also important to remind oneself that a bad script (or a weak story) can also bring what might have been a long and brilliant directorial career to an unhappy and untimely end pronto.

10. WORK WITH A PRODUCER?

As indicated earlier, my first producer was the great D. W. Griffith. Since that time I have worked often as my own producer, and many times with other producers. Some were of great help to me, but many others might well have ruined me had I acted on their suggestions. There are more "relatives" in producer spots than in any other category, largely due, I believe, to the fact that a producer can't fail. If his picture flops, it is always the fault of "That stupid (or stubborn) director."

And, of course, the producer always gets the last word. If the film is good, he takes a bow. If it's bad, there's always that ready patsy, the director to blame.

It's a pity that the truly fine producers are destined to suffer—prestige-wise—for the foibles and follies of these incompetents. A good producer may be counted upon to service the director in every possible. That's his job: preparing everything in advance, so that when shooting starts the director can devote his total energy to the task of getting his story on film, with no unnecessary hold-ups. The producer is the only one who can take this extra load off a director's back.

As I say, there have been many times when I have felt a great sense of relief and gratitude that I have been fortunate enough to draw an experienced and knowledgeable producer.

There's a lesson to be gained from all this: when you agree to do a picture that has a producer already committed, research that producer. Study his credits, talk to other directors who have worked with him, learn whether you can trust him if the going gets rough, and if you can depend on him for real help, or if, on the other hand, you must be prepared to fight with him every inch of the way.

11. USE A DIALOGUE DIRECTOR?

I have never used a dialogue director. I've never felt the need to do so. I've always made it a practice of taking the actors out by myself and asking them to "let me hear it."

In this way I not only made sure that the actors knew their lines, but if there was any reading that was not exactly what I wanted, then I would hang in and work it over with the actor until he had it right on target. I've found that this saved a great deal of time in shooting. It usually meant that I could print the first or second take, whereas if a dialogue director were to try to correct a reading, he might be as far off base in what he got the actor to do, as the actor was in the first place.

There is another point that is particularly pertinent in my individual case: I've always thought of my film as *moving* pictures. Most of the pictures I have made have contained far more *action* than dialogue.

12. WRITER OR PRODUCER ON THE SET?

Absolutely not. I never had the writer or the producer on my set while I was either shooting or rehearsing. My reasons seem obvious: for the sake of comparison, the captain of a ship would never stand for the owner or a stockholder to be around while he was on the bridge or quarterdeck.

13. WORK CLOSELY WITH THE CAMERAMAN?

Before I started shooting a film, I always spent many hours with my cameraman, discussing the script, sequence by sequence, giving him my ideas as to the type of lighting I wanted for each sequence, and explaining my reasons for desiring the specific effect in each instance.

For comedy, I had a set formula: flood the scene with light. Comedy—whether it's a facial expression, a spoken line, or a broad physical action, is no good unless it can be seen in minute detail.

As for the advance planning of camera movements: unless we were able to do our planning in the actual set or on the exact location where the action was to take place, advance planning—other than the most general—was simply not practical. Even in the actual sets, the blocking could be only the roughest. Until I got the first team (actors) on the spot, actually playing the scene, it was impossible for me to anticipate the moves they would make.

14. SUPERVISION OF CASTING?

I maintain absolute control all the way. Getting back to the ship's captain, an able captain would personally select every man in his crew; lives might depend on any one of the least of them.

So, in a picture, the mood, the tension or conviction of an entire scene or sequence can be sabotaged by a bad reading from an incompetent one-line bit, or even by the presence of some extra who does not look as though he belonged in that environment. He can distract the viewer's attention just long enough for you to lose your audience interest.

Remember, the picture is *your* responsibility, no less than the ship, her cargo, passengers and crew, are the responsibility of the captain. That's something well worth keeping in mind. As a director, the duration of your *professional life* may well depend on how conscientiously you assume that responsibility.

15. PREFERENCE OF ACTING STYLE?

I would rather work with the natural actor—the one who works from instinct. However, with experience, any good actor acquires a technique. That technique is the thing which makes it possible for him (in the theatre) to give a fine, balanced performance night after night, even in a long-run play.

To me, the "method" actor seems to get off on the wrong foot. I have encountered many young actors and actresses who seem to project so much "method" that it tends to make every character they play appear to have been cast from the identical mold. If they ever had any natural ability, their "method" work seems to have pretty well smothered it.

However, there are a few super-stars who are "method" actors, but who seem to have been able to assimilate all the good the "method" had to offer, and to adapt it to their own natural talents. Dustin Hoffman is a stand-out in this area.

16. PRECAMERA WORK WITH ACTOR?

This would depend entirely on the actor with whom I was dealing, and also on how well I knew him and his talent range. If I were not familiar with his approach to his work, or his attitude toward it, I would certainly get to him as early as possible, to tell him what I was looking for in the character he was doing, before he had a chance to form a totally different image, and one that did not coincide with my over-all plan for the picture.

If, on the other hand, he was an accomplished and prominent actor, or a star of real stature with whose work and thinking I was familiar, I certainly would let him exercise those qualities for which he had been chosen. However, this does not mean that he would be allowed to run hog-wild. There are times when even the best of them must be held down. That's what the director is there for.

17. IMPORTANCE OF REHEARSALS?

Regarding a full-script rehearsal with the entire cast, I've always said that I don't agree with too much rehearsal, and neither does the budget. From experience, I am totally convinced that too much rehearsal does indeed flatten out spontaneity, and we would do well to remember that spontaneity is the element that gives the audience a strong sense of reality—the feeling that, as they're watching, it's actually happening for the first time. If we can catch our audience up in that spell, we've got it made!

18. ADHERENCE TO SCRIPT?

No, I did not always insist that an actor adhere meticulously to the script—lines and business. When suggestions for a change were made, I listened to them carefully, tried them on for size, and if they worked, and I was convinced that they could in no way injure the structure or characterization, I played ball with the actor.

I knew from long personal experience, as an actor as well as a director, that occasionally there's one of those lines or bits of business that seems awkward to the actor, and he is inclined to give too much of his attention to that particular line or bit, to the detriment of the scene as a whole. If an actor comes up with something that will make my scene play better, or flow more smoothly, more power to him. But I'll be the judge. It's still *my* picture.

19. EDITING SUPERVISION?

The selection of a cutter has always been a matter of utmost importance to me. Once I was satisfied that I had a competent and conscientious man, I followed the general pattern of the director you refer to (who, incidentally, was a very close friend of mine to the day of his death).

I found that an imaginative and creative editor would often come up with a cutting sequence that was not at all what I had visualized, but was very effective.

Of course, the final judgment as to which cutting order to use was entirely mine, but there is no doubt in my mind that giving a top editor his freedom can prove very beneficial to the picture. In any case, if the thing your cutter tries doesn't work, you've lost nothing but a minimal amount of time—just the few hours it will require to get it put back the way you'd planned. Of course, a preview of the film will tell you in no uncertain terms whether or not it works.

There is no substitute for a preview before the paying public. A professional or studio preview is a waste of time. This gratuitous comment may not sound like anything that is remotely connected with your question. However, experience has convinced most of the old-timers that the average audience—the people for whom your picture is made—should be the best judges of what they like or dislike.

Of course, the preview system is not so kind to the director's ego, but if he, with his cutter, sees the film play before an audience, they're much more likely to wind up with a picture that is an ego-pleaser for everyone connected with it.

20. ROLE OF MUSICAL SCORE?

Musical scores are of tremendous importance in helping to arouse the audience to a high level; whether we are trying for sentimental impact, suspense or the ominous, or even a mood of life and love and joy, music increases impact.

However, I believe that in comedy, music has injured more film than it has ever helped. Obviously, I am not talking about the Walt Disney-Mickey Mouse effects.

21. INVOLVEMENT IN PREPARATION OF MUSICAL SCORE?

As in every other department that affected my picture, I was always right on top of the composer during the preparation of a score for my show; of course, I often sat in on recording sessions (particularly when I wasn't too sold on the composer), to make quite sure that the music came in only when and as it should.

This is a point we must all watch zealously, to make damned sure that some over-ambitious composer does not decide to make his big reputation with this score, and at our expense. It's happened many times, but *not* to one of my films. If an audience is ever made conscious of a score, your picture has lost them.

22. WHAT SCENES SHOULD HAVE MUSIC?

No, I rarely got mixed up in that, except for the uncertain situations noted above. Fortunately for me, Max Steiner composed scores for most of my pictures, During his career, he won some seven Academy Awards. Who wants to argue with him about scoring?

23. SOUND EFFECTS?

Sound effects are of vital importance to almost any picture, as long as they are kept at convincingly valid and realistic levels. I am a stickler for realism. As a matter of fact, the sound technicians always insist that I be there at dubbing sessions, as they valued my opinion, and I called them the way I heard them.

COMMENT

I saw Hollywood's birth, its golden era, and its declining years.

We were never the lotus-eaters of legend. We performed an endless job of hard work, under hot lights and blazing sun, in snow and rain, or wherever the job took us—even riding a camera on an ice-floe.

I'm convinced that Hollywood's decline from glory is in no way the result of senility. On the contrary, it is a relapse, temporarily (I hope) into the immaturity of adolescence.

I suppose the record shows that I have filmed my share of murder, rape and arson, but what a difference between those elements and the sodomy, sadism and scatology with which many of today's films deal.

My chauvinist studs never doubted that they were males. The virile lover had no need for nudity to prove he was a man: sometimes he didn't even take his hat off.

In passing, let us note that the current increase in nakedness in film, threatens to wreck a lot of stellar careers. How disillusioning for the fan of a film hero to find that the tiger in his tank is merely a mouse! Naturally the star demands that only his best side be photographed, but even Max Factor cannot make a Chiquita banana out of a dwarf pickle. On the other hand, maybe there is a whole new facet of humor to be discovered in such a predicament—or perhaps I should have said "re-discovered!" To the anti-heroes of my *What Price Glory* and other films of that genre, sex was funny.

They were not without precedent; twenty-five hundred years ago, Aristophenes taught us to laugh at sex, and the French made a national industry of frustrated lovers. Our neophytes, however, too often look on sex as a matter of very grim substance. Oh well, boys will be boys, and sometimes boys will be girls. If that's their bag, so be it.

My only quarrel is with infantilism masquerading as sophistication. It is my somewhat optimistic hope that a new generation of filmmakers will outgrow this preoccupation with animated graffiti, and learn the ABC's of entertainment, which is at least the basis of that rare commodity: art.

Indeed, I feel that there is a good chance that these young people will learn, from life as well as from art, for each man in his time plays many parts.

Robert Wise

1. BACKGROUND?

I was a film editor before I turned to directing.

2. FIRST FILM JOB?

I started in the film business in August of 1933, as a college dropout of that Depression period. There was no money to go back to another year of college and no jobs to be found around the college town, so it was determined that I would go to California where I had an older brother working in the accounting office at RKO Studios, to try and find a job.

I was fortunate enough to land a job as a film porter in the shipping room of the editing department at RKO. For the next few years, it was a matter of working my way up through the department. After my months as a film porter, I became an apprentice sound effects editor, than a sound effects editor, and then a music editor as well. After two years of the sound effects-music editing, I realized this was rather a dead end and asked my boss, Jimmy Wilkinson, to allow me to move over to the picture editing side.

Eventually, I became an assistant editor and was fortunate enough to work with a top "master-editor" of those days, Billy Hamilton. Billy was one of the few editors around who was very progressive in terms of letting the young people learn and take a hand. Before I had been with Billy over two or three films, I was doing all the first cutting myself and, eventually, on the last few pictures that I worked with Billy, he insisted that I share editing credit.

Finally, I branched off on my own and was a full-fledged editor—worked with Garson Kanin on *Bachelor Mother* [1939], also with Gar on *My Favorite Wife* [1940], and then my two top assignments as film editor, and an experience that has proven invaluable to me over the years, was the film editor position with Orson Welles on *Citizen Kane* [1941] and [*The*] *Magnificent Ambersons* [1942].

While doing some of these films as an editor, I had the opportunity to do some second unit directing, and—on occasion—to direct a few retakes after films were finished shooting and the original director was unavailable. During this time, I had kept after the front office for an opportunity to direct myself. In the early fall of 1943, I was working on a film for that marvelous producer of small-budget horror films, Val Lewton, editing [*The*] *Curse of the Cat People* [1944]. Half-way through that picture, the director on it had fallen woefully behind on his schedule and was going to be replaced. I was told to take over—I was told on a Saturday to take over the following Monday. That was my start as a film director. I finished up the picture and have been directing since that time, since 1943.

3. YOUR GOAL IN FILMMAKING?

My philosophy regarding the films I make is really two or three fold. First comes the matter of entertainment, and I use "entertainment" in its broadest sense, not a definition that implies only something that will make people laugh in order to enjoy themselves. I consider entertainment as anything that involves an audience and gets them caught up in the story, the plot, the characters, all aspects of the story you're telling.

As a strong, what I like to call "byproduct" of that story that, hopefully, will catch people up and involve them, I hope the story will have some comment to make. (I prefer the use of "comment" rather than saying "message.") It should have some comment to make about man and the world he lives in, his condition, his life, his laws, his government, his goals, etc. I think it's recognized that no story can be told, no matter of what nature, that doesn't really have something to say. So, as a strong "by-product" of the story I choose, I look for that additional comment of what it has to say about man and his world.

There is one other point that I would like to make about film, and it relates to what I have just said about comment. (I don't really know, Tay, whether this belongs exactly in answer to this question or not.)

I consider film a universal language. We know our films are shown all around the world; we know we see films from many other countries, and in my view there is no single art or means of expression that is so universally understood, and has such around the world as film, as motion pictures. I believe it is one of the most effective ways in which peoples of the world can get to know and understand each other better, to illustrate the very, very many things that people around the world have in common as against those few things that we have in disharmony.

So this is a very important aspect of films and filmmaking, and film power. It is not a final determinant in material I select to make for my films—not all carry great weight as far as a "one-world concept" is concerned—but I certainly value very highly that aspect of any story subject that happens to contain this element.

4. IN WHAT GENRE DO YOU SEEK A STORY?

As far as the genre is concerned, I have no special genre that I investigate for the films or stories that I'm seeking for film material. As most people do, I basically like a story that catches me up—that's the first thing that any story must do as a film possibility for me—catch me up as the reader, as the audience—get me involved, get me into the whole thing; into the plot, into the characters, to hold me in it before I, then, would think to go further with it as a possible film vehicle. It has to have cinematic possibilities, of course, and all the other things that are entailed. It has to have commercial possibilities. But, first of all, the story—in whatever genre—must catch me up.

5. STORY SOURCE?

Like a lot of people, I presume I look to any source I can for stories on which to base a film. That's the big challenge for all of us who direct and produce films, the matter of finding exciting, original, cinematic material.

I will look at and take on material from all sources-from original screenplays, books, stageplays, short stories, even, occasionally, a radio show—just any material in any genre of writing that might offer the opportunity of developing into an ongoing, successful, exciting and cinematic screenplay.

You open yourself up to all the possibilities for sources of stories for films that you can. When you finally find one that hits you, regardless of what source, you then proceed to try to get the proper screenplay and make your film.

6. USE A SCRIPTWRITER OR DO IT YOURSELF?

Since I am not a screenwriter myself, I must have my screenplays done by professional screenwriters. I have one rather strong feeling about this. I prefer generally not to have the man who has written the original material—that is, of course, unless it's an original screenplay—but let's say if I purchase a novel, I'd rather not have the original author do the screenplay.

This is because I feel more often than not, that the original author will be so close to his material, will be so involved in it, he will not be able to see where it needs to be pulled together, what needs to be eliminated—all the cutting, excising and rewriting that might be necessary to make a first-rate screenplay out of his material. This is not a hard and fast rule, of course, and there have been very good examples of original authors and playwrights doing the screenplays on their own material, but I generally prefer to have a man fresh to the material do the screenplay.

7. CLOSE COLLABORATION WITH THE SCREENWRITER?

I have already established that I use professional scriptwriters. I don't work with the scriptwriter as a co-writer. I generally have long, in-depth story sessions with the screenwriter before he starts to work, letting him know all the thoughts I have on the transference of the story to screenplay and getting the ideas that he has at this early juncture.

We kick ideas and approaches around in these story sessions and then I let him go ahead and do his treatment, if he likes, or go directly into screenplay, if he prefers. I let him write himself out and give me everything that he can think of, or wants to put into his first draft. From there on, I work with him in cutting down and polishing, and with the rewrites in finally getting the script in the best possible shape for a shooting script.

Depending on the film, I may have ideas for delivery of certain sequences, particularly in a visual sense. I often write these up, in my own form, and turn them over to the writer to put into script form.

Case in point: the whole opening of *West Side Story* [1961], the helicopter shots coming in over New York, and gradually working over Manhattan to the West Side and into the playground—an opening that has been very favorably received from the time it first came on the screen was my idea. In order to simplify the matter of explaining the idea to Ernie Lehman, the screen writer, I simply sat down one day and wrote up the opening sequence, and gave it to Ernie, who then worked it over and put it into proper terms for the script.

I've done this in several instances. They usually are visual and action sequences, not sequences that involve dialogue.

8. PREPLAN OR IMPROVISE?

I like to have all the action and business worked out as fully as possible in the script before I start shooting. I like to have all the indications that occur to the writer put into the early drafts, indications of business and actions for the characters. Sometimes I will trim some of this down so it's not excessive in the shooting script, but I like a good, full script.

Then, as do most directors, I allow myself room to improvise beyond that, beyond what is down on the written page. Then, when the actors are on their feet, but the action as described doesn't work well, and we see chances to improve it, we improvise from what we start with in the script. But I am a director who very much likes to prepare fully every aspect of films as much as possible.

9. MOST IMPORTANT COMPONENT OF YOUR FILM?

Shakespeare said it the best for all of us: "The Play's The Thing." There's no doubt in my mind that the one specific component involved in the creation of a film that is the most important, is the story. I feel that is the major decision any of us make-that is when we say "This is the story I'm going to make into my next film." We never escape the strengths of that original story, or its weaknesses. I might work better than the next director, or I might cast it better, or I might get a better screenplay or I might do a worse job than another director, but neither of us, I believe, will ever escape the strong influence of that original decision, the story we choose to make.

I don't mean to make it sound like all the other aspects of filmmaking are not terribly important and cannot add tremendously to that choice of the original story. All the aspects that we know, the script, the scriptwriter, the actors, the stars, the art director, the composer, the cameraman, the film editor, all the technicians, they're all terribly important—but none of us can escape the rightness or the wrongness of that original decision of "that's the story I'm going to make into my next film."

10. WORK WITH A PRODUCER?

I no longer work with a producer. I have been my own producer as well as director since 1959. I like being my own producer because it gives me more overall say on the film as the filmmaker, as against working with somebody else who has perhaps purchased the story, developed a screenplay, and then hired me to be the director. So it's a more fulfilling job and one that allows the director to realize all his intents for his film, if he is in a position to act as his own producer.

However, I would like to say that in those fifteen or sixteen years in which I functioned simply as a director and did have producers, I did work with some producers who were particularly creative, and contributed very, very much to the films which they produced.

One of these, a giant in his own right, was the man who gave me my chance as a director, Val Lewton. Although he gained his reputation making small psychological horror pictures in the early 1940s, Lewton did make a remarkable place for himself with his films. Val was a novelist in his own right, contributed tremendously to all aspects of the films that he produced, and yet was very supportive of the director. As a matter of fact, he gave many of us our first chances to direct. I was one, Mark Robson was another, Jacques Tourneur was another, all first-time opportunities as feature directors through Val Lewton, the producer.

Another fine producer who—much like Lewton—contributed tremendously to his films, to the screenplay, to the production, the casting, and the postproduction, was John Houseman, with whom I did *Executive Suite* at M-G-M in 1953.

A couple of others who come to mind who were particularly contributive were Charles Schnee, a writer-producer at M-G-M in the mid-50s. I did *Somebody Up There Likes Me* [1956] for him, and also *Until They Sail* [1957]. Another producer with whom I did a very successful film—one of the most talked about films of all I've made—is Julian Blaustein, who was producer of *The Day The Earth Stood Still* [1951].

So I am not one, as a director, who puts down the function of producer. I think there's a great range in the qualities and creativeness of producers. I have worked with some who, I felt, were more of a hindrance than a help, but certainly those that I have mentioned were most creative and highly contributive.

11. USE A DIALOGUE DIRECTOR?

I no longer use a dialogue director, or dialogue "coach," as we now call them. I haven't, I guess, for some fifteen-sixteen years. I did use dialogue coaches off and on in the early years of my directing career, particularly when I was getting started and was new at the game. I felt that the dialogue coach in that instance helped me with the actors in getting performances and readings. As time went on, I wanted the dialogue coach, when I used one, simply to get the actors up in their lines and to cue them.

12. WRITER OR PRODUCER ON THE SET?

If possible, I think it's helpful to have the writer on the set when one is rehearsing. This is true, particularly, if you're fortunate enough to have a rehearsal period before you start shooting the picture. I've had the luxury of this a few times in my career as a director, and it's always most helpful to have the writer there in case lines need to be improved and changed. On-the-spot help from the writer is very important, very contributive.

I've also had the situation where I literally didn't have the opportunity to have pre-shooting rehearsals, but did have the chance to get the principal actors together to read through the script, to listen to the lines, and to discuss the characterization, the dialogue and the action. We might read through the script two or three times and, here again, it is always most helpful to have the scriptwriter there for these readings so he can hear how his lines sound, and catch the clinkers and change and improve and rewrite on the spot

13. WORK CLOSELY WITH THE CAMERAMAN?

I do like to work with my cameraman before we start shooting. Very often, however, there's not the opportunity to have the cameraman present for very long before one actually starts shooting. I certainly talk over my scripts with the cameraman and discuss the style of lighting that might be called for in the film, discuss ways we can go with the film if we have the opportunity. If we need to make tests with some of the actors, we sometimes try lighting effects in some of the tests. We certainly have an ongoing and thorough discussion of the lighting.

However, the matter of pre-determining camera setups and composition, and blocking out camera movements, I generally do with a sketch artist. This kind of "story-boarding," as we now call it, takes weeks and weeks, and it's generally done with the sketch artist and the art director long before the cameraman really comes on the picture.

Once we have the cameraman on, I go over all these sketches, compositions, continuities with him as well as certain special set sketches that may have been made by the designer or the artist to indicate lighting ideas. I go over all these with the cameraman, get his responses, his ideas and certainly his suggestions so by the time the cameraman starts a few weeks before the film goes into production, we are all working together on this matter of the dramatic and mood lighting, and the set-ups and composition.

Now, once again, in this matter of preparing and planning, although I have composition and set-up and action sketches, I always leave room for change on the set. When I get into the staging of the scenes and find certain things as planned don't work as well as one thought they would when the actors are doing a scene, I always allow myself chances to change, to improvise, if need be, and to improve what we've put down on the sketches. But I like to go in prepared, at least at the start of a sequence, to know where I want to go in terms of the camera and compositions and the action.

14. SUPERVISION OF CASTING?

I supervise the casting on my films completely, all the way down to the one-line "bit" parts and even going into selection of extras in key sequences where extra types are terribly important. Of course, one depends very much on the ideas from the casting directors; they have made many fine suggestions about actors of whom I wasn't even aware. However, I simply don't allow casting directors to cast them; I look at film on the recommended actors, see other film they have been in; next, I interview them, if possible, have readings with the actors I'm interested in, and read with them myself. If need be—if it's that important—I make tests, so I don't leave any final decisions to anybody else. Any actor that's in a picture of mine has gotten my final okay and approval, and if there are some poor actors in the film, I'll take the blame.

As I said, on key sets where the looks and types of atmosphere people that we need are terribly important, I call for interviews of extras, and hand-pick my extras out of the interview calls. This is terribly important because all of those people up there on the screen are going to be getting your message and your film over to the audience. The actors are between you and the audience, and it's all-important that you make them just as right as you possibly can. You can't do that by leaving any of the casting decisions to somebody else.

15. PREFERENCE OF ACTING STYLE?

In considering actors, I generally prefer working with the "seasoned techni-cians," so to speak. Although many of the actors of the more "instinctive" type can be very effective and very good, I consider that acting is a profession, and is to be learned as most professions are. I felt film editing was to be learned, and that directing was to be learned, and I certainly am very much in accord with actors learning their profession, learning how to use their bodies, their voice, their emotions, all of themselves.

I have absolutely nothing but the greatest respect for the school of "method" acting. I think the "method" is abused sometimes, of course, but I have had very good luck working with actors who have gone through the "method" school. I would support it, for most people, and say that it can be very helpful for actors, if that is going to be their profession, to go to school and learn their trade.

16. PRECAMERA WORK WITH ACTOR?

I feel you've put this question in an either-or context, which is not in accord with my thinking and practice. My approach to working with actors is a combination of the two things that you mention. Before an actor has had too much of a chance to form his own opinion—let's say, he's read the script, he has formed his own image of the character and some of his thoughts about the script, but before he really starts to learn the role and learn the lines—I want to have a good, long discussion with him about the script, about the story, about the aims of the story, and—particularly—about his character and how I see it. I like to get the actor's thoughts about his character, I like to see whether we're in accord or whether he has things to suggest that would improve what I feel, or whether I can put to the actor aspects of the character that he hadn't thought of.

Before we start shooting, I like to be sure that, with all the characters, the actor and I are basically in accord with our feelings about the character, what he stands for, and where he is going. Once that is established, and we start rehearsals and shooting, I like to give the actor his head, let him experiment and play around and bring out all the things he feels in the scene in relation to the character. This is the area of improvising on the basis of a solid understanding between us before we start shooting, about what the character is.

I feel you must give the actor a chance—he is the one who is in there on his feet doing it, bringing the scene to life—you must give him a chance to explore and find out what will come out of his performance or his delivery of the character. Many times we find strong added values by doing this, values that we could not possibly get by sitting in an office and discussing or reading the script.

Sometimes you will find things that an actor feels and likes, that you don't like and you have to tell him it's not good, that you don't like it, and where it's wrong; sometimes he'll have an idea that's not quite right, but you can help him improve on it. So once you have established the commonality of your feeling about the character, then it is a matter of the director working with the actor to bring out and to enlarge and to enrich his characterization and his performance.

17. IMPORTANCE OF REHEARSALS?

I'm one of the directors who believes in a lot of rehearsal. I like full rehearsal of the script before we start shooting, if possible. I indicated earlier that I had done this a few times in my career. It doesn't often happen that one has the luxury of this kind of rehearsal, because of the economics involved. It requires too many actors being on salary before you start shooting. Very often, many important characters are normally not picked up until part way through a shooting schedule, so the matter of extreme, heavy cost is involved in this question of having full rehearsals before you start shooting. However, when it is possible, I find it very, very helpful in all aspects of the production.

When I get into actual shooting and rehearsals of a given sequence, I like enough rehearsals to really get the whole scene working well, and to give everybody a chance to know where it is, see where it is, to help the cameraman, and all the other technicians. There's a limit beyond which one should not go in rehearsals, because you do start to lose the freshness in the scene. The decision of how much you rehearse, I find, has to do with the individual qualities of the actors. Some actors love a lot of rehearsal and improve with it; other actors, I find, really don't give everything in a performance until you start rolling the camera; so the amount of rehearsals, to some extent, really is determined by the particular actors with whom one is working.

I think it's unfortunate sometimes when an actor won't give a full performance in a rehearsal. It just means you have to start making takes earlier and, very often, in order to get a set-up you want to print, you end up making eight or ten takes when you should have had five or six of those still in the form of a rehearsal. But that's the way it goes, and you have to adjust your approach, it seems to me, to the requirements of a given situation and the actors involved.

18. ADHERENCE TO SCRIPT?

No, I don't insist that an actor adhere meticulously to the scriptlines and business. I accept the position of most actors that a slight change here and there, without damaging anything, can many times bring more realism, more truth, more color to the character he's portraying. I'm always very careful that such changes don't in any way affect the plot or the story or do anything that will be reflected as wrong any place else in the story; but, certainly, if one or two slight changes make it better for an actor and makes the performance more truthful to his character, I believe very much in helping him do that.

19. EDITING SUPERVISION?

Of course, as an ex-film editor, I supervise the editing of my films completely from beginning to end, and place tremendous importance on the value of film editing, and the postproduction work on my films. Certainly, I run my rushes carefully every day. I don't dictate to my editor, by any means, how he should first-cut the rushes. If I have something that I think is of particular value in the rushes, a line reading or a closeup that feels very effective, or a certain angle I think that part of the scene must be carried in, I will indicate those things to the editor as I run rushes. Then I let him go ahead and put his sequences into his first cut, do the best he can in getting it effectively up on the screen for me.

After that, it becomes a process of running the film with him, and working it over, looking at out-takes and trims and other film, and recutting, revising, and sometimes restructuring until we get the very best that both the editor and I can bring to the scenes and sequences in the picture. It's a constant process of change and revision. Often, the more you do in changing and trimming and pacing, the more you find to do. One thing leads to another. So it's an almost never-ending process with me.

20. ROLE OF MUSICAL SCORE?

I believe the musical score is very vital to most films I've done. I feel that it shouldn't be approached with the thought of "What do you need music for there?" but rather, "What can music bring to this sequence, what can it add?" I think that's where it is, to approach the matter of the score in terms of what added dimensions it can bring, the added emotion, the added underlining for you that can enrich your film, or accent your film, or help bring out values you want to have recognized.

21. INVOLVEMENT IN PREPARATION OF MUSICAL SCORE?

When you ask, "Are you deeply involved in the preparation and recording of the musical score for the film?" I don't quite know what you mean, Tay.

I'm involved to the extent of the choosing of the composer, and this is a very vital casting on a film, and a difficult one. The composer is going to come later on to the film, and do your score; although he may at the time of preparation play a piano rendition of themes or pieces of underscoring for you, you never really get the full feeling and effect of what he's going to do until he's recorded his music on the stage with the orchestra.

Since the score is one of the last things done on a film, you're very often stuck with whatever music you get, whether you like it or not. So I've always considered the casting, so to speak, of a musical director, the composer, one of the most vital and touchy ones on the entire film.

I do always, when he's recording, make my comments and give my reactions to the music. Then I follow through very fully and very completely in the dubbing room with my films, not only as to the musical score, but all the sound effects, the looped dialogue, everything. I am very demanding and a perfectionist. I sit by the hour, by the day, by the week in the dubbing room to be sure of everything that is put up on that screen, to be sure that the soundtrack is just as right and as effective and contributive to the film as it can possible be.

22. WHAT SCENES SHOULD HAVE MUSIC?

As both producer and director, I do exercise the final control as to which scenes are to be scored, and which not. Of course, I take the sensitivities and the feeling of the composer very much into account in this. I feel he knows what he's reaching for in his music. There are instances where a composer will feel a scene should be scored that I don't necessarily think should be, or haven't thought of as being scored. Most often, in an instance like this, I will let him go ahead and score it, because if it doesn't work and I feel it's wrong when I get in the dubbing room, we can always take it out. But if he is right, and it's something that should be scored, it's too late down the line to get some music in the sequence. So if there is a difference of opinion about whether something should be scored or not, and if a composer feels strongly that a given sequence should have music, I certainly support him in scoring it.

Occasionally, by the same token, I will insist that a certain sequence that he may feel does not need music, or would not be aided by music, _should_ be scored, and he will do it. So it's a give and take proposition with the producer-director and the composer as to where the music goes, but it usually sorts out very well.

In the final analysis, I do have the final say as to where it goes in a film, in the dubbing room. I don't have any fixed rule by which I determine this for myself, but just take it on an individual basis on the needs of an individual film as it comes along. Some films need more music than others, and you have to sense that, and feel it for the individual film as it comes along.

23. SOUND EFFECTS?

Of course, as an ex-editor and particularly as an ex-sound effects editor, I feel very strongly about the importance of sound effects in pictures, all pictures. Like everything else in film, effects should not be overdone nor should they be forced in when they don't belong, but they bring a great sense of reality, of the "being" of something, to a picture when they are properly used. I'm very, very involved in this part of the film.

As I mentioned in preceding answers, I work very closely with the sound effects people. I schedule a very detailed and comprehensive reel-by-reel running with the sound effects men to discuss what I want in each sequence, what kinds of effects should be there, get their ideas, and their thoughts on the sound effects, and have a good, all-out exchange of ideas on this aspect of the film.

Certain films have stronger needs for sound effects than the average. I'm just finishing up a film now about the old German Zeppelin, _The Hindenburg_ [1975], and I think we have a marvelous looking film.

We have visually recreated the _Hindenburg_ just beautifully up there on the screen, but it's not really going to come to life, and be flying in the air until we get the sound of those four giant twelve-cylinder diesel engines running, and the wind whistling by the nose cone, and the varying aspects of the sound of those engines in different parts of the ship. It's really going to come to life, and be the _Hindenburg_ only when we get those very special and very required sound effects into the film.

William Wyler

By
Tay Garnett

1. BACKGROUND?

Before getting into the film business, William Wyler worked in a chain-store system (a haberdashery) in Paris as an apprentice. His duties included sweeping out, wrapping packages and rearranging displays, all of which bored him intensely. Finally he quit and went home to Mulhouse [Alsace-Lorraine].

His mother greeted him with the news that his cousin, Carl Laemmle, was in Zurich, and they were going to visit him.

Cousin Carl was an authentic movie mogul, with his own studio (Universal) in Hollywood. The company also had a large distribution branch, headquartered in New York. The Laemmle name stirred wildly dancing visions in Willy's mind—he could imagine a dazzling future. When Cousin Carl offered Willy a job in New York, at twenty dollars a week, Willy grabbed it before Cousin Carl could entertain second thoughts.

His first job in New York was that of an office boy, carrying inter-office memos and film cans around. After a year of very hard work, he managed to wangle a transfer to the Universal Studios in Universal City, which—he was told—was just over the Cahuenga Pass from fabled Hollywood.

2. FIRST FILM JOB?

William Wyler's first position in the actual filmmaking business was, once again—the job of office boy. He didn't mind; he was working directly for the casting office, which gave him ample opportunity to hang around sets where shooting was going on. He spent a great deal of his time watching the various directors at work. He liked what he saw, and realized that *he must become a director!* The logical way, of course, was to become an assistant director, on location with a director who made *twelve two-reel Westerns in six weeks.*

Soon after that initiation, Willy left Universal for M-G-M where director Fred Niblo was making *Ben-Hur.* He was preparing to shoot the chariot race sequence, and needed every assistant director he could find. Willy managed to be useful in the thick of choking dust and rampant hooves.

Word got back to Universal that Willy had been an assistant on *Ben-Hur,* actually, the rumor said, Willy had been Fred Niblo's right-hand man. That the rumor was without foundation, as much Hollywood rumor has always been, did nothing to lessen Willy's new-found prestige. He was summoned back to Universal, where he was assigned to serve as assistant director to Bill Craft.

The film was a two-reel Western; Craft, who had directed far more important films, was bored. They were on location when Craft yawned and announced that he had a dental appointment. Fixing an eye on Willy, he said, "You know what happens here. You shoot it." Craft mounted a nearby horse and rode away, leaving Willy staring at the megaphone Craft had shoved into his hands.

Next day, at the studio, no-one seemed to know that he had shot day's work, but Willy knew. *He had directed!*

Next, he was assistant to director Arthur Rossen. They were in the midst of a two-reel Western, when Rossen received word from his agent that Paramount wanted him to direct a "Big One." In leaving, Rossen recommended that WIlly be allowed to finish the Western.

When this was brought to Mr. Laemmle's attention, he decided that if Willy was to be given a chance to direct, it should be on a *complete* picture. So, William Wyler, director, was assigned to make a two-reel Western.

3. YOUR GOAL IN FILMMAKING?

It goes without need of emphasis that Willy Wyler loved making films. His aim was, always, to choose material that would lend itself readily to adaptation for a motion picture that would appeal to a large percentage of the movie-going public. Entertainment was his prime objective.

In time, he learned that a story involving elements of social significance—a current controversial issue, or touching on some imminent problem that people had been unwilling to face—carried an impact that brought vastly more importance to his film.

No matter what picture he did, it was always designed, according to his most fervent belief, to illuminate the good of our nation.

4. IN WHAT GENRE DO YOU SEEK A STORY?

It can be safely stated that Wyler, during his fifty years in the picturemaking business, has used story material from every conceivable genre. He has done comedy, drama, melodrama and action pictures, westerns, cops-and-robbers and whodunits. You name it—he's done it.

Regardless of category, wherever he found an idea or story that convinced him it would make a good film, he grabbed it. Truly good story properties are rare, and he regarded himself as lucky when he came across one.

5. STORY SOURCE?

In the silent picture days, the material was almost entirely limited to stories written directly for the screen. Directors were given no choice. When they were handed a script, they shot it.

The advent of sound broadened their horizons materially. It didn't take Willy long to realize that a play or novel, having achieved public acceptance in one medium, must have a far better chance of being successful in the new form, than a wholly untried "original."

Also, in adapting a play, there seemed to be far less chance of losing its success factors than in converting a novel to the video/audio medium. As a consequence, a great portion of Wyler's finest films started as plays.

6. USE A SCRIPTWRITER OR DO IT YOURSELF?

Wyler was not a writer; consequently, he always hoped to get the best screenplay writer available. Often, particularly when working with a producer like Goldwyn, Wyler had very little to say in this area; the writer often had been selected by Mr. Goldwyn long before Willy started to work on the project.

There is a possibility that Willy's lack of writing talent has been an actual advantage to him. Certainly, he could evaluate a finished script more objectively than would have been possible if he had participated in its development from its inception. There are a number of extremely able and successful directors who are writers, but the director of the future, according to Mr. Wyler, would do well to note that such men often employ other writers to work with them in this phase of preparation.

Directing is a rugged, exciting job; any help one can get is calculated to provide a bit more breathing-room, and perhaps an added nudge toward that ultimate goal: a fine picture.

7. CLOSE COLLABORATION WITH THE SCREENWRITER?

Most certainly, Wyler always wanted to see everything the writer could bring to a picture; consequently he encouraged the writer to express himself fully on paper after a thorough briefing. This system resulted in a *first draft screenplay.*

When it came to the final polish, the writer always worked under Willy's close supervision. This meant, advance in-depth discussions of each scene. The writer went into each scene knowing exactly what Willy expected to accomplish, how it related to the character and to the story structure as a whole.

There have been occasions, such as in the making of *Jezebel* [1938] when, in Willy's opinion, the script required a complete rewrite—the fresh viewpoint of another writer. That was done.

8. PREPLAN OR IMPROVISE?

Of course, Wyler always wanted everything the writer could dream up, put down on paper before Wyler started to shoot. That included action and business. An able writer is bound to come up with valuable action-business ideas.

However, regardless of the merit of the script, there are times on most pictures when the director must improvise, usually with action or business.

Referring to *Jezebel*—in it, Julie Marsden [Bette Davis] is a spoiled and willfully wild aristocratic New Orleans belle. She openly flouts convention and mortifies Preston [Henry Fonda] by insisting that he dance with her, when he should be dancing with his wife [Margaret Lindsay]. Julie practically drags him onto the floor. He is embarrassed and thoroughly enraged. His wife watches in outraged dignity, while others leave the dance floor in disgust. Julie's ploy has backfired. She tries to leave the floor, but Preston is coldly determined to make her pay for her gauche behavior. She pleads with her eyes, but he holds her relentlessly.

That scene, in the script, consisted of only a few descriptive lines. It came late in the picture, where Willy needed a strong emotional moment. By the time he had worked it over, he had developed it into an extremely moving scene—without one word of dialogue! Just the movement of the dance...horrified faces of onlookers ...Julie's wretched humiliation ...the wife's hurt, but contained fury....Preston's fierce determination...all played against the gentle lilting dance music. It was one of the most moving scenes in the picture.

9. MOST IMPORTANT COMPONENT OF YOUR FILM?

It seems evident from Wyler's approach to filmmaking, that in his opinion story, scriptwriter, film editor, stars, cast and cameraman—all, are of vital importance. Yet the real picturemaker—the dominant force—is, of course, the director. Ultimately, it is his responsibility to adjust and reconcile all these diverse components—to mold them into a harmonious whole.

In the creation of a motion picture, the single indispensable thing is that element which, to a great degree, predetermines the quality quotient of the completed film: *the director's advance visualization.* Yet, before the director can translate that vision into film, he must penetrate its outer facade, study the inner structure, to determine the function of each element within.

Obviously, it is these individual elements whose combined efforts have produced the contours, strength and grace of the completed whole. Of course, these components translate themselves into stars, cast and members of the crew; working in unison, with a single objective. The director's visualization is the blueprint by which they are all guided.

Because a director's materials, being neither animal, mineral, or vegetable, but rather tempers, talents and temperaments abounding in ego, his job is never an easy one. However, the joy of seeing a finished film that duplicates in detail, his original concept, produces an euphoria which—like twilight sleep—eclipses the pain of delivery.

10. WORK WITH A PRODUCER?

Wyler has worked with many producers, among them a few highly able men. Of course, there were many others! However, it has been Willy's *glory* and his *misery* to have done a number of pictures with Sam Goldwyn. Beyond doubt one of the truly great producers, Mr. Goldwyn was, however, a very difficult man—a strong man, as well as a sensitive man—bull-headed, but with a built-in sense of good taste. He was a lavish spender where the good of a picture was concerned, paid top money for story properties, writers, actors and directors. That was the glory aspect.

As for the *misery:* Willy quarrelled with Sam Goldwyn frequently and fiercely. Several times he walked off pictures, in the heat of argument, and left the studio, swearing he'd never come back.

Somehow, he always went back. Sometimes Sam would see the problem Willy's way. On other occasions, Willy would have a second thought, and wind up agreeing with Goldwyn. Wyler and Goldwyn had one immutable cause in common: each was fighting for the best picture he could make. By the time their show was previewed, Willy was—usually—completely mollified. It's awfully hard to stay sore when you've just had a really successful showing, and most of Wyler's films with Sam were gratifyingly successful.

So, in the race between misery and glory, it was glory by ten lengths, going away!

11. USE A DIALOGUE DIRECTOR?

Wyler did not use a dialogue director. His script supervisor was always able to run dialogue with the cast, to make sure they knew their lines.

As for the idea that a dialogue director might bring "other values to his operation," Will did not believe there could be two directors working successfully on a picture. Certainly, he did not want anyone else giving readings to any member of his cast.

12. WRITER OR PRODUCER ON THE SET?

Wyler liked to have the writer on the set while the cast was rehearsing; if a line didn't work, or an actor found it difficult to read, an experienced writer was handy to have around.

As for producers: the really good ones rarely came on the set (that does not include Sam Goldwyn) and, if they did visit, they concluded the thing for which they had come, and left.

The good producer (still excluding Goldwyn) never talks to the director or cast, on a set, about anything concerning the film in work. The experienced man knows that such a breach of courtesy could cost the picture both time and money, and quite possibly a degree of quality, by pulling an actor right out of his character or the situation. The Fail-Safe conclusion is, most definitely: *no producers on the set!*

13. WORK CLOSELY WITH THE CAMERAMAN?

Wyler worked with many excellent cameramen, but he did more pictures with Gregg Toland than with any other. When they were planning to do a film, they worked very closely together. Gregg was as interested in the story as Willy was. Jointly, they planned camera movements, angles and lighting effects, all soundly based on solid dramaturgy as affecting character, mood or pace.

Of course, this preplanning could only be done in a general way. Until one had the actors on the set in actual rehearsal, it wasn't practical to let anything get too set. The scenes themselves supply the cues for most of one's moves.

Gregg Toland was vitally important to the whole Wyler operation. Knowing what Willy wanted in every set-up, Gregg would exercise that magnificent creativity of his. He always found photographic ways of bringing out the precise thing Wyler was looking for.

It was on *The Little Foxes* [1941] that Wyler and Toland really struck a bonanza. Because of the peculiar nature of the play, to have approached it from the usual point of view would have involved an inordinate number of close-ups. In *Foxes,* it would have destroyed any flow the film might have had. What Willy wanted, boiled down to simple mechanics, was more focal depth—to be able to record visually, both *action* and *reaction* in a single camera set-up. Gregg worked it out. By greatly intensifying the lighting, he was enabled to stop down radically, which gave them vastly greater depth of focus. Then, by using a wider angle lens (35mm), Gregg was able to carry the depth required.

That was wonderful, but it brought with it an entire new set of staging problems. The wide-angle lens made everything appear farther from the camera than it actually was, so Willy was forced to work his actors closer together than they would, normally, be. Yet it was a great step forward. Now, Willy could film long scenes, getting actions and reactions in the same shot. The added depth allowed them to save the close-ups for the places where they were really needed for emphasis. There was another big bonus: *they could film full scenes,* rather than doing the whole thing in bits and pieces.

Willy always considered a fine cameraman to be one of any film's greater assets.

14. SUPERVISION OF CASTING?

Convinced that there is no such thing as an unimportant part—and that included one-line "bits"—Willy stayed right on top of casting. He hung in there until he was convinced he had the best cast possible for that particular picture. On occasion he even hand-picked extra people for types calculated to enhance a particular mood for which he was striving.

Of course, an able casting director can be of great value in suggesting actors; usually they came up with several names for each part, any one of whom might conceivably play it. But remember: as a rule, the casting director has read the script only once, hurriedly, whereas a director has been living with it for months. So, even though he has been given a good idea of what a director is seeking for in each part, he can't possibly know the character in depth as the director does.

The Little Foxes was probably one of the most perfectly cast films Wyler ever made. Of course, he exercised a tremendous influence on all the casting.

15. PREFERENCE OF ACTING STYLE?

Willy believes that, to be a good actor, one must have a sure instinct for acting. However, before one can qualify as a truly good actor, one must develop a technique. Then, once having found the key to a character, the actor will never again stray from it.

There has never been a truly fine actor who didn't have an abundance of both technique and instinct. John Barrymore, Walter Huston, Bette Davis, Katharine Hepburn, Lord Laurence Olivier, Gregory Peck, Olivia de Havilland and Greer Garson, to name a few with whom he has worked, were loaded with talent which, through work and study, they had learned to use to its maximum potential through technical control.

Wyler's opinion of "method" actors? Every experienced actor, consciously, has a method that is entirely his own. We've had many young actors and actresses— "method" actors from New York—who were so consumed by "the method" that they fell into a pattern. The "method," or their application of it, overshadowed characterization. On the other hand, many of our predominant stars have studied under such teachers as Lee Strasberg and Sandy Meisner.

16. PRECAMERA WORK WITH ACTOR?

As for discussing a part in depth, if Willy knew the actor well—perhaps having worked with him on earlier occasions—he could visualize exactly what the actor could bring to a part. If, however, Wyler knew the actor only from having seen him in other director's films or plays, he must discuss the character fully with the actor before signing him. Obviously, Wyler couldn't tolerate any hang-ups over a difference in ideas regarding characterization, once shooting had started.

Of course, there were occasions when, despite a very thorough knowledge of the range and capabilities of an actor, Willy failed to prevent a costly conflict. For example: his violent controversy with Miss Davis on *The Little Foxes*.

Miss Davis was convinced that Tallulah Bankhead's interpretation (in the theatre) was the only way the part should be played. Wyler was equally convinced that Miss Bankhead's interpretation was completely black-and-white—no grays. What Wyler wanted was a gentler approach—a far more vari-colored, multi-faceted characterization.

It would seem reasonable that a director, having lived with the script for months, must have a more valid assessment of the values latent in every part, than that of an actor who has had only a brief time to digest it. In addition, no actor can possibly visualize the director's structural view of the finished film.

Willy has said many times that he considers the director's first responsibility to be the guidance of his actors. No director can *make* people act. He can't say, "Make this face here, or that face there." But, if one reaches an agreement with any good professional actor about what goes on *inside the character,* the right expressions will be the inevitable result.

17. IMPORTANCE OF REHEARSALS?

Mr. Wyler has probably tried every known approach to getting the maximum benefit out of rehearsals. If one has a small cast and a story that plays mainly on studio sets, the theatrical type of rehearsal is often feasible. If it's an outdoor or action picture, such rehearsals are impractical.

On *The Best Years Of Our Lives* [1948], Willy adopted a completely unorthodox rehearsal plan: as each new sequence came up, he rehearsed it for a full day before shooting. Willy and the actors sat around a table and discussed the scenes so as to give the cast a feeling of ease with what they were doing. Then Willy hammered away at it: scolding, wheedling, nagging, until he had each of them giving every nuance and color-tone the scene called for. The next day he rehearsed again, fully, when they were on the set.

Willy has been accused of shooting a lot of unnecessary takes. He did shoot a lot occasionally; however, there was always a reason. Usually it was a matter of getting his ideas through clearly to everyone in the scene. It was never remotely conceivable to Willy Wyler than one might settle for anything less than the best.

18. ADHERENCE TO SCRIPT?

It is true that some actors find certain word combinations difficult. In such cases, when Wyler was convinced that the difficulty was real, and not just an ego trip for the actor, he'd watch rehearsals, including the suggested changes. If convinced that the changes did not alter the mood or intent of the scene, he'd agree. There were times, with really fine actors, when scenes were actually made to flow more smoothly by such substitution.

19. EDITING SUPERVISION?

True: the late John Ford made a big thing of not viewing his rushes. He knew exactly what was on that film, but more importantly, you may be sure that he had discussed each days' work with his cutter before the rushes were run. Consequently the first cut was precisely what Ford had visualized and conveyed to the editor. When it came to the actual fine-comb editing, Jack was right on top of it every minute up through the final preview.

With Wyler's own films, he has been fortunate. He has had either Danny Mandell or Bob Swink, both extremely capable editors, on most of his important films. Each man knew what Willy wanted, always, and gave him exactly that. This would seem to indicate that, in Wyler's case, a mutually responsive director/editor relationship was vital to the ultimate quality of the picture.

There is one very real danger in connection with cutting—a danger most directors have faced at one time or another: that of falling in love with one particular scene or bit of business to the point of emasculating one's overall perspective. No matter how dramatic, well-played or entertaining a bit may be, unless it is an essential instrument for advancing the play's structure, it will probably serve only to distract the viewer's interest from your story line. This is a difficult lesson to absorb, but it's a must!

20. ROLE OF MUSICAL SCORE?

Wyler considers a fine score to be an absolute essential to the full realization of the values in most films. He always fought to get the services of the finest composers.

Having chosen one such, he ran the film with him, giving him every thought he had regarding the scenes he believed were in need of help from the score, and pointing out other moments where he believe that any music at all might defeat his purpose.

He learned that the truly great composers were easiest to work with—they grasped the dramatic intent quickly, and knew how best to augment it. After a complete meeting of the minds, the composer was on his own until he was prepared to audition for Willy.

21. INVOLVEMENT IN PREPARATION OF MUSICAL SCORE?

Wyler's involvement in the preparation of a musical score seldom went beyond the point mentioned in the preceeding answer.

However, he did attend the recording sessions—as an observer.

When it came time to dub the music into the picture, he became deeply involved. Here, they were dealing with the delicate balance between dialogue, sound effects and musical background: if the music was allowed to intrude itself into the consciousness of the viewer, even for an instant, the chain of enchantment was ruptured, and the drama had to start all over again, building from scratch.

22. WHAT SCENES SHOULD HAVE MUSIC?

Wyler demanded absolute control over which specific spots were to be scored, and which were to be played completely without music. He believed that every director should do this for his own protection.

We have all seen an occasional scene—well staged and beautifully performed—left dying for lack of music. But, far worse, we've seen many highly dramatic, or deeply emotional moments destroyed by the strident efforts of an over-zealous composer.

23. SOUND EFFECTS?

It seems extremely doubtful that Mr. Wyler could ever have bought that bit: "We who have directed silent pictures are inclined, perhaps, to overestimate the importance of sound effects, particularly in 'action' sequences."

If there is a doubt in anyone's mind as to the importance of sound effects, let that person run the best gun-fight, barroom-brawl, or an automobile chase without a soundtrack. That experience would be an instant doubt-remover.

It is conceivable that some directors, at one time or another, have made the error of expecting to get added impact by heightening the volume of sound effects. As a matter of fact, we've all seen this done with great effectiveness—as a single gunshot at a tense moment, in the dark.

However, it is William Wyler's contention that the more closely we can reproduce reality, the better our chances for a truly fine film.

Sergei Yutkevitch

1. BACKGROUND?

I began my career as a stage director and scenic designer. Most of what I learned in that field I owe to the great Russian stage director, Vsevolod Meyerhold.

2. FIRST FILM JOB?

I began my work in film as an assistant director and set designer. My first master was the well-known director Abraham Rom. During those years [1926-1928], the production staff was very small—consisting of the director, cameraman and two assistants.

The second assistant was expected to do and be everything from carrying the camera tripod, to hunting for props, and manipulating extras in large crowd scenes.

3. YOUR GOAL IN FILMMAKING?

I am sure that film represents a great deal more than merely another form of entertainment. Personally, I enjoy a purely "entertaining" film—just as I like to read "who-done-its." But I believe that the film has fully caught up, in its ability to affect its viewer, with the impression evoked by a literary work, or a stageplay, or even a musical composition. I would be very glad if some of my films were considered in this category.

I would hope to widen the viewer's perception of life and the world around him, so that—after the final fade-out—something remained with him which had enriched his psyche. This is a measure of its aesthetic value.

But film, being a medium seen by hundreds of millions—unlike other art forms-must be judged in terms of its ethical values. A basic law of dialectical materialism states that, in such a case, quantity becomes a new dimension of quality.

Considering the enormous force to influence minds and hearts of humanity, a filmmaker bears a responsibility in no way comparable to any other creative worker.

4. IN WHAT GENRE DO YOU SEEK A STORY?

In seeking a story on which to base a film, I am always hopeful that I may find a fundamental idea, in any category, which contains the possibility of enriching the viewer's knowledge and understanding of life, and to some degree, fortifies his ability to cope with life's intricate problems.

5. STORY SOURCE?

Among my films are both original designs and adaptations of already existing library works. Personally, I much prefer to work on an "original," which gives me a greater freedom in my own field.

6. USE A SCRIPTWRITER OR DO IT YOURSELF? / 7. CLOSE COLLABORATION WITH THE SCREENWRITER?

On all of my projects I prefer to work with a writer, either a full-fledged collaborator, or with myself in the role of supervising script editor. In any case, the final scripts, invariably, are a definite reflection of my own thinking.

8. PREPLAN OR IMPROVISE?

I insist, always, on having a fully finalized script before the camera starts turning—which does not preclude a certain amount of improvisation, sometimes dictated by the nature of the location, or other production surprises.

9. MOST IMPORTANT COMPONENT OF YOUR FILM?

The most important element in any project must be the scenario. Consequently, this demands the greatest creative sympathy between the writer and the director. Equally as important is, not only the individual ability of each member of the cast, but the complete mutual creative understanding of all concerned.

10. WORK WITH A PRODUCER?

Since the film industry in the USSR is a state enterprise, a producer as an entrepreneur doesn't exist.

11. USE A DIALOGUE DIRECTOR?

Dialogue is very important. I prefer speech that fits the personality of the actor who has to deliver it.

[Ed. note: It is clear that Mr. Yutkevitch did not understand the question. Probably the dialogue director is unknown in the USSR.]

12. WRITER OR PRODUCER ON THE SET?

Certainly, the presence of the author of the screenplay on the set during shooting doesn't bother me at all. Actually, there are times when I find it most helpful for him to be there—in case of an unexpected need for a dialogue change here or there.

13. WORK CLOSELY WITH THE CAMERAMAN?

Preparatory work with the cameraman in advance of shooting is an absolute necessity, so that he is completely familiar with the director's approach to the pictorial framing of the story.

14. SUPERVISION OF CASTING?

All of the actors in my films, from leading characters down to the lowliest bit player, are cast by me personally.

15. PREFERENCE OF ACTING STYLE?

[Ed. note: This was not answered, probably because there is no "method" acting in the U.S.S.R.]

16. PRECAMERA WORK WITH ACTOR?

In working with actors, I prefer the role of coach to that of a "dictator." Actually, an actor can find full realization only on the stage. In films he functions softly, as a very fragile and sensitive tool in the hands of the director.

17. IMPORTANCE OF REHEARSALS?

I find rehearsals desirable, but only up to a certain point—before the performance begins to get "set" and loses the improvisatory quality during actual shooting.

18. ADHERENCE TO SCRIPT?

My theory is that the actor is an independent creative artist. As such, he is entitled to some degree of freedom. Any slight alteration of line or action, which does not conflict with my visualization of the story development but will bring vitality or added color to the character, is acceptable.

19. EDITING SUPERVISION?

All phases of final editing, I perform myself, with the assistance of my permanent editor. I consider film editing to be the most decisive and interesting part of the entire filmmaking process.

20. ROLE OF MUSICAL SCORE? / 21. INVOLVEMENT IN PREPARATION OF MUSICAL SCORE?

I am against special musical scoring of my films. I use music only as a counterpoint element—always written in pure musical form—like a fugue, sonata, etc., but never as an illustration or stressing of mood as in American films.

I think that the exaggerated use of music in a film is a sign of lack of confidence on the part of the director in the eloquence of his work.

I am not against music on the screen, but I do admire the work of Buñuel and Rom, who do not use any music at all.

23. SOUND EFFECTS?

Unlike music, I consider sound background of the highest importance, and devote a great deal of time to sound effects—but again, not so much as part of realistic "noise," but rather as counterpoint to developing action.

Fred Zinnemann

1. BACKGROUND?

Studied music, found I had no talent.

Studied Law at Vienna University, got bored with it. Went to see movies instead of going to lectures.

Decided to become a film director after seeing Stroheim's *Greed,* Eisenstein's *Potemkin,* Dryer's *Joan of Arc,* and King Vidor's *The Big Parade.* This was in 1927. There was hardly any film industry in Austria at the time. The idea of becoming a film director seemed totally outlandish and impossible. I'm still surprised that it worked out eventually.

2. FIRST FILM JOB?

It seemed essential, in order to be able to enter this promised land, to get first of all a solid technical background. I therefore joined an old friend, Gunther Von Fritsch, who had already enrolled at the then new and excellent Technical School of Cinematography in Paris. From there, the timetable went roughly as follows.

1927/1928	School in Paris
1928/1929	Worked as assistant cameraman in Berlin
1929	Came to Hollywood, tried to join cameraman's local; no success
First job:	Extra in *All Quiet on the Western Front.* (German soldier and French ambulance driver)
1930/1931	Personal Assistant to Director Berthold Viertel (Fox)
1931/1932	Personal Assistant to Robert Flaherty (in Berlin, preparing to shoot a documentary in Russia. It never came off, but taking part in Flaherty's preparations was a fascinating and important experience for me.)
1933	Worked with Busby Berkeley and Gregg Toland in a very minor capacity: helping to prepare camera angles for dance numbers in the Goldwyn film *The Kid From Spain* (starring Eddie Cantor).
1934	First directing job: *The Wave,* a documentary feature for the Mexican Government.
1935	Wrote a film treatment with Henwar Rodakiewicz, a Mexican

story entitled *Bonanza.* It was sold to M-G-M but nothing came of it in the end, and the story joined M-G-M's vast slagheap of unused "material."

1936   A brief three-day job, working as Technical Advisor for William Wyler on the final sequence of *Dodsworth* which took place in a café in Vienna.

1937/39   Three years as shorts subjects director (M-G-M) Pete Smith, John Nesbitt's "Passing Parade" and "Crime Doesn't Pay" shorts. *An excellent preparation for feature directing.* Afterward, I directed a number of "B" pictures for M-G-M and one "A" picture, *The Seventh Cross* (1944) with Spencer Tracy.

3. YOUR GOAL IN FILMMAKING?

I like to make pictures for my own enjoyment—with a story I find exciting and with a cast of talented actors. The activity of making films is, for me, a source of pleasure in itself. Needless to say I always hope that the picture will entertain the public. Sometimes this hope is fulfilled; on other occasions, the film lays an egg.

I have no underlying objective beyond entertaining an audience.

4. IN WHAT GENRE DO YOU SEEK A STORY?

My range in the choice of subjects is fairly wide. I like suspense stories [*Seventh Cross, High Noon,* 1952; *The Day of the Jackal,* 1973], especially if they involve a chase or pursuit. There are certain themes that interest me very much, particularly the theme of individual conscience [*From Here to Eternity,* 1953; *The Nun's Story,* 1959; *High Noon, A Man For All Seasons,* 1966]—especially if the story is about the clash of a single person with a powerful institution (the army, a religious order, the monarchy). I like stories which show in an entertaining way a close and affectionate family life [*The Sundowners,* 1960]. Also, I like subjects with strong documentary flavor [*The Men,* 1950; *The Search,* 1948; *Day of the Jackal*].

I'm very limited when it comes to comedy and musicals. My imagination doesn't function along the lines of musical numbers, and I lack that special sense of absolute, sharp comedy timing which is indispensable to this genre.

5. STORY SOURCE?

I have no absolute preference, but favor short stories or short novels because of compressed situations which level characters and relationships with economy and imagination.

Good plays are, of course, also an excellent starting point, although they depend too much on the spoken word.

6. USE A SCRIPTWRITER OR DO IT YOURSELF?

I must have a writer, because I'm hopeless at trying to write good dialogue, Besides, I am always thankful for someone with a true dramatic instinct.

7. CLOSE COLLABORATION WITH THE SCREENWRITER?

I like to leave the writer alone while he is working on the first draft; I like to get his original, personal contribution without interference by anyone. (So far as I am concerned, this goes also for actors, cameramen, editors, production designers—in brief all creative people who have a part in the making of the picture.)

I am, of course, always available if during the work on the first draft the writer wants to have a discussion with me. After the first draft is finished, I work very closely with the writer on the final version.

8. PREPLAN OR IMPROVISE?

I need to have the skeleton of the action very clearly defined; I improvise upon it as much as possible from then on. I like to take advantage of the endless possibilities and choices which occur during the shooting of a picture; they can enhance and bring added life, spontaneity and passion to scenes which may have been worked out in an atmosphere of cool, calculated detachment. And very often one couldn't ever imagine or dream up the possibilities that present themselves for free.

9. MOST IMPORTANT COMPONENT OF YOUR FILM?

The following components are, to my mind the five essential creative elements of each film. They are all of equal importance and equally indispensable. They occur in overlapping, successive stages, as follows: 1) story (plus shooting script 2) casting 3) production design 4) camerawork and visual style, and 5) editing.

10. WORK WITH A PRODUCER?

Yes, I work with producers sometimes. It depends on the circumstances—if, for instance, a producer owns the rights to the story I would like to direct (for example, John Woolf in the case of *Day of the Jackal*).

A good producer can be of enormous help, and can take a great deal of work off the director's shoulders. Truly fine producers have always been rare. Look at the requirements: excellent talent for organization, financing, administration and pro-motion of film. Good showmanship. Good taste. A passion for movies. Knowledge-able as to casting and story values. A good deal of cunning, to be used for defense against predatory distributors. If possible, he should have good editorial instincts. Should be an excellent host in order to cope with stars and public relations. Should be reasonably honest.

(Tay: if you know someone who combines all these qualities, please send me a cable.)

11. USE A DIALOGUE DIRECTOR?

No. Because I believe that direct contact between director and actor is very important. An infinite number of nuances can be filtered out and lost if there is communication through a third personality. I do use a specialist dialogue coach when there are technical questions, such as teaching the actor a special accent.

12. WRITER OR PRODUCER ON THE SET?

No. There should be only one man on the set who calls the signals, and that man should be the director. Nothing is more destructive to the discipline and morale on a set than to have a debating committee wasting time while the crew and cast stand around all geared up, full of steam and ready to go. It is deadly to see creative energy slowly wilting away while a scene is being debated to shreds on a "live" set. If discussions are necessary, they should take place in an office away from the set and not on production time.

13. WORK CLOSELY WITH THE CAMERAMAN?

I work very closely with the cameraman and production designer—sometimes jointly, often separately. The important thing for me is to establish the visual style of the picture long before shooting starts—possibly before the sets are fully designed.

I worked, for example, with Floyd Crosby, the cameraman on *High Noon* in this manner. We agreed that the picture should be shot to give the illusion of a newsreel—had there been newsreels in existence at that time. To that end, we studied a great many contemporary photographs, especially the work of Matthew Brady. Floyd make a particular point of using flat, diffused front-lighting. No filters, of course, and a grainy texture. Up to that time it had been the norm to have a nice, panchromatic, grey sky, with pretty clouds is possible; but he was purposefully burning up the negative where the sky was. As a result, the figure of Gary Cooper, who was deliberately dressed in black, stood out, and was etched very sharply against the background.

Another sacred cow of the period, which we disregarded, was the rule that the star must always look young and beautiful/handsome, even if this meant washing all the character out of the person's face. Floyd photographed Cooper as a middle-aged man, without making him look pretty, and so got the maximum of character out of him.

I believe that, subconsciously, this style contributed a good deal to the overall effect of the picture. It was interesting that every morning after rushes, there were screams from the front office because of "lousy photography"; there were also veiled hints to the effect that Floyd Crosby should change his style or be replaced.

Many men would have caved in under the pressure, but Crosby stuck to his guns, and fortunately I was able to back him up.

14. SUPERVISION OF CASTING?

To me, casting is of enormous creative importance. It requires a certain amount of imagination, especially if one wants to "cast against type," i.e., to use an actor in a part which seems to run counter to his image. (Example: Donna Reed playing a prostitute in _From Here to Eternity_ [1953], Deborah Kerr playing a nymphomaniac, and Montgomery Clift as a boxing champion, in the same picture.)

In any event, I like to be involved with the casting even of one-line "bits," and sometimes of key extras.

15. PREFERENCE OF ACTING STYLE?

It depends on the part. I love actors if they have talent; I hate them if they have no talent. Very often I like to work with non-actors, provided they are not self-conscious. (i.e., _The Search; The Men._).

[Views of "method" acting]. It is all a question of talent. I find that talented actors come from all kind of schools. Certainly, some towering talents have come from the Actors' Studio. I have worked with many of them, and have been very much impressed by most of them. They are enormously self-reliant. The one quality many of them lack is self discipline.

16. PRECAMERA WORK WITH ACTOR?

In the second paragraph, you explain clearly the way of working with actors which I happen to prefer: I like to have a very brief general discussion with the actor after he has read the script, but only in order to indicate a sort of framework so that he won't scatter his creative energy by working on extraneous things. After that, the preparation is up to the actor; but I am always available if he wants to talk, and especially when he says that he is ready. As a general principal, I abhor talking a character or a scene to death.

17. IMPORTANCE OF REHEARSALS?

The type of rehearsal varies according to the kind of picture I am making. Painstaking rehearsals are obviously essential in the theatre, but not necessarily in motion pictures. I agree that too much rehearsal can make a filmscene go flat and mechanical, and kill all spontaneity. I like to shoot rehearsals, especially if the mechanics are accidental and imperfect. I think that elaborate rehearsals stem from, and are a part of the theatre. It happened to me on several occasions that actors who "hit the top" in rehearsals had difficulty in trying to generate the same emotion weeks later, when we were shooting the scene. Very often they tried to work from the *memory* of the emotion, rather than to evoke the emotion itself. One can get by with this on stage, but a film performance is diminished by it.

18. ADHERENCE TO SCRIPT?

I don't believe that every line of dialogue is written in stone. I don't mind if an actor changes lines and business so long as something more truthful and more spontaneous will emerge.

19. EDITING SUPERVISION?

I like to see the rushes once, preferably the day after shooting. After that I never look at he film again until after the editor has made his first cut.

I always ask the editor to keep up with the shooting schedule, so that I'm able to see *his own* first cut about ten days after I've finished shooting. From then on, we work very closely together, until after the final previews of the picture in a theatre. My view as to the importance of editing? You can make or break a picture in the cutting room.

20. ROLE OF MUSICAL SCORE?

The importance of the musical score depends entirely on the type of film in question. I believe that, until fairly recent times, most pictures were desperately over-scored, and while the music itself may have been good, the effect of sobbing violins over an emotional scene would almost invariably drain that scene of all its emotional content-just as sombre, ominous music would telegraph the fact that something ghastly was about to happen.

Referring to some of my own pictures: while Dimitri Tiomkin's song and music undoubtedly made an enormous contribution to *High Noon,* the same composer's score succeeded in killing several important scenes in *The Men.*

21. INVOLVEMENT IN PREPARATION OF MUSICAL SCORE?

Not really. I like to listen to the various cues while there is still time to make changes, but that's about all. I don't make suggestions very often.

22. WHAT SCENES SHOULD HAVE MUSIC?

Yes. I don't have a fixed rule for anything.

23. SOUND EFFECTS?

Concerning the importance of sound effects: it cannot be stressed enough. I think that the imaginative use of sound effects is still an open, and relatively untried field—especially when one thinks of the brilliant beginnings and the imaginative techniques in pictures such as Fritz Lang's *M,* and René Clair's *Under the Roofs of Paris.*